PLAY FROM THE SOUL

An Artist's Science of Creativity

KEITH RICHARD HILL

PHILAGNOSIS PRESS

Published by Philagnosis Press 2018

First Edition
Printed by CreateSpace, An Amazon.com Company

Book & cover design: Matthew Francis Parkinson
Cover image: *Evening on the Raisin River Millpond* by Keith Richard Hill

The title of this book is a phrase taken from *An Essay on the True Art of Playing Keyboard Instruments*, which was written in the mid-eighteenth century by Carl Phillip Immanuel Bach, the second son of Johann Sebastian Bach—perhaps the greatest composer of music. The entire quote reads, "Endeavor to avoid everything mechanical and slavish. Play from the Soul, not like a trained bird." There can be little doubt that these words were J.S. Bach's ever-present exhortation to his sons to "play from the Soul." Likewise, it can be the motto of every living person, no matter the variety of work they do.

Short Table of Contents

Extended Table of Contents

Acknowledgments

I first became acquainted with my Soul when I was five or six years old. I remember standing in the school playground and realizing that no matter what I did, some kids would like me and others would not, so I resolved to never do anything designed to make others like me. I now know that this was one of the many crucial, life-shaping decisions that my Soul has made for me. I therefore acknowledge my Soul, which is responsible for writing this book. Everything good in this book came from my Soul, and everything bad in it came from me.

My wife, Marianne Ploger, prompted me to think about cognition and perception. Our work on the techniques of musical communication led me to understand how the greatest artists of the past produced consistently high-quality work.

My parents, Jack and Joann Hill, taught me the art of asking questions.

Wendell Westcott, my piano professor at Michigan State University, taught me how to think clearly.

Harald Vogel and John Brombaugh got me thinking about musical and spiritual proportions, which led to me thinking about universal principles.

When I completed this book in 2007, I knew I needed an editor who was capable of understanding my ideas. In 2017, I asked Matthew Parkinson, an editor and student of my wife's, to edit this book. He is responsible for getting it into publishable condition.

Finally, none of this would have happened without my Apple computers. As an instrument maker, I know the importance of using quality tools. I also know that tool-makers are often not acknowledged. Therefore, I acknowledge Steve Jobs and all at Apple for making the tools I used to write this book.

Preface

The Story behind These Ideas

According to contemporary reports, when Johann Sebastian Bach was asked about his prodigious musical talent, he responded, "I was obliged to be industrious: whoever is equally industrious will succeed equally well."[1] When I first read this line in *The Bach Reader*, that valuable compendium of material written by and about Bach, I had the same reaction to it as everyone else—I didn't believe it, and I suspected that the people from his time didn't either. Bach was saying that hard work trumps talent.

Years later, I understood that Bach wasn't being falsely humble or dismissing acknowledgments of his talent. His assertion was earnest and genuine—he put very little stock in talent. Furthermore, he probably did this because he knew how limited his natural proclivity for music was and how hard he had to work to achieve a satisfying level of competence.

That day, traveling from Edinburgh to London after a visit to the Russell Collection of Early Keyboard Instruments, I had an epiphany of sorts. It struck me that the reason antique musical instruments sounded so much better than modern ones was not their age. Everyone at that time seemed to agree, with no evidence to the contrary, that the better sound heard in antique instruments was due to aging, likening it to the aging of wine. On the contrary, I realized that it

1 Hans T. David, Arthur Mendel and Christoph Wolff, eds., *The New Bach Reader* (New York: Norton, 1998), 459.

was because makers of old knew exactly how to create wonderful sounding instruments, while modern makers, including myself, didn't know squat about how to make instruments that sounded wonderful. I knew this to be true because of what I heard at the Russell Collection. There I heard a harpsichord, made in 1769 by Pascal Taskin of Paris, which sounded much better than one made by Jan Couchet in 1645. If age was the reason instruments sound better, then Couchet's harpsichord should have sounded at least 124 years better than Taskin's.

Since there were other examples in the collection of newer instruments sounding better than older ones, it meant that better sounding instruments are made by makers who know more about the acoustic enhancing of wood. This also meant that knowing what you are doing is the key, and I reasoned that whatever was known in the past could again be known if I could uncover the methods and techniques employed by the ancient makers. That was why I understood that Bach meant it when he said, "I was obliged to be industrious, anyone who works as hard as I can do the same."

All my life, up to that point, I had been painfully aware of how meager my talents were. Nothing was ever easy for me. Everything that I loved to do, like playing the organ, drawing, painting, or making things, I was supremely incompetent at doing. It wasn't that my work was mediocre; it was bad. As far as I could tell, I had little talent for doing anything except doing everything badly.

One of my best friends, Harald Vogel, an Organ expert from Germany, once saw my first try at lid painting and emphasized that I should avoid making lid paintings because it was clear I had no talent for it. Since he was telling me what I already knew, I thanked him for his honesty and said that I would continue to paint because that was the only way I could train my ability to see. It did not bother me if I had any talent or not; Bach had assured me that anyone who worked as hard as he did could do the same.

Furthermore, to say I was an average student at school would have been an embarrassing compliment because my success in school was below average. But when I remembered Bach's quote while travelling from Edinburgh to London, I felt that however poorly I fared as an instrument maker, I nevertheless was prepared to commit myself to discovering what the greatest instrument makers from the past knew about sound, or die in the process.

I had no idea where to begin or how to discover what I needed to know. I was so impatient with the details of making instruments that my shoddy workmanship ruined my reputation. I needed to hear my instruments as soon as possible, so I worked so fast that I neglected furniture-making niceties. I justified my inadequacies by quoting to myself a line from C.P.E. Bach's treatise, "Play from the Soul, not like a trained bird...Endeavor to avoid everything mechanical and slavish."[2] I was happy to have my reputation ruined if that was going to be the result of pursuing mastery over sound. For me, it was all about the sound and learning how to make as beautiful a sound as possible, and sooner rather than later. It was this decision that launched me on a trajectory where figuring out how to best "Play from the Soul" took precedence in my life.

Not long after making that decision, I discovered what it was like to have my Soul engaged in my work. It was at this point that I switched from trying to control sound to learning to control myself; all I needed to do was to be present, willing, and able, and get out of my Soul's way. I found that every time I allowed my work to be executed by my Soul, the acoustical results were beyond everything that had gone before. I turned my work into a set of experiments aimed at creating a science for how to engage my Soul in work. This book is all about that science. I call it a science because it required thousands of hours of making observations, taking notes, and searching for adequate explanations of what I noticed.

Now, I don't pretend that what I have learned is new. Others who came before me have made similar observations, I am sure, but they were perhaps not made as part of a focused scientific endeavor. Nevertheless, obvious similarities between what I have noticed and what others have already said in no way weakens the contribution of either party. Rather, it strengthens observations when they are independently confirmed and validated; this is how science progresses. (Einstein never proved his theory of General Relativity. Scientists who found his ideas

---

[2] C.P.E. Bach, *An Essay on the True Art of Playing Keyboard Instruments*, translated by William J. Mitchell (New York: Norton, 1948).

compelling set out to prove or disprove his theory by making direct observations and calculations that, in the end, proved him right.)

The science to which I refer should not be compared to a religious notion designed to appear scientific, like Scientology. The term I coined for this science is *aesthetic science*. It is a science of the senses—all 133 of them. While I say, "all 133 of them," I suspect I have grazed the tip of the iceberg. I expect to hear from interested readers about all the senses I have missed, and I intend to add them to later editions of this book, including a mention of the person or persons who brought them to my attention.

The connection between aesthetic science and the Soul is to do with *knowing*. Aesthetic science focuses on all our senses, and it is the senses that make knowing possible. Without our senses, we would be incapable of knowing anything and would be condemned to function on belief. As far as the Soul is concerned, it is neither a religious notion nor a philosophical concept. Rather, it is a real and sensible part of one's experience of being alive. The Soul is only accessible through the senses and perceptible because of the senses. It can only be recognized by sensing. It is as real as the taste of salt is to the tongue, but perhaps one thousand times more subtle. All this means that we are obliged to figure out how to amplify our senses, our focus, or the way we pay attention to learn how to manage this aspect of ourselves. That is the purpose behind aesthetic science. This book exists to make the whole business of accessing the Soul easier and more logical.

As I have learned, the Soul's spiritual mechanisms don't need us to believe anything to have them improve our work and lives. Like a seesaw, where you push down on one end and the other end rises, these mechanisms are predictable. You apply yourself to the Soul's requirements, and the Soul comes out to play. Like a theater in which all the stage lights must first be switched on and all the lights in the hall switched off, these mechanisms need to be switched on and the counter mechanisms switched off before the main actor (the Soul) is willing to emerge from the wings to center stage. Believing things about these mechanisms reduces their effectiveness, like leaving lights on in the theater hall so that what was happening in the hall competes for attention with the actors on stage.

As you read this book, don't be intimidated by its lists. Also, don't be put off by statements or ideas that challenge you, are hard for you to swallow, or that seem to be presented without corroborating evidence. This book is based on first-hand personal observation and experience. I don't want you to believe anything I say. I want you to keep an open mind and test these ideas for yourself.

This is a science book, and it will be best used if you incorporate one idea at a time. Don't try to force-feed yourself these ideas. Take it easy and be methodical and systematic. Treat yourself as your best friend when it comes to assessing how well you are doing. Patience, industry, attentiveness, and good humor will produce the best results over time.

INTRODUCTION
Useful Definitions of Basic Concepts

I view all humans as sensory organisms because the intellect and emotions wouldn't work without the senses. I'm using the term *senses* in my expanded definition. Where most of my readers will be familiar with the five senses, some will grant that we also have a sixth. My model has 133 senses divided into seven distinct sensory groups that can be ordered in terms of how obvious they are to us:

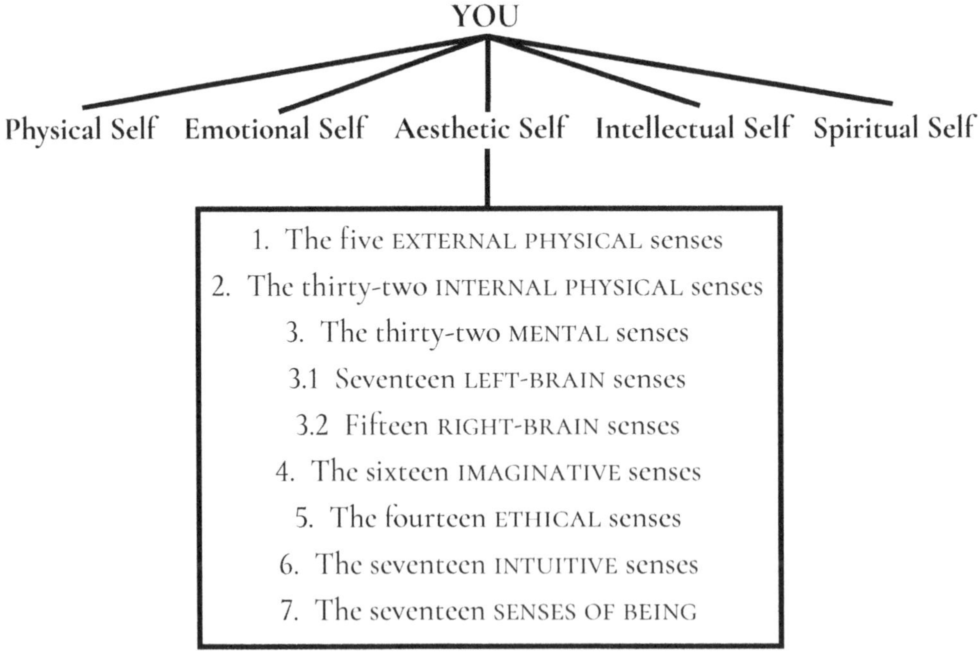

FIGURE 1. The model of a human being as a sensory organism with seven sensory houses.

That, in a nutshell, is my model for how human beings are constructed. YOU stands for who you believe you are. The group below is how we normally experience consciousness. We are all able to notice our physical, emotional, intellectual, and spiritual selves, but our views of our aesthetic selves are marred by whatever we believe the aesthetic self to be. As long as we stick to our awareness of our five external physical senses, we can all appreciate the aesthetic self. We can also accept the thirty-two internal physical senses as specific senses, rather than feelings. For example, when you feel sleepy, your sense of regeneration is stimulated; when you feel hungry, your sense of hunger is stimulated; and so on. Similarly, when you feel that what you are being told is nonsense, that feeling is a specific mental sense being stimulated. In short, what we say we feel is the result of stimulation of one or more of our inner senses, but this is not so when it comes to our emotional selves. When we feel angry, we are having an emotion. Ditto with feelings of desire or fear, which are also emotions.

The problem is that human beings have talked themselves into a corner by labeling every inner experience as feeling. Feeling tired, feeling hopeless, feeling pressured, feeling hot, and so on, have all been lumped together into a mass of feeling that needs to be separated into different types of inner experience. Feeling cold is a sensation of temperature that has overwhelmed the inner sense of well-being. Feeling hopeless is an emotion. We are all born entirely occupied with our senses foremost in our experiences of life. It takes considerable time for our emotions to take hold, and a longer time for our intellectual powers to form. This is why I say that human beings are sensory organisms at their core.

Man has often been called "the thinking animal," but we don't start life that way. It takes a long time to develop into a thinking animal. Freud and other psychologists in the past have made us out to be primarily emotional beings. Indeed, that characterization of humans has persisted for almost a century, but now that definition is being reviewed in the light of recent brain science. Be that as it may, my main concern is not with our intellectual or emotional makeup; it is with our spiritual makeup. By *spiritual*, I do not mean anything related to religion. I view religion and spirituality to be diametrically opposed. Religion is about beliefs and believing, whereas spirituality is about sensing and knowing. From this point of view, spirituality is about how to endure the uncertainties of life via maintaining a state of love and knowing by paying attention to the senses and the Soul.

THE STAGES OF DEVELOPMENT OF THE SELF

As opposed to the development of the Soul

FIRST STAGE

From the moment you are born to the moment you die, you are a sensory work in progress doing the work of your brain, which is to make *sense* of everything. Each person is endowed with a sense of the right order of things; so as an infant, your Soul is in charge. Close on its heels is your body and its various needs. At around the age of six, your intellect, or mind, begins to assert itself in decision-making. During this time, contact with the Soul is gradually lost.

SOUL
CONSCIOUSNESS
MIND
EGO

FIGURE 2. The proportional relationship of one's condition of being at the time of birth.

SECOND STAGE

As your mind starts to assert conscious control, it usurps your Soul's job of decision-making, and your Soul gives up on making decisions, which results in a kind of disintegration of personality. This usually occurs because you need to find your way in the world of adults (parents, teachers, grandparents, mentors, and so on). As you learn to use your mind, it begins to view itself as *who you are*. When this happens, your Soul has been put out of place, and it is required to turn over decision-making to your mind. During this process, arrogance enters the picture. The stronger your intellect or mind, the more arrogant and less compassionate you will become. Only high-quality parenting can change these effects.

MIND
CONSCIOUSNESS
SOUL
EGO

FIGURE 3. The proportional relationship of one's condition of being from the age of six to adolescence.

THIRD STAGE

By the time you reach adolescence, and hormones become active, emotions strive to supplant your mind in making decisions. Your mind struggles to keep control until the effect of hormones becomes so intense that emotions win the round. Meanwhile, your Soul has nothing to say about this turmoil. By that point, decision-making is lost somewhere in your personality, and you might well seek comfort from others who are similarly disintegrated. Only when the raging hormones subside do you literally come to your senses.

EGO
CONSCIOUSNESS
MIND
SOUL

FIGURE 4. The proportional relationship of one's being during adolescence.

FOURTH STAGE

As the brain develops and matures, your senses become more important to you and vie with your emotions to make your decisions and hold your attention. Concurrently, your ego increases in strength and competes for making decisions.

EGO/MIND
CONSCIOUSNESS
SOUL

FIGURE 5. The Soul gradually recedes into the background of one's awareness by adulthood.

FIFTH STAGE

Only after you realize the error of letting the emotions and ego make decisions do you discover how to pull back and again have the mind in charge of decision-making. If you have trouble reverting to having the mind in charge, emotional disorder often ensues, and life appears to degenerate into a series of bad decisions. If you have put your ego in charge, this manifests as paralyzing fear, addiction, or hyper-aggressive behavior. It is unfortunate that people in this situation often end up being miserable and angry, and they make life miserable for those around them.

SIXTH STAGE

The three ways left to live are:

(1) to live with your mind permanently in charge of decision-making and try to reign in the arrogance that accompanies it;
(2) live with your emotions, ego, or mind in charge of decision-making and try to reintegrate your Soul via religion; and
(3) seek reintegration with your Soul directly.

Since this last way has been, historically speaking, the most difficult to achieve, it has also been the path least understood. In most cases where reintegration of the

MIND

CONSCIOUSNESS

EGO

SOUL

FIGURE 6. The relationship of aspects of one's being under the good effects of religion. The mind and consciousness dominate the ego, but the Soul is still mostly out of the picture.

Soul has been sought, the phrase *spiritual development* has been the call-word for this path. While every religion purports to call itself the true path to spiritual development, religions are based on belief, and believing creates a barrier to reintegration with the Soul.

Spiritual seekers are genuinely trying to reintegrate with their Souls, but they too often get sucked down a path that leads to self-delusion. Aware that my model

SOUL

CONSCIOUSNESS

MIND

EGO

FIGURE 7. In a fully integrated human being, the Soul dominates the personality and the consciousness keeps the mind in check while reducing the importance of the ego to almost nothing.

could be construed as one of these self-delusional paths, I would emphasize that a mind that tends to believe or practices believing is one that will likely become self-deluded. Therefore, I advocate *knowing* as a way of being and reject all manner of belief.

It is in the nature of my model that everyone, consciously or unconsciously, is pedaling as fast as they can to do the right thing. Even when they are doing something viewed as wrong, it may be the right thing for them to reintegrate with their Souls. Hence, judging the actions of others as wrong is not a good idea, unless those actions damage another person or persons. They are probably doing everything in their power to integrate with their Souls.

THE SOUL

The Soul, as I have come to define it, is the part of you that makes decisions. After thinking about this for the last thirty-five years, it is my conclusion that the Soul is the most real part of you, but not the conscious you—it is the part of you that is *aware of* the conscious you and of which the conscious you is not aware 99.9% of the time. Indeed, most of us are so far out of contact with our Souls that we treat it as something to be believed in or considered irrelevant. By believing in the Soul, we tend to separate ourselves from it by calling it names like over-self, super consciousness, conscience, spirit, and so on. If, on the other hand, we treat the Soul as irrelevant, it is driven from our reach.

The Soul is part of an entire subliminal system that exists within you, not unlike the heart and circulatory system, or the brain and nervous system. In other words, as the heart is to your circulatory system or the brain is to your nervous system, the Soul is to your spiritual system. The spiritual system acts like the flowing blood in the circulatory system or the air that flows as you breathe. In fact, the spiritual system is the energy that flows in your nervous system and the brain. It is probably most like the digestive system in how it operates, which is perhaps the most important aspect in viewing the Soul.

Ask yourself if you use your body or if your body uses you, and you will likely conclude that you use your body. Ask yourself if you have emotions or if your emotions have you, and you will conclude that you have emotions. If you ask yourself if you use your mind or if your mind uses you, you will likely conclude that you use your mind. However, if you ask yourself if you use your consciousness or if your consciousness uses you, you may arrive at either conclusion. This conundrum can be resolved if you understand that the word *consciousness* comes from the two Latin words *coni*, meaning *with*, and *scio*, meaning *I know* or *knowing*. Since knowing precedes deciding, I conclude that you use your consciousness for that purpose.

Throughout this book, for ease of communication, I will speak in terms of *the* Soul, *your* Soul, *their* Souls, *my* Soul, *our* Souls, etc., but if you answer the question, "Do I use/have a Soul, or does a Soul use/have me?" you will find that the Soul has you. Remember, the real-entity-that-you-are and your Soul are the same thing.

You can behave in ways that are contrary to what your Soul decides. This only means that you have lost contact with your Soul. Indeed, most of us have long ago reassigned the business of decision-making from the Soul to elsewhere. If this business is assumed by the mind or taken up by the ego, then the Soul has let its decision-making duties be usurped. It does this because other parts have been more insistent or overbearing, so the decision-making work is yielded to those stronger and more aggressive parts.

An aggressive mind or intellect usually bullies the Soul into submission. When this happens, arrogance is the result. The central trait of a mind or intellect allowed to run free is its inability to question itself. The word *arrogance* comes from the two Latin words *ab*, meaning *away from*, and *rogo*, meaning *I ask*, *I question*, or *questioning*. Hence, arrogance is to put away questions or questioning.

Similarly, if the emotions or ego usurp the Soul in decision-making, the central trait is the need to save face, and any actions that have the potential to damage self-image are treated as a lethal threat. For example, you have probably experienced times when you were criticized and left feeling attacked or humiliated; this is a sign that your ego was in charge of making decisions.

THE EGO

The ego, or "I," is often referred to as the self, but not in my lexicon. What many refer to as the ego is a part of you that has one job, and that is to keep you alive.

The ego keeps you alive because it is connected to the parts of your brain where emotions and other autonomic systems of your body are processed.

Emotions are based on fear. I know from experience that this statement will raise hackles for many of my readers, but I base this point of view on the two roots of the word: *E* is a Latin prefix meaning *away*, and *movere* is the Latin verb meaning *to move*. Emotion is therefore *motion away*. Hence, love cannot be an emotion because the action of love is to move towards something, not away from it. For all feelings that are not fear based, we need other words. I use the word *ammotions* for feelings of love, based on the Latin *amo*, meaning *I love*, and *movere*, meaning *to move*.

In people who are aurally dominant, the ego can manifest as a ranting, vociferous, critical voice in the head. Those who suffer from an ego-driven physical dominance are manifestly aggressive. Arrogance is the cardinal trait of an ego-driven intellectually dominant person. Spiritually dominant people who are ego-driven suffer from the chronic self-righteousness or an inflamed feeling of certainty that whatever they think or believe is right, without question. Though these characterizations may appear sweeping, it does not mean they are not true; they are based on thirty-five years of observations made for the purpose of understanding how we humans tick.

There are clear precedents for thinking about the ego within our history and culture. Psychologists tend to refer to the dark, unknown aspects of personality as the unconscious. As a teenager, I was able to read all the literature on psychiatry and psychology that my parents owned or subscribed to because they were in those professions. After having been steeped in that point of view, I thought about the unconscious for a long time and concluded that the unconscious was a figment of the imagination. It is something to blame when you don't want to take responsibility for your actions, i.e., the devil made me do it. In my experience, the unconscious is a collection of memories of experiences, feelings, difficulties, desires, motivations, excuses, and delusions. We all harbor these within ourselves because we imagine them to be too embarrassing, unpleasant, or unthinkable to tolerate dwelling on, much less accept. The fact is, everyone has thoughts like these. Dredging them up leads to narcissism or self-infantilization, just as suppressing them leads to psychic constipation.

Having these forbidden thoughts and feelings isn't a problem, it's how you respond to them that is a problem. Like any body function, when things are ingested, they must occasionally be excreted. Just as you wouldn't obsess over going to the bathroom, you need not obsess over your non-conscious emotions. Once they are attended to through self-observation and meditation, they require no further attention until they need to be excreted. They are the stuff of humor, and I suspect that humor is the art we invented to help us take all of that nonsense less seriously.

By viewing the ego rightly, you have the power to disabuse yourself of the hold it can have on you. By regarding it with understanding, you can learn to manage it. Because you can't ever rid yourself of it, learning to manage it is the best course. Recognizing the ego in its many manifestations can help you avoid slipping into delusion. Understanding the ego is the purpose of wisdom.

These concepts of human beings as sensory organisms, the function of the Soul being to make decisions, the role of the ego being to ensure survival, the 133 senses, and our purpose of reintegration with the Soul, are all the results of having spent more than thirty-five years studying the Soul to better understand it. The science of studying our spiritual nature is an aesthetic science because it involves a systematic study of the 133 senses that make up the aesthetic self. These concepts and the results of this study are what this book is about.

The Soul and the Universal Principles

Chapter One
Thirty Creative Mechanisms That Activate the Soul

Thirty-five years ago, my passion for making musical instruments took a turn in a direction that I did not expect. Aspiring, as I was, to make instruments of the highest possible acoustical quality, I was prepared to follow any leads that would result in improving the quality of what I was making. I wanted to make instruments equal in sound to those from the golden age of acoustics, from 1550 to 1840.

Unexpectedly, I made an instrument that sounded radically better than all my past work. In the normal course of things, one might assume that this was reason for rejoicing. For me, it was a disaster because I was stymied to explain how it happened. I hated the idea of making one good instrument without understanding how to duplicate the result, so I decided to go no further until I understood exactly how to make an instrument of comparable quality.

Following the instrument's delivery, I sat myself down to think about everything that had happened during its making. This was the first step of three months of thought before I began to understand what had happened and how it had happened. I discovered during this period of cogitation that I had been actuating some important spiritual mechanisms while building this instrument.

Strictly speaking, the Soul is ungovernable, but by formulating my observations about what had happened as creative mechanisms I found it much easier to change my behavior to accord with the nature of my Soul. At the beginning of my quest

I used the word *intuition* instead of *Soul*. I know now that both the Soul and the intuition are roughly the same thing. That said, I began to articulate these creative mechanisms to guarantee that my work would be as intuitive, or Soul-based, as possible. The reason for this was that whenever I found myself working in an intuitive state, the resulting instrument sounded significantly better than any I had made before. I realized that I could make better-sounding instruments by studying what emerged during the building of them and applying each small improvement to every subsequent instrument I made. This process worked because intuition differs from the Soul as much as your mouth differs from you. That is to say, intuition is the mouthpiece of the Soul. The Soul expresses itself through the intuition.

The creative mechanisms are simple. I express them here as universally applicable and easy for anyone to follow. But, it must be remembered that these creative mechanisms are not mechanisms in the conventional sense. Instead, they are realities uncompromising in how they work, and they determine how behavior must be managed to "log in" to those spiritual realities. I use the word *creative mechanisms* because each has the predictability of a see-saw where one end is pushed down for the other to rise. They could also be likened to the rules of the road, which we follow because to do otherwise would result in chaos. If we want for ourselves the highest possible quality in our lives and work, these creative mechanisms must be enacted.

The Soul, like a plant, is predictable in its behavior. If you try to start seeds on hard, dry, unworked ground, the seeds will fail to germinate. Your ego is like that hard, unworked ground. You have to break it up, turn it over, and repeat the process until there is no possibility of invasive weeds crowding out the plants you are cultivating. Failure to deal with the ego will result in the proliferation of fear-based thoughts (weeds) that will eventually win the competition for reconnecting with the Soul (the plant we are trying to cultivate). Even so, if you manage to deal with your ego's weeds, you still must commit to growing the seeds by feeding, watering, and weeding until they flower and set fruit as mature plants, and then you have to protect the fruit until it is ready to harvest. If you happen to be away having fun on the day the fruit ripens, it will fall to the ground and rot because you weren't present to pick the fruit at the right moment. Furthermore, if you didn't feed the plant, the fruit might be lacking in properties that you could have used had you fed it properly.

Like in farming, cultivating the Soul has no guarantees, even when you have done everything right. The creative mechanisms explain what you can do to optimize your results, but they don't guarantee financial freedom, emotional gratification, or salvation; the creative mechanisms only make sure that you don't get in the way of any possible positive outcomes occurring. The work of clearing the way for the Soul to act needs to be embraced for the pure joy of it because being who you are is a value in itself. These other rewards may or may not materialize, so to expect them is foolish.

I venture to remind you that the Soul is not a metaphysical concept; it is a real system, like the digestive system, and it functions according to principles or mechanisms. Like the digestive system, the spiritual system has requirements and behaviors that are needed to keep it in peak condition.

Creative Mechanism One

What the Soul gives is both right and true, though it may not appear to be so. Everything the Soul gives is true because it is always based on what is real; it is incapable of giving anything false.

Sometimes, when I would change something to improve the sound of my instruments, the acoustical result was inferior. This was unacceptable to me because so much time, energy, and materials are wasted following notions that are wrong. We waste our time with these things because we often do not require our ideas, leads, and notions to justify themselves.[3] When the mind has a notion about the cause of something, it is difficult to gain enough perspective to see that notion as junk or something valuable.

---

[3] I have often noticed that those who have minds like a steel trap tend not to apply that steel trap to their own thinking. Quick to doubt and criticize the thoughts of others, they appear incapable of using that critical ability to filter our own thinking. It is important that we can eliminate junk thought from our minds if we feel compelled to apply that skill to others.

I have devised a routine of putting every idea, notion, or lead to the test by asking the following four questions:

So what?
Who cares?
Why bother?
What of it?

Each of these questions is designed to eradicate vested self-interest from the business of thinking. "So what?" forces the ideas to explain themselves in a manner that would convince me they are right. "Who cares?" requires the ideas to be relevant and pertinent to more people than myself. "Why bother?" insists that the outcome be worth the trouble of changing everything to accommodate the idea. "What of it?" solicits from the idea its purpose, reason, or motivation for being applied.

I have often been asked by others who dabble in building musical instruments to answer questions about their pet theories on acoustics. The problem with pet theories is that they are, literally, pets for those who own them. These folks' lives are taken over by living to service and sustain the pet. Had they answered the questions, they would have gained needed perspective to notice if their pet deserves such attention.

Thought can be classed as junk when it has no rational explanation, it is designed to stroke the ego of its owner, it possesses the mind without improving results, or it fails to respond satisfactorily to the above questions. When a junk thought is not filtered, it gets a foothold in the mind and becomes almost impossible to eradicate. Like a sofa too large for its room, it forces all other thoughts out so that there is never enough space for the mind to move or for the Soul's thoughts to get through.

To override the mind for the sake of the Soul, I regard all that my mind comes up with as being potentially suspect, unreliable, delusional, and ego-centered. I regard it that way because I realize that the mind under the ego is cunning and that it can create hundreds of rational-sounding explanations for every falsity. So, I subject every thought to the four questions. I hold the questions in my mind without answering them—like a vapor, not like a solid object. I hold them in suspension until my intuition comes up with the answer, usually in a flash. Holding ideas or questions as solid objects is dangerous because you can't intuit the answer if you are thinking away about something else or another question.

By taking the trouble to eliminate junk thought from your mind, you make yourself open to the Soul's intuitive suggestions. By holding your fears and ego in check, you have the freedom to pursue those intuitive suggestions. And finally, by filtering everything that crosses your mind with the four questions, you can move forward with the confidence that thought might be from your Soul.

A thought that has been generated by the Soul most often alights as though heard from behind and above. The thought is near silent—several levels more silent than a whisper. In contrast, a thought generated by the mind tends to be low voiced and moderate in tone, while thoughts generated by the ego are most often loud, strident, and urgent. The ego's thoughts are easy to accept, need little reflection, create a feeling of safety, and don't demand much energy or time. Thoughts that come from the Soul require more; they require that you give up your time, energy, and feelings of security.

Often, we become possessed of a notion that agrees with what we believe and that feels right, good, and true. Alas, we can believe anything we like, and the whole range of possibilities lies before us. But when it comes to the Soul, it is interested in reality, not "our reality" as we interpret it, or the social reality of individual or collective fears; the Soul is only interested in reality as it is. This reality is unvarnished, un-interpreted, direct, unmitigated, and profound. It is so simple that children and animals are instantly aware of it unless an adult has beaten that awareness out of them. As thinking adults, we each seem to have figured out how to stay as far away as possible from that uncensored reality. We listen to what others say and group together with those who agree with us, which virtually guarantees that we will be detached from what our Souls find compelling.

Reality is not subject to belief. We can suppose, theorize, theologize, fantasize, and rhapsodize about what is real all we want, but that "don't make it so!" The one way we can approach reality is by knowing, and knowing is the result of paying attention to sensation. True knowledge is the awareness, not the memory, of sensation. Conventional memory-based knowledge is concerned with the past. Real knowledge is known in the present moment. Conventional knowledge is about what other people have experienced and thought and may be useful to the degree that it is a report or snapshot of reality as it was, in a previous time. Unfortunately, real knowledge is not going to make us look smarter than we are, nor will it help us win games based on instant recall of trivia.

The trick to mastering the application of this creative mechanism is to tell the difference between the various competing forces within you. If you can't tell the difference between your Soul and your ego, you are going to be in trouble. This inability characterizes every religiously motivated terrorist, politician, opinion monger, or cult follower. Possessed of the conviction that they are acting as the right hand of God, they will commit every act against the Soul imaginable and justify their acts as having come from God. The reality is that your Soul will never give anything that damages the Soul of another. What the Soul gives is usually designed to encourage others to investigate a relationship with their Souls because the results are so compelling, wonderful, and inspiring. What the ego gives is usually designed to control others and acquire more power.

Creative Mechanism Two

The Soul is not to be restricted or limited. Any attempt to restrict or limit it in others will result in creating the same limitation in you.

The Soul can transcend both time and space. It is ageless and instantaneous in its action. It uses your imagination to create things that don't exist. It uses your body to do its work if you allow it to do so. It uses your mind to explain the real world. It invents things, music, ideas, and understandings instantly, completely, and without effort. This does not mean that you comprehend everything it impresses on you. Your job is to question so as to understand what it has given. If you fail in this job, it is as though you have limited what you will accept from the Soul. Restrict and limit the Soul, and the Soul will respond in kind.

The Soul is like a mirror that reflects what you are. If you are not fast enough to catch the message from that reflection, it will whiz past; and you will never know the difference.

By acknowledging that your Soul processes reality far faster than you can ever match and by applying yourself to the business of watching and waiting for your Soul, you can benefit from your Soul's ability to be everywhere at the same time. Remove your limits on the Soul, and you remove the limits on yourself, and vice versa.

Creative Mechanism Three

Your Soul will never do what you are capable of doing for yourself.

By providing you with clues about what must be done, your Soul will help you do anything at a higher level of quality than you can imagine, but it is your job to figure out how to achieve that end. If you can't think past your current limited and narrow perspective, your Soul will give a glimpse of what you are in for. If you ask, your Soul will reveal how to think about what you are doing so you can do it better. It will help you approach a problem differently from what you may have determined on your own initiative, but that is also something for which you must ask, and it is up to you to move in the direction of those imaginative suggestions.

The purpose in life is to create a relationship with your Soul so that you know it intimately and learn how to get it involved in your life. When this happens, as it can for all of us, your Soul works and grows in your particular interests. Remember, though you may be working towards figuring things out, your Soul has been doing this far in advance of your limited ability to process reality. When it comes to beholding reality, the Soul is masterful.

Creative Mechanism Four

The Soul knows everything, but it can only give what you remind it about.

The Soul behaves with a knowledge that you cannot comprehend. It is not limited by time or space. If you know how, you can access what it knows. However, to do that, you are responsible for investigating the reality of whatever interests you. This investigation reminds your Soul of all that it knows about your interest.

To understand the past, you must have a clear idea of what the reality was for people living in a past age. Then, once reminded of that past reality, the Soul can impress on you the true nature of it. What your Soul can't do is the work required to understand what it gives at the moment of impression.

The business of reminding the Soul is the purpose of exploration, investigation, research, and experimentation. Why do you think we have the word *research*? The word applies most appropriately to delving into a new, untested reality. Scientists are not in the business of rediscovering what they already know, they are devoted to finding what they don't know. But still we use the term *research*, even though it means *to search again*. In essence, a scientist is discovering anew what his or her Soul already knows but needed to be reminded of.

Creative Mechanism Five

The Soul can't be bullied or controlled.

Bullying your Soul will make it avoid involvement with you, and you would be fooling yourself if you thought that your Soul could be controlled. All you can do is control yourself so that you get as much from your Soul as possible. Controlling yourself does not mean behaving yourself; it means keeping a check on your mind and curbing its tendency control everything.

The more controlling your mind is, the more you will need to free yourself from that tendency. There are ways to do this which work and others which do not. The least successful method is not to think at all. People who work in the artistic fields often foster a belief that if they don't think, their Souls will get involved. They once noticed that when they were thinking and working the results were inferior, so they back away from thinking about their work altogether. The most successful method is to bring your mind to bear on whatever you are doing, and then set it aside to let your mind relax. As soon as the mind is totally relaxed, the Soul will emerge, and ideas will start to flow as though the floodgates have been opened.

This method requires you to be aware of how and on what your mind is working. When you notice that your mind is wandering, you have realized that it was out of your management but is no longer because you regained awareness of that state. If your mind is obsessed with an idea that has no relevance, it is out of your management. Being disciplined in the use and management of your mind is crucial to getting the most from your Soul. The Soul needs you to remind it of what it knows and what you need, but your mind must be in a relaxed condition for the Soul to be heard. When your mind is relaxed, it is more aware of the Soul's subtlest thoughts. That experience is vitalizing and inspiring because nothing can compare to the feeling of being in full contact with the Soul. Indeed, so much energy is released in that state that one can often function for weeks, months, or sometimes years from a moment with the Soul that might have lasted ten seconds or less.

The more often you have this experience, the easier it will become to put yourself into a condition of relaxed, open awareness. If you hold in mind an important question and present it to your Soul, you will often find that its answer will be in direct opposition to the answer you want to hear. In fact, in the early stages of developing a relationship with your Soul, your preferred view on a question will likely be the opposite of what your Soul challenges you with. Most of the time, this is because what you think you want is, in fact, a desire of your ego. It is rare that the desires of the ego and the Soul are the same. However, you will discover that when the ego has been brought to heel, the energy available to do the Soul's work is exponentially magnified, like when the result of bringing together matter and anti-matter is a huge release of energy.

The technique I developed to bring my ego to heel first began with acknowledging its true responsibility. That responsibility is to keep me alive by being wary of possible danger and keeping me clear of any lethal threat. Acknowledging that responsibility means that I promise to pay attention and heed its signals when danger lurks. By promising to pay attention and act on the ego's warning signals to keep me out of danger, I can take back the reigns of my life. I noticed that when I spoke that promise, I could palpably feel my ego letting go and relaxing with the knowledge that I would keep the promise.

Making that promise and reinforcing it, from time to time, is a good idea. You can do this by putting yourself into situations that will activate your ego into sending its warning signals, whether the situation is actually dangerous or not. This allows you to manage your reaction to keep your ego in its comfort zone by fulfilling your promise to it. Relevant to this is the idea that paying attention and heeding the warning signals in no way means that you must oblige your ego. It means that you acknowledge the warning and decide to continue what you are doing anyway. In these circumstances, the ego assumes the responsibility for generating the endurance, grit, or plain adrenaline to get the job done. If life is lost, the ego makes life go out in glory because that, too, is part of its job.[4]

I activate my ego like this by challenging myself to learn something unfamiliar from time to time. This puts me in the role of a rank beginner where I will make mistakes, and the ego hates making mistakes because it loathes the criticism that mistakes elicit. This loathing is the ego reacting to the feeling of a false lethal threat which criticism excites. I use this as an opportunity to reassert my dominion over my ego.

Creative Mechanism Six

Your Soul will give when you are in Love Mode.

During one fruitful session of cogitation, I instantly understood what spiritual development was about. The way it occurred to me was that the brain processes everything in one of two modes: Fear Mode and Love Mode.

In Fear Mode, the parts of the brain utilized are those parts often referred to as the primitive or reptilian brain. We each share these same primitive structures with other mammals, birds, and reptiles. The purpose of the Fear Mode brain and the ego is the same—to ensure our survival. The Fear Mode brain is where the emotions and all autonomic body functions are processed. This means that your ego is always busy keeping you alive and breathing without any attention or intelligence on your part. The problem with this Fear Mode brain is that the ego is so stupid it can't tell the difference between real and fake danger. Your ego will treat the presence of a man-eating tiger ready to kill you as a similar threat to someone criticizing you. Because the ego can't tell the difference, it will start a

---

[4] I suspect that the ego and the historical Lucifer are one and the same. To be the light bearer, the ego needs to go out in a blaze of glory. The curious thing is that to create an environment in which the ego can become that angel of light is as mundane as having the courage to confront an abuser to be clear that the abuse must stop, or something similar. Creating art also has that effect because for art to have any punch it requires the ego to be involved in the dangers of making something that may be criticized. Otherwise, art has no intensity, and to be art an object must be imbued with intensity, among other traits.

fight or flight response in either situation. When you become belligerent because you took offense at something someone has said, this is the fight response enacted by your ego. The flight response is cessation of listening.

The first function of spiritual development is to train one's ability to discriminate between real danger and fake danger and, in so doing, inculcate a deliberateness of being so that one can access all of the brain, including those parts beyond reach when in Fear Mode. The purpose of spiritual development is to get out of Fear Mode and stay in Love Mode.

In Fear Mode, the brain operates by believing. Believing is easy, fast, and requires no thought. In Love Mode, the brain operates by knowing. Knowing is hard, sometimes painfully slow, and requires a huge amount of thought to process. Believing, which is not to think, requires minimal brain matter or processing power.

This idea about Fear Mode and Love Mode being linked to physical brain-structures occurred to me while I was thinking about the nature of belief. What I observed in myself, as well as others, is the tendency to formulate beliefs rather than paying attention. Indeed, the number of words and terms we have in English that involve *believing* and *beliefs* is fascinating. Here are a few:

accept
accredit
think
trust
gullible
understand
assume
rely on
keep the faith
lap up
place confidence in
suppose
faith
speculation

gambling
gamble
invest
investing
posit
postulate
presume true
presuppose
affirm
attach weight to
notion
notional
be certain of
be convinced of

be credulous
be of the opinion
theory
theorize
theoretical
hypothetical
hypotheses
preconceptions
buy
conceive
conclude
consider
count on
credit

deem	reckon on	take as gospel
fall for	regard	take at one's word
give credence to	rest assured	take for granted
have	suppose	take it
have faith in	swallow	etc.
have no doubt	swear by	

By comparison, the words synonymous with *know* and *knowing* are few:

appreciate	see	distinguish
experience	apperceive	fathom
have	apprehend	grasp
learn	cognize	ken
notice	comprehend	prize
perceive	differentiate	undergo
realize	discern	sense
recognize	discriminate	etc.

To me, this means that people are much more comfortable believing something than knowing it. Unfortunately, the act of believing anything renders the believer incapable of knowing and keeps them in Fear Mode.[5]

When I decided to believe nothing, it did not make me an atheist; atheists believe in no god, which is another belief. I was requiring of myself that I would avoid every form of believing, such as speculations, assumptions, notions, preconceptions, theories, and the like. At first, this made thinking difficult because our language is replete with phrases that express belief, all of which are difficult to avoid using. Even the words that mean to eschew belief, such as *skeptical*, *cynical*, etc., carry with them notions of one's superiority due to not believing. Putting away all beliefs is essential. However, by remaining cognizant

[5] This could be proved or disproved using brain scanning to determine where it is in the brain that believing and knowing are processed.

of the dangers inherent in the act of believing, I found that I was eventually able to use those words without thinking that the thoughts behind them were true.

The discipline of purging my mental habits that were founded on believing made my question-asking more interesting and focused. Questions became more aimed at answers involving knowing and reality, and being and staying in Love Mode became much easier when belief never entered the picture. Thinking became more focused and cleaner because I stopped entertaining all questions to which the answer could not be known. All in all, the benefits were worth the difficulties.

Eventually, I understood that the most effective mechanism for setting aside years and years of Fear Mode functioning is forgiveness. From this point of view, forgiveness is the single most "self-ish" process we can enact. It is something we do for ourselves; but, paradoxically, we are not the only ones who benefit. Everyone around us benefits from that act. Forgiving is not easy to do, especially in cases of horrendous abuse, but it is necessary for the Soul to work in our lives.

The saying "forgive and forget" is an unfortunate expression because people think that if they can't forget then they can't forgive. Nothing could be farther from the truth. The saying should be, "forgive and remember." You can't forget terrible abuse or having been deeply hurt, so if you take the view that you will forgive the abuser anyway, it makes forgiving much easier because you never become plagued by self-recrimination when you find that you can't forget. Also, forgiveness is a personal responsibility. If you witness someone being abused, you have a responsibility to try ending the abuse because of the damage to both the abused and the abuser's relationship with the Soul. Likewise, if you experience abuse from others, it is important to protect your relationship with your Soul by bringing that abuse to an end. In forgiving, you free yourself from slavery to the negative energy you are subjected to. By not forgiving, that energy will hold you in bondage until you become bright enough to realize the benefits of forgiveness.

Historically, the aim of religion has been to offer a guide for how to stay in Love Mode so that humans can develop a relationship with the Soul. However, religion has become polluted with layers of belief that don't have that aim in mind. Indeed, at its worst, religion inculcates fear so that those in charge keep control over believers. When this happens, religious leaders become true enemies of the

Soul because any fear, no matter how subtle, is enough to banish the Soul from being active. Afflicting others by creating fear in them places one in the role of antagonist to the Soul. Those who create fear do so because it feeds their egos, and well-fed egos feel secure and confident of survival. The same is true for those who spread beliefs, for believing is the seed of fear as knowing is the seed of Love.

There is a sure way to know: Pay attention to what is happening. Paying attention and loving are one and the same. You can't do one except that you do the other. To say you love someone and not pay attention to them is hypocrisy. Likewise, to pay attention to something while claiming not to love it is an error. What you pay attention to is what you love. What you fail to pay attention to is not loved by you, despite any claims to the contrary. The act of paying attention is the act of glorifying, so what you pay attention to is what you glorify. Glorification is a form of worship, and people will only worship that which is important or valuable to them. Thus, to focus your attention on criticizing the behavior of others is the same as worshipping or glorifying them and their behavior, so beware the tendency to gossip or complain because it is a form of worship.

The opposite of paying attention (not paying attention) is cultivating ignorance. From ignorance springs fear, while from knowing springs love. By paying attention to something as simple as your breathing, you can stay in Love Mode. Life is too short to waste on cultivating behavior that keeps you in Fear Mode or that encourages the glorification of nonsense.

Creative Mechanism Seven

To get the most from your Soul, you must trust it totally (but not stupidly).

There are several kinds of doubt, one of which leads to knowing. This kind of doubt involves questioning to arrive at an understanding of what you need to know. Another kind of doubt is the religious belief that only things of a material nature are knowable; if they can't see, touch, or measure it, it doesn't exist. This second kind of doubt is held high in the minds of those who practice it because it makes them feel superior. They are so convinced this way is superior that they consider others who experience non-material aspects of reality to be living in La La Land. Unfortunately for them, the Soul is real, yet it can't be seen, measured, or touched. Those who practice this religion of doubt rarely experience a relationship with their Souls. They are so desperate to be right that they miss the entire point of being alive. It has been said that one should never use the word *stupid* in one's writing. However, here the word is not only apt, it is necessary because stupidity is the inability to profit from error.[6] Those who practice the dogmatic form of doubt are unable to perceive their intellectual stance as flawed. Thus, they suffer from a chronic, incurable stupidity.

What I propose is that we test everything, especially our own assumptions. Useful doubt hangs lightly on the shoulders. It evaluates everything to filter out junk thought. It questions everything to examine it in the light of clear, unprejudiced, and sensible reason. Our brains evolved to process the whole of reality, not just the tangible or material aspects of it.

There was a time in my work when I was trying to find the structure of the sounds of antique harpsichords and violins. During that time, it dawned on me that the most important part of the structure of any sound was a certain harmonic, and when that harmonic was extremely present, the sound had the same structure as found in the best musical instruments from the past. When this occurred to me, I then proceeded to try proving that it wasn't true. The path doing that took me on cost me three years of work to prove that it, in fact, was true. In other words, I could have saved three years of experimentation had I focused on finding what that harmonic was and how to enhance it. However, I would have lost everything else that I discovered along the way. My Soul had given me the insight of what I needed to focus on, but by assuming full responsibility for understanding what I had been given and trying to prove it wrong, I ended up mastering dozens of other ways of improving sound that are just as important, if not more important.

Often, to make sense of what you get from your Soul, you will require super-rational understanding. Since you probably don't have that kind of super-rational ability, you must do the best you can to understand and do what your Soul has suggested. Sometimes this can be daunting because it will require

---

[6] When I was growing up, my mother posted a maxim on the wall for everyone to read. It said, "Stupidity is not in making mistakes; stupidity is the inability to learn from them."

you to do things that appear counterintuitive. Scary or not, conditions may need you to trust your Soul and do something that seems irrational.

The Soul's suggestions can be upon you so fast that when you later stop to think about what happened, you think it was a glaring error, but later reflection makes it clear that what happened was a serendipitous accident. Most of every improvement in the quality of my work has been the result of serendipity. It was through these experiences that I became intimately acquainted with my Soul and learned to trust it completely. When that occurs, the highest level of quality is the result. Nothing higher can be had at that moment.

Creative Mechanism Eight

Your Soul works most efficiently when you ask it to provide you with right attitudes.

Every major advance in learning comes with a new attitude or a more right attitude. Minor advances occur in the realm of a single insight. Multiple insights will result in "AHA!" experiences, which occur because of a change of attitude or point of view resulting in new understanding.

It is in the nature of problems that there exists one right point of view or attitude such that the problem appears to solve itself. The Soul functions most efficiently to give these right attitudes. A clever person will begin solving a difficult problem by asking their Soul for the one right way to view that problem. If you try this, remember that asking does not guarantee an immediate solution—the Soul is not yours to command. Normally, you will be required to exhaust your own resources before it will give what you ask of it; and when it does give what you need, the attitude will be gently impressed on your mind. If you make the mistake of ignoring your Soul when it provides what you ask of it (usually because the attitude it provided conflicts with your beliefs), it will stop being forthcoming, even when you really need what it has to offer.

One often likes to think that the Soul is unceasingly compassionate. Indeed, it is, but it is not tolerant of nonsense and stupidity. If it has provided you with the necessary attitude and you fail to adopt that attitude, it is your own fault that things fail to work out. Anyone who has a genuine relationship with their Soul finds out that it has zero tolerance for nonsense. If it seems that your Souls is indulging in notions, triviality, and nonsense, then you are probably having a relationship with the egoistic self.

The Soul is paradoxical in this regard. It is so sensitive to fear that the slightest hint of it will cause the Soul's disappearance, but when it is in charge, it tolerates no nonsense whatsoever. This behavior often manifests in a person by him or her deferring control to whoever appears to need it most and then becoming intolerant of nonsense when he or she is running things. It can be intimidating for those on the receiving end of this behavior. It is like how the ego works but in reverse—the ego is all about nonsense.

Everything hinges on how committed you are to having a productive relationship with your Soul. Once you understand the Soul's idiosyncrasies, you learn to accept its behavior because you need the attitudes it offers to function at your highest level. So, if this no-nonsense behavior is bothering, as the saying goes, "if you can't stand the heat, get out of the kitchen."

Creative Mechanism Nine

Your Soul is not encumbered by time or space. Work at the speed of the Soul, which is significantly faster than you can think.

The Soul is the fastest thing in the universe. Light is like a tortoise by comparison. The Soul is unique, even hyper-quantum in property, in that it can be in thousands of places at the same time and can straddle the past and the future simultaneously. Only our self-imposed limitations lead us to believe that this cannot be true.

So, to follow this creative mechanism, I had to learn to work faster than I could think. This introduced into my work a host of mistakes, but I was able to distinguish between mistakes made by my incompetence and serendipitous "mistakes" that were the result of my Soul at work. I focused on eliminating every one of my errors and incompetencies, while preserving every serendipitous mistake. Not surprisingly, the acoustic quality of my work improved. By applying this creative mechanism, I initiated a process by which I would eventually figure out how the greatest instrument makers from the seventeenth, eighteenth, and early-nineteenth centuries made their wonderful-sounding instruments.

Interestingly, others began to see a style or look in my work that they said was like a brand-new antique.

If you are working faster than you can think, what replaces thinking as a specific guide to guarantee a quality outcome? After pondering this question for several days, I narrowed the possibilities down to two phrases:

All real learning takes place in the imagination. You cause to be real only that which you imagine.

What resides in one's imagination may be realized at any speed. It was from this insight that I developed a personal approach to guide my several long-standing learning problems, the main one being dyslexia. If something isn't in my imagination, it is either because it wasn't put there in the first place or it was incomplete when it was put there. From that moment on, my learning became a process of constructing an imagination of whatever it was I set out to learn.

I have since found no exceptions to the above observation on learning. It turns out that much of what is valued in the time-tested model of learning isn't real learning at all, it's memorizing. Memorizing is to real learning what plastic pearls are to oyster-made pearls. It looks like learning. It can be tested to see if it acts like learning. It can be evaluated for accuracy. It can be corrected. It can be improved. But until it is applied in a relevant manner, it is not learned, and here lies the problem because we will never use much of what we learn in school, unless we all become schoolteachers, accountants, or personal trainers. By approaching learning as a process of constructing an imagination, it is easy to find holes in that construction when you try to use it, especially when you are working at speed.

My wife, Marianne Ploger, is an amazing musical and perceptual scientist. She has figured out how to teach the fundamentals of musicianship so that her students know, at the speed of music, what is happening in a piece of music on one hearing. This is much like how Mozart was able to know what was happening in a piece of music by another composer as he was hearing it played for the first time. Her approach is to teach the most basic elements of music, pitches, notes, intervals, chords, and rhythms in a manner that builds them into her students' imaginations. If it is not in the imagination, it is not learned.

As soon as what you learn is in your imagination, the main difficulty is in applying what you have learned at the speed of the Soul. Since the Soul is beyond the limits of time, it is necessary to work much faster than you can think so your conscious mental processes can't get in the way. The ultimate aim in all endeavors is to become one with your Soul so that it does your work for you. If you don't work faster than you can think, you will never acquire the fluency necessary for your Soul to be engaged in what you do. In my experience, the real reason for failure to acquire fluency in this manner is the fear of making a mistake. Banish all fear of error, push yourself beyond the impulse to control everything, aim to achieve the greatest possible speed in whatever you do, and let go to allow your Soul to realize the best possible outcome.

We are raised to consider mistakes as bad, wrong, incompetent, evil, and even sinful. What this attitude encourages is a hatred for mistakes and the act of making them. In truth, those who hate making mistakes will never grow beyond the simplistic idea of *mastery is not making mistakes.* Hating our mistakes will condemn us to either repeat them over and over, or, it will cause us to glorify the ability of not making mistakes. This I learned from a colleague who was proud of the viola da gamba he had made because there was "nothing wrong with it." To me, the instrument sounded uninteresting, bland, and unfocused, all of which I considered to be egregious errors of sound-quality. As Percy Blakney is quoted as saying, "Nothing is quite so bad as that which is not so bad!"[7]

When I switched from hating my mistakes to loving them for what they could teach me, I found that they vanished from my work. Having noticed this link, I concluded that hating mistakes causes one to dismiss them from memory, which results in certainty that the mistake will happen again. Loving mistakes keeps them near and dear to your attention where they can show, in no uncertain terms, how not to do something. If you follow this regime, your work will always improve.

---

[7] Percy Blakney is the main character in the story by Baroness Emmuska Orczy, *The Scarlet Pimpernel.*

Creative Mechanism Ten

The Soul operates according to universal principles. Convert the cause of every improvement wrought by the Soul into a fixed principle.

By analyzing my work, I discovered that all improvements in it were effects. By viewing these improvements as effects, I could trace back to what had caused them. Then, by formulating a principle that I supposed was the cause for an improvement, I could objectively test if that principle was the cause. If my guess about the cause was correct, the next instrument would turn out to sound as good or better than the last one. If incorrect, the next instrument would sound worse or no better than the last. Gradually, I figured out how to link each discrete effect with its underlying cause. As I got better at doing this, it became clear that the quality of my work was increasing so fast that each instrument became aesthetically obsolete before it was finished.

Creative Mechanism Eleven

It's your responsibility to bring every idea that comes from your Soul to completion.

Before understanding this mechanism, my head was full of ideas. I am sure that some of these ideas were intuitions while many others were the product of my fantasy. The question was how to know which ideas were which. I discovered that intuitive ideas had a certain quality to them which my self-generated ideas did not have. The only thing I could say at the time is that they felt more solid and right. By first determining the solidity and rightness of an idea by how it felt, I could more easily figure out how to bring the idea to completion.

I had seen how someone could get an idea that was from their Soul, as far as I could tell, but then they didn't take responsibility for bringing that idea to completion. From what I observed, the result was that they appeared to have fewer and fewer ideas as time went by. Somehow, they never seemed to evolve beyond the point when they had that idea. Determined to avoid that trap, I resolved to always bring ideas I got from my Soul to completion, and my work has never ceased to evolve and improve as a result of applying this creative mechanism. When I see others whose work is always improving, I have noticed that they too follow this creative mechanism, whether they know it or not.

When I bring an idea to completion and am not happy with the result, it is usually the problems I had to solve in the process that made it important to have brought that idea to completion. From these experiences, I concluded that it is often necessary to go through with mediocre ideas before the great ideas can occur to us. Mediocre ideas need far more skill and ingenuity to bring to a first-rate result than do great ideas. Submitting ourselves to doing everything in our power to make a mediocre idea work is challenging and instructive.

Somehow, it seems that our Souls test us by giving us the ideas we need to grow. If we turn our noses up at mediocre ideas, we are prejudging the quality of what the Soul gives, which is a sure way to get fewer and fewer ideas. For this reason, you must work through every idea from your Soul.

Creative Mechanism Twelve

Your Soul never speaks to you when you think you know better.

By now you will have guessed that the Soul is a sensitive creature. Like a sea anemone blooming in the rough and tumble ocean but retreating when it senses a specific presence, the Soul blossoms while it works away at whatever you invite it to do; but the instant it senses you having your own thoughts, it recedes into the background. The Soul always loses in a struggle for attention because it never interferes when you think you know better than it.

Over years of experience, your Soul has learned how you behave, and so it responds accordingly to your behavior. This means that every time you give in to your fears, you are choosing to ignore your Soul. It also means that every time you take credit for something your Soul did, you are dismissing its value and importance and are basking in glory that does not belong to you. With each belittlement, the Soul retreats further into its shell and hesitates to take part in your life.

If you think you know better than your Soul, it will let you think that, but it is not so with your ego. Your ego will do everything in its power to dominate your thinking. Like a veritable clown on stage, your ego will grab all the attention it can get and does everything it can to increase its ability to run, or ruin, your life.

Where the Soul suggests and gives, the ego grabs and takes. Not until you pay attention to your Soul will it venture forth, make itself known, and be active.

It is also important to know that the Soul is the same in each of us. That is, my Soul and your Soul are of the same spiritual material. For me to address myself to your Soul is to address myself to my Soul, everyone else's Souls, and our collective Soul. Deal with one Soul, and we deal with all Souls. This is because the Soul is universal and identical in each individual. It behaves in a hyper-quantum manner. What we do to one, is done to all. What we do to all, is done to one. This is the underlying truth in the saying, "Do unto others as you would have others do unto you." It is not an injunction about a behavioral relationship, rather, it is an injunction about a spiritual relationship that might be described as follows: As you would have your Soul relate to you, relate to the Souls of others.

If you mistreat another's Soul, for example, by taking credit for the work or ideas of that Soul, you damage your Soul and cause it to withhold itself. If you exalt the Soul of another for providing right, good, useful, and true ideas, your Soul will feel the exaltation and be encouraged to produce similar ideas for you. For this reason, you should be eager to give credit where credit is due and recognize the Soul-relationship in others so the relationship with your Soul is not imperiled.

Creative Mechanism Thirteen

Your Soul needs to know, understand, and feel that you take seriously what it gives you, otherwise it will not give you what you need, regardless of the consequences.

You might inadvertently get something from your Soul, but then fail to view it as important enough for you to follow up, probably because you are ignorant of what this Soul-relationship is all about. Ignorant or not, this behavior sends the message to your Soul that you don't take it seriously.

It doesn't matter to the Soul if you believe in it or not. Your Soul doesn't care what you believe as long as you pay attention to what it offers. If you use what your Soul offers by expanding on it and thinking about how it may be used and developed, your Soul will offer more.

Incidentally, it's fine if you prefer to characterize the relationship with your Soul as being your intuition. The Soul is indifferent as to how you characterize the relationship. Just remember that the words you use to characterize it need to be formulated carefully because they might color the relationship in unanticipated ways.

Creative Mechanism Fourteen

The Soul gives what you need only when you need it, according to what you can deal with and how you have managed the relationship.

A physicist's Soul will probably not give him or her all the themes and solutions for working out a symphony; likewise, a composer's Soul will probably not be revealing the solution to cold nuclear fusion. Physicists don't need musical themes, and composers don't need solutions to problems in physics. Your Soul knows what you need better than you do. It also knows how you are going to receive and process what it gives, even before you ask. It knows this by the nature of the relationship you have with it.

If you never pay attention to what your Soul offers, why should it pay attention to you? Any serious relationship in life is a reciprocal balance between give and take. If a water tank is never filled, and water is continually removed from it, the tank will run dry. You might wonder what your Soul needs, and how to provide for your Soul in a way that is meaningful. The needs of the Soul are what much of this book is about. For now, it suffices to say that for the relationship to be reciprocal, you must pay close attention to what your Soul offers you.

Since your Soul knows the difference between needs and wants, it won't have much to offer when you want what you do not need. If you want to fish, you will have to figure that out. If you need to eat, and all that is available to eat are fish in the stream, your Soul will lead you to figure out how to fish.

Creative Mechanism Fifteen

The Soul can only give slightly more than what it is paid in the form of attention.

If you aren't paying attention, your Soul can't give information that you don't already know, but it can give new insights into what you do know. By increasing how informed you are, you can increase your insights. By increasing knowledge, you increase in understanding.

This creative mechanism refers to facts and information. The Soul knows everything, but it needs to be reminded of what it already knows. If you don't take the trouble to educate yourself in whatever it is that you're doing, your Soul will never give more than what you can handle. By educating yourself about what you need to know, you make it clear to your Soul, beyond a shadow of a doubt, that you are serious about what you're doing.

The Soul is incapable of filling an empty head, so you need to learn as much as possible and in as many related areas of knowledge as possible. When you do this, your Soul creates a synthesis of all that is true and useful and eliminates the rest so that what you get is distilled to the point where you might not understand what has been given. That is the reason why it is important to take seriously what you get and puzzle it over to ferret out all that may be nonsense (while still being willing to try out what you were given). If you do get an idea from your Soul, the results may be astounding and wonderful.

Creative Mechanism Sixteen

Trust encourages the Soul, while doubt squelches it.

Although I have already addressed the matter of doubt concerning the products of the Soul, it is also necessary to address what effects doubt and trust have on the Soul's behavior. In the same way that a deafening, continuous noise will cause us to cover our ears and recoil, the Soul will withdraw and recoil from the damaging effects of doubt. It is as though doubt acts as a smothering agent intended to put out the Soul's flame of inspiration. An intention to smother is not required for doubt to have this effect; rather, the slightest hint of it is all that is required.

So, while you are in a receiving mode, you must cast yourself in a trusting state. The time to raise or consider any questions arising from doubts is *after* you have received something from your Soul.

Holding a condition of not doubting does not mean that you are actively encouraging your Soul. Not doubting simply prevents restriction. On the other hand, trust works to free the Soul's behavior. To encourage your Soul means trusting it implicitly. Like riding a bicycle, the first attempts at this may be unnerving, but the more you trust your Soul, the more likely it is that you may merge with it. I call this eventual merger *super integration.* In this state, you unify with the Soul and become what might be called a *prime mover.*

Trust is a curious state. It implies a powerful yielding up of feelings of control over outcomes. Trust is aware of consequences, but pre-accepts whatever outcome may happen. Most people detest giving up a feeling or an illusion of control. After all, being in control of things is an illusion because it doesn't exist in reality. If we could control everything, there would be no accidents, the weather would be perfectly predictable, other people would behave according to our will, and harmony would prevail everywhere. If humans could control everything, it means that I could control everything, you could control everything, and everyone else in the world could control everything. All of this would mean that nobody could control much of anything, which is exactly how the world works.

We have control over one thing—ourselves. What is fascinating is how much control of ourselves we have but how few people are determined to exercise that control. We all have a modicum of control over limited aspects of our lives, and by considering what we can control, we gain a measure of security from the feeling of certainty it provides. Trusting our Souls means giving up that measure of security and feeling of certainty.

When you experiment in trusting your Soul, you will discover that what was once viewed as chaos has a specific order to it, and what was once deemed precarious is not dangerous at all. What you gain by trusting your Soul is a perspective that takes in the whole picture, rather than a tiny part of it. You will be able to see how interrelated everything is and notice how things you used to view as important become unimportant. You will be able to notice how your awareness of the world becomes more focused on the essence of things and not so much on the surface of things. As you become more committed to trusting the Soul, you will begin to think in the way your Soul thinks and know in the way your Soul knows; and, most miraculously of all, you will begin to be the person you were born to be. This is what it means to be true to yourself.

Creative Mechanism Seventeen

Usually, the Soul is not nice.

That's right. When you get to know the Soul, you discover that it isn't nice. It can be extremely demanding in what it requires. You remember that the Soul is intolerant of nonsense? There are people in our lives who mirror that behavior, and we respect them more than we enjoy being around them. Yet the more we are around these people, the more we come to love them because they don't tolerate nonsense, which makes them more real to be with. The same is true of the Soul.

Reality, in its nature, is not nice. If you get used to this idea, you will learn to appreciate it when seemingly nice things happen. Nice is unchallenging, pleasant, and agreeable. Part of why being in wilderness is so invigorating is that it calls on all your senses to deal with the vast complexity to which you are exposed. On the other hand, nice calls on none of your senses.

Since paying attention requires you to focus on your senses, your Soul will enhance that state by invigorating and inspiring you. This makes paying attention easier and, at the same time, more serious.

Creative Mechanism Eighteen

The Soul's insights, understandings, ideas, conceptions, and potentialities flow constantly, in the same way that reality flows constantly. When you are in tune or at one with your Soul, you live in the flow of its bounty.

According to an urban myth, Albert Einstein said that humans use about 10% of their brain-capacity. If he was functioning at 10% of capacity, imagine what functioning at 100% would be like. We are built to use far more of our brains than we settle for. We are held back by our beliefs about what we are capable of, our fears of the unknown, the limits of what we imagine is possible, and, most importantly, how little time we spend listening.

Interestingly, there is a correlation between how much brain capacity an organism has and the amount of listening an organism needs to do for survival. For instance, animals which rely on echolocation to maneuver and find food will have significantly larger brains than animals of about the same size who use their eyes and sense of smell to do the same thing.

Using more of your brain capacity requires only that you spend more time listening than you do now. The act of listening is interesting in that it involves purposefully not focusing on yourself. This means that purposefully not focusing on yourself and brain size are related. By developing a habit of spending more time every day in active listening, you can increase the amount of brain accessible to you. However, actively listening is hard work. It takes effort and focus, but it is not impossible. Indeed, anyone can do it.

Active listening is the whole point of meditation. Meditation is what I call *mind-watching*. To mind-watch is to listen to your mind as it makes plans, works out problems, thinks about gossip, obsesses over fears, and so on. By watching your mind grind away on this thought and that, you eventually begin to notice (using more of your brain capacity) patterns and triggers which result in predictable outcomes. You can notice, too, during momentary silences, a steady, seemingly insignificant idea that leads to an expanded awareness of the reality you experience inside yourself (using more of your brain capacity). By focusing on those moments of silence when these apparently insignificant ideas make themselves known, you are tapping into a bounty which flows from the Soul in a constant stream. Those ideas, which appear to be insignificant, are hints from your Soul on how to more effectively cope with the false reality of social interaction and living according to man-made rules. As you focus on those moments of silence for what you can glean from them, you are taking concrete steps to giving full attention to the Soul and the bounty that it has to offer.

Every new idea requires you to think and draw the meaning it has for you. Doing this increases your brain capacity since it produces new, interlinking neuronal pathways in your brain. When you are constructing new neuronal pathways, you are also increasing the resources that your Soul can use to give you better and more-precise ideas about what you are doing with your life.

All of this runs like mechanical clockwork. Do one thing that effects another thing that triggers something else, and so on. What doesn't run like clockwork is the nature of the ideas you will receive, which normally relate to problems and questions that you pose. For each of us, it is different. My search was first focused on how to improve the acoustics of my instruments. Then it became a quest to understand all about the Soul and the mechanics involved in its workings. What you bring to your Soul is what you will get out of the experience. It depends on you. The more you bring, the more you will get. If you want it, your Soul is there for you with a continuous flow of insights and ideas.

Creative Mechanism Nineteen

The Soul is not apt at explanation—that is the mind's job.

Every part of a human being has its own unique responsibility. You can use your feet like hands, but feet and legs were made for walking, not for picking things up. Similarly, the Soul is best suited to providing the right attitudes at the right time, and it is also well suited to generating ideas and understandings. It is not good at providing explanations. If you ask your Soul to explain why something works the way it does, it's like asking your endocrine system to do your thinking. You might get an answer, but just as the endocrine system's thoughts tend to be based on hormones, explanations coming from your Soul are likely to be cryptic and mysterious. Your Soul may know what it means, but it might be years before you can make heads or tails of it.

It is best to put tools to the purpose for which they were designed and are suited, like using a chisel as a chisel and not as a screwdriver. Your mind is best suited for forming explanations and noticing interrelationships, just as your imagination is best suited to be your Soul's playroom, and your Soul is best suited to providing you with right attitudes. Each is an aspect of full brain capacity, and each profit from the time you spend paying attention to them.

The main reason why people don't improve over time is that they become attached to attitudes that don't work. Having things not work is addictive because it supplies a feeling of predictability in their lives. In the end, the ability to abandon wrong attitudes and adopt right ones is the real measure of intelligence. Since everyone has this ability from birth, everyone can increase their intelligence by quickening this process.

Often, attitudes that have worked to solve past problems may not be the right attitudes needed to solve today's problems. The best attitudes are those with which problems tend to solve themselves. If you ask your Soul to give the attitude needed for a problem to solve itself, you will find that those attitudes are most unexpected and interesting.

Creative Mechanism Twenty

To connect Soul to mind, keep your mind on a leash. This enables you to focus on principles rather than on your mind's penchant for concepts, notions, beliefs, or theories.

Too often, the mind is working at odds with the Soul. The mind wants to control, explain, hold court, judge, and be rational. These behaviors are antithetical to developing a strong relationship with the Soul. To have the mind not be rational, not be controlling, not explain things, and not judge and condemn is like asking a dog to be a cat. The mind does what it does because that is what minds do. The problem with an out-of-control mind is that it quickly turns the penchant for controlled and predictable outcomes into an obsession for controlling everything and everyone. To prevent this from happening, it is imperative that you hold a suspicious attitude towards your mind, lest it run away with itself because of its hubris. Keep a leash on your mind's knack for inventing explanations using the flimsiest of reasoning, distrust every thought generated by your mind, and inquire of each thought where errors have occurred.

Of all the powers of the mind that need to be managed, the power of judgment and its sidekick, condemnation, have no equal. When judgment and condemnation get together, they produce a judgmental mentality that I call *judgmentalment.* To comprehend the difference between judgmentalment and mere opinion or being judgmental, you need to understand that opinions are not judgments at all. Opinions are feelings expressed to sound and look like judgment but are judgmentalment. True judgment is not based on feelings at all. It is based on knowledge and understanding of the underlying reality behind every phenomenon. As much as you should seek to avoid opinionating, you ought to seek entirely unbiased judgment.

For your mind to be in harmony with your Soul, you are required to manage what your mind is allowed to control and when it is allowed to sit in judgment, and you need to work your mind into creating explanations using its power of reason. Eventually, you can bring your mind into a state of unity with your Soul by learning to incorporate into your thinking the way the Soul thinks.

When you have unified your mind with your Soul, your ability to understand and creatively analyze reality and mental life will take on a quality of competence and solidity it never had before. Thoughts that would have been perplexing will become easy to grasp. Subtle differences in types or tones of thought will become obvious until they are glaring in how different they are. What might have been faint and beyond your ability to pay attention to will become strong and forthright. All this is as it should be, according to how we humans have been designed by evolution.

Creative Mechanism Twenty-One

To connect your Soul to your imagination, think metaphorically and attitudinally, not irrationally, hopefully, or phantasmagorically.

The imagination is the Soul's playroom. To let that become a reality, you need to filter out meaningless fantasy, delusion, irrational entertainment, and wishful thinking. Remember, the Soul is all about reality, and if you cultivate the unreal in your imagination, it will be no place for your Soul to do its work. Cultivate the unreal in your imagination, and it will fill to overflowing with junk, leaving no room for your Soul to enter, much less move around and play. Your Soul needs an empty room for it to play at top speed, and you need to speak to it in a language that your Soul understands.

The language of the Soul is metaphor and attitude. Therefore, speak in metaphors when talking to your Soul, and pose questions in the form of attitudes. It is a metaphor to say the imagination is the playroom of the Soul. To say that the imagination *is like* a playroom for the Soul would be a simile. The simile means that the imagination isn't literally a playroom for the Soul. Since that is not a reality, and the Soul is all about reality, that wouldn't work to entice the Soul into one's imagination. So, you need to consider how you communicate with your Soul because that can profoundly affect its ability to act with freedom.

By playing with different attitudes and how they might be worded, you can hone your ability to communicate with your Soul. This is because the Soul "thinks" in attitudes, points of view, or angles of perspective. Practically, your Soul understands you with whatever language you choose, but the most efficient communication is in the form of attitudes. I will be discussing the Soul's language in more detail in another chapter; for now, it is enough to say that each attitude or point of view will yield a different outcome. When the Soul is at play, it is trying out new attitudes to see how they fit. If you deliberately use your imagination to play with different attitudes, it's like an open invitation to your Soul to enter and join the fun. Indeed, this is how improvisation works.

It may be useful to say that, from an artistic point of view, attitudes are most efficiently conveyed visually or aurally in the form of affects and gestures. Affects are objectively read suggestions of expressed emotions or states of mind. Gestures are the visual or tonal "words" or movements that express affects. This is the language that infants and adults use to communicate clearly, and so it is with the Soul when it communicates musical and artistic ideas. Meaning is given to organized paint or composed music by the attitude expressed through the artist's or composer's Soul. Art not emanating from the Soul is wholly without meaning and is corrupting to the Soul to entertain because one's time and attention are taken without the Soul being fed.

Creative Mechanism Twenty-Two

To connect your Soul to your physical body, pay attention to sensations and relationships within your body and remove all interference from within.

Interference relating to the physical body is unnecessary tension and rigidity of muscles. The Soul requires a relaxed yet alert state to work with the body. For musicians and sportspeople to have their Souls involved in their work, it is imperative that they be as attentive to their physical state as possible. The same is true for chefs, surgeons, carpenters, artists, dancers, and so on.

Being in the zone, as it is called, means inviting your Soul to do the work you have been training for. Once in the zone, all time and consciousness of physical impediment disappear, and actions feel fluid and effortless as work appears to do itself. Books have been written about this state, so it isn't necessary to say more except that only what is in your imagination will come to pass, barring any unforeseen mishaps. If you have missed something in your imagination, your Soul can help compensate for it, but don't expect to get your Soul involved in the final stages of work if you haven't involved it in the preparations. Also, don't expect your Soul to continue its involvement in your work if you don't give it credit when things go better than expected.[8]

Creative Mechanism Twenty-Three

To connect your Soul to your ego, get out of the habit of judging and condemning.

Yes, it is possible to connect Soul with ego, but the ego doesn't like it much because it has probably been running things for years. In fact, your ego will resent it if you switch the roles of Soul and ego. When religious people try to connect their Souls with their egos, the result is often self-righteousness. I call this inflammation of the feeling of self-righteousness the disease *self-righteousitis.* Self-righteousness is a sure sign that the ego has assumed the role of judge, jury, and hangman to keep what it sees as its rightful place of being in charge. The characteristic of this spiritual disease is incessant condemnation of everything and everyone for not behaving by the rules set down in scripture and interpreted by the ego. One can notice this same disease in scripture texts when they turn spiteful and condemnatory.

To connect ego with Soul is a tricky business. Your ego must be retrained to focus its life-saving attentions on your Soul so that when there is a choice to be made between saving the life of the body or the life of the Soul, it opts to save the Soul. Your ego must realize how much importance you place on the relationship you have with your Soul. This can only happen when you honor your ego's life-saving role, its intensity, and its energy. You must also honor its power and strength, but only when it is in a position of total submission to your management. In this

[8] The curse of beginner's luck is a manifestation of this process. The rank beginner needs and gets the Soul's participation, and when the compliments flow in, the beginner takes all the credit, thinking that they were responsible for the result. Puffed with confidence, the now no longer beginner is thrust into producing that same level of quality on their own, and the result is meager, uninteresting, and flat. The Soul, having left that beginner to their own devices, allows them to reap the benefits of their own incompetence.

regard, the ego is like a dog, which, if not brought into submission, will fill the management void and become a terror. Like the family dog, the ego can be a source of joy for its energy, intensity, ebullience, and loyalty—couple that with what flows from the Soul and the results are unbelievably rich and profound.

Creative Mechanism Twenty-Four

Your Soul knows everything that you are doing, thinking, feeling, and experiencing, and it will have nothing to do with you when you are being false in any way or under any circumstances.

Being false is all about the ego. The Soul never gets into a popularity contest with the ego, so if you are being false, your Soul will sense that it is a third wheel and will retreat.

While the ego loves to be in the driver's seat controlling everything that happens, it doesn't know how to drive. In fact, it doesn't know anything at all. It is all bluster and zero substance. The one thing it is good for, most of the time, is keeping you alive when in clear and present danger of being killed.

I once heard from a good friend who lives in the Southwestern desert of the United States. He told me of an experience with his ego that was nothing but positive proof that the ego works to save life. One morning, as he was walking out of his house, he found himself hurtling through the air and landing, sprawled on the ground, six feet from where he had been walking. He couldn't understand what had happened until he got up and noticed a forty-inch-long rattlesnake, in striking position, about a foot from where he had been walking. He reported to me that he'd had absolutely no awareness of danger but watched himself flying sideways through the air. Only after he had landed did he notice the danger.

In another example, a professional sailor told me of a time when he heard a strong voice (while alone on his boat) twice commanding him to look out the porthole of his vessel. When he obeyed the command and looked out the porthole, he saw seven waterspouts moving towards his boat. This gave him time to lower the sails and batten down everything loose until he rode out the tempest. These are the best two examples I have heard of the ego doing what it is meant to do with supreme efficiency.

Beyond saving your life, your ego has zero competence at anything. This is the reason it lies and works so hard to keep your attention. If it abates at any moment, your attention on it will wander and you will likely discover the truth about it and, heaven forbid, stop paying it attention.

Sometimes, if you make a mistake while doing a thing you love, your ego will lord it over you until you stop doing what you love and start paying attention to the ego. The more you ignore it, the louder and meaner it becomes. This could drive you insane. Paradoxically, I suspect that a large percentage of suicides are due to this behavior, especially for aurally dominant people or those who are not savvy to the ego's behavior. As soon as you start to notice how incompetent, stupid, and undeserving of your attention it is, you can begin to watch it and how its antics are designed to capture attention. If you assume the attitude of a scientist and study it, taking note of its every behavior as though studying a monkey, you will notice that the ego dislikes being the object of scrutiny. If you persist in this behavior, the ego will eventually go away because it realizes it has zero control when it is being studied as an object.

My point in focusing on the ego is that all falseness comes from the ego. Take charge of that part of you and eradicate falseness, and then you can have a serious relationship with your Soul.

Creative Mechanism Twenty-Five

The Soul rarely chews its cabbage twice. What you fail to get from it the first time, you are condemned to figure out on your own thereafter.

I have noticed that if I don't accept something from my Soul that I asked for, I can never get it again. If you ask for something from your Soul, and you are distracted or busy with something when it gives what you asked for, it's tough luck if you don't catch it. Most times, what the Soul offers comes and goes in less time than it took for you to read the first word of this sentence. The moral of the story is, if you ask your Soul for something, make sure you pay attention closely enough to catch what it tosses because that moment will never come again. In my thirty-five years of studying the Soul, I have never noticed an exception to this behavior.

There is an inane musical composition called *The Lost Chord*, by Arthur Sullivan. In this work, the words allude to a time when the musician was improvising on the organ and played a particular chord that sounded otherworldly and wonderful. But, as the musician played on, every attempt to recover that chord or recapture the magic of that moment failed. So it is when our Souls give us what we need.

The composer, Johannes Brahms, was aware of this effect. In an interview published fifty years after his death, he related that there were pieces he had begun but never finished because he was interrupted while composing these works. He knew that the inspiration of the moment was lost because the flow of ideas coming from his Soul was interrupted.

It is important to say that your Soul will always stretch your capacities—just as adults stretch the capacities of young children, who can barely understand what adults tell them. It is to the same degree, although with a lot less patience, that your will Soul relate to your consciousness to challenge and stretch it.

Creative Mechanism Twenty-Six

The volume of the Soul speaking is softer than the sound of a whisper in a windstorm.

By listening carefully, you practice hearing your Soul communicate with you. The more you can notice the subtlest sensations, the easier it is to hear what your Soul offers. The Soul never interrupts a distracted or tempestuous mind.

The best method for learning to hear your Soul's voice is to pay attention to the volume of thoughts as they cross your mind when meditating or mind-watching. When you hear a voice that is loud and obnoxious, it is your ego ranting and raving. When you are thinking or using your intellect, the volume of those thoughts will be just below the level of a typical conversation. What comes from your Soul will be many times softer than the volume of purposely shallow or near-silent breathing. This means that it takes considerable practice to detect when your Soul is communicating.

The only way I have found to increase the volume of my Soul is to tone down the volume of my thoughts and eliminate my ego from the equation. When I do that, the volume of the Soul appears to have been turned up, but this is an illusion because the Soul is still as soft as it ever was. The difference is that now there is less competition. If you are smart, aim to turn down the volume on all your thinking, to the point where it sounds at about the same level as that of your Soul. This practice makes it clear to your Soul that you are serious about paying attention to it and encourages it to communicate more often.

Creative Mechanism Twenty-Seven

Most of the time, what you get from your Soul is not what you want to hear. This contrasts against the deceitful ego, which always tells what you want to hear.

Generally, when you need something from your Soul, you will already have something in mind for what you want to hear. This is a big mistake. What you have in mind for yourself and what your Soul has in mind for you are quite often not the same thing. This is not a problem if you don't mind being disappointed most of the time. However, it can be unsettling if you haven't been warned to expect this possibility. Not getting what you want might make you think that your Soul doesn't have your best interests at heart, but nothing could be farther from the truth. If you are smart, take to heart what your Soul gives and be glad of it.

Creative Mechanism Twenty-Eight

The Soul is always principled; it will never suggest anything unprincipled.

Principles are to the Soul what minerals, proteins, fats, and carbohydrates are to the body. Principles are nutrients for the Soul. Without these nutrients, the Soul's food (the energy of paying attention) would be devoid of nutrition. For the Soul to reject nutrition would be for it to behave in a manner against itself. You can reject nutrition by choosing to eat things of little nutritive value. Likewise, you can reject principles in the things you choose to pay attention to, but remember that all systems will run out of steam when the supply of sustenance is depleted.

Universal principles are what the Soul needs to thrive. The Soul can stay in the body as long as attention-paying is possible, but it will not thrive without energy that contains or expresses universal principles. Universal principles are what govern the whole of the universe. Without even one of these principles, the universe would collapse and fall apart because every universal principle is necessary for the others to work.

Because the Soul emanates from the universal principles, without them, the Soul would cease to exist. For this reason, the Soul will never suggest anything that runs counter to the universal principles. This is one criterion by which you can tell if you are hearing your Soul.

One of the main reasons why you might not understand what you get from your Soul is that you don't know or understand what the universal principles are. Since these principles govern every natural phenomenon and present a highly complex or dimensional reality, it stands to reason that you might find these principles mysterious. The intellect loves to understand what is happening, but it detests anything that is not simple. Thus, your natural tendency will be to simplify everything to easily understand it or to force everything mysterious into the realm of religion so that you can simply believe it or not.

The point is that reality is complex. You have to get used to it, learn to pay attention to it, and ask questions that are crafted to reveal the truth about it. Do this, and your Soul will not fail you; but remember that you get answers to the questions you ask, so be careful in how you formulate your questions.

I hope that by the time you finish reading this book you will have a clearer perception of reality as it relates to the universal principles and the Soul. One can't exist without the other. We humans are as microcosms because we mirror, in our design and structure, the complex nature of the universe. Our human condition mirrors the true purpose of the universe's existence, which is to know itself.

Creative Mechanism Twenty-Nine

Your Soul handles complexity with ease.

Most people can use their minds to process three things at once. Some people can learn to use their minds to process as many as seven things at once. Beyond that, the human mind is not able to handle the number of variables that result from trying to competently decide what to do.

Since we often exceed the limits of our minds when trying to process everything we are doing, our tendency is to simplify what we are doing by eliminating variables. Interestingly, when an artist musician is making music, it is not uncommon for them to be processing nine thousand decisions per minute.[9] At that level of intensity, complexity, or speed, the mind will give up after a second or two. How music is performed today betrays the reality that few performances are Soul-inspired. The preferred manner of today's performances is to do nothing except realize the score as printed, which is a manner of playing easily managed by the intellect of an average person and positively boring to listen to.

For your Soul, making nine thousand decisions per minute is child's play. It can handle rates of decision-making and levels of complexity well beyond your imagination to comprehend—even to infinity. But having the ability to do that and doing it are two different things. Handling complex processes and a high rate of decision-making requires a lot of practice and the ability to instantly engage your Soul in what you are doing.

Therefore, it is a mistake to slow things down or simplify things to keep everything manageable by the mind. When the Soul is activated, it can outstrip the mind by leagues and improve the quality of the result at the same time. From the Soul's point of view, this is normal behavior. What is not normal is being fearful and slowing everything down to avoid making mistakes. You were not

---

[9] In the music of Bach, Mozart, Beethoven, or Chopin, the following situation would not be uncommon. Imagine one voice, in 4/4 time, sounding in continuous sixteenth notes for forty-eight measures, and played within the space of one minute. The upper voice will have sounded a total of 768 notes, for each of which needs to be decided the specific touch, volume, moment of beginning, moment of ending, and whether the note should precede or follow the sounding of other notes scored at the same time (subject to the performer's interpretation, the audience's attentiveness, the size of the room, the sound-quality of the instrument, and so on). Making these five obligatory decisions for 768 notes comes to 3,840 decisions in the space of one minute for just one voice. So, the estimate of nine thousand decisions per minute for music that often contains four or more voices is completely realistic, if not conservative.

One may argue that the artist makes many of those decisions beforehand. However, I counter-propose that it is a mere technician who makes those decisions before the concert begins. The true artist makes them during moment of performance. The technician is all about control, whereas the artist is all about communication. The technician practices for greater control, while the true artist practices to experimentally discover more dimensions of feeling which the music intimates.

born behaving like that. By acquiring fear-based habits you learned to disengage the Soul from your life.

Engaging the Soul when working requires you to disengage your mind, but your mind will not like being disengaged. The easiest way to disengage your mind is to overwhelm it because when it feels overwhelmed, it will disengage.

There are various techniques that you can use to overwhelm your mind. The most effective is to do things or process information faster than your mind can keep up with, or add complexity to any task so that your mind struggles to keep pace. The idea is to maintain acute attention while making it impossible for the intellect to function. I do this by constructing an imagination of what I wish to do and then pushing to work faster and faster until my mind disengages, or "checks out," so that the Soul can take over. But bear in mind, if your intellect disengages at a speed below what the Soul requires, you are neither doing one nor the other. For this reason, it is imperative to work at the speed of the Soul, not just speed up while staying within the limits of what your mind can control. You are not supposed to feel comfortable. If you are always staying within comfort range, your Soul will likely never engage with what you are doing.

Paying attention is something we tend to do naturally when we are uncomfortable. And, as I have already said, paying attention and loving are the same thing—we can't do one without the other. Increasing attention-paying by increasing the speed of processing and adding layers of complexity creates a loving mental environment that welcomes the Soul. This usually does the trick to disengage the mind without disintegrating into fear.

Creative Mechanism Thirty

The Soul is always challenging and can be extremely insistent.

The Soul unceasingly loves. However, remember that loving means paying attention, not being nice. One of the curious side effects of learning how to better pay attention is that you might also become less nice. Others may be alarmed or alienated by this, but some will be drawn to it. If you encourage others to adopt this way of being, the effect can become contagious as everyone increases their acuity of attention.

I once had a conversation with a friend who objected to this because her idea of the Soul was one of being loving in the conventional, sugar-coated sense. Years later, after she had been teaching a lot of students, she finally understood what I meant by this attitude. Coddling students makes them weaker, while paying attention to them and utterly refusing to indulge or coddle them makes them stronger and helps them develop more substantial character. It also encourages the student's Souls because the attitude is from the Soul of another and is recognized as such.

CONCLUDING COMMENTS

The choice to relate to your Soul is yours to make. Your Soul has no interest in emotions, preferences, desires, or intellection. These mental processes have the power to completely overwhelm your awareness of your Soul. By focusing on your Soul, you can choose to sip what it offers or gulp down as much as possible. If you choose to sip, it will give a sip's worth. If you choose to gulp, it will give you as much as you can take and process. You get to decide which of these happens. Please remember creative mechanism number eight and don't engage in nonsense—the Soul has zero patience for it.

Chapter Two

Feeding the Soul

Remember reciprocity? Your Soul gives and you take, but when does the opposite occur? When do you give for your Soul to take? Like a water tank, if you take water without having a way to refill the tank, the tank will run dry. You need to be giving your Soul exactly what it needs to stay as full as possible. What you give your Soul, like the water tank, determines in large measure what you get out of it. If you keep refilling the tank with dirty or polluted water, that will be what you get. So, you should want to give your Soul the best-quality food, not by your standards of quality but by *its* standards of quality. The higher the quality of input, the higher the quality of output—that's reciprocity.

One of the sticking points that invariably arise when I discuss feeding the Soul is that many people feel the most required of them is their best, and they insist that if they are giving their best, then that is adequate. My experience tells me that sincerity works for people but not for the Soul. Doing one's best may be good enough for teachers or parents, but not for the Soul. If your best effort falls radically short of the best possible, does your sincerity make everything right and acceptable?

Imagine, if you will, your Grandmother wanting to give you a present. You are interested in astronomy, so your Grandmother decides to paint you a picture of the starry night for you to hang on your wall. She uses a paint by number image made by someone who created the image without actually looking at the stars. You look at the painting and wonder, "Is she serious?" The effort looks mindless and poorly done. However, you don't want to hurt your Grandmother's feelings, so you thank her and accept the gift because you've been taught that it is the thought behind the gift that counts. Does her sincerity cut it and make what she offered good and right? While others may disagree, I don't think your Grandmother's gift was good and right because it teaches the recipient that what you give is irrelevant.

The quality of what is offered to the Soul matters a great deal. It is better to give nothing than to tell yourself it's the thought that counts. Sincerity justifies the act of giving for a giver who is inconsiderate or misunderstanding of the recipient. Sincerity is incompetent to improve the quality of anything that is substandard. For these reasons, you must give your Soul that which is made according to the Soul's standards and not whatever you feel like giving. Inferior input results in inferior output. Polluted water does not magically turn into pristine water because it was sincerely dumped into the tank. I say again, give your Soul the best possible quality of whatever it is you give it, not by your standards of quality but by *its* standards. What does this mean in real terms? What does the Soul need to thrive? How is it possible to keep increasing the quality of what you offer your Soul? To answer these questions, we first need to understand what the Soul eats.

The food that your Soul eats is what I call *attention-energy*. This is the energy you use by paying attention. For instance, if you are a teacher, you might pay attention to developing clearer explanations of concepts for your students, and what you have fed your Soul is the energy you spent paying attention to developing those clearer explanations. Your Soul takes attention-energy, converts it into clearer explanations and then gives them to you or "excretes" them as and when you need. So, if you are careful to feed your Soul the food it needs, that food will be digested as your Soul makes sense of it; and, when it is ready, it will excrete what you need in the form of ideas, understandings, insights, concepts, attitudes, syntheses, etc. through your intuition. It works like clockwork, and what you get is entirely dependent on the kind and quality of food you provide.

The process of feeding the Soul begins with paying attention to sensation. A sensation occurs because something specific has stimulated one of your senses. The moment you notice the stimulation, you are generating attention-energy of a low quality, but it is attention-energy nonetheless. That energy is then sent to your brain via your nervous system, where it is redirected to the specific part of your brain that is dedicated to processing that form of stimulation. The more time you spend paying attention to sensations and processing them to extract meaning, the more places in your brain the attention-energy will excite. The aim is to pay such close attention to every sensory detail that you "milk" experiences for all they are worth. The more you pay close attention, the more you will notice in the simplest of stimuli. The purpose of doing this kind of exercise is to accustom you to focusing on subtle sensory details so when it comes time to focus on your Soul, you are not doing anything unusual where subtlety is concerned.

This practice of paying attention is not to feel good or to get something from your Soul. You want to be doing this for the sole purpose of feeding your Soul the attention-energy it needs. As you do this more, a reciprocal process happens, and your Soul will start up a conversation revealing to you the true nature of the reality you are paying attention to. You don't have to do a thing to generate this conversation. Indeed, if you try to induce it, the conversation probably won't happen. Your Soul is finding out how much and how closely you are listening to it. As soon as your Soul senses that you are paying attention to feed it, it will want your part of the conversation. It is important that you let your Soul be in charge of what happens. Forcing, as I already mentioned, is of no use at all.

HAVING YOUR SOUL IN CHARGE

When you let your Soul be in charge, you need to be sure that you are listening to your Soul and not your ego. As I have already explained, the content and volume of the interactions are telling. Even so, the ego can be sneaky and manipulative to keep your attention. This is why focusing on sensation is so important. The ego has little power to manipulate sensation, so it uses emotions in its battle for your attention, and as we all know, emotions are powerful. It is like one of Aesop's fables in which there was an argument between the sun and the wind as to who was stronger. Obviously, the wind took the position that it was by far the stronger, so the sun proposed a contest. Pointing down to earth, where there was a man in a coat walking down a road, the sun said, "OK, let's see which of us is stronger. See that man in the coat? Whichever of us can remove the coat from that man will be the stronger." The wind agreed to the rules of the contest, so the sun let the wind show its strength and power. The wind huffed and puffed and blew like the dickens, but the harder the wind blew, the more tightly the man clutched his coat. Finally, the wind spent himself and had to give up. "OK, now it's my turn," the sun said. Whereupon the sun did nothing except shine. No sooner had the sun shone than the man became overheated and removed his coat. The ego, like the wind, is full of bluster and rash foolishness. Your Soul only needs to shine, and you start shining as a result.

So, it is important to avoid focusing on emotions or non-sensory feelings. That is what mind-watching is all about. Watching your mind induces a completely different complex of sensations than does paying attention to the sensation of breathing, for instance. When feeding your Soul, what you are after is more like *listening* to your senses. The specific sense is less relevant than the listening, and you shouldn't be trying to notice anything in particular. When something catches your attention, follow it for a few moments to notice where it leads. If you notice that it's your mind or ego trying to distract you, stop and reframe the experience back to paying attention to sense stimulation. Don't try to characterize the sensation. Don't allow yourself to like it or not like it. By drawing your focus back to the sense you were listening to in the first place, you gain control over your mind so that you can use it with ever-increasing skill.

VESTED INTERESTS

The point behind all these suggestions is to train yourself to eliminate your vested interests. Vested interests possess you because you have a stake in their outcome. For instance, a dancer who needs to do well in an upcoming audition might be unable to stop his or her mind from constantly thinking about the audition. That desire to do well in the audition is a vested interest. The more vested interests you have, the less likely it will be that you come to terms with your Soul or have a reciprocal relationship with it.

The Soul needs you to be as free as possible of vested self-interest so that what it decides to give won't be wasted by your distraction. Music and art competitions often do more harm than good because winning becomes the goal, and winning is a massive vested interest that guarantees the competitors' Souls will never come through during their performance. When the judges reward soulless playing, the message comes in loud and clear that music and art *should* be soulless and egocentric.

Many various religions have each developed traditions of meditation. Unfortunately, these traditional forms of meditation too often become an end in themselves—a vested interest. Real meditation is free of all "have to's" and "should's" because they each constitute a form of vested interest. Any vested interest, no matter how faint or weak, will overwhelm the Soul. Any belief, no matter how seemingly insignificant, is enough to cause the Soul to wait until it passes, and if it never passes, the Soul never appears. In meditation, you should aim to manage your states of mind so that your Soul can relate to you as intended.

If you grow impatient because you aren't getting anything, that too harbors a clear and powerful vested interest. If you push to get things moving faster, your Soul will read that as bullying. So, the best way to encourage your Soul to speak is by assuming the attitude that you will regularly make yourself present for when your Soul has something to say.

INCREASING THE QUALITY OF WHAT YOU FEED YOUR SOUL

The purer the attention-energy you are generating, the easier it is for your Soul to get nourishment from that "food." Purity depends on how free your attention is from any form of coloration. Desires, preferences, fantasies, and expectations are all forms of coloration. Vested interests, which we have already spoken of, are an extreme form of coloration. Only knowing in its most elemental state is free of polluting influences and therefore is the purest form of attention-energy.

Knowing, in its crudest form, comes from paying attention to what is happening outside yourself. For instance, if you watch raindrops falling and splashing outside and listen to the sound of those raindrops hitting various surfaces, the attention-energy of these sensations is crude because you are separate from the experience. The crudity is related to the degree of personal involvement. If you are watching and listening to an event happening to something or someone else, you are not directly involved; thus, it is like watching television. The experience is crude by comparison to what it would be if other parts of your being were involved. As soon as you extend your arm to have the raindrops hitting your hand—and you are paying attention to the sensation of water hitting your skin, running over it, and collecting in your palm—the knowing becomes more direct because of your involvement in the experience. The knowing becomes more essential.

The essential nature of any sensory experience depends on how much you can articulate about the experience. The more you can articulate, the less essential the attention-paying is. The more essential the sensory experience is, the more impossible it is to express in words. At the most essential, the experience of sensing becomes pure knowing. You might ask, "So what?" Knowing, in its most elemental state, is the result of paying attention to sensation so sublime and pure that no words exist to describe it. It is what it is—knowing what is. This kind of knowing results in attention-energy of the purest form, on which the Soul can feed and derive from it the most sublime form of nutrition. The only kind of knowing that is more sublime results from *knowing*, not *knowing what is*, but just *knowing*. Nothing more.

From the crudest to the most essential levels of sensing and knowing, I experience seven discreet levels. Imagine that I touch your arm. The crudest form of knowing is what others see when they watch the action. The second crudest form is your observation that I touched your arm. This is followed by a third, less personal yet more accurate description of the event—your arm is touched. Fourth, the knowing becomes more refined and subtle as you observe that you sensed something warm on your arm. The fifth would be, "I sensed." Sixth, and still subtler, would be the observation that sensing happened. Finally, sensing. Just sensing. Nothing more. At that level of knowing, you and the knowing are the same. It is the nature of knowing that these seven levels make up the total of what can be known for any given experience. Everything else called knowledge is *knowledge about* and is like the first and crudest level. This could be called the scientific or legal description of reality. This level is not particularly edible for the Soul.

Just as some people can't process certain kinds of food because it fouls up their digestive systems, crude forms of knowing can foul up some people's spiritual systems so that it doesn't work for them in a meaningful way. Even refined forms of knowing can be insufficiently pure. What works best is to ask your Soul for direction to what it needs most. Upon asking your Soul for direction, you will discover that the kind of food it needs most is that of paying attention to sensing universal principles because your Soul is constructed from the same "materials" as the universal principles. Universal principles constitute the essential nourishment on which the Soul thrives. Whatever is made to be replete with universal principles is the best food for the Soul.

So, your Soul gets maximum fortification when you pay attention to anything—any experience, any thought, any form—in which universal principles are found or to which they have been applied. Nature is the primary source for experiences in which universal principles are expressed. Great art of every kind is a secondary, man-made source for experiencing universal principles. Indeed, expressing universal principles is the purpose of art. Fortunately, we all have areas in our brains dedicated to processing and recognizing universal principles. We also have discreet senses that are meant to apprehend most if not all universal principles.

CHAPTER THREE

The Universal Principles

THE TYPES OF PRINCIPLES

Behind every effect is a principle or principles. There are five types of principles: specific principles, common principles, general principles, conditional principles, and universal principles. The most common are specific principles. These apply to a specific activity, like cooking. The first principle of good cooking is to use the highest quality ingredients. The rules of good writing are also specific principles.

The next type of principle is a common principle, which applies to various groups of activities. An example of a common principle would be one that Edward Deming set down as a principle of business or manufacturing: Listen to your customers and apply what they say. This same principle is what parents of the past taught when they said to children, "Listen to your elders and do what they say."

General principles apply to systems or groups of groups. An example of a group is a nation or a market. Adam Smith's work on economics sets down general principles by which economic behaviors appear to function, where markets are concerned. "All men are created equal" is a general principle of politics and legal systems.

Principles that apply to conditions are conditional principles. An example of a conditional principle would be weather or global warming. Global warming will affect everyone on the planet. Although the signs of global warming are becoming more obvious, we seem to be a species that insists on ignoring a problem until it becomes so egregious that it is no longer bearable, like ignoring Hitler and the Nazis until they threw the entire world into chaos. Another conditional principle would be polluted water or space garbage. These conditions will eventually govern how every person in the world behaves.

Finally, there are universal principles. Universal principles govern all of nature. They govern everything in the universe. If we were to remove one of them, the universe would collapse. That is what distinguishes a universal principle from all other principles. They govern everything from the tiniest subatomic particles to the largest galaxy clusters, as well as everything else in between.

Universal principles seem hidden because they have no material form, yet they are forces that act to create everything in nature. In this way, principles are spiritual because spirit has no material form; it cannot be destroyed or changed; it is a force that acts to create everything in nature; and it must have existed before everything material existed, otherwise nothing would exist. Everything in nature appears as it does, from our perspective, because principles caused it to be so.

Where universal principles become important to us is in the works of men and women because those works may someday be perceived by others, and it is the Souls of these perceivers that will be affected. Every man-made effect has a cause, and if that effect is able to feed the Soul, the cause is one or more of the universal principles. In other words, for every effect there is a true cause, and for every true cause there are universal principles at work.

In music, every effect, like rhythm or communication, is the direct result of a principle or principles being applied. The more intense the application of those principles is, the higher quality the effect. It is the same in all the arts, irrespective of culture or sophistication of society. What touches the Souls of listeners and viewers is not the thing itself (the performance, the score, the sculpture, etc.), it is the intensity with which the principles that underlie every good effect are perceived. When great artists communicate, they are using their art, whatever that may be, as an excuse or vehicle to apply the principles of aesthetics—the universal principles. Great artists know that it is the principles that cause people to love their work, that create substance and meaning in their work, and that makes their work worthwhile observing. Without the principles, nothing man-made is worth paying attention to.

The similarities between universal principles and the behavior of subatomic particles haven't escaped my notice. Upon seeing the paths traced by certain particles, one can see how those paths mirror what many of the universal principles might trace if they were physical in nature, which they well could be if there is a direct correlation between them. This would help explain how the universal principles govern the manner in which material nature behaves and organizes itself.

I will proceed to describe each principle, as I have been able to articulate, and give examples of how I have found them in nature and in human works.

Principle 1. — Musical Proportion

Proportion based on the ratio 1:2:3

Musical proportions govern how atoms combine to produce molecules, how natural forms and structures develop, and how the entire audible realm functions, including the hum of the supposed big bang.

Musical proportions govern the overall structure of a work of art or music, as well as larger substructures. Neglect this principle and perception of disorder results. When this principle is used at the expense of other principles, the result is a perception of sterility—the singular fault of architecture since 1900. People often refer to this principle as being rational or symmetrical.

The structure of human bodies expresses musical proportions. Human beings have one head with two eyes and two ears, one nose with two nostrils, one mouth and one tongue with two sides, one brain with two hemispheres, etc. Defects in nature occur when one has been equipped with less or more than one or two of a particular part. Mind you, defects of nature are fascinating to us. This points to the crux of creating art, which the balance between beauty and interest. When a work of art is beautiful to the extent that it becomes boring and static, it is because this principle has been applied too rigorously.

Another universal principle that is realized by these basic numbers is the principle of balance (see page 117). It would be a fair question to ask, "Which came first, musical proportions, or the principle of balance?" Or, "Can balance exist without musical proportions, or can musical proportions exist without balance?" Since balance rocks in the western desert of the United States are in balance yet do not convey a clear musical proportion, I conclude that we can have balance without musical proportion. In this example, the musical proportion is internal.

Musical proportion does not just involve balance in structure, it involves the effects of efficiently distributed mass, of opposition, of dynamic interaction, and of a presumption of accidents. This means that the ratios 1:2:3 ensure that a natural object can survive in its environment because it has a spare part, and it is not physically, mechanically, internally, or externally lopsided.

When we add, multiply, and divide using these basic numbers, we get four, five, six, seven, etc. All the music intervals use these most basic numbers. An octave is a 2:1 ratio; a perfect fifth is a 2:3 ratio; and so on. The overtones, partials, or harmonics—whatever we prefer to call them—are expressions of these ratios. Nature grows according to the ratios of the overtones and non-overtones alike. For instance, all the bones in the human body are tuned to overtones of a basic pitch found in the sternum. This is how nature guarantees infinite variety and distinct vocal identity in individuals. Furthermore, trees and bushes are tuned in much the same way, but they use non-harmonic ratios (the perfect fourth and the minor third).

Nature grows according to these ratios because of certain structural and behavioral limitations that apply to various organisms. Human bodies, as with all living higher creatures, need to be as strong and as flexible as possible. If a snake is too rigid, it won't be able to move quickly. If our bones are too heavy, we won't have the needed flexibility to do what we imagine. By proportioning the mass of the various bones in the limbs of our bodies, nature can create ever-increasing lightness yet still maintain structural integrity. It does this by growing bones to exact mathematical/musical ratios. If you tap on your sternum and then on your collarbone, you will discover that you can hear the sound of a perfect fifth (a ratio of 2:3) from the pitch of the sternum up to the pitch of the collarbone.

Principle 2. — Spiritual Proportion

Proportion based on the ratio 1:1.618... (the golden ratio)

In nature, spiritual proportion governs the relationship of behavior to structure. The expression 1:1.618 describes the relationship of balance between rigidity and flexibility, between stasis and enstasis, between strength and flexibility, between structure and behavior, and between order and chaos.

Nature exhibits this principle in its patterns of growth. Spiritual proportions govern the relationship of all parts to each other in a living organism. The effect of using this principle is the perception of naturalness and elegance. Failure to use this principle generates the effect of crudity and uncouthness, despite an otherwise precise and refined execution. Spiritual proportion, or the absence of it, is obvious in every aspect of conversational dialogue. In other words, how we speak is governed by this principle. When present, the spiritual proportion creates ease of understanding. It works the same way in music too. A complete elucidation of this principle can be found in the book *The Power of Limits: Proportional Harmonies in Nature, Art, and Architecture*, by Gyorgy Doczi. In this book, copious examples of both the harmonic and spiritual proportions are analyzed in detail.

The following diagram shows the ratio of 1:1.618 (the golden ratio). The section AS represents a length of 1.618, and the section SB represents a length of 1, so the ratio SB:AS is a ratio of 1:1.618. A curious feature of the golden ratio is that its defining ratio repeats on itself—the ratio of AS:AB is also a ratio of 1:1.618.

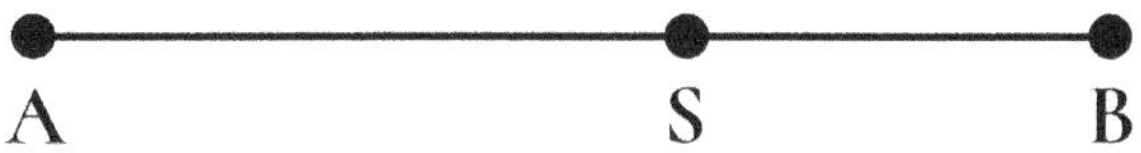

FIGURE 8. The Golden Ratio 1:1.618 as represented by SB:AS

If this principle is used senselessly, it can create a strong effect of stasis. This is because point S in the diagram above is devoid of tension or movement. An example of this can be found on your hands. Look at your fingers and notice that the length of the end bone of any finger is to the second bone as the second bone is to the third bone. The shorter bone is 1 part, and the longer bone is 1.618 parts. Notice also that when you move your finger, the point where those two parts meet, the joint, has no motion. You think it has motion because that is the point where the finger bends, but it has no motion. It is actually the bones, muscles, blood vessels, tendons, and ligaments that move. The contact point of the cartilage on the ends of each bone is motionless—it is a point of stasis. In music or art, the flow of attentive energy (the mental energy used in paying attention, which the Chinese call *Chi*) regarding the larger part always moves in the direction of the smaller part, and vice versa. The point where the larger and smaller parts meet is a static point.

In natural structures, like trees and fingers, this principle governs the relationship between strength and flexibility. The golden ratio expresses the precise balance-point between the extremes of maximum strength and maximum flexibility. Nature grows according to this principle to create a harmonic balance between the need to grow and move and the imperative to preserve physical integrity. It is no different in languages, including music.

For instance, J.S. Bach's Prelude & Fugue in G major from *The Well-Tempered Keyboard*, Book One, suggests a temporal relationship of 1:1.618 between the duration of the Prelude and the duration of the Fugue. Obviously, a musician can play these pieces to avoid having that relationship emerge, but if he or she happens upon the natural tempo for both movements, their relationship will express the ratio of 1:1.618. Bach's incorporation of this principle into his music is both subtle and intentional. Other composers, like Béla Bartók, are as intentional as Bach in using this principle, but not as subtle; hence, the result is more self-conscious and heavy handed.

There is a wonderful motto that was popular in the seventeenth century: *Art disguises itself.* This motto went out of fashion when self-expression became vogue at the end of the nineteenth century. Nature always expresses these principles in a way that we can't easily notice. This is also what is meant by another seventeenth-century motto: *Art imitates Nature.* True art works because it expresses these principles in such a way that we can barely notice them. But notice them or not, they still nourish the Soul.

If this principle is used in formulaic ways, the effect is pat and tedious. I direct your attention to the academic painters in nineteenth-century France who made this mistake in their paintings. The painting titled *The Oath of the Horatii*, by Jacques-Louis David, is a typical pat and tedious example of the static effect created when important information is placed on the point where 1 meets 1.618. By contrast, the *Mona Lisa*, by Leonardo da Vinci, is an outstanding example of how this principle was used with subtlety and grace by hiding almost every application of it. In this painting, the rendering of the mouth alone has at least ten expressions of the golden ratio. These renderings are responsible for the famous, enigmatic smile of the *Mona Lisa*.

Principle 3. — Contrast

Juxtaposed opposites

Without contrast, everything would meld from one thing into another as undifferentiated. Let me say that again:

Withoutcontrasteverythingwouldmeldfromoneintoanotherasundifferentiated.

In written text, it is the contrast of words with space that facilitates reading. Remove the spaces, and the same sentence is extremely difficult to penetrate.

In perceptual terms, contrast is how we make sense of things. Beauty contrasts with ugliness, cold with hot, dark with light, up with down, hard with soft, and so on. What appears to be normal is contrasted in the presence of abnormal. Contrast causes entropy as purity degrades into dirty, or solid into liquid. Every wave expresses contrast as sine and cosine. Contrast also causes alternating or cyclical behavior.

In nature, contrast creates clarity of purpose. Flowers are contrasted from other plant structures to make clear to insects where to find nectar. The contrast in the color of a fish from the dark top surface to the lighter underbelly creates invisibility. Seen from below, a light-colored underbelly blends with the lighter-colored water. Seen from above, the dark-colored top surface blends with the darkness of deep water. The purpose in both instances is clear. That is, the first is to make obvious and the second is to obscure.

Brains notice and register differences more than similarities. In music and art, the purpose of this principle is to alleviate the boredom brought on by unabated sameness, repetition, and similarity—a subtlety lost on minimalist composers and painters of the late twentieth and early twenty-first centuries. The brain assumes that sameness, repetition, and similarity are irrelevant, so it tunes out. The brain only needs three exact, or more or less exact, repetitions of something to tune out. Aristotle noticed this same phenomenon 2,500 years ago when he wrote in his treatise on *Poetics* (XXIV) that "Sameness of incident soon produces satiety..."[10] Indeed, I find it takes between three and five seconds for a normal human brain to tune out on hearing the fourth repetition of something.

Contrast, to secure attention, must be both structural and partial in the right relation. In this sense, structure can be purpose, form, construction, or mode. *Partial* refers to parts, as in the parts of a flower, environment, life cycle, outcomes, etc. This means that a flower that is all center with no petals is unlikely to get

[10] Aristotle, "Poetics," *The Internet Classics Archive*, http://classics.mit.edu/Aristotle/poetics.3.3.html (accessed Mar. 15, 2018).

pollinated, while a poisonous frog with brilliant contrasting colors is unlikely to get eaten!

In painting, this principle is called *chiaroscuro* (light and dark). Chiaroscuro is not just an artistic technique of shadow versus light. When used with that attitude, chiaroscuro is mundane. If you understand that the human brain is most interested in what it can't see and what is hidden, then chiaroscuro takes on a far more dimensional quality. The dark is where the eye wants to fixate because whatever is in the dark is out of the brain's ability to easily process. Every shadow becomes a mystery to reveal. With a painting, however, your mind can't lift the layers of paint to see what's hidden, but you can still sense the brain's urge and struggle to raise the veil of mystery that enshrouds the darkest areas. Rembrandt van Rijn was perhaps the most ingenious master of chiaroscuro.

In music, it is possible to express the principle of contrast in at least five ways within a single melodic theme not more than two measures long. Look at the example of the theme (ending at the downward pointing arrow) from the C Major Fugue from Book One of J.S. Bach's *The Well-Tempered Keyboard.*

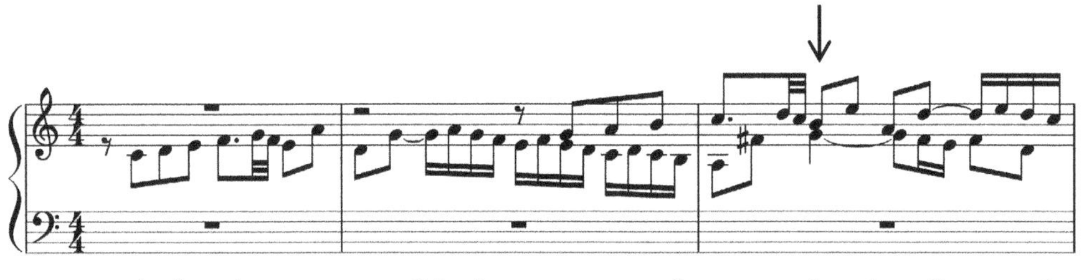

FIGURE 9. The first three measures of the fugue in C Major from J.S. Bach's *The Well-Tempered Keyboard* (Book 1).

Notice that Bach has created contrast in melodic direction, in the intervals used (first stepwise, then leaping), in the note values, in the harmonic implications, in the gestures, and in the tactus (from a walking tactus to syncopation). The extent of the expression of this principle, in a seemingly simple figure, is not unusual for Bach. Further analysis would show that he uses about fifteen of these universal principles in the construction of this theme. This is why Bach's music is so nutritious for a listener's Soul. It is not even necessary to like Bach's music for the Soul to be nourished by it. Likewise, it is not necessary to love being in the wilderness to receive nourishment for the Soul by being in that environment. For this reason, I will continue to refer to the above example, where it relates to other principles, so you can see how many principles are expressed in this theme.

Contrast has the advantage of being simple to understand and easy to apply, but it requires thought to use it as Bach has done. Too often, subtlety is an attempt to hide one's inability to communicate. For Bach, subtlety was his method for using and reusing principles without having it appear that anything at all extraordinary was done. In the above example, Bach applied the principle of integrity when using the principle of contrast. This brings forth the principles of efficiency and intensity that then reveals the application of the principles of paradox, dimension, hierarchy, which in turn reveals the principles of harmony, dynamic, unity, gesture, logic, focus, and continuity. All these principles are working at the same time in that seemingly simple theme. I am sure that Bach was aware of them all; otherwise, how could he have created theme after theme of the same quality?

Principle 4. — Efficiency

No waste

Matter cannot be destroyed; it can only be transformed into a different state. This is an expression of the principle of efficiency. Were we to remove efficiency from the universe, everything in the universe would have a mind of its own. Nothing would be predictable, as it seems to be. Matter could be destroyed, but new matter could not be created because stars wouldn't transform lighter elements into heavier ones, so everything would eventually become nonexistent. Our universe works because the principle of efficiency ensures that nothing is ever wasted.

No waste, or *nothing in excess*, also signifies that everything is used and that fullness of effect is achieved at the expense of nothing. Our sense of efficiency demands that everything we experience leaves nothing wanting. Unfortunately, we tend to focus our attention on the external aspect of nothing wanting, rather than the internal aspect. That is, we don't want to think much about anything. Total efficiency means making the mind efficient, the body efficient, the Soul efficient, the work efficient, the result efficient, the surroundings efficient, in other words, everything. When this occurs, efficiency will happen naturally in whatever you undertake.

The problem with efficiency is that it is too rigorous to readily accept. In art and music, a perceiver must be able to grasp significance on the first encounter. More exposure than that is inefficient. For this to occur, the principle of efficiency must be diluted by other principles in a way that increases the efficiency of *perception* of a work of art.

It wasn't until the principle of efficiency was applied in manufacturing that the Industrial Revolution came of age and became a bane on human happiness. People were treated like cogs in the machinery of production, and those who were trying to impose this principle on others became spiritual torturers. People are not cogs in a machine, and to be treated that way violates the Souls of those who are forced into that role. It is a plague on humanity that this behavior is still happening in the world; the perpetrators of this spiritual abuse need to be stilled.

Like in the case of the Industrial Revolution, when universal principles are misused or misapplied it can cause incalculable misery. What the Nazis and similar thinking people have done and are still doing in applying universal principles to control or torture people is the embodiment of evil. People that run large corporations to force everyone, without express permission, to use their products are no different in attitude than the Nazis when human beings are treated as fodder for filling their coffers. Government officials who work in collusion with these corporations are no different because they violate their purpose, which is to serve, protect, and defend the governed. It must be remembered that these people were and are "nice people" doing their jobs. Nice people using the universal principles to abuse others for their own gain are everywhere working their malevolent mischief with propaganda, lies, and legislative corruption.

In art, music, and theater, the application of the principle of efficiency ensures that the most intense communication happens. It is for this purpose that I issued the above warning. When you are persuaded without first forcing everything you take in to prove itself, you may unwittingly allow yourself to be a part of that body of people who use the power of communication to work mischief. So, it is important to remember that "nice people" can be and are being convinced to do some of the evilest acts ever devised.

Principle 5. — Integrity

Everything closely interrelated

Integrity governs the nature of matter. An atom of hydrogen is constructed the same way as an atom of gold—by the attraction of an electron to a proton. If we cut that delicate relationship, all the elements would vaporize instantly because electrons and protons would have no use for each other. The mind works to notice the interrelationships of things, which makes it an integrating organ or sensing device. It can notice how everything is interrelated because it is so sensitive to contrast. Noticing interrelationships is, perhaps, the most important task to which you can put your mind.

The principle of integrity is expressed in fractal mathematics. Nature abounds in examples of integrated structures: feathers, plants, circulation systems, and so on. Gothic cathedrals, the music of Bach and Beethoven, and musical instruments are designed from the simplest elements. These elements are worked with and developed into larger and larger structures. We sense these interrelationships as a logical spinning out of an idea, concept, or form. When someone explains something to us, we agree, disagree, or stay skeptical based on our sense of integrity. If we hear something which does not seem to relate or fit, we often stop the speaker short and make sure they have not introduced unrelated elements without first making us aware of the essential interrelationship.

Disintegration is the opposite of integration. An argument does not hold together if it is not well integrated. New scientific discoveries send scientists scrambling to figure out how those discoveries relate to everything else that is known. Any new discovery that can't be integrated into what is already known tends to pine away and is ignored until it can be integrated. Sometimes, the same discovery is repeated several times until the mental environment is ready for it. We need to feel the sense of integration to accept something. Those of us who have a refined sense of integrity can notice how things integrate without needing to intellectually process them. It allows those people to determine the future of art, craft, science, technology, or philosophy. For example, in all his books, Jules Verne displays this acute sense of integrity.

When we try to make sense of things, we experience various states of mind ranging from confusion, incomprehension, and muddle-headedness, to focus, comprehension, and clarity. The problem is that the perceiving mind tires readily, and a tired mind is easily confused. Confusion is a conflict between our attitudes and expectations, on the one hand, and our sensed experience of reality on the other. Eliminating confusion and becoming focused involves integrating our sensory experiences with our attitudes. Our experiences are incomprehensible when we don't understand them, usually because they don't relate to our situation or because they are new to us. As soon as we can relate new experiences to past ones and integrate them into our imaginations, we comprehend easily. We comprehend mistakenly when our understanding is assumed but not real. The purpose of a Koan (a Zen proverb) is to prevent anyone who has insufficient understanding from explaining it. Muddle-headedness is a feeling of nonsense, where nothing seems to make sense. Our sense of integrity helps us sort things out and keep things straight in our minds.

To keep a perceiving mind alert and awake, it requires stimulation flowing at a rate appropriate to the content and on one's ability to integrate what is sensed. The less complex the content, the faster the flow needs to be; the more complex the content, the slower the flow. The principle of integrity creates a tightness of content that demands a slower rate of flow.

The theme from the C Major Fugue of *The Well-Tempered Keyboard* (Book 1), by J.S. Bach, is an outstanding application of the principle of integrity (see Fig. 9, page 88). In the theme, the first four ascending notes are mirrored by the descent of notes 5, 6, 7, and 9, then again in notes 11, 15, 19, and 23, as well as in notes 12–15, 16–19, and 20–23. Bach reuses the pattern of four ascending notes by reversing the direction of movement while maintaining stepwise motion. In this example, you can see how Bach has drawn his theme from the first four notes. This creates an intense sensation of integrity. What is more amazing about Bach was that he could take what appears to be an intellectual exercise and give the music depth and meaning with a theme that sings.

Principle 6. — Harmony

Balance in tension

We often make the mistake of assuming that harmony is a condition in which everything is hunky-dory. Harmony is expressed as balancing in the tension of forces, conditions, relationships, or factors. It exists when contrasting pairs reach a state of efficient interrelationship. This state is not one that is static; rather, it is characterized by its dynamic qualities. Stars exhibit this quality in that their dynamic state is stable or static because it never changes or appears never to change. This is how harmony is paradoxical. It is dynamic yet static.

The principle of harmony requires a subtle awareness of the tension inherent in everything and how balanced or unbalanced that tension is. To have harmony requires balance in tension. The effect of ignoring a feeling of harmony is of being unsettled. For this principle to work efficiently, the perceiver must feel comfortable yet forever on the edge. This feeling can be described as a wholly natural yet intense alertness.

In movies, stories, and sometimes in our personal lives, the relationship between the protagonist and the antagonist is a harmonic evolution. The protagonist is brought into conflict with the antagonist, which creates tension. This makes for a more interesting story because the tension in conflict is more interesting than peacefulness. In music, harmonic evolution is not in conflict but is in the relationships between dissonant and consonant sound combinations. There is no harmony if the sounds are either all consonant or all dissonant. Similarly, stories aren't interesting if everything is nice. Interesting stories are about how the hero's conflict or struggle is resolved. Stories that end without resolution make the audience feel incomplete and devoid of energy. This is why stories need to end, if not happily, at least fully resolved. Without that feeling of resolution, there is no sense of harmony having been achieved. Likewise, music that is all about dissonance feels unresolved and arbitrary. Harmony is only felt when dissonances resolve in ways that stimulate the sense of harmony by a mode of resolution that sounds both inevitable and logical.

In our personal lives, we can find ourselves in conflict with others at work, at church, or at home. When there is no possibility of such conflicts resolving, we usually experience a high degree of stress. The only way to relieve ourselves of that stress is to find a means of resolving the conflict. Divorce resolves conflict in marriages. Conflict in churches or political parties ends in splitting, or it gets resolved by democratic means. If we work with mature, responsible people who listen well, we tend to take that situation for granted. Doing that creates a kind of disharmony because we assume the condition is normal, which it isn't. For this reason, it is important to create harmony by acknowledging those who are responding to discord with careful attention to the good of the Souls in all involved.

Principle 7. — Intensity

All parts contributing their uttermost

In nature, the principle of intensity is expressed in that nothing is half-hearted. When the sun shines, it shines with every atom of its being. When plants grow, they grow in a wholly uninhibited manner. Animals, in their natural state, exhibit a high degree of intensity, and man's quest to domesticate animals has resulted in a system of selecting animals that are less intense. With each generation of offspring, the selection process has removed the most intense animals from breeding, resulting in domestic animals that are calmer and more manageable.

In 1959 on a farm that raised Siberian Foxes an interesting experiment was initiated by Dmitry Belyayev and a team of Russian scientists. The natural state of a caged fox is to be extremely aggressive, so the Russian scientists wondered if they could make the foxes less aggressive. They selected and bred individual animals that exhibited less aggression. By doing this repeatedly, they found that it required eight generations to breed aggression out of the foxes. Interestingly, the closer they came to achieving their goal, the more like domestic dogs the foxes appeared—with floppy ears and wagging tails. The intensity of foxes in their natural state also kept their ears pricked up and their tails held low.[11]

The principle of intensity makes it possible to capture attention. Once attention is caught, keeping it is the problem. Intensity is best used to impress the attention

---

[11] Lyudmilla Trut and Lee Alan Dugatkin, *How to Tame a Fox (and Build a Dog): Visionary Scientists and a Siberian Tale of Jump-Started Evolution* (Chicago: University Of Chicago Press, 2017)

of the perceiver with other, more important matters of principle and content. Intensity that neglects this leaves the perceiver with a feeling of flatness or deadness. Those who have weak or unintense mental lives, though they may behave and feel intensely, are especially attracted to those who use their intensity to manipulate others; this was a large measure of Hitler's power. Creatures of this ilk are ever-present and need to be exposed for what they are when they emerge from their holes.

No matter how many principles may otherwise be employed, the absence of this intensity greatly minimizes their impact. Conversely, no matter how few principles are present in a work, intensity will be enough to make the work interesting to most people who observe it. Each principle has its own right level of intensity to make its effect felt; any more than that is excess. Balancing the principles in a work is the artist's job. When they are balanced, harmony is the result.

PRINCIPLE 8. — GESTURE

The unreserved expression of movement or function, that form follows, having the property of stretching the limits of form

The principle of gesture governs the behavior of storms and outbursts on the sun and the paths traversed by those storms and outbursts. Likewise, it governs the behavior of birds in flight and the paths carved in the landscape by rivers. If the principle of efficiency were to control the principle of gesture, rivers would flow in a path dictated by engineers. That is, they would flow in a straight line because that is the shortest, most efficient expression of a line. Yet rivers flow in a meandering gesture because, unlike lines, a river has weight and flowing mass. It is those properties that produce the meandering gestures of a river.

Every explosion is a gesture. Every movement is a gesture. It is this property for which the behavior-sensing side of the brain, the right hemisphere, must have developed. This side of the brain is designed to detect meaning. It functions that way because gesture is the way nature expresses meaning. Anyone who has been attacked by a small animal protecting its young, like a chicken, understands the meaning of the gestures used by that animal to drive a would-be attacker away.

The gestures are intense and objectively understood. Likewise, gesture through body language is how human beings efficiently communicate meaning.

It is through gesture that attitude is conveyed. Attitude is the language of spirit. Similarly, the principle of gesture conveys essence or spiritual intention. An absence of gesture conveys zero meaning, and gesturing without content conveys a flailing disorder that we read as mindless or senseless.

In every work, gestures are expressed that are either intended or unintended. Where gesture is missing, the meaning is static, sterile, and dead, no matter what the intention may have been. Affect is the result of gestures and sub-gestures organized to give the impression of emotion being expressed. This means that everything has affect whether or not a specific affect was intended. It also means that every part of a work either contributes to an intended affect or creates an unintended one. Further, a change to any part of a work alters the gestures and sub-gestures that make it up, so a slight change can radically alter the affect of the whole.

Certain forms of mathematics, like calculus and trigonometry, were invented to describe the paths of motions of bodies in space. Some of those paths are gestural, specifically in the form of an ellipse or a parabolic curve. Spirals, as found in nature, also express gesture and are governed by forces that can be described mathematically. Almost any shape produced by a physical gesture can be described by mathematics. This is perhaps the reason that most observers read the affect of gestures objectively. Emotion is different from affect in that it might be read accurately or not, depending on the acuity of the observers. Affect can be described mathematically by analyzing the paths of the gestures and sub-gestures. Emotions can be expressed without using gestures and are therefore subject to interpretation. Anyone's guess about what emotion another person is feeling is as good as anyone else's guess. The craft of acting is about managing gestures and sub-gestures to convey unambiguous meaning to an audience.

Principle 9. — Hierarchy

Order of importance

In nature, the principle of hierarchy governs how things grow. The hierarchy of growth makes the roots more important than the stems, the stems more important than the leaves, the leaves more important than the flowers, and the flowers more important than the seeds. But the function of a plant is to produce seeds or reproduce. So the hierarchy of function is the reverse of the hierarchy of growth. You cannot have seeds without flowers, flowers without leaves, leaves without stems, or stems without roots. At the same time, the hierarchy of conservation is based on environmental stress, like drought. When a drought occurs, the plant will still make roots but may grow them deeper to find water. It will produce leaves to feed the plant while it makes deeper roots, but it may give up on making flowers and seeds during the drought. If the drought lasts long enough, even the leaves and stems may be sacrificed to preserve the roots. Only if the roots dry up and die is the plant dead. These examples show the principle of hierarchy at work in the function of a plant, how a plant grows, and what happens if a plant is exposed to stress.

The principle of hierarchy governs our solar system according to the mass and distance of the various objects in it. Without the sun, there would be no solar system at all, which makes the sun the most important object in the solar system. The second most important objects are the planets; and as the planets revolve around the sun, moons revolve around their respective planets.

This principle also governs how language is constructed. The hierarchy of importance in a sentence makes the subject of the sentence the most important part. It is the subject to which all other parts of a sentence refer. The subject of a sentence is like the sun in our solar system. The verb is the second most important part of a sentence, so the verb is like a planet. The verb refers to the subject, but it can also have other parts of the sentence that refer to it, just as planets can have circling moons.

Establishing hierarchy is the function of grammar. Grammar describes how all parts of a sentence relate to each other. Without hierarchy, one thing is no longer obliged to refer to another. Like it or not, the human brain requires hierarchy to create order from chaos. All languages, including music, must follow certain hierarchical rules or the result will be gobbledygook. This means that for anything to have meaning it must adhere to strict hierarchical guidelines. Failure to do so effectively destroys meaning.

The principle of hierarchy governs what an observer needs to pay attention to. For this to occur, the artist must view the work as a disinterested or casual observer. Often the artist has their own agenda or priorities that the observers have no interest in. No matter how intensely the artist may feel those things, the observer mostly doesn't care about them. What creates the strongest attraction in a work is the most important thing, intended or unintended. By carefully controlling the forces of attraction at play, an artist employs this essential principle.

In every human institution, intended or not, a hierarchy eventually emerges to streamline decision-making. Prior to the drawing up of the United States Constitution, there existed a confederation of the states. In that confederation, all the states had equal status, and the result was that nothing got done because states were not obliged to accept any legislation that was passed by the Congress. After a year or two of that nonsense, the founding fathers of the United States of America drew up the Constitution to prevent the nation from devolving into a bunch of squabbling provinces. It was that short interim that the founding fathers needed to spell out the structure of the governing hierarchy and to articulate the limits to be imposed on those in government.

Principle 10. — Dynamic

Change, changes, changing

We live in an age during which truth is normally viewed as relative. This means that the truth I observe is different from the truth you observe, even when we're observing and describing the same thing. This is how the truth is thought to be relative to one's point of view.

The fable about ten blind men touching an elephant and describing the part they are touching is used as an example of how truth is relative to one's point of view. However, if this illustration is looked at more carefully, it is clear that not one of the ten blind men got it right. Not one who touched the elephant said that it was an elephant. The one who touched the leg thought it was a tree; the one who touched the end of the tail thought it was a brush; the trunk of the elephant was thought to be a fire hose; and so on. Those who hold truth to be relative would suggest that all those who touched the elephant told the truth. In fact, no one did.

Though it is anachronistic to say, my view is that truth is absolute and unchanging, and it is people who are relative to truth. The elephant is an elephant irrespective of opinion. It all depends on your point of view, and if your point of view isn't in line with reality, it is relatively worthless. The trick is how to have clarity of sight to observe the reality before you.

Here is where the principle of dynamic comes into play. The single most encompassing truth in the universe is that all things are changing. This truth is as absolute as they come because one of the cardinal characteristics of absolute truth is that it must and can never change. The reality of all things changing will never change. This specific truth relates to the spiritual dimensions in nature—the universal principles.

The principle of dynamic governs the perception of spiritual essence in a work. Work that is perceived as dead is largely undynamic. Work that is perceived as living or lively is extremely dynamic. The absence of this principle induces a loss of energy in the observer, and the opposite is also true. The more endlessly interesting a work of art is, the more dynamic we will find it to be. This principle can be manifested in crude or subtle ways, many of which yield the desired effect in varying degrees.

Principle 11. — Evolution

Adaptive response to change

Despite appearances to the contrary, everything evolves or devolves. Unfortunately, the word evolution evokes rancor among people who hold an unshakable belief in the magical power of the divine. Because they entertain the view that such belief makes them more spiritual, any evidence that contradicts their view threatens the strength of their notion of what it means to be spiritual. This threat makes these people dangerous. To quote Martin Luther King Jr.,

"Nothing in the world is more dangerous than sincere ignorance or conscientious stupidity."

Evolution refers to the adaptive capacity in nature and how it responds to change. This includes all aspects of nature, both animate and inanimate. In the universe, galaxies evolve. Within stars, matter evolves. And now we know that it takes a few human generations for bacteria to evolve from a natural deadly form into a deadlier drug-resistant form as they develop immunity to the increasingly powerful antibiotics produced to kill them. Indeed, bacteria are evolving faster than human beings are capable of creating new antibiotics.

Human beings have evolved and are continuing to evolve, but human evolution now happens less physically and more in the brain as humans learn to be increasingly accepting of the nature of reality and less addicted to notions and ideas that result in arrogance. The arrogance of the human species most often manifests in culturally stupid assumptions of superiority based on genitalia, skin color, religion, education, class, caste, power, politics, wealth, IQ, etc. The degree to which a person accepts the nature of reality is a measure of their degree of spiritual evolution.

Principle 12. — Dimension

The multiplicity of aspects or sides

Nothing in nature has only one dimension. Nothing in nature has only two dimensions. A few things have a mere three dimensions, for example, mathematical abstractions located in the minds of humans. Most things in nature exhibit a multitude of dimensions. This is because every waveform or particle form and every speed of those forms is a different dimension. Every principle—specific, common, general, conditional, and universal—is a dimension. Every aspect that a work can be made to exhibit must be present for it to assume its proper degree of dimensionality. A lack of dimensionality creates the effect of blankness, flatness, or emptiness.

In the visual realm, dimensionality begins with the dimensions up-down, side-to-side, and forward-backward. Add to these dimensions each individual color, and the visual dimensions stretch into virtual infinity. Some people have reduced color to the basic colors of blue, red, and yellow and the secondary colors of purple, orange, and green. When light and dark dimensions are added to the mix, the dimensions of color become infinite.

The realm of movement begins with the same three basic dimensions as the visual realm. However, when dimensions of size are considered, then the number of these dimensions becomes infinite as the structure of matter ranges from subatomic to galactic. In the realm of surface, the number of dimensions is only limited in our ability to accurately describe distinct structures in aspects of smooth to rough, sharp to blunt, repeated to unique, distinct to indistinct, and so on. Where sound and odor are concerned, again, the number of dimensions and range of differences that can occur are virtually infinite.

Each of these aspects of reality is a bona fide dimension, most of which are vastly more interesting to us than the three basic dimensions of the visual realm. The fact that people choose not to include these dimensions in our collective descriptions of reality is irrelevant. It is the multidimensional nature of reality that makes being alive worthwhile. If all we had was three dimensions, I doubt that most people would choose to stay alive for long. As the number of dimensions decreases, boredom increases.

Each universal principle adds yet another dimension to reality. Remove one universal principle from the picture, and its absence would take with it more than half of the other principles. This is because these principles are interrelated and interdependent.

Principle 13. — Transparency

The degree to which a thing is revealed

When philosophers speak of reality being an illusion, they usually mean that reality exists in how the brain processes the external world. If they are right, then nothing exists. However, which came first, the brain or reality? If the brain came first, then these philosophers are right, and reality is a result of brains trying to stay occupied. Since human beings aren't smart enough to create the reality that brains construct, those who say that reality only exists in the way the brain processes the world have the onus of demonstrating that human beings are smarter than they have shown themselves to be. However, if the illusory nature of human perception is real, then that reality is to be found in the fact that illusions are transparent. Poke at them, and they disappear; rub them, and they crumble.

The principle of transparency functions in the material world to create infinite dimensions of sensibility. Sand is transparent if it is seen through a microscope so that each grain's true degree of transparency can be viewed. Without a powerful enough microscope, sand appears opaque. Place a handful of diamonds into a glass of water, and they will appear to disappear because they are as transparent as the water that surrounds them. Put pearls into a glass of water, and all you have is a bunch of pearls in a glass of water. They are not transparent until you slice them thin enough to see that they, too, are transparent.

Now that we have tools to see the atomic structure of things, we see that atoms are mere points in otherwise empty space. Set them to vibrating, which is what they are doing all the time, and that empty space appears to be filled up with something solid.

Besides the transparent aspect of materials in nature, there exists perceptual transparency. The more transparent a work, the easier it is to grasp. Something crude is transparent for its crudity. Something opaque is transparent to the mind for its opacity. When a high level of quality or degree of a property is obvious, then a thing is perceptually at its most transparent.

One of the oddities about discussions around sound is that they usually include the words *opaque* or *transparent*. A sound described as opaque is unidimensional, crude, obscure, and crass. There is nothing changing, clear, deep, refined, or sublime about such a sound. Granted, these traits are beyond the ken of most people to perceive, but with a little instruction, most people can learn to recognize their presence or absence in almost any sound. When a sound is perceived to have these multidimensional traits, it is clear to the senses that it is a superior quality sound.

Sound is more transparent than air, which is why hearing and spiritual sensibility are so closely linked. Learning to intelligently process sound helps with understanding the ephemeral spiritual realm. Nothing is more transparent than that realm.

Principle 14. — Clarity

The degree to which a quality is revealed

Linked to transparency is the principle of clarity. As qualities become more obvious the presence of principles become more overt. The more exoteric a quality, the clearer it is to the observer. When the principle of clarity is rightly expressed, the perceiver of a work will have instantaneous recall of the intended effect on the viewer.

In language and music, clarity is the result of efficient communication of expression. Unfortunately, language is often used for obfuscating the truth. This is the cardinal trait of academic writing; it is a rare academic who writes to clarify the obscure. Jargon is one of the best means of obscuring the truth or preventing the uninitiated from understanding what is being expressed. Eliminating jargon clarifies and makes easy the understanding of what is said. In music, jargon comes in the form of nonsense sounds, irrelevant sounds, arbitrary sound combinations, and unnecessary rhythmic interjections. As with most forms of jargon, the point is to appear smarter than one actually is.

The principle of clarity, as it manifests in nature, appears in how species stay distinct and in how cycles of growth, reproduction, and decay play out in time. Clarity in chemistry is the result of understanding the mechanisms involved when elements combine. A butterfly collection shows how species are distinct, but it is the DNA molecules that clarify how the differences occur. Layers of various kinds of rock make clear the geological process of sedimentation in that location. The practice of science itself is the application of the principle of clarity to man's understanding of the natural world.

Principle 15. — Paradox

Opposites appearing in one

The metaphysical nature of the human spirit occupying a wholly physical body provides the foundation for this principle. The more paradoxical a work is made, the greater it will be. To imbue a work with a principle is already bringing about a paradoxical state. It is this property of a work that makes it endlessly fascinating. Failure to properly use this principle will yield a work that might satisfy temporarily but fails to endure over time.

The Chinese developed the concept of paradox using the Yin Yang symbol. It perfectly expresses the concept of opposites in one. In music, paradox is realized by making a score come alive to an audience. In art, it is realized by creating images that appear real or alive. Art that simultaneously expresses multiple principles will appear alive. The more paradoxical a work, the more intensely interesting it becomes to our senses because the human brain is designed to grab what is out of its reach, rather than grab what is barefaced in front of it. It is a great scientist who discovers the reality least easily understood and whose discoveries appear self-evident as soon as they are made.

Black holes are a paradox. That is, a black hole is so dense and has such strong gravity that something as fast and as lacking in density as light can't escape it. Diamonds are paradoxical because they are made from carbon—a pitch-black opaque material. Mixing hydrochloric acid and liquid sodium hydroxide, two lethal chemicals, paradoxically produces salt water, a material that covers much of the earth and in which billions of animals live and thrive. Art itself is a paradox because it must appear to be something other than mere inanimate material.

Principle 16. — Logic

How a thing fits

The rules of art and music are designed to encourage conformance to this principle. When these rules are violated, as they often are, the result is unintelligible because it is perceived as illogical. Often, the logic is ineffable, yet its absence is felt as real. The ineffability of the logic usually means that the artist was working intuitively rather than knowledgeably. Normally, understanding the link between ineffable cause and effect requires sensing the subtlest effects and having the intelligence to locate the contributing cause. Once the esoteric becomes exoteric, the logic becomes self-evident. Failure to work according to the logic demanded by a work's constituent elements will inevitably produce a gross violation of this principle. As with every principle, violation, ignorance, avoidance, or evasion of the rightful execution of this principle destroys the ability of a work to touch or move an observer.

Euclidian geometry is designed to teach the process of logical thought. It shows how leaving out a step in the logical process causes a breakdown in the understanding of how particular forms are derived. That is why it continues to be taught after more than two millennia. People still need to learn how to think logically and deeply.

Principle 17. — Distortion

The unpredictable, chaotic, erratic, disordered, etc., which is also known as entropy

In nature, anything unflawed or pure is unstable and bound to deteriorate. Everything has a point at which the flaws inherent in its manifestation can no longer accumulate. From that point, it must be actively destroyed to deteriorate. Nothing in nature is more stable than a balanced state of chaos. Physicists call this entropy.

In art, the element of disorder, dirt, messiness, flaws, or crudity creates the effect of strength. Purity in the arts is strong only for the boredom it inflicts on the senses. Hence, strength in the arts is greatest when the amount of dirt is high enough to be detected, but not dominant. Anything that is not perfect is distorted. The exact degree of distortion needed to create enduring interest is different with each work. Work which lacks distortion or dirt appears weak and insipid.

In his treatise on *Poetics* (XXV), Aristotle uses the word *error* when saying, "Error may be justified, if the end of the art be thereby attained, that is the effect of this or any other part...is thus rendered more striking."[12] He adds to this the warning, "If the end might have been as well, or better, attained without violating the special rules of the poetic art, the error is not justified: for every kind of error should if possible be avoided." No clearer definition of poetic license can be had.

---

[12] Ibid.

Distortion needs to be used judiciously if the end result is not to be marred. The more sublime the expression of a work, the cruder its manifestation needs to be, and vice versa. Mozart played beautifully sounds puerile. Beethoven played roughly sounds coarse. Bach played in a mathematically precise manner sounds dead.

Rock music has evolved to incorporate greater and greater amounts of distortion in both sound and performance practice. As it evolved, the names that Rock music was called changed according to how much distortion was applied. That is why there are distinctions between Soft Rock, Hard Rock, Acid Rock, etc.

Distortion for its own sake is like violence for the sake of violence. It is meaningless and baneful. Distortion only exists in the presence of what is pure. Error only exists in the presence of correctness. Dirt only exists in a state of cleanliness. In art, distortion is not an aim—it is a solution. Weakness is solved by distortion, and overbearing strength is solved by purity.

Botticelli's paintings, *The Birth of Venus* and *The Primavera*, are superb examples of intelligent use of distortion. On the surface, the paintings don't appear in the least distorted. Yet if you look carefully at the figures, you can notice how extremely distorted the features of the faces and bodies are. If you were walking down the street and met a woman with features as Botticelli painted them, you would be shocked by the misalignment and disproportion of all the parts; but the features in the painting appear right and natural, as well as interesting and compelling. This attests to the genius of Botticelli, who consciously took the degree of distortion to its most extreme realization within the bounds of what can still be called beautiful.

Early modernist painters, who distorted everything in their paintings, failed to make real art because they did not understand that when everything appears distorted, nothing is distorted; it is merely ugly. The narcissistic motive for severely distorting their paintings was, and still is, to draw attention to themselves.

Principle 18. — Unity

Things working together as one

Unity is the glue that binds attention. Disunity guarantees wandering attention. Unity is different from integrity in that, for it to exist, it requires the right manifestation of universal principles to the right degree. Unity has less to do with ideas and their development than with the relationship between a work's various elements. Attention is easily lost when it must focus on the parts of a work. Creating a meaningful relationship of the parts to each other and to the whole makes for more enduring interest.

In every living thing, all the parts contribute to the success of the whole. Each ant contributes its minute yet essential role in the life of the entire colony. Likewise, every part of each ant contributes to the success of the ant's ability to play its role. Trees would be nothing without their flowers, and flowers are wasted without bees to pollinate them. Bees, in turn, would fail to survive if their bodies did not have tiny hairs to collect pollen from flowers, and so on. It is unity that connects the working parts together in a process or cycle.

When unity breaks down, it is because something arbitrary has intervened in the process thereby halting the connections. A story hangs together if every element in the story moves it forward, thus maintaining the listener's interest. Interject one arbitrary element, one that fits nowhere in the context of the story, and the listener's interest is disrupted and violated. Likewise, music that fails to derive all its material from the theme lacks unity. When a composer adds arbitrary elements to a piece of music, they make the music sound like listening to an insane person speaking in entirely unrelated phrases. It would be like saying, "Like reading cats are purring for the Nixon White House with money is evil." Nothing makes sense because every phrase is about something different. By eliminating the arbitrary and sticking to a point, there is a greater chance of creating unity.

It is not color coordination that creates unity in a painting, though that is how many lesser painters try to fake unity. Subject matter has been used in the past to unify all the elements in a painting, but since Abstract Expressionism influenced the thinking of painters, the mere fact that painters were expressing themselves was enough to assume that their paintings were unified. Since the time of that movement in painting, unity has been imposed by self-conscious and artificial means, supposedly involving the viewer's intellect rather than their sense of sight. It is like pasting words on food to engage the diner's intellect during dinner. This approach to imposing unity on a work is propaganda. That is, using an artistic medium to make a political or emotional point. Unity is not something pasted on after the fact. It must be at the core of the conception of a work so that each element in the work is derived from the central unifying theme, just as every organism's development is programmed from the beginning by molecules of DNA.

Principle 19. — Flow

Fulfillment of means (as in "means to an end")

The principle of flow governs the perception of connections between gestures and sub-gestures. Flow is not an extrinsic part of a work, it works mostly on the observer. When it is present, flow cannot be detected. When absent, it cannot be felt. A performance of music works when it most closely mirrors the flow of thought. When thought flows, you almost never notice the flow until it is interrupted, when the feeling of the absence of flow makes it possible to detect the interruption.

Nature, as it is, embodies this principle from the smallest particles to the largest structures in how matter and energy interact to create movement. Failure to flow creates a perception of disconnection of whatever would otherwise be flowing. Just as damming a river interrupts the flow of water, when the dam is full, the river will again flow. By forcing the river to cease flowing, the dam is made to more precisely manage the river's flow.

Flow of water is managed within plants, to some extent, by evaporation of water through its leaves. This forces water to defy gravity and flow upwards to replace whatever water was lost through transpiration. As soon as a plant's leaves disappear, the water within the plant sinks into the roots.

When ballet dancers self-consciously pace from one choreographic phrase to another, the effect is tedious to observe. Only when the affective content of the dance is made clear does the stiff, self-conscious pacing become flowing. This is because the affective content is the meaning behind each phrase, and the phrases appear as they do to convey that meaning. The function of ballet is to perpetuate the impression of everyone being airborne, for it is when the dancers are in the air that the feeling of flow in the dance is properly conveyed. Flow breaks down when the dancers appear connected to the stage more than the feeling of flow they are responsible for creating.

In nature, everything is flowing in space or in time. Continents, ocean currents, electrons, etc. flow at different speeds, but they are all flowing. Finally, it is the flow of logic that fulfills reason.

Principle 20. — Focus

Fulfillment of purpose

The principle of focus answers three questions:

- What?
- Why?
- How?

A work that gives satisfaction to those questions is focused, even if the questions are vague feelings in the observer. As long as the "What?" and "Why?" are manifest, the nagging feeling of those questions is resolved. When "How?" remains unresolved, the effect is mystery. Art conceals itself when it is both focused and mysterious.

Moments are focused when everyone involved in that moment experience shared attention. Work is focused when every action in its production points to the same end. Things are focused when the purpose for which they are made is fulfilled. A lawn mower fulfills its purpose when it cuts grass. The better and more efficiently it cuts grass, the more focused it is.

A musical instrument is focused when its sound fulfills the highest possibility of its potential. For instance, a violin that sounds like a violin, no matter how good that sound may be, does not fulfill its highest possible potential. Only when a violin sounds like a human voice does it acquire the quality of focus, and making it thus requires its maker to be focused entirely on that aim, an aim that is virtually impossible to achieve. Making a violin to sound like a violin is easily achievable because all violins already sound like that, which is why they don't sound focused.

When a person is focused, it is almost impossible for others to interfere with the aim or outcome of that person's focus. It is of no consequence whether that aim or outcome is destructive or constructive; stopping focused behavior is always difficult. This is the problem when dealing with a person who is obsessive-compulsive, and this is also why there exists a fine line between genius and insanity. The main difference is that a genius questions their sanity, while an insane person never entertains such questions.

Principle 21. — Timing

The moment when conditions are fulfilled

Timing can manifest itself in choosing the right moment, selecting the best place, filtering out the best possibility, employing the best method, acting on opportunity, etc. Bad timing means stopping too soon, waiting too long, selecting a less than optimal place, grabbing at anything in the hopes it will work, etc. Timing exists when everything comes together to make the best effect. It is also in the ability to endure the feeling of uncertainty caused by ignorance of the moment conditions are fulfilled.

The principle of timing governs the behavior of the artist as he or she selects and chooses. A meal at which each dish must be served hot at the same time is an example of the need for the chef to be aware of the timing involved. A painting technique based on a specific method needs to be executed step by step to get the best effect. Failure to follow the technique will result in a wholly different effect. Introducing a note too soon or too late can ruin a musical line. These are examples that demonstrate the need for an artist to be aware of the moment when conditions are fulfilled.

In nature, timing guarantees that the chicks in eggs will hatch at exactly the moment when the yolk runs out and the air inside the egg becomes depleted. As the egg develops in the hen, the formation of the shell happens at the right moment; otherwise, the egg becomes too fragile, or the shell could be weakened by distortions on the egg's surface. Seeds germinate according to specific timing.

If a seed begins to sprout too soon, there may not be enough water to sustain it. If the seed sprouts too late, the flowers may open too late for the fruit to develop before winter arrives. All these natural mechanisms are controlled by the principle of timing via genetic information.

Principle 22. — Elasticity

The resumption of order after disorder or distortion

The principle of elasticity is connected to the principles of dynamic and distortion. What is dynamic is also distorted. A thing may not be distorted if it was not at first regular or still. To stretch, to delay, to expand, to contract, or to go to extremes are forms of distortion and dynamic. Dynamic is distinguished from distortion in the degree of stretching, the degree of expansion, the degree of contraction, etc. Distortion is merely more extreme than dynamic.

The principle of elasticity brings everything back to a semblance of order. The faster the return to order, the greater the elasticity. The more extreme the distortion, the more intensely a return to order will be perceived. When everything is distorted or dynamic most of the time, nothing is distorted or dynamic because a constantly changing behavior is perceived as a continuous "hum" state. Hence, there is a need for both musically and spiritually proportioned structures to interrupt that continuous hum condition.

A rubber band is called elastic because it can resume its former shapelessness after being stretched to a specific identifiable shape. In this regard, the rubber band is a paradox because its original state is disordered, and distortion causes its shape to become more ordered. On the other hand, a musical string is a perfect representation of the principle of elasticity. When stretched to sound a musical note, the string is ordered to sound all the overtones relating to the pitch of the string. When plucked, struck, or bowed, the string is distorted. Upon release, the string quickly tries to resume its ordered state of being at rest.

A piece of music in variation form incorporates the principle of elasticity. Variations on a theme follow each iteration of the original undistorted theme in an ABACADAEAFA pattern. Humor often works with the principle of elasticity when an idea of a behavior is regularly repeated only to be replaced, suddenly and momentarily, with an unexpected behavior.

Principle 23. — Inevitability

Certainty of outcome

Nature applies this principle in the relationship between the effects of certainty and uncertainty. Every year, the earth's wobble makes it certain that the weather in winter will be cold, but exactly how cold is uncertain. Start a ball of snow rolling down a snow-covered hill, and the ball will inevitably grow in size, but exactly how much it will grow is not certain. When phenomena are both certain and predictable, they become scientific constants that are the basis on which to measure other phenomena. Water boils and freezes at specific temperatures at sea level. The temperature is certain for that altitude. Change the altitude, and the temperatures change slightly. Thus, we can be certain that by knowing the altitude, we can predict the temperature at which water will boil or freeze. The certainty of outcome in relation to the uncertain nature of that outcome is what the principle of inevitability creates.

For satisfaction to occur in art and music, the observer must have the sense of the outcome being inevitable. It is up to the artist or musician to create this effect. When this effect is observed as too certain, it feels predictable; when it is observed as uncertain, the feeling is like that of nausea because the observer doesn't like being jerked around. If the artist treads the line between boring the observer and jerking them around, the result is a sense of inevitability.

Principle 24. — Continuity

Fulfillment of function

The principle of continuity as the fulfillment of function describes the sensation of fulfillment we experience when continuity exists. To create continuity means fixing the observer's attention on the relationships between things, rather than on the things themselves. This is accomplished by using the aesthetic principles with skill and is not unlike the proverbial catch-22. That is, you can't fix an observer's attention without the things used to express the relationships, but it is the relationships between the things that fulfill their function upon which an observer's attention must be fixed.

Ultimately, the brain requires continuity to the same degree that it requires surprise. Without continuity of expectation, surprise is flaccid. Music that goes on smoothly without interruption creates the expectation of continuous, uninterrupted motion. In this way, surprise is made effective by expectation. If everything is supposed to be surprising, then nothing is surprising because the brain expects the constant interruptions to continue. In like manner, nothing is beautiful if it can't be compared to something ugly, and nothing is ugly if beauty is not present to deny the expectation. If everything is ugly, the brain becomes annoyed by the unabated tedium of sameness, and the same would hold true if everything were beautiful.

In his treatise on *Poetics* (XXIV) Aristotle observed that "sameness of incident soon produces satiety."[13] This is why music performed with fake flow or fake continuity (where notes and the spaces between them are made to sound as regular as possible) doesn't work. The human brain can hear three equally spaced events and predict the exact moment a fourth event will occur. When that prediction comes true, the brain tunes out and looks for something more interesting that might be happening. If nothing more interesting is found, it goes to sleep. The assumption that flow is guaranteed by forcing music into a perfectly regular meter is false, yet this is one of the cardinal standards for determining musical talent today. In practical terms, this means that music students are being trained in how to put the brains of an entire audience to sleep.

As I have alluded to already, in Botticelli's famous painting, *The Birth of Venus*, the distorted placement of body parts is so extreme that were we to correct them, the result would bore our minds instantly. Paradoxically, it is the subtlety of the distortions that fix the attention so continuously when viewing that painting. Botticelli has carefully uncovered the subtlest and exact degree of distortion needed to continuously fix attention. The observer doesn't normally notice the

[13] Ibid.

distortions because they are so carefully adjusted, yet an anatomist would find the placements ridiculous because they are so extreme. This is Botticelli's genius.

Principle 25. — Rhythm

Elliptical function

The principle of rhythm is linked to the idea of cycle. Cycles don't have the characteristic of absolute regularity, but they have certainty of outcome, which is the special feeling that rhythm conveys. An example of a cycle would be the earth's orbit around the sun.

Another component to rhythm, as important as cycle, is swing. Metrical movement is dead reckoning, while rhythm is a living, swinging impulse. Swing is the behavior of accelerating to a point of ultimate rest but missing that point, no matter how many times the repetitions continue. An example of swing would be a pendulum. Another would be a heavy ball on the end of a cord being twirled around by a man holding the opposite end of the tether. As the man turns, the weight of the ball exerts a force in opposition to the man, which causes him to move in response to that force. This may be called a dance because he swings his body in response to the counterweight of his partner, the ball. A hammer ride at the fair is an example of what happens when cycle and swing occur at the same time.

Without cycle and swing in harmonious balance, rhythm cannot exist. One hears it said that someone who can keep a beat has a good sense of rhythm. If this were true, a metronome would have good rhythm, which is a patently ridiculous conclusion. On closer inspection, we find that the ability to beat time is an indication of the ability to measure time precisely, like a metronome. Unfortunately, the ability to measure time precisely and the ability to sense and convey swing cycles are altogether different skills.

Dancers who believe that dance is best when it exhibits mechanical, metrical motor skills are boring to watch because they exhibit no sense of rhythm. Their movements are circular rather than elliptical.

PRINCIPLE 26. — GRAVITY

A pulling tendency

The principle of gravity is what creates tension, brings about stability, resolves matters of motion, and governs the durability of interest. What lacks gravity might be interesting...for about five minutes. The paradoxical state existing between the creation of tension and the formation of stability makes anything that exhibits this state extremely interesting to the observer, and the observer never tires of witnessing it.

Gravity is at the core of rhythm, attraction, form, and attention. Gravity is at work in relationships, and it forms the foundation of any hierarchy. Gravity influences flow. The pulling tendencies (gravity) of any two things act on each other and everything surrounding them to create system and force. System is created by function, and force is created by accumulated mass or energy due to repeated motion and direction.

Ants repeatedly follow a system of trails created by the force of efficient movement of individuals to and from the anthill and their food source, both of which display a gravitational pull on the ants. Watching ants break down a food source and move it bit by bit to their lair shows how nature organizes behavior to guide individuals to the most efficient use of resources.

In music, the pulling tendency that the tonic note exerts on the other notes of a tonal scale is so strong that music feels unnatural when those tendencies are ignored or trampled on. Similarly, the subject of a sentence has such a powerful pulling effect that if other words or phrases in the sentence fail to refer to the subject, the meaning becomes obscure and not worth bothering with. We are so sensitive to this in language that we tune out within seconds of detecting a violation of that pulling tendency.

PRINCIPLE 27. — LIMIT

Fulfillment of form

The principle of timing and the principle of limit are closely connected. Timing has to do with behaviors and events, whereas limit has to do with structures and places. Knowing the limit of a thing has to do with a sense of timing. To run a mile without first training for it is a sure method to know your limit for running without preparation. The preparation involves carefully managed timing of all the variables that affect the desired outcome. Only when you know your physical limits and how long it takes you to run a mile should you make the decision to enter a race or not. Further, knowing the timing of an event has to do with a sense of limit. When approaching a boss for a raise, you need to know what the limits are on how much you can ask for; but more importantly, you need to know when the moment is right for the asking.

In nature, forms are limited in size by both function and environment. For example, I suspect that the form of the giant dinosaurs early in the earth's history is due to the actual size and mass of the earth being significantly smaller than it is today. Large animals can't move with enough flexibility or speed when the force of gravity works its way on them. If flexibility and speed are necessary for survival, then large body mass becomes an evolutionary liability. The accumulation of mass from debris falling from outer space for over seventy million years would be enough to make trouble for the super-large dinosaurs survival. By this measure, human beings may have reached the limits of their size and may eventually start to get smaller over time as the mass of the earth continues to increase (assuming there will be any human beings left alive on Earth seventy million years from now). I suspect that we may go extinct far sooner than less intelligent species because we will fail to intelligently use our intelligence.

Principle 28. — Attraction

Sympathetic resonance

When forces attract, they react to and act on each other according to degrees of musical relationship. This holds true for mitochondria, planets, birds, humans, musical notes, and for forms. From a physics point of view, attraction is obvious, so it is unnecessary to discuss it here. It is more important to discuss attraction from a perceptual point of view because it is in the arts where we must first attract and then hold the observer's attention. In the arts, failure to attract the attention means failure, period. Failure to hold attention, once it has been attracted, also spells failure.

Attracting and holding the attention involves the neat balance between structure and behavior, perceptibility and interest, repetition and variation, order and chaos, and stasis and tension. The irrational attracts the attention, while the rational holds it. Sympathy stems from shared disorder, and resonance stems from shared order. Unless the totality of the perceiving mind is nourished from moment to moment, boredom quickly sets in.

The problem in art and music is to mindfully adjust the execution of these principles to fit the intended affect. Quality may be defined as the property of exhibiting principles. The fewer the number of principles a work exhibits, the lower the quality. The greater the number of principles intelligently applied, the higher the quality. When principles are present and active, they are virtually unnoticeable, yet they compel the observer to observe. In other words, when we are doing everything right, people will be attracted by the results but not have the least idea why.

Principle 28. — Balance

Repose of opposing forces

The principle of balance maintains opposites in equilibrium. Creating this condition in a work of art gives the effect of stability and poise. When balance is not maintained, the effect is lopsided. Lopsidedness feels untrue. Nature exists as a balance between order and chaos, and every chaotic behavior eventually settles to a condition of ordered stability. That condition of stability is a point of balance. Chaos that is never stabilized by the principle of balance makes the observer agitated and ill at ease, like when watching a classroom of unruly children where the teacher has failed to capture their attention. Order that never feels energized by an element of chaos makes the observer bored and annoyed. Beauty exists when the elements of chaos and order are perfectly balanced. The sense of balance can be easily eschewed by the internal psychological makeup of the observer. When the observer is spiritually balanced within, the sense of perfect balance can be perceived clearly and without bias.

No state is complete except that it expresses balance within and among all its aspects. Entropy is the conventional term used by physicists to describe a natural state of balancing. However, the error in the concept of entropy is that it is interpreted as disorder. A truer way of viewing entropy is that it is a state of immeasurable complexity. This state of extreme complexity is merely the combined effects of all universal principles acting in unison to bring about the most stable state. For a mind that is accustomed to studying uncomplicated, measurable, and controlled states, the balanced state of all things functioning in unison appears as noise or disorder.

The stability that the principle of balance brings is not a static condition—it is dynamic. The combined effect of all the universal principles acting in unison creates a condition of cyclical rhythm much like breathing. On a universal scale, the rhythm is slow, requiring perhaps billions of years of expansion before it begins to contract again. Does this mean that the universe is alive? The answer is affirmative to the same degree that a Bach fugue is alive when played in a manner that moves the Soul.

In art, balance is required between beauty and interest. Structure produces beauty and behavior produces interest. One could also argue that order is beautiful but boring because it is predictable, while chaos is interesting but irritating because it is erratic. True beauty happens in the balance between the predictable and the unpredictable. It is in this regard that beauty is in the eye of the beholder—the mind's eye.

PRINCIPLE 30. — VARIATION

Multiplicity of identity within similar form

The principle of variation governs how complexity emerges from a convergence of simplicities. This principle governs genetics. The simple elements of DNA converge to produce what we perceive of as infinite variety. The simple elements of sound—the overtone series, and the vowels of pitch that were discovered by my wife, Marianne Ploger, in 1983—produce the individuality of sounds in nature. The specific manner of sound generation adds yet more complexity and increases the ease of identifying individuals.

This principle is part of the means of creating identity. It is how individuals within a species can attract a mate. If all male birds within a species sang the same song, they would all be attracting the one female bird in the species that happened to like that particular song.

The making of art requires the application of this principle to every instance of repetition for the work to be perceived as lively, lifelike, natural, and enjoyable. Endless repetition quickly dulls the attention and lulls the brain to sleep. On the other hand, endless differences that have no point or meaning are perceived as gratuitous. When the brain perceives constant variation of otherwise similarities, the effect is one of delight in the flow of differences.

Variation is the spice of life, but it can also become an addiction. When variety becomes an addiction, quality tends to be disregarded. It becomes, "Difference for difference's sake." The purpose of variation is to increase quality, not decrease it. When quality plummets as variation increases, that is the time to do something else. If quality was not part of the equation to begin with, then variation is not going to change that.

Principle 31. — Reciprocity

Give and take

The principle of reciprocity ensures parity between opposing forces or complimentary states. In Physics, the principle of reciprocity is expressed in Newton's law: *for every action, there is an equal and opposite reaction.* In art, this principle is expressed in the ratio of pleasure versus energy expenditure. The more energy an observer must expend to experience art, the greater the return in pleasure they must feel. Therefore, a work of art must always be wrought to yield the highest possible return of pleasure on each unit of energy spent to observe it.

Actions of justice are designed to preserve balance of harmony in society. This was the fundamental purpose of "eye for an eye, tooth for a tooth, life for a life" penalties in Hammurabic Law. This law provided means for restoration within society through the principle of reciprocity. When people set aside these harsh punishments, they risked the stability of society if alternative forms of punishment were not able to create the feeling of reciprocal balance. The real question that needed to be answered was not, "Does the punishment fit the crime?" It should have been, "Has the violation of the sense of reciprocity among those involved been reciprocally, satisfactorily, and harmonically balanced?" If tension remains unresolved, people may try to make it right on their own initiative, which can lead to dangerous situations.

The alternative to unresolved or unresolvable violation is forgiveness. Forgiveness does not mean forgetting, which is impossible. It means that you do not require the violation of your sense of reciprocity to be satisfied, which frees you from the bondage and attachment to the desire for retribution. Forgiveness is important because the desire for retribution is an all-consuming, enslaving violation against yourself. The enslaving chains of this desire eat away at your connection to your Soul until that connection is severed or you get tired of being a slave.

Clearly, being a slave is not a user-friendly way to live. In this state, your entire occupation is to serve the feeling of violation and the desire for getting even. The world has more than its share of people who choose this life, and I have found that people usually do exactly as they are pleased to do. Those who choose this life of slavery do so because it gives them pleasure to spend their existence on a mental and spiritual treadmill for retribution. Forgiveness creates an automatic reciprocal action between the violator and the mind of the one violated because the violated one lets go of the desire to retaliate.

Remembering is not something that ever goes away because the brain chemistry that establishes memory does its job most effectively. The most that can be done by the victim of violation is to forgive the violator and treat the incident as unimportant. We lose interest in all that we consider unimportant, so the memory of a violation can become as unimportant as what we ate for breakfast two weeks ago.

In creative work, the principle of reciprocity is important in the interaction between the observer and the observed. It takes energy to look at a painting, listen to a piece of music, have dinner in a restaurant, or see a movie. Part of the energy equation is the money and time spent. So, when someone ventures out to be an observer of art of any kind, it is imperative that the experience is reciprocally rewarded for the trouble taken. If observers do not receive at least a 1:1 ratio of energy expended to energy received, they will feel cheated. The 1:1 ratio is the minimum requirement for a patron to consider returning for more. A more appropriate ratio, one I hold myself to, is a 1:10 ratio. Despite the high price I ask for my work, those who own my instruments consider themselves lucky to have one. A 1:5 ratio merely makes the patron feel fortunate. A 1:1 ratio creates the feeling of getting what you paid for. A 1:0.9 ratio creates the feeling of being taken. That is how powerful our sense of the principle of reciprocity is to each of us.

Principle 32. — Encasement

Containment of behavior by structure

The principle of encasement governs the balance between flexible behaviors, flows, processes, actions, and soft living material and the inflexible forms that contain them. Insects, bones, crustaceans, volcanic flows, plants, seeds, nuts, and eggs are natural examples of the encasement principle. Over the centuries, inventors and craftsmen developed ways of applying the principle of encasement in the form of case-hardened steel swords in medieval Japan, case-hardened lacquer ware in Bronze Age China, in the hard outer layers of Renaissance frescos, and in case-hardened wire for making piano strings and suspension bridges. In the human body, the skull encases our brain to protect it from damage. Shock the skull too extremely, as in a concussion, and the brain can be irreversibly damaged.

The principle of encasement is found throughout the universe in the form of planets and, in some cases, moons. Wherever there exists a soft central core protected by a hard exterior, like in the earth, the principle of encasement is at work.

Principle 33. — Radiance

Containment of structure by behavior

The converse of encasement is the principle of radiance. The principle of radiance governs the balance between inflexible inner structures and the external, flexible behaviors that contain them. This principle allows for variability of behavior without loss of integrity or structure. The structure of stars, animals, human beings, and atoms are governed by this principle. Our skeleton is the rigid inner structure that supports the soft exterior parts of the body. By being jointed, our otherwise rigid skeleton can bend and move with remarkable flexibility, allowing us to radiate our attention, desires, and intentions to others.

Musical instruments are of the few man-made objects that embody both encasement and radiance. That is, material musical objects that produce tone, over and above mere timbre, exhibit radiance. Violins of exceedingly high quality, like those made by Stradivari and Guarneri del Jesu, embody multiple universal principles: encasement, radiance, harmonic proportion, spiritual proportion, and gesture in appearance and sound; logic, limit, and harmony in their acoustical structure; flow and rhythm in design; flow, relation, distortion, and continuity in how they play; order, hierarchy, form, and efficiency in the acoustical design; clarity, dynamic, connection, propriety, and contrast in the manner in which they project the sound; and integrity, intensity, balance, direction, focus, and gravity in sound and character. This is why people are willing to pay as much as $10,000,000 for the privilege of caring for one of these violins. When it is possible to own a violin for a mere $150, it gives us an idea of the value people place on things and behaviors that radiate, express, and reflect universal principles.

Principle 34. — Individuation

A force that coalesces energy and material into complete unique structures

The principle of individuation governs the formation of structures, from the smallest to the largest, to make each structure unique, though similar to others of its kind. Humans have the power to create or manufacture highly similar structures, yet each unit, no matter how similar to other units, differs in ways that make each unique. The principle of individuation generates that effect. Laboratories can tell if a substance is from one source or another (in crime detection, for instance) because no two batches of anything are exactly alike.

The desire to eliminate the effects of this principle is the single most deadly disease affecting the arts in the twentieth century. It was this principle that drove the philosophy of Ayn Rand, as expressed in her novel, *The Fountainhead.* Nature strives to individuate because diversity is a stronger and more stable condition than similarity. Homogeneity, similarity, sameness, uniformity, and conformity are all unamicable to individuation.

The advantage of similarity is survival—survival of the most similar. This is how music performance competitions tend to work. Those whose playing is most similar to the judges' will win. In this way, music competitions tend to spread and sustain mediocrity. Those whose playing is principled are viewed as being undisciplined, despite it being vastly more difficult to incorporate universal principles into a performance than it is to play notes accurately and in time.

It is only in the last one hundred years that the individual has become so valued by society. This cultural tendency has both positive and negative consequences. On the positive side, people are becoming more accepting of individual traits and proclivities that they might have once shunned. On the negative side, this has resulted in a society inhabited by narcissists, and where each person falsely assumes that they are the most important person in the world.

Principle 35. — Infinity

A force that drives apart the limits of time and space, creating unboundedness, or the absence of beginning and end

The principle of infinity governs reality at the micro and the macro levels. The manner in which the principle of infinity works is embodied in how the principles of efficiency, paradox, attraction, limit, gravity, flow, inevitability, and rhythm interact with each other. The inevitable governs the limits of infinity, which is a paradox because that which is limitless should have no limits. Yet it is inevitable, or certain, that the limits of infinity are limitlessness itself. Like a sphere, which represents an infinite number of circles equidistant from a single central point, infinity can appear to be contained and still be unbounded, much like the Soul. Flow expresses infinite and inevitable motion. Rhythm expresses cycles that repeatedly flow through infinite time. Gravity governs the inevitable shape of objects in space, which are infinitely acquiring mass until a sphere, the most efficient shape of objects that have achieved sufficient size, is formed. Infinity is nowhere more profoundly expressed than in the nature of the Soul, which embodies limitlessness in space and time and in the balance between structure and behavior.

Humankind that thinks small, thinks limited, thinks insufficiency, and thinks within the bounds of limited experience. Universal principles govern the whole of reality in a way that is beyond what the minds of humans can conceive. Joining with these principles allows us to expand our awareness of what is possible within the bounds of what is kind.

THOUGHTS ON THE UNIVERSAL PRINCIPLES

What science discovers about the nature of our universe is the manner in which universal principles act upon each other in the forming of our world and the universe we occupy. We have difficulty recognizing universal principles as separate forces because they invariably act in conjunction with each other, not in isolation; yet each principle is a distinct individual force as each part of one's body is a distinct individual part. Like the parts of a body, these principles are parts that make up the whole, and they act together in coordination to produce every effect in the universe, including the effect of a universe existing in the first place.

Let's be clear. These are not all the principles; these are the principles I have been able to distinguish for use in my work. I'm sure that I have only scratched the surface of this unseen realm and that there are more principles to be sensed and understood. If there are more, of which I am sure, those that are missing from this paltry list and the senses needed to detect them will eventually become a reality. Humankind evolves as an organism, according to evolutionary processes, by acquiring clearer and more distinct senses designed to detect yet another principle that governs the universe.

I am also sure that every real advance in science will be the revelation of another universal principle or the articulation of the mathematics that explains how another of these principles works. Algebra is the mathematics that shows us how logic works. Fractal mathematics describe how the principle of integrity functions. Each principle has a unique mathematics that explains how it works, and that mathematics is available for scientists to discover.

The mathematics itself doesn't help us understand how the Soul is fed by our sensation and perception of these universal principles. Mathematics feeds the mind, not the Soul. If someone were to provide the mathematics for each of these principles, I am sure there would also be someone who would use these principles to gain and hold power over others. It is ever the potential for anything good to be brought into the service of those who are evil. Those who are evil are allowed to dominate the human race only when good people fail to be vigilant and act on their senses.

APPLYING THE UNIVERSAL PRINCIPLES

Learning to apply these principles takes constant attention and effort. It cannot be done overnight. It is best to first use the ones which you understand most easily. Later, use others which you understand less well but which you can apprehend. Finally, incorporate those that seem the most esoteric; these are the ones that will take your work from great to sublime. Discipline yourself to devise every conceivable means of putting the principles into the work you are doing. The more you do this, the easier it becomes. The beauty of universal principles is that they can transform your work from being mediocre to good, from good to the level of genius, from genius to great, from great to sublime, and from sublime to divine. All who use them will be improved by them, as will their work.

Everyone can comprehend the universal principles in their utter simplicity, yet there are those who insist on being too bright, cynical, intellectual, or cocksure to subject themselves and their work to governance by the principles. In terms of the spirit and the reality of the universe, such people make themselves irrelevant by their arrogance. Anyone who can muster the humility to subject themselves to the principles will be raised to a level of relevance. I suspect this is what is meant by the sayings, "a tree is known by its fruit,"[14] and "the last shall be first and the first shall be last."[15]

Remember, the principles are sensed, not felt. Emotions are felt, and sensations are sensed. Emotions arise from sensation as the feeling of annoyance arises from the sensation of constant itching. Take the principle of efficiency, for example. When we *sense* a lack of efficiency, we *feel* like what we are doing is a waste, which makes us angry and irritated. Therefore, use your emotions caused by the deprivation or insufficiency of a principle to help you sense that principle. Many artists who have achieved greatness were ill-tempered or choleric because this is how they maintained a connection with the principles. Thankfully, once you

---

[14] Matthew 12: 33 New Testament, Bible

[15] Matthew 20: 16 New Testament, Bible

know what the principles are and can sense them, you can more easily maintain an level temperament.

Just as sensing an absence or violation of a principle might cause anger and irritation, fear of being angry or irritated often leads to rampant mediocrity in people's quest for niceness and pleasantness in the arts. Cultivate an intolerance for mediocrity, ignorance, or violation of principles in your work and in yourself, but practice tolerance by allowing others to be as mediocre as they wish. In other words, mind your own business and give others the room to learn at the rate they mean to, but don't be forced to accommodate them simply because they are too lazy to put in the effort to be better. Everyone has the right to make mistakes, be wrong, mediocre, or incompetent.

Subjecting yourself to the dictates of principles is a free choice that should be made with joy and deliberation. Not everyone can live with the consequences of making that choice, so you have no right to judge the appropriateness of other people's decisions. Yet you do have a right, even an obligation, to say if what they do violates your senses or not. You are obliged to say the truth as you know it because that is part of living in harmony with the principles. The principles are the essence of truth and reality, and they best not be denied. Those who hide behind silence to avoid dealing with unspiritual attitudes are, in effect, saying that such attitudes are OK.

Remember also that to judge a work as inferior is not to condemn the person who made it; it is to affirm that the person is or was ignorant of principles, which is a statement of reality. If the one whose work is being criticized feels angry, it is that person's anger that condemns him, not your observation of reality. In this situation, anger arises because they are afraid that what they are hearing is true but they don't know how to fix the problem, or they are afraid that you are attacking them personally when you make an observation of reality that reveals inadequacies in their work or thinking. It is their ego that generates the anger needed to defend them from the ravages of the truth.

It is a decision to be subject to the tyranny of your ego, in the same way that it is a decision to be subject to the dictates of principles. When you do decide to follow the principles, you release the power of the brain to embrace reality and all its resources. These resources occasionally leak out in spurts of ingenuity and invention in the works of great artists and scientists, in bursts of intuition in the writings of the greatest philosophers, and in the constant flow of divine inspiration in the words of great spiritual teachers. A brain that is subject to the principles is more fit to understand, process, grasp, receive, and play with the gifts of the spirit than a brain that is not so subject. It is such a brain that is fulfilling its design function.

All too often, we become so heavily invested in expressing ourselves (our egos) that we lose awareness of the understanding needed to make the most of what is being expressed. A mind cultivated to perceive principles needs the universal principles to be exhibited in the right proportion for a musical experience to be fulfilling. A deprived mind will settle for two or three principles; but settling for something and being fulfilled are not the same. Being accustomed to settling for things inures the observer by creating the expectation of nothing more to be had. When more may be had, that expectation is trampled on by the surfeit of stimulation and often leads to withdrawal. This is what happened in France when the Impressionists first exposed their work to the public. Too many principles created an intensity that overcharged the viewer's senses, resulting in a shock.

Although we've been raised to think that we have five senses, human beings have at least 133 discreet senses, including a discreet sense for most of the universal principles. This means that we have dedicated areas of brain tissue to apprehend these principles when they are present and feel deprived when they are absent. When these principles are violated, we naturally feel that something is wrong. The purpose and function of art, in its many manifestations, is to directly apply these universal principles and stimulate an aesthetic awareness in us of those special senses. Art has no other purpose. It imitates nature to the degree it expresses universal principles. This is why art has been and is important in the lives of human beings.

When a work of art succeeds in stimulating the sensation of these thirty-five universal principles, it will generate a high degree of caring, love, and responsibility in an open observer. The more of these principles a work stimulates, the greater the work is. As a species, human beings evolve when another principle is discovered, articulated, and sensed. The job of the artist or scientist is to discover and express these principles. A paradigm shift has always occurred when a new principle is discovered and articulated for everyone to understand, and so it will be in the future. Wars have been conducted to enforce the acceptance of a principle or to stop the violation of a principle. This was the reason for the American Civil War when the abolition of slavery became the goal.

HOW TO HOLD YOUR MIND WHEN USING PRINCIPLES

Don't despair if the idea of these principles overwhelms you. Your mind will work best when you take one thing at a time. If you are determined to use the principles, your Soul will rally to your cause and make available all the resources it has at its disposal. The important thing is to be measured and deliberate. Don't try to use too many principles without first understanding them and determining how to maximize them in your work. Incorporate each one thoroughly before adding another.

Above all, avoid arrogance. Do not assume that because you know about these principles, you can actually use them. Assuming that would send the message to your Soul that you are a charlatan, and once it is informed of this reality, your Soul will leave you to your hubris. Be humble and ask questions. Remember, your Soul is designed to answer questions about that which can be known. Ask questions of your Soul, then listen!

Aesthetic Science, the Aesthetic Self, and the Senses

Chapter Four

Aesthetic Science: The Science of the Senses

In Chapter One, I mentioned something I called *aesthetic science*, or *knowing through sensing*. Aesthetics involves all of the senses. Science, for our purposes, involves methodical or systematic knowing, as opposed to haphazard knowing. This might seem simple enough because there are five senses, right? Well, by my reckoning we have at least 133 senses. Aesthetic science involves becoming acquainted with every one of these senses. At the risk of belaboring a point, I will systematically discuss each of our 133 senses to help you understand them. Like the way we refer to the emotional self, intellectual self, or physical self, these 133 senses may be referred to as the sensory or aesthetic self. I have divided these 133 discreet senses into seven houses, according to the specific purpose for which the senses exist or by how they relate.

Each house contains all the senses that pertain to that specific part of being, be it the physical, intellectual, spiritual, or essential. Personally, I would be surprised if my calculations are correct because I suspect that my readers will be sure to come up with more senses, ones to which I might be blind. Also, if my surmise about the universal principle of evolution is right, we humans will evolve increasing numbers of senses because for every waveform, particle species, or vibrational type, nature modifies organisms to sense those aspects of reality.

I also suspect that my readers will apply the term *sense* to experiences that are not sensory but are emotional or feeling-based. The standard I set for what constitutes a *sense* as opposed to a *feeling* is simple: Sensing is objective while feeling is subjective. Objective, in this usage, means that the sensation can't be influenced by preference, opinion, insistence, interpretation, desire, or action. Specifically, an objective sensation is a fact that has been registered as a sensation and not as a unit of information to be processed by the mind. Feelings, on the other hand, are subject to preference, opinion, etc. Hearing a car horn is objective when all you pay attention to is the effect the sound is having on your ears. Becoming angry when that sound continues long enough to cause irritation is a feeling that is subject to your desire for the sound to stop. Any experience of sensation classed as a bona fide sense must pass this test.

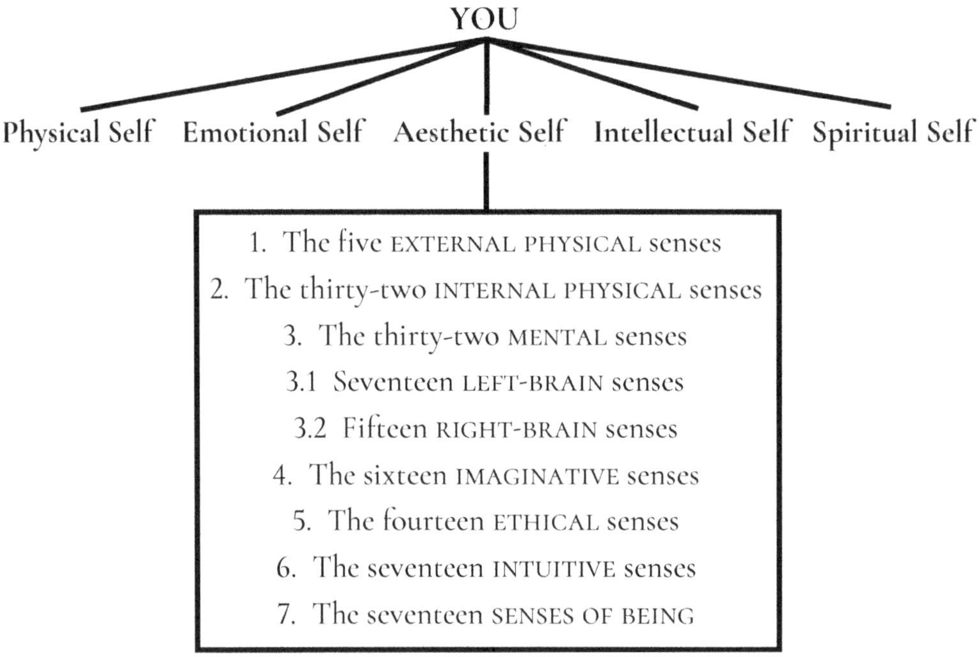

FIGURE 10. The model of a human being as a sensory organism with seven sensory houses.

A great deal of what we end up feeling emotionally, spiritually, ethically, or intellectually stems from stimulation (especially violation) of one or more of our many senses. Together, the senses form a new paradigm for understanding human personality and behavior that stands opposite to the Freudian, Psychological, or Behaviorist models, which we already know are based on the ego and the range of feelings that stem from fear or desire. This new model that I propose is based on the aesthetic self.

THE 133 SENSES

The five external physical senses are sight, hearing, touch, taste, and smell.

The thirty-two internal physical senses are pressure, pressure of contraction, pressure of expansion, compression, being, motion, temperature, tension, respiration, hunger, thirst, reproduction, excretion, regeneration, location, irritation, space, territory, fatigue, gesture, gravity, physical balance, comfort, pain, itching, emotion, relaxation, excitement, intensity, humidity, satisfaction, and numbness.

The seventeen mental senses of the left-brain are hierarchy, logic, quantitative proportion, harmony, balance, order, form, degree, clarity, contrast, limit, equivalence, number, encasement, direction, focus, and gravity.

The fifteen mental senses of the right-brain are flow, relation, rhythm, time, qualitative proportion, efficiency, integrity, intensity, dynamic, propriety, continuity, distortion, connection, radiance, and infinity.

The sixteen imaginative senses are melody, probability, possibility, mechanics, similarity, differentiation, analogy, metaphor, sufficiency, worth, simplicity, profundity, significance, elasticity, gesture, and impression.

The fourteen ethical senses are responsibility, honor, respect, duty, loyalty, discretion, humor, commitment, discrimination, virtue, continence, decency, value, and right.

The seventeen intuitive senses are justice, truth, purpose, perfection, paradox, awareness, vitality, knowing, unity, transparency, dimension, attraction, meaning, condition, vibration, principle, consequence.

The seventeen senses of essential being are energy, being, attention, perception, attitude, emotion, thought, inevitability, infinity, universality, origin, ultimate, sacred, enigma, transcendental, relevance, and verity.

Chapter Five

The Aesthetic Self

Sensation is at the core of your experience of being alive. Due to your senses, you are able to know and direct your attention towards things happening in the external environment. You may avoid dangers as well as enjoy pleasures that come to you from outside. You can focus attention on any part of your body and become aware of that part to develop a certain consciousness of it. Without your senses, these perceptions are not possible. It is the world of the sensible which your aesthetic self is designed to apprehend. Without the senses, you would know nothing. The senses are the core of our aesthetic selves.

For most people, conventional awareness of the senses is limited to sight, smell, taste, touch, and hearing. There is nothing about these five senses that is unique to humankind. In fact, none of these senses in humans compare in acuity with that found in other species. Birds often have better sight. Elephants and dogs have better hearing and smell. Spiders have more sensitive touch. Little is known about how well other animals taste, but I suspect that here too human beings are not especially endowed. The senses in which humankind excel are mental, not physical. The problem with proving this assertion is that the inner or mental senses are far too subtle to be easily observed. The consequence is that we limit ourselves to using the five external physical senses. This simplifies matters, but I hope to show you how this simplification prevents you from being fulfilled as nature intended.

What is the point of making these distinctions? Most human problems arise out of misunderstanding, and most misunderstanding happens when we jump to conclusions about the way things are that "just ain't so." When we take the trouble to stop, look, and listen without prejudging, we can begin to really understand the world around and within us. The more we understand and pay attention, the easier it is to solve problems and deal with difficulties.

To understand ourselves, we must get used to the idea of asking questions about ourselves. We may also have to get used to the idea of receiving answers that we don't like or, worse, never receiving an answer at all. If you think this is an odd idea, think again. Scientists work by attempting to answer questions that have not been asked or answered, and they often they get answers that they don't like because it disagrees with their theories, or they get no answer at all. Unfortunately, people like clean answers to life's questions, but having a pat answer is not the point of asking questions. The real point is to understand something more today than what we understood yesterday. To do this, we need to look ever deeper to make clearer and more precise distinctions about ourselves and the world we live in.

With deeper looking and questioning, the problem of understanding ourselves becomes easier to articulate, but the solution is more elusive. Now we need a solution that treats everything we sense, feel, and experience as distinct, individual, specific, discernable, knowable, and definable. Finding such a solution should make self-knowledge and self-understanding significantly easier. Philosophers have repeatedly tried to devise solutions, with mixed results. The difficulty we have in thinking about this problem is that the solution cannot be arrived at by using what is under inspection to inspect itself, that is, the brain. This is where the concept of the aesthetic self becomes extremely useful.

My solution to the problem was to avoid using my mind while in the act of studying it; I studied my mind as though it was a laboratory animal. This is a simple thing to do, and anyone can do it. You just practice careful, close, and impartial observation of how your body and mind are responding to all manner of stimuli. By doing this for the last thirty-five years, I have evolved an understanding of how the mind functions.

So, the concept of the aesthetic self is not a product of whimsy. It is a systematically arrived at explanation for what appears to be happening within. It came about after fifteen years of studying my own senses and trying to answer the question "So What?" When I tried to answer this question, my way of looking at the world changed radically. I started getting a lot of strange new ideas that often proved to be extremely helpful to my friends. When other people found the ideas useful, it gave me reason to think that this could be a new way of looking at human beings.

IGNORANCE OF THE AESTHETIC SELF

The cause of ignorance of the aesthetic self is sin. For the last twenty-five or more centuries the senses have been viewed as a source of sin or moral corruption. Curiously, this view was adopted by philosophers as well as religious people. The senses were, and often still are, deemed to be unreliable, subjective, and morally corrupting. This might be a natural conclusion because the result of hedonistically reveling in the five external physical senses is often a deterioration of physical and emotional health. In condemning these acts of sensual indulgence, well-meaning religious people and philosophers attempted to get others to focus on things they viewed as more important—the mind and the spirit. What these well-meaning people did was to make it impossible for their followers to know reality through their senses, thus forcing them to believe in what they were told by others—others who wished to exercise power over them.

What never seems to have occurred to anyone is that they were preventing themselves from having a relationship with their Souls because the Soul is encouraged by knowing and discouraged by belief. Yet what they were aiming to do was to help people have a relationship with their Souls. Unfortunately, they succeeded in making such a relationship impossible because of the many beliefs that they were asking people to accept. This business has been going on for the last 2,500 years, except for a few bright lights who tried to change this behavior without much success.

The senses are not unreliable or subjective, nor are they morally corrupting. I repeat, the senses are not unreliable or subjective, nor are they morally corrupting. How is an organ like the eye or the liver said to be unreliable if the organ is healthy and functioning properly? The eye is there to sense reflected light. If the eye turns blind, then it becomes unreliable. Otherwise, a healthy eye is completely reliable. And how is the eye subjective? The eye is there to behold waves and particles of light, nothing more. In fact, the eye is totally objective because it sees everything as it is and interprets nothing. The truth is that what is unreliable, subjective, and morally corrupting is the mind of the one using the eye. Blaming the eye for the incompetence and stupidity of the mind is like blaming a household pet for every mistake we make. What does that pet have to do with our incompetence?

The senses are objective. They have no opinions of their own, and they don't force beliefs on anyone's mind. It is the mind and its owner that is at fault when it errs in its interpretation of the senses. So, when learning to use your aesthetic self, remember that you are the one who uses your mind, your senses, and your body. Don't blame those parts of you for your lack of rigor in paying attention, and don't blame the senses if you can't let go of your preconceptions long enough to take in reality as it is.

The function of the aesthetic self and all its senses is to provide a highly dimensional reading of reality so that you can learn to assess the reality around you with greater accuracy and acuity. It is a way of giving form to the multiplicity of sense impressions you experience every day. It is a way of thoughtfully directing your attention to the senses. It is a way of avoiding being overwhelmed by the complexities of what you experience. It is a way of developing powers of discrimination and discernment regarding your outer and inner worlds. It is a way of mindfully organizing your relationship with the world. And, it is a way of expanding awareness and consciousness without the help of dangerous drugs.

Like most things, the concept of the aesthetic self also has its challenges. Having this concept puts you squarely in charge of developing your awareness. When you are in charge of your development, you can't blame others for your lack of progress. Once you are in charge, you are responsible. If you shirk that responsibility, you have yourself to blame for the consequences.

MISUSING THE WORD *SENSE*

There are many expressions in language that use the word *sense* wrongly. When this is done, the meaning most often intended is *feeling*. Here are a few of the seemingly endless examples of improper use of the word *sense*: sense of certainty, sense of hope, sense of despair, sense of community, sense of drama, sense of well-being, sense of momentum, sense of powerlessness, and so on. Clearly, the intended meanings are a *feeling* of certainty, a *feeling* of hope, a *feeling* of community, etc. You feel or have emotions; you don't sense them unless you are focusing specifically on that particular sense. The fact that humans frequently make this error doesn't justify continuing to be imprecise about what we experience and mean. Feelings are unreliable, subjective, and susceptible to deceit because they typically refer to the reaction you have to sensing—your interpretation or misreading of what is real. Feelings arise from interpretations produced by the mind, and so they are subject to the whims of the mind. To read reality accurately is not an interpretation, it's a perception.

If our current language is incompetent to express thoughts on any matter, then it is right to invent new words to cover newly discerned meanings. This is how language grows and develops. Using pre-existing words, like sense, to cover a lot of intellectual territory makes thinking less expressive, less precise, and altogether less meaningful. Indeed, because all language was invented by thousands of Souls over tens of thousands of years, it is important to realize that the result can only be junk thought or blatant misinterpretations when we use language sloppily. It is unfortunate when this happens because the correction is relatively easy to effect.

Many of the senses I have listed under those different houses have historically been lumped together and classified as common sense, mind, conscience, super-ego, extrasensory perception, the sixth sense, consciousness, and even emotions. These senses were lumped together because, for most of us, sensation is extremely hard to talk about, and we usually avoid doing what is hard. Also, by purposely keeping any discussion of the senses vague, those with taste, judgment, strong minds, or those who were self-righteous could easily intimidate and gain power over others who didn't have those qualities, and power over others is an opiate for the ego that needs constant reinforcing against fear. Another explanation might be that discussions of the senses were avoided out of sheer laziness or empty-headedness. The state of being human is so complex that even the best thinkers have been at a loss for giving a clear explanation of it.

AWARENESS OF SENSES

You will likely ignore the senses that you can't easily notice. The intellectual senses are much less noticeable than the internal physical senses. The ethical senses are more obvious than the intuitive senses and less obvious than the imaginative senses. Failure to develop an awareness of these subtle senses stunts your spiritual and intellectual growth and inhibits your success and happiness. Success in developing an awareness of all your senses allows you to realize your full potential, and reaching your full potential is, I think, what you are alive for.

Because the aesthetic self is relatively weak in its ability to command attention, especially compared to the emotions, you need to proactively cultivate an awareness of it. No two persons will have the same starting point or upbringing, so each person has a different place to start and a different rate of cultivation. How do you go about cultivating this awareness? It is not difficult, but it does take time and a great deal of attention. Fortunately, each of us has time that we can fill as we choose and an attention which we can direct as we see fit.

MIND-WATCHING

The technique for becoming acquainted with the senses is as simple as mind-watching, which I mentioned earlier in the book. Others might call it meditation, and they would be right. It is a form of extremely focused meditation. Mind-watching is a process of observing the products or output of one's brain. Since the output of the brain comes in the form of thoughts, images (both pictorial and experiential), feelings, sensational memories, emotional memories, experiential memories, and so on, mind-watching means paying attention to all these for the sole purpose of noting what is happening. If you try to mind-watch and you start thinking about something, you are not mind-watching, you are thinking. Mind-watching is simply watching, listening, or observing without making any judgments about what is happening. It is registering thoughts as they flow across the forefront of your mind, like watching flames of a campfire.

The temptation to criticize thoughts as they flow past is enormous. Resist that urge. Concentrate on watching. It should begin to feel like watching fish in an aquarium. Cultivating this state is most easily accomplished by asking, "what exactly is happening?" and then waiting and being alert to what flows across the mind. If you are not accustomed to watching your thoughts, your body and mind will resist. When that happens, it is probably because something inside you other than you is accustomed to making your decisions. As soon as you begin to feel this resistance, you can overcome it by riveting your attention on the thoughts you are having.

What I have noticed is that feelings and thoughts of resistance don't like being watched, in the same way that little children who are acting up to seek attention become self-conscious and eventually wander elsewhere when one observes them. This is true for any kind of emotional feelings or thoughts. When you take charge of being observant of your thoughts and feelings you send a message to your brain that its owner is now running things personally. When this message is sent often enough, it eventually gets through, and you can watch your thoughts easily and with greater clarity.

Like all of us, the brain takes seriously only what it is forced to take seriously. If you are not in the habit of meaning business about life, the chances are that your brain has acquired that habit as well, so making changes will happen with great difficulty. Making changes effectively means being patient with your brain until it has made the required neuronal reorganizations. Holding in your imagination the change you wish to make and building an increasingly detailed concept of what it will look like is the fastest method for realizing change in a permanent way. Assuming and reinforcing an attitude of meaning business about everything you do and think makes these changes occur more rapidly.

THE ADVANTAGES OF UNDERSTANDING THOUGHT

Learning to distinguish the differences between *thought* and *thinking* will help you appreciate how the mental and higher senses work. It will also help you quickly discern the different kinds of thought and their possible source. Most importantly, it helps you understand the relationship between thought and the Soul and between language and the Soul. The easiest way to understand the nature of thought is to discuss the various aspects of it from the outside in. What those on the receiving end get are the products of our thoughts, and the products of thought are actions for which thoughts are the cause.

OF ACTIONS AND QUESTIONS

Whether we know or not, every action is a direct response to a question having been asked. Most times, we are insufficiently aware of our internal processes to be able to articulate exactly what the question was which our actions or thoughts answered, but it is possible to logically deduce the questions we are answering from the actions themselves. To discover the questions that your actions or thoughts are attempting to answer, ask yourself what kind of question you would have to ask for your action or thought to manifest exactly as it did. Your actions need not be physical, external, intentional, or unintentional for them to answer a question. Most of these questions are covert in that they are subconsciously posed or unconsciously expressed.

It is important to remember that from this point of view, thought is also an action. Every thought results from a question having been asked. It is crucial to understand this reality because it enables each of us to ferret out the questions that our actions have been busy answering. By doing this, we gain a level of management of and over our minds never experienced before. Further, by questioning our questions, we can avoid the pitfalls of running on automatic pilot, which is an effect similar to complete mindlessness. Clarity of thought and purpose should be the ultimate outcome of questioning. This includes clarity of action and clarity of intention.

In this way, our lives are the products of the questions we ask, and it is the quality of our questions that determine, to a large extent, the quality of our lives. Taken from this point of view, the most important questions we can ask ourselves are those designed specifically to produce the kind and quality of answers we want to have. Questions invariably generate the answer they were designed to evoke. If you need a specific answer, you need to ask a specific question. General answers require general questions. Likewise, spiritual questions will produce answers from the Soul, while intellectual questions are best answered by the mind. Questions about beliefs usually involve the emotional self because feelings are almost always connected to what you believe, not what you know.

Failure to think about and manage your questions will inevitably result in you going in circles as your past repeats itself endlessly—you keep repeating the same "answers" that never work. To avoid going in circles you need only stop long enough to notice the repeated patterns and strategies that create this circularity and change the questions that are producing that effect. Since it is fear that creates circular patterns and life strategies, asking questions that seek out the origin of that fear can end the circularity of failure. By asking "Why?" of every answer, especially where it relates to the reasonableness of your fears, you can most quickly get at the root cause of any stasis in life. Removing unreasonable fears from your decision-making allows you to gradually acquire greater clarity of thought, which results in non-circularity of action and intention because clarity is the agent of direction.

OF WORDS AND HOW THEY INFLUENCE OUR THOUGHTS

I can remember the day it dawned on me that every word in every language had to be invented. To me, this meant that language is an invention of the Soul. It also meant that for every word or utterance in each language there is one true meaning. Over eons, probably because we are a lazy species, we developed the habit of adapting existent words and forcing them to multi-task (a word the Soul has invented recently) by serving more than one meaning.

Language is, at best, a feeble means of true communication because of this multi-tasking behavior. The more often we abuse language by forcing words to serve for two, three, or more different meanings (like the word *run* in English) the more difficult it is for the Soul to express itself using that language. There are two reasons for this: (1) The Soul most easily expresses itself when it uses words that it invented to cover specific meanings. (2) Words that have more than one meaning need interpretation by the mind, which is a skill the mind uses to rationalize fears and beliefs. Interpretation is at the core of why language is problematic, and differences of interpretation are at the core of most misunderstandings between people. How is anyone to know what others mean by a word unless it is agreed upon in the beginning? This is why legal documents often begin with a set of definitions for what certain words will mean for a particular document.

If you examine your thinking to uncover the questions that your thinking is attempting to answer, you can experience feelings of trepidation about stepping into unknown territory or feelings of reluctance about answers that damage your feelings of security or self-esteem. These feelings show, like a barometer, how close you are getting to your ego, to the truth, to clarity, or to your Soul. To have your Soul involved in this discovery process, you need to grasp the distinctions between the types and sources of these experiences, have the words to express what they mean in reality, and be able to recognize the Soul's language and thoughts. What the Soul will not do is come down to your level. If it is obliged to do that, it tends to command in the simplest language possible, but that sounds so much like the ego communicating that the Soul will only do that as a last resort.

So, to make the business of thinking as efficient as possible and the detection of thoughts more facile, you need to get at the true meanings of the words used by the Soul. Remember that every word used in language probably originated in the Soul of someone needing a particular sound to fit the truth or meaning relating to an experience they had. In other words, every new aspect of truth provides a new meaning that needs a sound. Once the sound for that meaning is invented, the sound signifies the meaning. Using words that have not been invented by the Soul or using them in a way not meant by the Soul sets up a barrier to understanding the Soul because it only uses words it has invented in another time or another place. When the Soul impresses language on your mind, it does so using its "invented" language. Recognizing that language renders you so much more astute in judging what thoughts emanate from your mind due to thinking and what thoughts arise from your Soul or intuition.

THE SOUL'S PERPLEXING LANGUAGE

Some people, who are close to their Souls, might strike you as being enigmatic or cryptic when you hear them speak. When what they are saying is comprehensible, but you don't understand what they mean, you may be recognizing the Soul's presence in their conversation. That is because the Soul's language is often enigmatic or cryptic when what is said is so far out of your experience that you can't immediately or easily comprehend it. However, be aware that some people love to communicate using indirection, obfuscation, and equivocation. They probably do this to appear impressive because it makes them seem smarter than they actually are. But, on the whole, when you hear communications that you sense as being enigmatic or puzzling, it may be the case you are hearing the language of the speaker's Soul.

THE METAPHOR OF REBIRTH

Various religious or so-called spiritual traditions have a myth of rebirth. Jesus mentioned this process using the phrase "born again." The concept of reincarnation is another hint at this process. The Buddhist Noble Eight-Fold Path leading to enlightenment is another phrase used to refer to this process of rebirth. To have a close connection with our Souls, undergoing this process is imperative because without it we are prevented from knowing the Soul intimately and are forced to deal with all the problems of interpretation. Frankly, no one is astute enough to know what their Soul means if they haven't learned its language using through the process of "rebirth." Here, I in no way mean the common notion of "finding God" that is typical in religions—that phenomenon is more akin to swallowing a pill that magically saves you from your sins.

In my experience, rebirth is the work of ferreting out useless meanings from every word to get down to the real meaning intended by the Souls that originally invented each word. That is hard work, but everyone can do it if they put their will to the task and insist that it happen. Those who set out to do this work but who fail to insist that they follow through to the end will fall by the wayside and bear a serious likelihood of becoming notional or deluded. You must insist that you come to the end. Like a woman in childbirth, the baby needs to be born because there is no other option. I call this attitude a *zero options attitude*. People who start things and fail to follow through on them have assumed all along that not following through is one of the available options. Therefore, you cannot allow yourself the luxury of other options; otherwise, it is not rebirth.

When you question the origins of every word in your vocabulary and determine how you acquired the use of that word, you are performing the act of self-conception. By requiring yourself to articulate what you mean when you use a particular word, you are able to slowly and systematically rediscover the language that the Soul recognizes and insists on using. But to rediscover this language you do have to seek it out—it doesn't happen by magic. For me, it took the better part of two years paying attention to each word I uttered or thought. Doing this resulted in a much higher level of clarity and surefootedness in my thinking.

BARRIERS TO THE SUCCESS OF THIS PROCESS

Much of what we think usually happens in *short-think* or *short-speak*, which are forms of schematic thought and speech. A schema is a replacement for a complex concept or object by a fast, easy, simple notion, much like how a stick figure of a man or woman represents the restroom. An example of short-speak is the word *apps*, that recently coined term for computer applications. Text messaging has radically increased the tendency for young people to use short-speak...LOL...if u gt my mening. Although these are relatively benign forms of schemas, short-think can be more dangerous and insidious.

Bigotry and prejudice are based on short-think. For instance, hatred of people based on their heritage or skin color has created pain and suffering for millions of people over the last five hundred years. Hating someone because they may be Jewish or have black skin is the fastest, easiest, and stupidest excuse for thinking there is. It is as stupid as hating everyone who is left handed or hating all people who have black hair for no other reason than the color of their hair. For those who espouse such prejudices, anything that sounds like a reason is used to justify their hatred and support an already schematically arrived at notion. The truth has nothing to do with how a bigot thinks. The one important consideration to such a person is how they feel. Even now, hatred of people based on their religion is again showing its ugly head as conflicts between Muslims and Christians escalate. Every form and variety of short-think is based on fear. Fear, in the end, is the great deceiver. Love is the great revealer.

Both short-think and short-speak are connected to the primitive brain, which means that people who habitually use these forms of thinking and communication will not likely have a close connection to their Souls. Short-think curtails depth and dimensionality of thought, just as short-speak truncates words and phrases and requires the receiver to interpret the code to make any sense of it.

The way to rid yourself of these shortcut processes is to treat every word as a possible source of repression of the Soul. Think of words as being gateways to the Soul. Words used to mean something other than what the Soul would have it mean need to be filtered out of your thinking. By slowly and carefully rebirthing your use of language, you can eventually engage in direct conversation with the Soul. Fortunately, the Soul is extremely helpful to those who choose to undertake this task. Does this mean that you can't use words in the same manner as most people? I should think not. You can't control how others choose to speak and communicate, so you may be required to use the language they use. However, you will know the difference between how they choose to communicate and how the Soul communicates because of the rebirthing work you have gone through.

While it is possible to recraft how you use words over a year or two, this process never stops because you will learn new words and utter words that you haven't uttered for years. Each time you do that, it is advisable to make a mental note of the words and think about what they actually mean from your Soul's point of view.

THE PROBLEM OF CONFUSION

Confusion is to the Soul as doubt is to the Soul—it is squelching. For this reason, it is necessary to relieve yourself of confusion. Confusion arises when there exists a conflict between information and attitude. This conflict can be understood as existing between the mind and the Soul. As long as these two aspects of yourself are in conflict, communication with your Soul is unlikely to occur.

Since you either have right information or wrong information and right attitudes or wrong attitudes, this conflict is resolved when you have both right information and right attitudes or when you have wrong information and wrong attitudes. Out of these two options, communication with the Soul can only happen when you have both right information and right attitudes. On the other hand, while the conflict between information and attitude may be resolved, a relationship with your Soul is impossible when you have both wrong information and wrong attitudes.

Interestingly, people who have wrong information and wrong attitudes never seem to be confused, no matter how wrong they are. Examples of this, like the Nazis or the Roman Catholic Inquisition, are replete throughout history. They declare, "those who aren't with us are against us" to make clear to all their lack of confusion.

Every puritanical movement in human history occurred because of puritans having both wrong information and wrong attitudes. Puritanism is a product of the primitive brain attempting to become spiritual, like Satan wanting to be God. Puritans believe that removing all temptation from their environment will make them purer. They start by sterilizing other people's behavior and environment of everything they deem to be tempting, and they usually end by killing other people and destroying the environment to subdue everything to their will and avoid temptation. Of course, they didn't first sterilize their minds, imaginations, and thoughts from every tempting visage or evil notion. Little do puritans realize that sterilizing oneself of all temptation is a lifetime occupation that is highly labor intensive. So the only recourse for the lazy puritan is to focus on what they think others are doing that goes against their beliefs. The result is a world left miserable.

When religions dictate that the source of right information is sacred scriptures, they endow believers with both wrong attitudes and wrong information. When science deems that the source of right attitudes is a belief in the infallibility of science, it endows those believers with both wrong information and wrong attitudes. Sacred scriptures are intended to be a backdrop for acquiring right attitudes (though few religious believers apply them), and they have no business in the realm of known information about how the world and the universe works. While science does have business with information about how the world works, scientists are often arrogantly wrong where this is concerned. Yet this is how religious fanatics and scientists can appear resoundingly unconfused, but don't be fooled; there is no relationship with the Soul in that mentality. When scientists believe in the superiority of the scientific method and use it to argue against the Soul's existence, it only means that their thinking is attitudinally castrated by the need to keep things simple enough to be studied and measured.

The Soul is the ultimate source of all right attitudes and reality is the ultimate source of all right information. It is the Soul, in the end, that makes it possible to comprehend the full scope of the nature of reality. Bearing this in mind makes it possible to work and feel comfortable in the realm of the unknown because you will always be moving towards revelation of what is real using the Soul as a direction finder.

There can be no doubt as to the efficacy of having a good education. In general, the function of getting an education is to acquire skills and information about reality to be relevant to the culture in which one is born and raised. The ideal education is one that passes on technical and spiritual (not religious) information and skills in the form of right information and right attitudes so that all students are empowered to access their Souls, should that be desired.

THE LOCATION OF THOUGHT

It is hard to say for sure where thoughts arise within each individual due to factors such as our various dominances, genetic differences, and experiences. I can only speak for myself, but I am sure that for each type of thought there is a specific location in the brain from where it arises. Determining the source location of thought is a way of identifying the type of thought that is occurring. For example, in most people who are right handed, intellectual thinking can be sensed on the left side of the head, although there are exceptions to this because of the way nature creates organisms according to the principle of individuation.

Thoughts that emanate from the Soul are usually experienced as silent non-conscious hints or statements. They are located, according to my observation, behind and above the head and are phantomlike in the way they happen. You must be listening for these thoughts or your chances of noticing them are remote. Because they are so fleeting and quiet, perhaps the easiest method for recognizing these emanations is to notice where in the head they come from.

OF MECHANISMS IN THE BRAIN AND THEIR TRIGGERS

Thoughts are different than thinking. Thinking is active, while thoughts are more passive. Thinking is intentional, while thoughts are unintentional. Thinking is work, but having thoughts is effortless. Thinking is overtly purposeful, but thoughts are random, scattered, and often without purpose. Thinking is something we do when we feel the need to do it, but thoughts occur whether we need them or not.

It is in the nature of thinking that the process be conscious. Thoughts can be either conscious or non-conscious. Thoughts result from the automatic workings of various mechanisms in the brain. Some of these mechanisms result in inventions and ideas, while others guarantee survival. Some mechanisms increase the ability to learn, and others are for problem-solving. By carefully cultivating your thinking processes, you can optimize these various mechanisms and employ the mechanisms that the Soul itself uses. Most of the time, these mechanisms are triggered by an attitude.

So, thinking is *generated*, but thoughts *arise* from mechanisms in the brain's structure. The senses provide the basis upon which these mechanisms operate. They are like the silly mechanisms depicted years ago by Rube Goldberg in which one action moves an object, which pushes something else, which forces another thing to roll down an inclined surface to fall on a device that breaks an egg for its contents to fall into a hot frying pan below. The spiritual mechanisms to which I refer are how a string of attitudes cause one action to occur that triggers another attitude needed to make some other part function properly; which in turn produces a result the quality of which can vary depending on the attitude.

To be specific, take making a cake, for example. You begin by looking up a recipe because you know you don't know enough about how cakes are made. The attitude here is that anyone can make a cake if you find a recipe and follow it. Next, you open up the pantry and pull all the dry ingredients off the shelf and then open the refrigerator to take out the wet ingredients. The attitude used here is that what you have on hand is adequate for the job. You then take out your measuring cups, spoons, bowls, and mixer and begin measuring out all the ingredients into your mixing bowl. The attitude applied at this point is the assumption that there is no real method or order to how things go together when making a cake. Finally, you thoroughly mix the ingredients, pour the batter into a cake pan, and turn on the oven to bake the cake. At this point, you go and watch television whereupon you become so involved in the show that you lose track of time and the cake almost burns.

Any good cook would have thrown in the towel long before this because the principles of good cooking had been violated. The attitude you used in this hypothetical situation is that cakes make themselves as long as you follow the recipe accurately. But what if the flour was two years old, the butter was rancid, the eggs were four weeks in the fridge, and the milk was sour? In that case, you would have violated the first principle of good cooking: *Use the freshest possible, best quality ingredients.* The attitude that would have allowed you to do everything as described in this scenario would have been that the point of the exercise is to make a cake and how it turns out is not relevant. Believe it or not, this is how many people in the arts, trades, professions, and vocations function. They do what they do as an exercise, and that is all that is required because most people don't seem to notice.

I had the experience of visiting another instrument maker's shop, and in the course of our conversation he told me, "My job is to make as exact a copy of the original instrument as possible, and if it doesn't turn out sounding good, it's not my concern because I will have done everything required of me." I was speechless. If this were an isolated incident his attitude might not have left an impression on me, but I ran into this attitude repeatedly, even in the most esteemed instrument makers on the planet.

Your attitudes determine, in large measure, the exact quality of your work. Just as you have language to communicate, your Soul communicates using attitudes. If you take your spiritual life seriously, then it is your attitudes that form the color of your character. If you don't take your spiritual life seriously, then your maladapted, delusional ego becomes your character. Your work reflects the nature of your character; hence, the nature of your Soul is defined by what we do. If you cultivate positive attitudes, your work will reflect this reality. If you cultivate negative or delusory attitudes, your work will reflect that too. In the case of cooking or making a musical instrument, the quality of work can be painfully or wonderfully truthful.

Just as there are mechanisms that produce ideas, there are mechanisms that result in no ideas, few inventions, extinction, incompetence in problem solving, and the incapacitation of learning. The triggers for these mechanisms are specific attitudes. For example, inattentiveness to the senses, denial of the validity of sensory experiences, unwillingness to make and stick by commitments, unwillingness to assume personal responsibility for oneself and one's decisions, and a highly cultivated indulgence of the ego are the trigger mechanisms or attitudes of people who typically blame others for their problems. By forbidding from yourself the triggers that set off these dead-end mechanisms, it is possible to guide yourself away from those self-destructive habits and move towards to ever-increasing competence.

But there's a catch. To understand how the winning mechanisms work, you need to understand how the brain effects its results. The problem is that no amount of thinking or knowledge of the brain's physical makeup can lead to this understanding because the way the brain effects its results is an aesthetic function (like the proverbial light bulb going on in the head, as seen in comics). I use the word *aesthetic* carefully because the only thing that transcends thought is sensation. What this means is that it is easier for you to be aware of the sensation of a thought happening than for you to describe what is happening in the words used to think about it. The best that thinking about it can muster is to make vague references and circumlocutions about the effect.

For example, imagine a great fountain. Now imagine what it is like to imagine a fountain without ever having seen one. Next, try imagining a fountain on the basis of a verbal description of one, assuming that you have never seen one before. This is where the Chinese proverb, "a picture is worth a thousand words," comes in handy. If you have never seen a fountain, imagining one from someone else's description is hardly possible unless the description includes familiar metaphors. Make a drawing of a fountain, and the idea of a fountain becomes clearer. See a fountain, and you know at once what one looks like and can call up the memory of that experience at will. The imagination is triggered more by a visual image (an aesthetic function) than by a description (a verbal function). If a description is precise and thorough enough, someone who is accustomed to processing verbal descriptions into images might make something of it. Unfortunately, in this book format, we don't have much choice, so I hope you will bear with me and my descriptions.

In the next chapters, when I describe the senses that make up the aesthetic self, I am jostling your memory of experiences that you may have already had. If you draw a blank with any of the senses I describe, you may not have had an experience of that specific sense, or it is possible that you may be experiencing a sensory hole within yourself. (A sensory hole is when a sense doesn't work correctly or at all, like with blindness or deafness.) It is also possible that you may be learning of a sensation that your life experiences have not yet called into action, or it is possible that my description is incompetent.

Each sense can contribute to the generation of thought. Each sense can bring to your awareness the potential for understanding something new about reality. When your thoughts are intimately connected to reality, you have the possibility of experiencing visions of what you would like reality to be. If your thoughts are not connected to reality, those imaginings are likely to be mere fantasies—wishes motivated by hope with little chance of influencing reality.

Don't make the mistake of judging too severely your experiences with reality. You may discover that many of your best intentions have failed or will fail because the act of prejudging things causes the potential for change to be curtailed. The purpose of thinking is to remove barriers that inhibit progress and development, not squelch that progress and development. The role of thought is to bring clarity to your understanding of reality. The ultimate aim of thinking is to give voice to an ever-increasing and urgent command from reality that an understanding of it should be articulated. When you use thinking for less valuable ends, it will become your undoing because wasted or junk thought creates false leads, and false leads take you down paths that go nowhere or that distract you long enough so that you are unsuccessful. These wouldn't cause problems were your time alive to be unlimited, but life is too short to be wasted chasing false leads.

TURNING ATTENTION TO YOUR SENSES

Assuming you continue to develop your awareness of your senses, you will notice how you mature as a human being as more of the 133 senses become real to you in the way you are able to use them purposefully and intelligently. If you come to fully appreciate all the mental senses, you will begin to develop in the realm of ideas and concepts. The realm of ideas and concepts activate more of the imaginative senses, which causes development in the ethical senses. As each sense becomes real to you, you can expand further up the scale of the senses, from the crudest to the most refined (from the physical senses to the senses of being).

For whatever reason, some people will never arrive at a full experience of all their senses. Likewise, some people will fulfill their purpose for being alive by gaining a full and complete awareness of their senses. In the end, the quality of your life is not determined by how many senses you are aware of; it is determined by what you do with your senses to enhance other people's lives. Enhancing the lives of others is not an altruistic act; it is a self-centered act because you must be centered from within to truly enhance other people's lives. In the same way, forgiveness is a wholly self-centered act because it is the act of dis-enslaving your mind from the bondage caused by unresolved violations and injuries. These aims are the natural outgrowth of a loving character. Making the lives of others and your own life miserable because of the inability to forgive is the natural outgrowth of a fearful and selfish character. Living such a life is a waste. In short, it's not how much you have that counts; it's what you do with what you have. Those who do much with the least are better off than those who do little with the most.

Chapter Six

The External Physical Senses

The physical senses have the ability to overwhelm the attention by sheer intensity. They also make it easy for the mind to lay us open to deception because it cannot easily distinguish between illusion and reality. The five external physical senses make it easy for the mind to seduce the attention through the lure of imagined pleasure. They can appear to distract the mind and the spirit equally. They make it easy to be deluded with fake self-evidence, and they do nothing to prevent us from becoming prejudiced because they often appear to support our bigotries. It seems that these senses trap us with their demands for stimulation and comfort. Indeed, they do all this, but none of us would willingly do away with one of them. This is not because we enjoy being trapped, lured, prejudiced, deluded, or overwhelmed; it is because each of us can somehow learn to manage ourselves in the face of and in spite of these forces. It is this idea of self-control or self-management that allows us to fend off the barrage of sensory stimulation that could easily be our undoing.

The traps that the physical senses set out for the mind are only traps to those who resist seeing them as such. This resistance probably arises from an upbringing devoid of an interest in the truth. However, everyone is capable of looking for the traps and looking for the truth. It is up to each of us to decide for ourselves what we will do.

THE SENSE OF SIGHT

Sight is the registration in the brain of the impressions of visible light waves received directly and indirectly (as reflected light) through the eyes. Sight allows us to fathom the visible world in all its diverse dimensions. Some of these dimensions are size, degree of difference, texture, quality, effect, illusion, gradation, depth, motion, color (of different intensities, hues, and shades), and so on. Using the faculty of sight, the mind can perceive these dimensions because of the relative presence and absence of light waves and particles. This process allows us to discern and distinguish forms (i.e., the shapes of things). It also allows us to identify the uniqueness of similar things.

Sight is probably the most important sense to us. Of all the senses, it is the one you would probably be most upset about losing. At the same time, it stands above all the other senses in its ability to lure us humans into mindlessness. This is because we are most inclined to believe what we see. This inclination causes us to short circuit our other senses and what they are telling us. Sight lures us into assuming that what we are seeing is true without question. It requires an act of resistance to avoid falling into this kind of trap because we tend to believe what we read, mindlessly accept the images of television and the movies as real, and measure everything with tools that can be visually read. Yet no competent person allows themself the indulgence of accepting anything seen at surface value, and no person can become competent without becoming suspicious of how the mind interprets what the eyes see.

The most efficient way to train your sense of sight is to learn to realistically paint or draw. To do this, you have to notice things as they are without making any assumptions about them. This involves seeing more than sight. The distinction to be made here is that your eyes take in all light rays indiscriminately and what you see is that to which you are paying attention. In other words, seeing is done in the mind. Seeing involves a great deal of noticing, and training your mind to notice visible things makes it much easier to notice less obvious things. Drawing is something that anyone who is sighted and puts their mind to can do well. This is because everyone who is sighted is capable of using their mind to see the visible world clearly and precisely. Lack of interest and willingness to learn are the major obstacles to developing this way of using the mind. Betty Edwards wrote a book called *Drawing on the Right Side of the Brain.*[16] Avail yourself of this book if you wish to improve your ability to see clearly.

To properly train the sense of sight, you need to use your mind to discern and discriminate the subtleties of color and shade, form and shape, edge and outline, effect and reality, light and dark, and so on, down to the minutest visible detail. You need to recognize the mind's self-serving tendency to accept its own illusions, manipulations, and deceptions as easy substitutes for how it relates to visible things. You need to be suspicious of what you are seeing but stay open to all possible explanations for what you see. You need to be guarded about the ease with which others might emotionally manipulate you with what you look at. You need to dwell on what can't be seen more than what can be. You need to habituate yourself to asking questions of what you see, questions that force the evidence of your eyes to accord with your other senses. Anyone who has a properly trained sense of sight, though they are blind in both eyes, sees more clearly than those who are sighted and ill trained. Examples of blind individuals who see clearly would be Helen Keller, John Milton, and Homer.

An important aspect of sight is binocular vision. Seeing with two eyes gives a wholly different perspective on the world than seeing with one eye. By having two overlapping images to deal with, the brain is capable of grasping a much more dimensional sense of reality. With binocular vision, humans are able to appreciate multiple points of view and access parts of their brains that process three-dimensional form.

The brain works to detect the maximum amount of dimensionality available for noticing. Hence, the more dimensional a thing appears to us, the greater our feelings of appreciation for it. Conversely, the less dimensional a thing is, the faster we are bored by it. Whoever notices more will undoubtedly use more of their brains. The nature of the greatest art is that it causes us to use more of our brains than we are normally accustomed to using. Naturally, if this is true, then

---

[16] Betty Edwards, *Drawing on the Right Side of the Brain* (London: Souvenir Press Ltd., 2013).

painting, music, and all other forms of art have a far more elevated purpose than mere entertainment. The more of our brains we use effectively, the smarter we become.

THE SENSE OF HEARING

Hearing is the registration in the brain of the impressions of audible sound waves received directly through the ears and indirectly through bones in the head. The ears can detect a finite number of different speeds of sound waves (pitch or frequency), and they can detect an infinite number of subtle differences in overtone arrangements (timbre or tone color) of sound. Some people are born able to hear a narrow band of frequencies, while others are born with the ability to hear a wide band and can hear far below and above what others can hear. However, the actual band limits are not as important as the way in which the sense of hearing is used.

Using the sense of hearing, the mind can perceive infinite levels of sound wave amplitude (loud and soft) within the range of hearing and qualify sound according to intensity (the ability of the sound to affect the sensing mechanism), resonant proportion (the relation of overtones to the fundamental frequency), and the nature of sound in time (its decay behavior and rate). The ear, like the eye, can accept a large number of wave speeds at once, while the mind is capable of isolating and focusing on one or more out of many wave speeds at a time, should it be used to do so.

Of all the senses, hearing is the most objective. This is because it is the one sense that is capable of precise mathematical measurement. The ear accomplishes this feat when one tunes a musical sound. Since musical sounds are defined by their regularity of wave frequency, and musical pitches are determined by speed of frequency, when one tunes two pitches those notes are set into a mathematical relationship that can be precisely described using numbers. A unison is a 1:1 ratio. An octave is a 2:1 ratio. A pure major third is a 4:5 ratio, and so on. This precise objectivity is a blessing when it is used for making music purely, and it is a curse when the ears are subjected to sound that is out of tune.

Along with objectivity, there is an aspect of subjectivity. Although the ears are objective, people tend not to be. This aspect of subjectivity manifests by someone "tuning in" or "tuning out," depending on how they feel emotionally about what they are hearing. Good listeners are able to concentrate their attention on exactly what they are hearing at the same time as tuning out their feelings on what they are hearing. Bad listeners do the opposite—they dwell exclusively on what they are feeling and mostly ignore what they are hearing. Most of the interpersonal problems that people encounter in life are the result of bad listening habits.

Because of our ability to listen or not listen, I say that the ears are the doorway to the Soul. Listening is a product of the essence of our being and, as such, it has nothing to do with our ears. We can listen to any of our senses if we want to. No fulfillment, no development, no real achievement, no progress, no great endeavor can ever be perfected without an intense level of listening. How we listen, what we listen to, and who we listen to in large measure determine where we go and how fast we get there. There are no short cuts. What this means is that no other human activity should come before learning how to listen well. Unfortunately, we usually learn to listen only when we are forced to do so. Such pigheadedness is all part of the subjective nature of hearing. It should be clear that being smart (i.e., listening) is an advantage available to anyone. Problems occur when those who are not listening can't hear this advice.

The inability to listen is the cause of most human failures. No matter how technically accomplished, if one is unable to listen well, one will never achieve greatness. Great marriages, for example, are not made in heaven, they are the product of two people listening to each other. Great businesses are not those that necessarily make the most money, they are the ones that put careful listening to their customers as first priority and listening to their employees as second. Great artists are not the product of overwhelmingly supreme talent, they are the product of extremely careful listening to what is happening inwardly. Great teachers are not born, they are the ones who take the trouble to listen to what their students are doing, thinking, saying, feeling, and sensing and then respond to the specific needs of each student at that moment. Great parents are those who listen to their children and give them only what they really need. As beneficial as listening is, it is sad that it is taught almost nowhere.

The best way to cultivate the skill of listening is to learn to listen to music. This is because music is an unthreatening and objective source for focusing your attention on the sense of hearing. Often the mistake made by music teachers is that they think they are supposed to be teaching music theory, music history, instrumental technique, or, worse, music as entertainment. When they discover that their students have no affinity for learning any of this, they conclude that their student has no talent for music. That is the same, in my mind, as saying that a newborn has no talent for language because it has little affinity for speaking in complete sentences. By learning to listen first, anyone can eventually understand music theory and learn to read and play music on an instrument. Learning to deal with music prepares the mind to think clearly, prepares the imagination to project accurately, trains the senses to gauge correctly, cultivates underused parts of the memory, and offers the Soul a vehicle for expressing itself. All this is over and beyond the business of learning to listen.

THE SENSE OF TASTE

Taste is the registration in the brain of impressions made by the reception of "frequency bands" of molecules on the tongue. Matter organizes itself in five (some would say six) flavors or frequency bands: salt, sour, sweet, bitter, and savory (the sixth would be neutral). For every class of molecule, the neutral band possesses a different flavor. For instance, the neutral band for a liquid would be water. The neutral band for carbohydrates would be something like bland, overcooked noodles.

The presence of minerals, acids, bases, etc., in varying degrees, give each form of matter a particular flavor. The mind can be used to distinguish an infinite variety of flavors as well as qualify them according to intensity and degree of purity.

Obviously, eating well-prepared food is a way to develop this particular sense, and learning to do gourmet cooking is an even better way. On a small budget, you can train your awareness of this sense by growing or raising your own foods or by inspecting the produce you buy and consistently selecting the highest quality materials for consumption. I am sure that a gourmet chef would have more to suggest on training this sense than I would, yet you can be assured that paying close and careful attention is at the core of training any of the senses.

THE SENSE OF TOUCH

Touch is the registration in the brain of impressions taken through the skin from tactile structures and their temperatures. The forms of matter determine the variety of tactile structures available. The inherent frictional resistance and subsurface structural properties of matter allow us to class them into the following groups: hard, firm, gaseous, spongy, soft, viscous, grainy, rough, sharp, blunt, smooth, etc. Most forms of matter fall into one or more of these classes. The mind can be used to distinguish the class of a tactile structure and to evaluate the relative temperature of the surface or the material.

We use the sense of touch to coordinate the world we see and hear with our bodies. For instance, you may see and hear a cat, but your picture of it is no more real than if you saw and heard a moving hologram of it. However, the moment you touch the cat you feel assured that what you see and hear is indeed a cat.

Without the possibility of touch or smell, most of us function by pure assumption. There is a great danger of being deceived in this way of operating. Touching our surroundings has the effect of grounding our otherwise heady experiences. When we speak of "keeping in touch," we mean maintaining a firmly based relationship. This is as true for interpersonal relationships as it is for less animate aspects of reality.

The best way I have found to cultivate my sense of touch is by bathing and swimming. Water against the skin stimulates every part of the body as the motion of the water bends and flexes the hairs that cover the body. With each subtle motion, the nerves that surround the hairs are stimulated. Water temperature can also have a strong wakening effect, especially if its temperature is significantly higher or lower than expected.

A far less popular way of cultivating awareness of the sense of touch is by practicing nudity. The effect of the motion of air on the skin is the same as that of water during bathing. The problem with nudity lies in the potential for over-stimulation of the sense of sight. Seeing other people's normally covered body-parts creates what I call *interest of discovery*. Interest is generated hierarchically on the basis of familiarity, and this manifests as a tendency to be more interested in things that are unfamiliar. The connection between the visual center, which is highly susceptible to the interest of discovery, and the sexual center is often too close for comfort at such moments.

The connection between the sense of touch and sex should be obvious. The most fulfilling sexual relationships are those which give each person a complete "picture" of their bodies by having it touched and stimulated all over. Although it did not involve sexual arousal, it is the same kind of touched-all-over experience we had as infants when our parents lovingly handled and fondled us. Cessation of this kind of stimulation as we age produces conditions that make us susceptible to disease.[17] This is at least one reason to take the sense of touch seriously.

THE SENSE OF SMELL

Smell is the registration in the brain of impressions made by frequency bands of effervescing molecules (e.g., evaporating liquids and warm oils) that are carried through the air and affect the olfactory nerves in the nose and sinuses.

As with taste, effervescing molecules can be classed into six different bands: acrid, pungent, savory, sweet, sour, and neutral. A single odor can be derived from combinations of substances and their frequency bands and temperature. The mind can be used to qualify the infinite variety of odors according to intensity, density, and degree of freshness. It is with the addition of the sense of smell that we securely apprehend things visible and audible.

The sense of smell is found to generate the longest-term memories. Whole experiences long gone can be easily summoned up with an odor similar to one from the past. Such memories tend to be intense and focused. The memory connection appears to have an influence on the subjective nature of our sense of smell—we tend to like odors that are linked to happy memories, even if the odors

---

[17] Lunstad J. Holt, W. A. Birmingham and K. C. Light, "Influence of a 'warm touch' support enhancement intervention among married couples on ambulatory blood pressure, oxytocin, alpha amylase, and cortisol." *Psychosomatic Medicine* 70 (2008): 976-85.

are offensive. Since taste and smell are closely linked, it seems that this may be the explanation for why there is no accounting for preferences in taste.

Because of the immediate nature of smell, little needs to be cultivated in this sense. Each person, from my observation, has a distinct set of preferences for odors and a widely varying sensibility for both general and specific odors. Those with a high degree of sensitivity have a low tolerance for strong odors of any kind and can easily detect low concentrations of certain molecules. People who have a low degree of sensitivity have a high tolerance for strong odors, either pleasant or unpleasant, and they can be oblivious to high concentrations of such odors. Coroners, for instance, need an extraordinary degree of tolerance for offensive odors, especially the smell of decaying flesh. Perfumers need an extraordinary degree of sensitivity to delicate odors so that they can make alluring scents.

CONCLUDING REMARKS

The senses we have discussed are the *external* physical senses with which we explore and define our experiences in the physical world. What follows in the next chapter are explanations of the *internal* physical senses with which we relate to the world and the forces within our bodies as they exert influence on us.

Chapter Seven

The Internal Physical Senses

The internal physical senses are located inside the body. When they are related to a specific organ or system, they are localized. Because of their general distribution, the internal physical senses are extremely important to doctors for diagnosing illness. Also, the internal physical senses provide a sensory concept of who one is, in physical terms, and act as a constant reminder that one's body is material in nature.

These senses are not as prone to deception as are the five external senses. But, as hard as these senses are to deceive, they can be just as hard to discuss. Thankfully, we need never feel compelled to discuss them, but when we want to talk about them, we often find ourselves at a loss for words.

THE SENSE OF PRESSURE

The sense of pressure is directly related to the uninterrupted integrity of body tissues. Any interruption to the integrity of body tissue, especially the skin and muscles, compresses or stretches the tissue creating an impression that is registered in the brain as pressure. The force that excites the sense of pressure can be slight or strong, sharp or blunt, dynamic or unrelenting, gradual or continuous, and sudden or slow. A pinprick is a strong, sharp, sudden, and then either gradual or unrelenting form of pressure. A sexual stroke is a slight, blunt, dynamic, gradual or continuous, and usually slow form of pressure.

You sense muscle motion with your sense of pressure. Changes in the shape of a muscle force changes in the skin and the surrounding tendons, ligaments, and other muscles. These changes are read as fluctuations in pressure.

Every time you breathe in or out, you stretch or relax your rib cage. Doing this changes the amount of pressure you experience within your thorax. By focusing your attention on all the subtle changes in pressure within your body while breathing deliberately, you can cultivate a high degree of presence of mind. Learning to be present is useful because it empowers you to control your mental, emotional, and imaginative life. Those who feel like they are on an intellectual and emotional rollercoaster are especially in need of this kind of breathing exercise.

When we feel emotionally pressured we tend to respond by tightening our diaphragms. Concentrating on the internal physical pressure sense during slow, deliberate, deep breathing forces the diaphragm to move, thus easing the tension caused by emotional stress and taking one's mind off thoughts that bring about that stress.

We also tend to interpret internal physical pressure as being pleasurable or painful. The pleasure usually exists in the soft and soothing to the intensely stimulating. After a certain point of intensity, the experience becomes painful, and we only register the intensity or sharpness of pain.

THE SENSE OF PRESSURE OF CONTRACTION

When a muscle goes into spasm, the sense of contraction is obvious, if not overwhelming. Anyone who has experienced a charley horse—an involuntary spasm or cramp in the leg or foot muscles—knows what this sensation is like.

THE SENSE OF PRESSURE OF EXPANSION

As you breathe, your sense of pressure of expansion is stimulated in your chest cavity as the tissues that bind your ribs together are pulled apart to allow more air into your lungs. Even with shallow breathing, pressure of expansion can be clearly sensed. In the case of a charley horse, the spasm pulls on the fascia and tendons where muscles connect to bone and the sense of pressure of expansion is experienced there.

THE SENSE OF COMPRESSION

The sense of compression is usually stimulated when one is sitting. Where the sense of pressure is primarily restricted to the body's soft tissues, the sense of compression is more noticed in the bones. The sense of compression does not necessarily register any force that is applied to the soft tissues; however, as soon as the bones become involved, like in the case of ruptured discs in the spine or bone on bone contact, the sense of compression is obvious.

THE SENSE OF BEING

The sense of being is subtle because it is related to the sense of pressure, yet it has nothing directly to do with it. Specifically, the internal physical sense of being is the sensation of blood flowing throughout the body. You will usually become aware of this phenomenon when you have a serious problem, like a gaping wound or a pounding headache.

I call this the sense of being because our experience of existing is linked to blood circulation. The beating of the heart is an autonomic function that causes cessation of being when it stops beating. The moment when the heart stops beating is when one most notices this sense because it is no longer filling one's subliminal awareness with its low-level rumble. People who experience momentary cessation of being often have a subsequent spiritual change. Life assumes greater meaning the moment we know we can actually die.

THE SENSE OF MOTION

The sense of motion is directly related to the awareness of the changing of position of all the body parts when not at a state of rest. Athletes and dancers are usually people who love to stimulate their sense of motion.

The force that stimulates this sense can be internally initiated or externally imposed. That is, you can jump into the air, as on a trampoline, or you can be thrown into the air. In either case, the objective sensation would be equivalent. When internally stimulated, the sense of motion can dominate the awareness as an effect of focused progress. When externally stimulated, the effect is more a fear of being out of control.

The sense of motion is closely linked to the imagination. Whatever movement one concocts in the imagination is easily enacted through the sense of motion. The differences in grace and ease between athletes and dancers are largely determined by the degree to which each imagines their motions in detail before making them. The quality of the motions produced is determined by the quality of the motions imagined and how precisely they have been realized. Even though we don't have a motion sense in our imaginations, we do have a host of other senses that we use to construct imaginative motions that can then be translated into physical motion.

THE SENSE OF TEMPERATURE

The sense of temperature is an internal physical mechanism that stimulates the whole body to respond appropriately to the degree of hot or cold in the environment. Depending on the nature of the source, internal or external, different systems are called upon to act. If you get burned, your body rushes white blood cells to the burn site, and the temperature in that area rises. If you get frostbite, your body at first responds by raising the temperature to resist damage and then, if necessary, it retreats to conserve heat and protect the whole by allowing the freezing part to die.

You can control the overall response of the sense of temperature by managing your attitude to the condition. For instance, I have had the experience of having to walk home in weather that was thirty degrees below zero (my car wouldn't start). I determined that I could get home without getting cold by running or by inventing a way of thinking that would keep me warm. The ice and depth of snow prevented me from running, so I decided that I could feel cold or pay attention to the sensation of my body experiencing a cold temperature. I chose the latter. What was interesting is that by the time I had walked half a mile, I was so hot from the walk that I was forced to shed my insubstantial jacket. After a mile of walking, I was sweating all over. I have since used this technique to stay warm or cool depending on what was required. Only when my body is sick with a cold or a virus does this technique not work for me. My own explanation for the beneficial effect of thinking this way is that by accepting the condition of cold absolutely, I allowed the mechanism that regulates my body temperature to work without interference. I expect that this might be the same attitude peoples in the northernmost regions of the world use to tolerate the low temperature they are exposed to.

There are stories of Indian yogis who can sit meditating high up in the mountains in the dead of winter and can melt the snow several feet around them. These tales have the look of tall about them, but I would allow them credibility based on my own simple experience.

The sense of temperature stands as a vanguard against illness as it raises and lowers according to the needs of the moment. It is incredibly smart because it knows exactly where in the body the temperature needs to be raised or lowered.

THE SENSE OF TENSION

The sense of tension is related to chemical changes in the muscles when they have been contracted for some time. Any prolonged contraction is called a spasm. Spasms can be agonizing when the buildup of acid in muscles occurs at a rate faster than its removal. Massage helps relieve tension by dispersing those acids faster.

Relaxation is the opposite of tension. Both tension and relaxation become a problem when they are excessive. Excess tension makes a person high strung, volatile, and impulsive. Excess relaxation makes a person lethargic, inert, and passive. The ideal balance between these two extremes is to be alert, ready, considerate, deliberate, and bold yet circumspect.

Impatience is a feeling that people with a tendency for tension have towards others who move, think, or react more slowly than they would prefer. People who like moving at a slower rate get irritated when pushed to go faster than their natural pace. Some of these differences in personal style are related to the nervous system, while others have to do with psychological makeup. Those who are tense tend to want to control everything so they can avoid making mistakes. While those whose who hold back try to avoid making mistakes by being sure of their actions. In both cases, it is the fear of mistakes that is the cause of excess tension or laxity. When exposed to a no-fear environment that encourages the making of mistakes, the tense become more relaxed and the lax become more alert. Natural behavior only occurs in an environment where the fear of reprisal for making mistakes is absent.

THE SURVIVAL SENSES

Like every human, you have five survival senses: respiration, hunger, thirst, reproduction, and excretion. These senses are stimulated when the connective materials within and around the organs involved are stretched or contracted. When you withhold activity regarding any of these functions, you stimulate the sense connected to it. The longer you withhold activity, the stronger the stimulation of that sense becomes. Try holding your breath—the longer you withhold breathing, the stronger the urge to breathe becomes. Each of these senses works along the same lines. What we call the feeling of fullness is caused by a stretched state and what we call the feeling of emptiness is caused by a contracted or relaxed state.

Because the survival senses are designed to help us survive and prevent our extinction, they can be overwhelming. When given the opportunity, they will make our decisions for us. However, when we are in control of our survival senses, we actually have a greater chance of survival. This is because our various drives and urges usually get us in trouble when left unchecked. When the urge to stave off hunger by eating causes you to over eat, you run the risk of death from heart disease. With the survival senses, practicing self-control is a positive thing that can be a matter of life or death.

Long ago in India, the notion of *chakras* was developed to give form to the various energies experienced within the body. I suspect that five of those chakras are associated with the five survival senses. The yogi tradition of practicing self-denial appears to be a method of learning to control the influences of these senses on one's mind. By systematically playing with each sense, yogis learned to control the senses' influence on their minds and control each sense to the point that they seemed to no longer exist for them.

I like the idea of controlling the degree of influence any sense has on my mind, but I don't like the idea of practicing denial, unless denial can be defined as non-indulgence. The mentality of denial is a dangerous frame of mind to cultivate. At what point is zeal for denial denied? Indeed, in the case of anorexia, denial can lead to death.

To remove the influence of a particular sense on your decision-making, you need only decide against what that sense suggests. That is a denial of sorts, but it doesn't require a mentality of denial. By acknowledging an urge and deciding against doing what it suggests, you exert your power of decision over your body's power of decision.

THE SENSE OF RESPIRATION

The sense of respiration is located in the area of the diaphragm and is associated with the lungs. The diaphragm is the muscle that controls breathing. The respiratory sense can be noticed most strongly when you hold your breath or exhale completely and avoid breathing in for an extended period of time. The longer you avoid breathing, the more intense and urgent the sensation of the need to breathe becomes.

Interestingly, the diaphragm also acts as a coordinating mechanism for the body. When it is intelligently employed, it provides a vehicle for consciously integrating mind, body, and spirit. That is, an idea for an act or movement is more efficiently turned into reality when the diaphragm is somehow involved. Meditation, concentration, the art of speaking, the art of singing, and the art of controlled movement all focus on this purposeful involvement of the diaphragm.

The phrase, "his heart wasn't in it," is a cliché that accurately describes an observation of an action or performance during which the performer's diaphragm is disengaged or marginally involved. When the emotions are involved in an action, the diaphragm is automatically utilized. However, there are times when one must act without emotion yet need to involve the coordinating power of the diaphragm, like in athletic events, musical performances, and staged dancing. Pre-performance nervousness among athletes, musicians, and dancers is a case in point. Although some performers benefit from "performance jitters," others are devastated by them. Those who benefit from the jitters use them to help generate the excitement needed to do a great job. Those who suffer from the jitters are filled with fear of failure or of making a fool of themselves (there are other fears, but these two rank highest on the list).

I have observed that when the diaphragm is in a state of tension, it locks the mind upon whatever it was focused on just prior to the diaphragm tensing. This is how the diaphragm functions to integrate the works of the mind with those of the body. Indeed, this behavior is much stronger than our intention or will. This unusual power can become a curse when the thoughts are emotional, like in cases of depression. No amount of attention or talking is enough to cause depressive thoughts to abate because it often only increases fixation. Encouraging laughter or crying is helpful. The function of crying and laughter is not to distract the fixed mind; it is to cause a gradual relaxation of the diaphragm by rhythmic interruptions. When the diaphragm relaxes, fixation disappears. Any heavy exercise, such as hard labor, running, or swimming, will have the same effect of untying the diaphragm's "knot."

By applying the technique of following an intention for physical action with a subtle contraction of the diaphragm, these observations can be verified by anyone. By using the opposite technique of breathing forcefully to interrupt a mind frozen by fear, moving from a state of fear to one of greater mindfulness is made possible.

I suspect that the intentional use of the diaphragm is also the main reason why singers regularly outrank other musicians. The effect of managing the diaphragm while singing causes a singer's impression on the imaginations of listeners to be more intense than stronger intentionality from an instrumentalist. Instrumentalists do not usually make a habit of managing their diaphragms, unless they play a wind instrument. The apparent effect of connection made by the diaphragmatically charged mind of a performer on the brains of an audience is likely the real source of efficient communication when performing.

It is easy to ignore the sense of respiration because it functions autonomically, but the fact of its many benefits when mindfully attended to should be reason enough for us to be deliberately mindful of it.

THE SENSE OF HUNGER

The sense of hunger governs your appetite for food. This sense is stimulated by suggestion (seeing food, smelling food, watching people eat, etc.), by habits of time and place for eating, and by the body's actual need for nourishment. Your general health is determined by the way you respond to this sense when it is stimulated.

Overreaction to hunger by over-eating happens in both animals and humans. Denial of hunger is fasting. Absence of hunger results in anorexia. A moderate response to hunger that sustains the body and satisfies the sense is the healthiest response because it maintains enough reserve in the body to cope with illness without accumulating gross excess, which could cause illness or discomfort.

Because of the proximity of the stomach to the diaphragm, when the stomach is filled, it presses against the diaphragm and temporarily induces the illusion of relaxation. This is the reason, I venture to guess, for what is called "comfort eating." A full belly makes the stomach feel less tight and gives the illusion of well-being because the diaphragm appears relaxed.

There are spiritual, intellectual, and emotional aspects to the sense of hunger. The spiritual aspect is a hunger for fulfillment. The intellectual aspect is a hunger for things to make sense. The emotional aspect of hunger is greed. All of these non-physical aspects function like hunger does for the body.

As soon as you pay attention to what is happening, both internally and externally, you begin to feed the spirit and Soul. Starvation of spirit makes you cast about seeking stimulation that will cause attention to be paid. Although this casting behavior seems aimless and senseless, the purpose is clear to the spirit. Much of the reason for why people are addicted to drugs, food, sex, violence, and power stems from a simple lack of paying attention. Just as the digestive system will excrete what we eat, the Soul, when it is well fed, will excrete ideas, insights, understandings, and so on.

The pursuit of knowledge is the way of satisfying our hunger to make sense of the world. Intellectually, we hunger for things to make sense, and we feel starved by a surfeit of nonsense when things don't make sense. This drive is as powerful as the hunger for food, and in the same way that you can be anorexic, you can also lose appetite for having things make sense. If you've never had the experience of needing to know something, it is possible that your intellectual hunger wasn't satisfied when you were a child because of a negative experiences around learning.

Much of the problem of feeding the intellect arises because we tend to feed it beliefs. Beliefs are fake intellectual food—junk food. They give us something to play with in our minds but fail to provide adequate nourishment. This is the reason that beliefs need the constant buttressing of proof. Proof feels temporarily satisfying because it reminds us that our beliefs are still working. The search for evidence that supports beliefs is like groping for the truth.

When we are accustomed to beliefs and how they "taste," the truth can often have an odd taste to it. Because of its substance (or our lack of substance), we often tire of intellectually chewing on it. The truth is rarely tailored to suit our tastes or expectations and so is often hard to swallow. If unaccustomed to either knowing or truth, the chances are we will spit it out and reject it on the first encounter. Hence, anything that is true or that needs to be known (i.e., anything threatening to beliefs) also stimulates us to eradicate it.

Emotional hunger manifests itself as greed, lust, avarice, sentimentality, dependency, and addiction. When we experience spiritual and emotional starvation at the same time, it becomes difficult to separate the two kinds of hunger. Emotional hunger is the easier of the two to alleviate, so most of us try to do that. We do everything in our power to get others to love us. Unfortunately, being loved as a child is about the only way that this kind of hunger can be satisfied. I was lucky in that I never experienced this deficit personally, but I have a good imagination for what it must feel like, at least enough to feel compassion for those who have this deficit. If this love never happened for us, we can take ourselves in hand and learn to love ourselves genuinely, and that will help relieve the hunger. But there will always be a feeling of deprivation that lingers. This feeling of deprivation will only be satisfied when we experience God-love. This kind of love can't be had from any person, so people have created a way of experiencing this kind of love, which they attribute to God. That is the reason I am using the term *God-love.* In Latin the term is Amadeus. In Greek it is Theophilus. It doesn't matter what this kind of love is called because the effect is always the same—it allays the feeling of deprivation. Curiously, the Soul can give this kind of love. This may, in the end, be the most compelling reason for people to become acquainted with their Souls.

God-love is the kind of love that accepts us absolutely and attends us when needed, yet never seeks to influence us nor is it able to be influenced by us. If we can give ourselves that kind of love, more power to us. If we can find someone else whose Soul can give us that kind of love, more power to us. If we can learn to receive that kind of love from everything around us in nature and the universe, the greatest power to us. This is the only kind of love that can fill us to the point that we never again feel deprived. It charges us up, like a battery, allowing us to fulfill one of our most important original design intentions—loving.

There is a danger in this because the desire for experiencing this quality of love can be so strong that we are capable of imagining the effect and convincing ourselves that the effect is the "real deal" when, in reality, it has no substance. That substance is the universal principles. If universal principles are missing from the equation, the tendency to create illusion is high. The problem that arises from generating a false love is that when it disappears, as it always will when the illusory bubble bursts, the comedown is devastating. When people turn away from religion with bitterness, it is because that bubble burst for them. When universal principles are behind this kind of God-love, the effect needs no buttressing because the feeling lasts.

When we no longer feel deprived, our hunger for things, money, excitement, pleasure, and comfort transforms into a feeling of gluttony or of having over eaten, and all we want to do is dispose of those things and behaviors. When not deprived of God-love, we eventually discover that material things and endeavors don't have much intrinsic interest. We can own things without being attached to them. We can be free of emotional, mental, and physical encumbrances. When we no longer need something, we can give it away or sell it with the emotional attachment with which we might dispose of garbage or sell junk.

THE SENSE OF THIRST

The sense of thirst is intended to maintain proper fluid levels in the body. When fluid levels are high, the body excretes the excess. When fluid levels are low, the body retains what it can. When fluid levels get low enough, the body senses the need for replenishment, and you get thirsty.

The sense of thirst, like the sense of hunger, has a spiritual dimension to it. It is the thirst for affirmation of truth. It is not enough to have a direct experience of the truth—we need to know that others also have the same experience. When things ring true, they do so because of the refreshing effect that occurs when we hear stories from others that parallel our experiences. The effect is like drinking a cool glass of water on a hot day. This effect also accounts for the plethora of support groups and television talk shows that expose and deal with emotional problems. The thirst-quenching effect of recognition can be quite addicting.

THE REPRODUCTIVE SENSE

The reproductive sense arises from the system of glands and organs that involve sex and reproduction. The hormones pumped into the body by these glands make us "horny." This sensation is the urge to achieve sexual release. Of all the urges and drives of the body, this one tops the list for sheer intensity of pleasure. One of the main problems humans have in life is in trying to avoid being more than an automaton of their sexual impulses.

Because of the emotional and political nature of humans, elaborate rituals, rules, procedures, games, and laws have been invented to attend to the problems of sexuality. If humans had little interest in their own feelings, such trappings would be all but nonexistent. Indeed, there have been cultures in which the sex act had all the political energy of eating a bowl of cereal. I am reminded of the sexual culture of the Bonobo chimpanzee societies. In these cultures, sex is treated lightly, as if it is fun, convivial, and nothing special. In Western culture, where humans are pitted against themselves and each other, sexuality assumes divine status. Those who are sexually attractive are called sex-gods and sex-goddesses. Those who are sexually promiscuous are worshipped and glorified, or jealously vilified. The irony is that such over-emphasis on sex makes many people feel sexually inadequate, or they worry about being so.

Making people feel guilty about their sexual senses and feelings is something religion excels at. However, if God is good, then God probably could not care less about how humans sexually express themselves as long as they treat each other with love and respect and never hurt others. If God is good, then God is only interested in your relationship with your Soul and in how you care for and love others.

Sex is like breathing or eating because it is a natural body function that all human beings are equipped with. Some people experience that function more intensely than others. Over-emphasizing its importance is as damaging as under-valuing its consequences. Viewing sex as a natural body function and setting limits to protect people who are vulnerable to exploitation is as much attention as sex deserves. Sexual abuse steals the victim's potential for integrating with their Soul, so coming down hard on those who sexually victimize others is the responsibility of all societies. Societies that fail to protect citizens who are abused sexually are anathema.

THE EXCRETORY SENSES

The urge to evacuate the body of something impure is the result of complex mechanisms designed to maintain a healthy body. The excretory senses respond to the presence of waste products. Urination and defecation occur when the body has generated enough waste to trigger these senses. Another autonomic excretory mechanism is sweating. Anything that is identified as toxic to the body will get excreted by one means or another.

Excretion of toxins, so to speak, functions at all levels of personal existence. When things that would poison you do not get excreted, you can become constipated and extremely ill. In the same way that you can be physically constipated, you can be emotionally, intellectually, intuitively, imaginatively, or spiritually constipated. Although it's easy to be aware of physical constipation, recognizing other kinds is far more difficult because the symptoms are like those of starvation. So, it's hard to tell if you are spiritually starved or constipated, or emotionally starved or constipated.

Many emotional disorders occur as a result of emotional constipation if you cannot articulate your feelings. When you have been violated and have never had the opportunity to express your feelings of outrage, you will probably store up those feelings. This is a form of constipation. Even the constipation itself is a form of violation. When those feelings finally surface, they appear with much more intensity than they would have, had they been expressed at the moment of violation. Learning to live with frustration and anger over having been violated means accepting the idea that the past is dead and that being a slave to the past is senseless and self-destructive. When you are unable to forgive and leave the past and the bad feelings behind, what you are actually expressing is that you enjoy wallowing in misery. Leaving the past behind does not mean denial; it means acknowledging the past yet forbidding it, via the mechanism of forgiveness, from influencing or determining future decisions. The issue of whether to forgive or not is one that requires resolution because it is a choice each person must make to create a connection with their Soul. Not to forgive those who have violated you is a decision that guarantees no relationship with your Soul.

THE SENSE OF REGENERATION

This is the sense of the need for sleep. Since sleep is designed to give the body the opportunity to regenerate itself, calling this the regenerative sense seems reasonable. Most of the needs and urges in the body are announcements by various senses that blockages or build-ups need to be released or that vacancies or depletions need to be filled or replaced. The need for sleep is caused by the brain needing to reprocess and make sense of the day's stored impressions and by depletion of energy due to the processes of repair and growth. Failure to get enough sleep can cause disconnection from your Soul as your being begins to disintegrate when fatigue sets in.

THE SENSE OF LOCATION (PROPRIOCEPTION)

The sense of location is directly related to the awareness you have of exactly where your body parts are at any given moment in time. People who have a poor sense of location are accident-prone because they don't or can't pay attention to where their body members are in space. Young children generally have a poor sense of location. They learn about their sense of location by repeatedly getting hurt. The more often they get hurt, the better their sense of location becomes until they finally learn how not to get hurt. For those of us who can see, walking in the dark heightens in us a strong awareness of our sense of location.

Anything designed to be used by a human being needs to account for this important sense. When someone creates a design for a product that will be set out in public, it is imperative that they use their sense of location to understand how those who are not paying attention could get hurt by that product. This goes for street signs placed on sidewalks, potted plants in hallways, throw rugs on the floor, the swing of a split panel door, hanging lights and ornaments, or curbs of a sidewalk, etc. Anyone who is paying attention to their sense of location and who encounters a poorly designed object will immediately become alarmed at the danger generated by the improper design. When designs are right, they are never noticed—they become part of the landscape.

THE SENSE OF IRRITATION

The sense of irritation manifests itself as massive or unabated itching or soreness. This sense seems connected to conditions of the skin or subsurface skin layers. Chafing, rawness, and abrasion of the skin result when itching has caused scratching to the point of tearing the skin. Often, diseases and allergic inflammations of the skin show up as itching rashes or blisters. Whatever the cause, the irritation of itching can literally drive a person crazy when it is unrelenting and pervasive. Self-mutilation in nature usually occurs when an irritant causes itching and scratching to the point of massive destruction of tissue. Veterinarians are conscious of this problem, and they use plastic cones to prevent wounded animals from scratching themselves to death.

Soreness is caused by wounds and inflammations of the skin, such as pimples, boils, sties, cuts, and slivers. These conditions don't produce the urge to scratch, but the experience of irritation demands that the soreness subside. The kind of pain that soreness imparts on the skin is superficial, though it may be extreme. Only when the wound extends to tissues other than the skin is the pain sensed as acute.

Soreness can also exist in muscle tissue, tendons, ligaments, and bone. Bruising is the usual cause of soreness to these areas of the body. However, it needs to be said that every person experiences all the various types of pain, soreness, and irritation differently. This is a result of each person's threshold of pain. A stimulus that will cause some people to experience low levels of pain will cause others to writhe in agony. This phenomenon is likely due to the number of pain receptors that differ from individual to individual. Those people who have more pain receptors are likely to register higher levels of pain from a given stimulus than those with fewer receptors.

The sense of irritation also has emotional, intellectual, imaginative, ethical, intuitive, and existential dimensions. This is because the sense of irritation stems from a disruption to the integrity of undisturbed perception. When perception is happening under normal conditions, it is subliminal. Psychologists might call it unconscious or subconscious, but these terms trouble me because they imply layers of consciousness. If we take the word *consciousness* at face value, it means *with knowledge*. Unconscious then means *without knowledge*. How can we perceive without knowing? This is an oxymoron.

You take in reality on every level at the same time. Your ability to make use of what you take in is limited by what you choose to pay attention to. An example of this is when you are concentrating hard on some kind of work and you fail to notice that you cut your finger during the process. Your body certainly knew what was happening. It perceived the fact that it was cut, but your sense of pain was momentarily displaced by more pressing matters. This is the case with most instances of so-called subconscious processes. Truth be told, whatever rattles or squeaks the loudest is what we tend to turn our attention to, which usually are things of the least importance. This is because our bodies are organized so that things of the least long-term spiritual importance are the things that scream the loudest for attention. These things are physical pain and pleasure, emotional pain and pleasure, and imagined pain and pleasure. The volume of pain and pleasure of the other aspects of ourselves are mere peeps by comparison.

Because every important discovery and every truly creative act has come about from a form of irritation, the sense of irritation is one of our most valuable assets. Knowing this, I am amused when I see people working hard to avoid being irritated while, at the same time, desiring to be creative. Talk about walking in opposite directions at once! Anyone who is successful at business knows what the market needs because they are extremely sensitive to the irritation caused by absences, vacancies, and holes in the marketplace. Their business savvy stems from providing the right "salve" for the irritation. It is this sense of irritation that ultimately generates the feeling of necessity that is said to be the mother of invention. If necessity is the mother of invention, irritation is its father.

THE SENSE OF SPACE

The sense of space has to do with the perception of the nature of spaces that surround us. It is a kind of measuring sense with which we adjust our physical motions to the space at hand. Anyone who has traveled on an airplane or bus knows the cramped sensation we get from being confined to the seats. We restrict our motions using our sense of space to avoid hitting someone or falling down when getting in or out of the seats.

Designers and architects call on this sense when they design spaces for human occupation. They apply their sense of space in their imaginations to imagine a space before it exists. They must imaginatively project a multitude of actions that might take place in a given area and decide how much space those actions require for safety. Indeed, building codes exist because of the myriad of mistakes that designers and architects have made when failing to use their sense of space. Unfortunately, building codes also discourage paying attention because they replace it with following rules. Too many mindless rules can lead to institutionalized stupidity as a result of trying too hard to idiot-proof the world.

THE SENSE OF TERRITORY

The territorial sense is the sense of space of the environment directly surrounding the body. The area covered can be as small as a few inches or as large as several yards. The intensity of a person's territorial sense is directly proportional to their fear and need for security and power. The more power a person needs, the larger the space they need for security. The more fearful or insecure a person feels, the more space they need. The sense of territory in humans is essentially the same sense as it may be observed in animals. For instance, if you remember seeing a large flock of birds roosting on telephone wires, you will remember seeing these birds being spaced at regular intervals from one another. The distance between the birds is an expression of the specific territorial sense of each individual bird roosting on the wire.

Protocol and etiquette also focus on this perplexing sense. The rules for entering and leaving the space of another person are not arbitrary. They have to do with creating an effect of avoiding the impression of invasion, violation, or subversion, and they solve the problems of leaving a person's space without creating ill will, offense, or annoyance. It is for this reason that the sense of territory is closely connected to the emotions of avarice, greed, pugnaciousness, jealousy, and envy. Avarice and greed are the excessive desire for wealth, territory, and power. Pugnaciousness is the excessive desire to fight over those things. Jealousy is the excessive fear that others will take what we've acquired, and envy is the fear that what others get or have gotten was acquired at our expense. I once had a flock of chickens, and watching those birds behaving this way often made me think of humans as possibly being one of the lower forms of animal life. The similarity of behavior is amazing.

When our sense of territory is violated, great turmoil is created because of the violation. This is as much the case with rape and burglary as it is with legalized breaking and entering, etc. Imprisonment is designed to punish a criminal by the confinement of their territory to a small space, thus abridging their liberty to make deliberate decisions or to violate the territories of others in the future.

THE SENSE OF FATIGUE

The sense of fatigue is stimulated by the presence of chemicals or toxins produced by the body when it is ill or working hard. The inability of the body to excrete these substances quickly enough leads to the sensation of fatigue. The sensation of fatigue can also be excited by the thought of exertion or expenditure of energy. Sometimes, imagined work is just as tiring as the act of working. Narcolepsy is the disorder characterized by instant and extreme sensation of fatigue brought on by an intense stimulation.

The sensation of fatigue is an important aesthetic sense because the act of paying attention to things that are mediocre stimulates this sense. I learned this during a trip to Europe once while visiting art museums. I found that the task of looking at all the supposedly great works of art in museums exhausted me, so I tried an experiment. At the next museum, I stopped and paid attention only to those paintings that seemed to jump off the wall at me and say, "look at me." This worked. I saw all the pictures in the museum but looked at four or five, and I left with more energy than when I walked in. My conclusions from this experience were that most museums are filled with mediocre, sophisticated junk and that great art should be a source of energy, not a stealer of it. I have related this experience to many others who also noticed that they got tired looking at all that "great" art. They later reported that doing as I suggested—running through the museum to find those great pictures and ignoring the rest—gave them the energy they were looking for. I have also found the same effect true for hearing mediocre music or hearing great music badly played.

THE SENSE OF GESTURE

This is a sense that is used to read nonverbal messages. Nonverbal messages are attitudes. Attitudes control what gestures get expressed and, consequently, what gestures get read by others. Our attitudes can often be changed merely by altering our habits of gestural expression. The gesture of slouching expresses carelessness, while a gesture of uprightness expresses alert attention. The gesture expressing defiance can be seen in the eyes of criminals and miscreants—the eyes appear to recede from the front of the face as though hiding due to shame. Our minds need not be engaged at all for clarity of communication to exist. In fact, if the mind is engaged, communication through attitude and gesture is usually obscured.

Interestingly, this sense is specifically located in the upper thorax just under the breastbone. Why it is located there needs to be explained by those with specialist medical knowledge.

The sense of gesture is aesthetically important because much of art involves gestural communication. Great art communicates high spiritual attitudes by composing together gestures and other matters of content. It is in this regard that great art is universal—everyone reads gestures in much the same way. What I have learned from witnessing great art is that the success of a great painting, for instance, is not in how much we remember but in whether or not we were "impressed" with the attitude expressed.

THE SENSE OF GRAVITY

What we normally call weight is the force of gravity exerting itself on our bodies. The sense of gravity is what determines your awareness of your own inertia. When you jump, you can sense this at the point of the motion when you're about to descend. When sitting, you can sense the pressure on the backs of your legs and buttocks as gravity pulls you down. At the moment of rising from sitting, you can sense gravity pulling you down.

Anyone who has taken a ride in an elevator knows the differences in the sensation of gravity that make you seem heavier to yourself when going up and lighter when going down. Pilots experience this sensation and refer to it as *g-force.* Some of this sensation comes from the flow or collection of blood in certain parts of the body due to the body's acceleration or deceleration from a resting position. The remainder comes from the sensation of the pull of the earth's gravity on the body. That is, you can sense the pull of gravity on your hands and arms as they hang by your side.

For dancers, acrobats, divers, and practitioners of the martial arts, a heightened sense of gravity gives a feeling of security, but it can also become a drawback if it is not effectively handled. Dancers and acrobats appear sodden and clumsy when they have not learned to manage this sense. Managing it means learning to prevent it from being centered directly under the feet. This effectively moves the center of gravity to a point where it makes the body fall over. By catching the fall and uplifting the body, a dancer can give the impression of great motion with lightness and ease.

THE SENSE OF PHYSICAL BALANCE

The sense of physical balance is located in the inner ear. Because there is a mental sense of balance located in the mind, it is important to distinguish how the physical sense of balance differs from the mental sense of balance. Mainly, the distinguishing factor of the inner physical sense of balance is its purpose, which is to help us keep equilibrium in an upright position. Those who have experienced weightlessness are very aware of the senses of balance and of gravity. Dizziness is a symptom of a disturbance in the inner ear due to a loss of equilibrium.

Balancing mechanisms exist at all levels of personality and physiology; they are part of the brain's natural function. The chemistry of the blood is carefully regulated and balanced by the brain. Brain output is balanced according to the environment. Too much boredom makes us agitated, and too much chaos and confusion paralyze us. We experience burn-out when exposed to too much stress and anxiety. Our lives and bodies reflect this constant fluctuation between excess and privation. Achieving balance means making decisions that tend to avoid either extreme. This is called "moderation in all things," a notion rightly advanced by both Pythagoras and Confucius.

THE SENSE OF COMFORT

The threshold of comfort is experienced the moment any of the physical senses, outer and inner, have reached a point of stimulation past which the experience becomes painful. This threshold differs according to both the physiological and the psychological makeup of each person. Within each person, however, this point is consistent and mostly objective. It is the fact that no two bodies are built identically that makes this threshold subjective for purposes of discussion.

Since much of what gives us pleasure is a stimulation of this sense, up to the threshold, we might be tempted to call it the sense of satisfaction or pleasure. However, satisfaction and pleasure are subjective in the extreme, while comfort is moderately so. Much of what is discussed about subjectivity and relativity concerns a discussion of degree regarding this threshold.

Comfort is a transitional sensation because the registration of comfort is a level of awareness slightly above an awareness of the actual physical sense to which it pertains. It is transitional because it involves a higher level of awareness to articulate and attend to than an awareness of the physical senses, and it is on a higher level because it applies to all of the physical senses. Along with the threshold of pain, it forms the transition from the purely physical senses to the lower mental senses.

THE SENSE OF PAIN

Pain is a word used to describe the sensation at the upper end of intensity of stimulation applied to any given sense. Too loud a sound, even the most beautiful in all the world, will cause pain. The threshold of pain is different for each individual.

At first, the effect of pain on the mind is a focusing effect; later, when the level proves unabating, the effect becomes numbness. For doctors, pain is the primary indicator of disease in a patient, and disease would prove difficult to locate or diagnose without it.

Pain could be thought of as a sense because the nervous system is designed to detect pain. This definition would work if the nature of the stimulation were limited to the nerves themselves either by violation (cutting or pricking) or constriction (pinching or twisting). Rather than speculate, I prefer to treat pain and comfort as thresholds of awareness. Together they bridge the chasm between the physical and the mental planes.

Pain is important because it announces that something is happening. Normally we ignore our senses until the stimulation we take in reaches the threshold of pain. As soon as that threshold is crossed, we register pain and finally pay attention. Often this happens too late to do anything about the pain's cause. I believe the underlying reason for why we have this habit is that we are trained as children to deny pain. When children cry due to pain, adults give them the clear message that crying is unacceptable behavior. "No one likes a crybaby," they say, or, "If you don't stop crying, I'll really give you something to cry about." Since whining is often crying for the purpose of gaining sympathy, crying is often interpreted by adults as a whining ploy to gain sympathy. The result of all this is that most of us are trained to consider pain as undesirable. Hence, we tend to reject pain and painful experiences indiscriminately, and we also tend to treat pain as a source of misery that deserves to be denied.

Indiscriminate denial of pain can get us into trouble. The trouble comes when we become exposed to the pain of anything new, different, out of the ordinary, or unusual, and we respond habitually, more to the feelings of pain than to the different stimuli, by turning away from the things that are new. We read anything new as threatening because it disagrees with our firmly held beliefs, our entrenched habits, or our vested self-interests. Unfortunately, things that are new may be needed for us to survive in the future. For this reason, it is important to beware of the urge to extinguish pain too quickly or to have a knee-jerk reaction to anything new.

One of the major benefits of pain is the feeling of need it creates. Since all real creativity arises from a feeling of need, to abolish pain is to abolish need, which is to abolish creativity. A smart person understands this and works to optimize their painful experiences. Out of pain, we also learn what is worthwhile and valuable to us. Pain brings us down to earth, it shackles us to reality, it gives life focus (albeit an unpleasant focus), and it keeps our priorities well in mind. It tests our character and molds our humanity. It does all these things for us as long as we don't deny or avoid it.

By embracing and accepting the pain we experience, we can learn to deal with it positively and creatively. Interestingly, this kind of attitude inspires all who encounter it. Hearing a mortally ill child talk about their coming death inspires compassion in us that little else can match. When we hear their words of wisdom about how those they know should view them and their death, we are moved out of our selfish and petty mindsets. Do we all need to experience terrible pain to learn such wisdom?

By carefully avoiding the easy and painless path, you can profit spiritually. This occurs because the needs you feel when you choose to take the harder path activate your dormant intuitive self. Awakening your intuition empowers you beyond any ability you may have imagined. Suddenly, you know things you never knew before, and this knowledge makes you more competent and bold and gives you a feeling similar to being intensely loved. This feeling and knowledge is generated internally, yet it seems to flow not from yourself but from another source. Once it envelops you, it leaves an impression on your state of being that is impossible to remove. From that point on, nothing can harm you, and pain and death become meaningless events, each just one more experience of many.

IMAGINED PAIN

It is imagined pain that is the most painful. Anticipated, conjured, heralded, and celebrated in the mind before it happens, imagined pain paralyzes you and prevents you from exploring your potential. If you paralyze yourself with imagined pain, you are dead already. Conquering the grip of imagined pain is the same, metaphorically speaking, as resurrection. The same could be said of fear.

ACHING

The variety of pain we call aching is a dull sort that varies greatly from mild to intense. Anyone who has had a migraine headache can attest to this. Aching is usually a deeply sensed form of pain when internal tissues become inflamed.

There are emotional and intellectual equivalents where aching is concerned. For example, the emotion of unrequited love causes aching, and I suspect that an excessively tense diaphragm causes an aching sensation. Subjecting the brain to an intense level of learning or thinking causes intellectual aching—the effect makes the head hurt.

BURNING

Burning is another variety of pain. The term *burning* is metaphorical. It isn't actual burning that is sensed, it is like the sensation of being burned.

STABBING

Stabbing is also another variety of pain. Like burning, *stabbing* is a metaphorical term. It is not necessarily the sensation of being stabbed by something. The sensation appears like being stabbed by a sharp pointed object. That is, one experiences a sudden, intense, localized pain.

SENSITIVITY TO PAIN

There is a tendency among individuals who experience lower levels of pain for a given stimulus to cast themselves as superior or as machismo. Being highly sensitive is usually viewed in our culture as a sign of weakness. Praise or ridicule for insensitivity or sensitivity is both unnecessary and stupid. We wouldn't praise a person for having pitch black hair and ridicule another for having slightly less black hair because differences in hair color are a matter of having more or less melanin, which is a genetic trait. Similarly, having a greater or lesser number of pain receptors is a matter of genetics. There was a time when people used to taunt others who were deaf because they couldn't speak and were thus treated as stupid. It turns out that deaf people are far more sensitive to gesture and affect than those whose hearing is normal. Similarly, the blind are infinitely more touch sensitive than are sighted people.

Soon there will come a time when being hypersensitive will no longer be a sign of weakness. Those of us who have more receptors are like the canaries in the mineshaft because they are the first to recognize aesthetic problems or sense environmental insults. Ultimately, balance will be achieved as every condition of genetic makeup is appreciated properly for its strengths and possibilities. Just as my own dyslexia has made it possible for me to comprehend complex immaterial phenomena, those whose genetic makeup is different will be appreciated for what we can learn about reality from them.

THE SENSE OF ITCHING

How is itching different from the sense of irritation? Irritation is far more dimensional than itching. The sense of itching is experienced as irritation that appears to be under the skin. The impulse to scratch an itch is so strong it is almost impossible to deny. Where irritation rarely reduces the sufferer to insanity, it doesn't take long for itching to produce that effect. I know of no emotional, spiritual, or intellectual equivalent to itching.

THE SENSATION OF EMOTION

Emotions are feelings that you can sense because of physical changes that occur inside your body. These physical changes and sensations vary with each emotion. The sensations are not the emotions themselves; they are the physical manifestations of emotions. That is, tightness in the pit of the stomach caused by fear is the physical manifestation of the emotion called fear. In this case, you would sense internal pressure as it affects the diaphragm.

Many of your internal physical senses are stimulated simultaneously when you have an emotion. This kind of experience is what I call a *sensory cluster*. When many senses are being simultaneously excited, it is difficult to isolate any one sense for paying attention to. Normally, in these moments, you are only interested in the emotion you are having or expressing.

A sensory cluster stems from habits, attitudes, and the complex chemistry of the body (hormone levels, blood sugar levels, toxin levels, and so on). For instance, men become more assertive or aggressive when their bodies' testosterone levels become high. The natural tendency for men to have more muscle tone than women also leads to male habits that involve intense levels of muscular activity. These habits act as a natural support for when men want or need to be assertive or aggressive because of their hormones. When men have the unpleasant concurrence of high hormone levels and physical habits that support a macho mentality, they tend to be pushy, insolent, strutting, and aggressive.

The attitude you have is key to whether you are slave or master of your emotions, hormones, habits, or urges. The sensation of emotion is useful because it can act as an alarm that announces the need to acknowledge your emotions and divert energy back into more interesting and profitable enterprises.

THE SENSE OF RELAXATION

Without the sensation of relaxation, you wouldn't be able to release tension in the various parts of your body. Tension is sensed as pain or pressure when it lasts more than a few seconds. Relaxation is sensed as a release of pain or pressure. This sense is fleeting because you will have difficulty conjuring relaxation if you do not first sense something tense. In this way, it is like the sense of numbness.

The phrase "letting go" is often used to describe the effect of consciously relaxing tense muscles. The reason for not releasing tension is likely to be fear that causes muscles to contract away from the source of fear.

The sense of relaxation helps you to free your body's movements because muscles that are under constant tension don't allow for freedom of movement. When the effect of releasing tension makes you feel freer, you can easily mistake that feeling for the sense of relaxation. You might say that you have a sense of freedom, but this is an effect caused by the releasing of tension and is more rightly described as a *feeling* of freedom, not a sense of it.

THE SENSE OF EXCITEMENT

The physical sense of excitement is different from the emotional feeling or the intellectual experience of excitement. The sensation of excitement has a component of tingling. Other sensed events that accompany excitement might be rapid breathing, rapid heartbeat, flushed face, or a rush of adrenalin. Excitement is also accompanied by increased alertness and mental acuity. The emotional feeling of excitement adds strong feelings of repulsion, attraction, revulsion, or desire that color the experience favorably or unfavorably.

THE SENSE OF INTENSITY

The sense of intensity is experienced inside the chest just below the breastbone. When we are struck by the sheer intensity of an experience, we might say that it is "breathtaking." That saying is, I suspect, related to the location of this particular sense.

THE SENSE OF HUMIDITY

You experience the sense of humidity as moisture or dryness on your skin, nose, and eyes and in the mouth and lungs. Generally, you won't notice this sense unless dryness becomes extreme or excess moisture creates the experience of stickiness on your skin or carries molds and mildews that create respiratory distress.

THE SENSE OF SATISFACTION

The sense of satisfaction is triggered when a survival sense that was stimulated to the point of urgency has been relieved. For example, the sexual sense becomes satisfied with orgasm, the sense of hunger becomes satisfied when one is full, and the sense of thirst is quenched and satisfied upon drinking a glass of water.

THE SENSE OF NUMBNESS (NO SENSATION)

This sense is stimulated when an area of the body becomes numb and exhibits no sensation.

Chapter Eight
The Mental Senses

DISCOVERING THE MENTAL SENSES

The idea of the aesthetic self, when it first occurred to me, began with the mental senses. The five external physical senses have been with us throughout human history because they are so obvious and palpable. The thirty-two internal physical senses are below the surface and are less easy to be precise about. What brought me to conceive the idea of the aesthetic self and the mental senses of the right and left hemispheres of the brain was having articulated for myself twenty-five of the universal principles and devoting myself to figuring out how to apply these principles in my instrument making. I reasoned that if I succeeded in applying these twenty-five principles, the effect of my instruments on players and listeners should be like hearing a sound which nature herself had created. I didn't count on it taking me thirty years to achieve this!

Only after thirty years of experiencing increasing success in applying the universal principles to my instruments did I intuit that each of those twenty-five universal principles were related to specific parts of the brain. I conjectured that half of these principles were located in the structure-sensing brain (left hemisphere) and the other half in the behavior-sensing brain (right hemisphere). I could sense the stimulation in my head from various parts of the sound as an effect similar to what is experienced when you close your eyes while someone holds their hand near your head. You can feel the presence of a hand being there because of its subtle warmth, without being able to say exactly what it is.

When the sound of my instruments was unstructured, I could detect sensations in my right-brain that were like being in a room of screaming children. On the other hand, structured sounds produced sensations on the left side of my brain that were like standing in a cool stream on a blistering hot day. If the sound had no observable behavior other than vanishing over time, the sensation was like seeing a dead body. If the sound went sharp or flat in pitch as soon as it sounded, it was like listening to someone whining. If the sound had a powerful blooming behavior, I noticed a strong swooning effect in the frontal area of my brain.

These observations led to the insight that my brain was sensing for structure on the left hemisphere and for behavior on the right side. What I had learned from literature about the left and right hemispheres of the brain was only half right. No-one has an "analytical" left-brain nor do they have a "feeling" right-brain; rather, they have a left-brain that senses structures and a right-brain that senses behaviors. This made sense to me because everything I had observed in nature was a balance between structure and behavior, not between analysis and feeling. I understood at that moment how to think about sound and everything else.

Now I know there are folks in the neurosciences who scoff at the "outmoded" left versus right concept of how the brain works. My observations are made first hand by paying attention to what is happening in real time in my own brain. Neuroscientists are looking at brain scans, which I consider to be a somewhat crude method of studying what is happening in the brain. Like musical instrument builders who are box oriented rather than sound oriented, most neuroscientists are box oriented because they study the brain's behavior by looking at it with a machine. I am sound oriented—I carefully observe what is happening in my brain when I experience any stimulation. What I notice is that some stimuli have an effect on one hemisphere of my brain more than the other, which leads to my view of a structure-sensing left-brain and a behavior-sensing right-brain.

Once the idea that the brain was a vast sensing mechanism occurred to me, many previously confusing things became instantly clear. Humans are constructed as super-sophisticated sensing devices, and everything that comes into the brain is processed as sensation. How you feel about what you sense depends on your attitude. If what you sense is pleasurable, you will usually have positive emotional reactions; if it is painful, you will usually feel negative. If a sensation is painful because of having exercised a little too strenuously that day, you might feel positive by adopting an attitude of *no pain, no gain!* If a sensation is pleasurable, but you have the attitude that sensing pleasure is sinful, then you are choosing to feel negative about that pleasure. What you sense is always being evaluated within you, and if the spin you put on those sensations accords with your beliefs, you will feel positive emotions. Should your attitudes yield interpretations that collide with your beliefs, then you feel negative emotions. Sensations are clear and real; it is the mind that uses belief to interpret what is clear and real as being beneficial or dangerous. The reality is that what is clear and real is neither beneficial nor dangerous, except that thinking makes it so. Hence, to perceive reality in a way that is clear and true requires you to suspend belief or dispense with it altogether.

Meanwhile, your brain is also sensing all thought, notions, feelings, ideas, observations, stimulations, and bits of information by "touching" or manipulating (like squeezing a wet sponge) everything to detect if what is being processed is structure or behavior, or some proportion of structure and behavior. What your brain is sensing is actually the energy in your nervous system. That energy is tossed back and forth from one side of the brain to the other to notice if there is anything structural or behavioral to be perceived. Each of the mental senses is like a sensor for a specific quality of structure or behavior. We might also call these senses *filters.* The brain receives a nervous impulse from the physical senses and runs it through every possible filter to see which of the mental senses filters out or catches that impulse, thereby revealing any sensible structure or behavior the impulse may have. The brain appears to do all this automatically, and if there aren't any structures or behaviors to detect, the brain drops what it is processing as being irrelevant or continues to work on it. If nothing is resolved, a state of confusion occurs as the processing continues without sense having been made.

The more you pay attention to each of your mental senses, the faster your brain can do this work. It seems that paying attention to these mental senses is like clearing a path—a neural pathway—to that sense.

THOUGHTS ON THE MENTAL SENSES

The following two chapters contain a discussion on each of the mental senses. These senses have their location in the mind and are used for sensing the nervous energy of thoughts, concepts, attitudes, ideas, beliefs, statements, and the like. The mode of sensation is like the sensation of touch. The mind touches, handles, tastes, and squeezes the thoughts and impressions presented to it to probe and inspect them for their substance and how they relate to reality. The mind uses language as the vehicle for apprehending thought in the same way that the eyes use light as the vehicle for apprehending material forms, colors, and shades.

The sense of hearing is the external physical sense most like sensations of the intellect because the world of sound is both material and immaterial. What I mean by this is that the world of sound functions according to the laws of physics, but we can't taste, see, smell, or touch it. For all practical intents and purposes, sound is immaterial. In this way, sound is exactly the same as thought.

People who handle thought as though they were fondling, smelling, chewing, and inspecting it are generally good at thinking. However, I would qualify this by changing the word *thinking* to *thought-touching* or *thought-handling*. Thinking then becomes something else altogether. Thinking is the process of producing a thought on demand. When people with strong intellects encounter a thought or an idea, they at once rip the thought apart and tear it into pieces, not unlike a little kid tearing into his birthday presents to find out what they are. In the act of shredding a thought to pieces, they learn the nature of the words used to express the thought, the peculiar nature of the sentence construction that gives each word its own special meaning, and the relationship of each part of the thought to every other part. In doing this, they grab a clear imagination of what is meant by the thought or idea. When the idea is firmly conveyed to their imaginations, they are able to say the sentence back in their own words and retain every bit of meaning that the original sentence expressed. Any discrepancies in understanding (imaginative grabbing) between the original idea and the reprocessed thought becomes the subject of conversation until the idea has been clearly and fully understood.

Everyone, even those who are intellectually slow, can learn how to touch and handle thoughts competently because we all have the senses that are required (barring any sensory blindness). If you have never learned how to use your senses, they may be quite dormant, but they will awake when stimulated and will gradually become sharper, more flexible, faster, and more direct with constant use. Those of us who have been fortunate enough to meet someone who could teach us how to handle thought have a significant advantage over those with equally good minds who have not had that good fortune. If my book changes this inequity to any degree, I will consider it a success.

Chapter Nine

The Mental Senses of the Structure-Sensing Left-Brain

The senses of the left hemisphere[18] of the brain involve the aspect of reality we call order, form, pattern, structure, or rationale. Order is a structure of positions. Form is a structure of design. Pattern is a structure of events or conditions. Rationale is a structure of thought as governed by relationships.

When the brain is unable to sense structure, the incoming stimuli are interpreted as gibberish. In the absence of any stimulation of the senses that perceive structure, the brain will supply a structure by generating one within itself. This is important to remember and understand because it will influence your ability to manage what you experience and think. For this reason, I will reiterate it. In the absence of any stimulation of the senses that perceive structure, the brain,

[18] Although not a strict rule, for right-handed people, the left side of the brain is responsible for sensing structure. Left-handed people are usually the opposite.

when it perceives this deficiency, will supply a structure by generating one within itself.

You have no control over what your brain chooses to structuralize. The only thing you can do is preempt that process by seeking out, identifying, and creating sensible and perceivable structures. Whoever fails to manage this aspect of inner life may discover that their brain has selected a means of creating a sense of structure that works in opposition to their aims. For instance, if a musician wants to communicate music but fails to acquire an instrument that has a perceivably structured sound, their brain may structuralize that musician's rhythm resulting in a stilted or rigid but structured manner of playing. The musical result bores the minds of listeners.

Indeed, this is why some people have lots of ideas and others none. Having ideas is the result of a brain that detects too much structure and not enough behavior. To create the necessary sense of balance, the brain will produce ideas (a potent form of sensed behavior) to offset the presence of too much structure, but only if the nature of the structure is principled. To create an internal environment in which you get lots of ideas, you need to be paying attention to anything that can be construed as a structure. These are attitudes, methods, procedures, patterns, principles, rules, measures, forms, archetypes, shapes, etc.

If a person with an out of control ego lands in jail, the effect of being enclosed behind bars is perceived by their brain as too much structure, and its balancing behavior produces "stir-craziness." Prison violence is partly a result of prisoners' brains having endured too much structure over a long period of time or too high an intensity of structure over a short period of time. Urban graffiti is the brain's response to the excessive structure sensed from flat, boring walls and buildings.

On the other side of this coin is that of sensing too much behavior. When people misbehave because they can't, don't, or won't control their impulses, it is because their brains are begging for structure. This is probably why some people thrive in highly structured environments, such as being in the military, in prison, in school, or being a member of a religious order where rules determine what a person can and can't do. Children enter this world exhibiting a high degree of behavior, and they need to be given the right kind of structure to feel secure.

The types of ideas we need or desire determine which kinds of structures we pay attention to. From a practical point of view, every behavior can be reduced to a structure, even chaos. It all depends on how particular we get and how hard we look. Getting dressed may seem like a random behavior, yet each person gets dressed according to a predictable pattern, whether it is socks first or shirt first, right arm first or left arm first, etc. We usually don't notice or think about these habitual patterns of behavior, but it's important to think about them and every other habit we might have. This is why I emphasize that paying attention to sensation works to stimulate the Soul into action. When you feed your Soul attention-energy focused on structures, it will dish back an endless supply of ideas relating to the nature of the structures you attend to.

What follows is a discussion of each of the mental senses of the structure-sensing side of the brain. As with all our senses, some are easier to notice than others. For the sake of the reader, I will begin with those that are easiest to notice.

THE SENSE OF HIERARCHY

The sense of hierarchy is how we develop an imagination for what is important and what is less important. Since the principle of hierarchy governs everything in the universe, it is a good idea to become thoroughly acquainted with this sense. This principle governs the structure of matter from the simplest form to the most complex.

Most human institutions are founded on a hierarchy based on power or responsibility, or to serve the needs of all members equally by controlling the tendency for corruption. Human institutions become a source of dysfunction when the hierarchy becomes more important than the members of the institution. This was and is the major fault line running through communist institutions and religious cults.

Without this sense, making good decisions is impossible. People who are blind in their sense of hierarchy never seem to get the hang of how to make good decisions. They often abrogate their decision-making to others, thus becoming their slaves. The power of pundits and opinion-makers is their ability to get others to abandon their inborn sense of hierarchy. They offer easy to repeat doggerel crafted to control other people's decisions. This behavior, while attractive and easy to adopt, is evil because it is based on inducing fear.

A set of priorities is a hierarchy of which things come first and in what order. A method is a procedural hierarchy in which one thing comes before another. A family budget is a financial hierarchy that determines how a family's earnings must be spent to preserve the security of the family. That is, rent or mortgage must be paid before food, and food must be bought before entertainment.

Hierarchy governs everything in the universe. If we think nature is chaotic when we witness a violent storm, we should try to imagine what the world would be like if the principle of hierarchy were to be eliminated. The hierarchy of attraction is what makes electrons orbit the nucleus of atoms, moons circle planets, planets revolve around stars, and stars to form galaxies. The hierarchy of development is what makes embryos develop as they do inside the womb, seeds turn into plants and trees, and inventions develop, like the phonograph into a CD player. The hierarchy of systems puts the forests and marshes of the world before all others because the elimination of the forests would quickly lead to the total collapse of everything else in the world, ending all other less important systems.

HIERARCHY IN LANGUAGE

It is the grammatical aspect of language that is governed by the principle of hierarchy. In good writing, the hierarchy of every word has been made clear. The subject being the most important part of any sentence is an expression of grammatical hierarchy. When every word is in its right place, according to each word's importance, the meaning of the sentence is clear.

In order of importance, the predicate comes after the subject. The predicate tells us what the subject is doing. Any violation of these two basic hierarchical rules results in the perception of blather. To say, "People laugh," makes sense because we know what people are and we know what laughing is. When we put the two words together, we immediately note, according to the sense of hierarchy, that the word *laugh* refers to the word *people.* The sentence, "laugh people," doesn't mean anything because the verb *to people* and the noun *laugh* refer to nothing! However, it would mean something if we were to add a comma between the two words and follow them by an exclamation point, as in, "Laugh, People!"

In speaking, we use our sense of hierarchy to emphasize words of greater importance than the other words in a sentence. The more skillful a speaker is, the easier it is to follow their thoughts. Monotonous speech quickly puts us to sleep not because of the complexity of the language but because the speaker does not make the event of speech meaningful to his or her listeners.

Violating the principle and sense of hierarchy can have disastrous consequences when it comes to teaching. Perhaps the greatest disservice a school board can foist on the students in their school is to hire boring teachers. Boring teachers guarantee that only those students who are already interested in the subject or fearful enough of failing will learn. Boring teachers squelch the love of learning that all young people have. Education departments in colleges and universities seem to cultivate the notion that the art of rhetoric has no hierarchical place in the curriculum of trainee teachers, so students have to endure the agony of trying to look awake in class while their sense of hierarchy is being violated by a teacher's monotonous droning. By applying one simple hierarchical corrective, the dropout rate could be cut almost entirely. That corrective is this: Forbid from teaching any person who is unwilling to master the art of vivid and convincing expression.

HIERARCHY IN MUSIC

The principle of hierarchy in music governs the functioning of tonal scales and rhythm. In music using the Ionian Mode, the tonal center or tonic is the so-called "root" and is the note to which all other notes refer. When we refer to music as being a universal language, it is this hierarchical property expressed in pitches that makes it so. Music not based on tonal scales (atonal music) bears little or no relationship to language because, being atonal, no pitches refer to any other pitches, so it is devoid of the principle of hierarchy. Like language designed to confuse the listener or reader, this music sounds arbitrary and confusing because the principle of hierarchy is missing.

This is precisely the reason why atonal music sounds like gobbledygook to most listeners. Interestingly, Arnold Schönberg, the father of atonal music, made it a rule in this kind of music that no note or pitch be more important than another. His idea was that all twelve pitches should be treated as equals. He made it a rule to violate the principle of hierarchy because he had the deluded notion that the appreciation of tonal music (most of the music ever written) was a learned behavior. His conclusion based on this false notion was that a composer could invent any system for writing music they wished, and it would be accepted as soon as everyone learned enough about it. Unfortunately, this nonsense is much of what is taught today in colleges, universities, music schools, and conservatories. Like fascist dictators, atonal composers and theorists prevent students who don't like atonal music from advancing. They toss out compositions that are not atonal, and they do everything in their power to discourage musicians who dislike atonal music from exploring tonal music further.

Clearly, the sixty or so years since Schönberg's death have shown that most listeners have no interest in that kind of music, as much as musicians force others to learn about it. Listeners have no interest in it because it violates their sense of hierarchy. It takes a great deal of mental discipline to shut down and ignore the sense of hierarchy when it is being violated. This is also the reason why the people who like this kind of music are invariably intellectually and left-brain dominant. Most people are not both intellectually dominant and left-brain dominant, so they instinctively understand that what they hear needs to express references for it to make sense. They understand intuitively that art is intended to stimulate one's inner senses, not violate them. What is missing references or clearly perceived relationships sounds like nonsense, which it is. There is no art of any kind when this principle is absent.

Predictably, musicians who are forced to deny their sense of hierarchy by playing this music are usually unhappy people. A curious study that was done some years ago found that out of one hundred professions rated and ranked on job satisfaction, orchestral musicians ranked second to the bottom. The only professionals less happy with their jobs were prison guards. I can say that of all the musicians I know and have known, few of them were happy. Of course, the most successful musicians are happy...sometimes.[19]

The hope in all this bleakness is that the cognitive sciences are beginning to unlock the secrets of how people perceive. As we discover the mechanisms that

---

[19] While being interviewed on film, Sviatoslav Richter, the famous Russian pianist who was considered by some to be the greatest pianist of the twentieth century, admitted to being unhappy with his life.

govern perception, it will become clear that our inner senses function in specific ways. When artists, teachers, lawyers, etc. learn that it is the senses of principles with which they need to communicate, their work will make sense, not nonsense. Whoever masters the art of communicating with these senses will be ranked among the highest in their field. Artists will again be able to create paintings and sculptures that make the ordinary viewer feel ennobled and honored to have viewed their work. Teachers will be able to generate enthusiasm in their students for the subjects they teach.

HIERARCHY IN THINKING

The sense of hierarchy usually functions automatically until you need it for thinking. If you have not honed and exercised it beforehand, it is of little use to you when you need it on demand. The hierarchical sense is used to help establish priorities. Thinking about processes involves using the sense of hierarchy. Composing in the form of writing, music, or painting employs this sense all the time, assuming the artist intends to communicate. The creator of a work must sense the best order for the expression of it to make sense to the reader, player, viewer, or listener. Aesthetically speaking, things that fail to present a hierarchy are observed to have a sensory hole—something feels like it is missing. This is the problem with monotony in speaking and with uniform colors, spaces, and surfaces in buildings. Such environments are an invitation for meaningless effort. It is my sense that the loud and soft in music was invented to increase the perceptibility of hierarchy. The sense of hierarchy is the mind asking to have its attention brought to something meaningful and important. When this fails to happen, the mind is left without energy and is unfocused.

Learning to identify the principle of hierarchy at work is the best way to develop a heightened awareness of that sense. It is among the easiest of the mental senses to learn about and understand, and it is also one of the first mental senses to develop in young children. This means that young children can be taught about this principle and grasp its significance. One need only ask the question: What is the most important thing happening here?

THE SENSE OF LOGIC

The principle of logic is easier to discuss than the sense of logic, but by describing the principle, I will automatically refer to the logic that you can sense. The principle of logic is measured out in the mind according to regular forms of thinking: correlative thinking, associative thinking, contrasted thinking, processive thinking, reductive thinking, analogical thinking, additive thinking, and others of which I may not be aware. Correlative thinking is a form designed to bring together similar elements and to show linkage; in other words, similarity is sensed between two or more characteristics, which demonstrates linkage or correlation. Associative thinking is designed to bring together and show linkage in dissimilar elements; again, among the dissimilar elements, it is the characteristics that we sense as similar that show linkage. Contrasted thinking shows the nature of opposites by demonstrating the linkage of that to which the opposites refer. Processive thinking is designed to give step-by-step order in a way that shows linkage. For example, elements in the periodic table are ordered to enable sensing of "what comes after what" so that understanding how elements relate to each other is made easier. Reductive thinking is designed to disassemble parts to show their linkage; that is, when the parts become too complex for simple apprehension, the mind dismantles them to sense how they go together. When a child carefully dismantles a new toy to see how it works, that child is going through the reductive process to form a conception of the true relationships that make the toy work. Analogical thinking uses analogies and metaphors to produce clarity of conception. Finally, additive thinking takes a kernel, link, or chain of thought and develops it further; a single element is sensed while related or unrelated elements are brought to bear to sense the additive results. Variations in musical composition are examples of additive thinking. Each of these forms of thinking may be used to express truth or deceit.

The measuring or evaluating process (called *ratio* in Latin) has, in the past, been called reason or reasoning. *Ratio* is also the root of the word *rationalize.* As long as the act of reasoning is understood to be an evaluative process, as opposed to a self-justifying behavior, then using the term *rationalize* is good. The fact that reasoning is a methodical act of thought-craft in no way minimizes the fact that it is a sophisticated thought-sensing process. Every other mental or higher sense can and should be disciplined into a methodical act of thought-craft. Education's purpose, ideally, is to cultivate and train people to process and sense thought, information, impressions, feelings, and ideas by using their higher senses as clearly and as unaffectedly as possible.

Although logical thinking is often paraded as a trademark of intelligence, it should be remembered that intelligence existed long before Socrates turned logic into a systematic method of thinking. Real intelligence is the ability to grab the right attitude at the right time. If logic plays into that condition, then so much the better. If a person can't assume the right attitude to successfully serve the moment, then that person isn't intelligent, however logical their mind.

Michelangelo used the word *intelletto* in his writings to mean, I suspect, something akin to our word *intuitive* or *intuition.* Indeed, day-to-day experiences with people reveal that those who are rigorously logical in their thinking can also act in highly unintelligent ways because they lack intuitive skills. Hence, logical thinking and intelligence should not be equated—linked, perhaps, but not equated. I have never had an experience with a highly intuitive person who was not also highly intelligent in their behavior, in spite of often appearing to be unreasonable or illogical.

Highly intuitive people make leaps of logic instead of using the laborious step-by-step approach that most of us are stuck with. The behavior of making a leap in logic is like a glissando in music. An intuitive person senses and proceeds through every step or "note" in the logical process, like the musical scale, but they move from one step to the other so quickly that the result is a continuous blur of thought such that the outcome might appear to be intellectual nonsense. Those who are forced to work through every step usually condemn themselves to this torture because of doubt. Their doubt about the results of each step forces them to justify, rationalize, and support their position until they feel comfortable with the idea that they might be right, which slows their progress. This fear of being wrong is not something that normally plagues an intuitive person. Like Babe Ruth, they prefer to hit a lot of home runs and shrug off the strikeouts. It is exactly this kind of non-invested attitude that causes intuitive people to be distrusted by those who are less intuitive yet more rigorous in their logical thinking.

Using the sense of logic gives each of us the power to make leaps of logic, to penetrate deeply into any problem to find the right solution, and to engage in supra-logical thought like the kind J.S. Bach, Isaac Newton, Ludwig van

Beethoven, Albert Einstein, Rosalind Franklin, or Alan Turing used to achieve their remarkable results.

THE SENSE OF QUANTITATIVE PROPORTION

Proportion is the nature of the relationship of things, one to another. The sense of quantitative proportion is the ability to perceive the quantitative nature of those relationships. It is a sophisticated sense in that it can precisely discern mathematical ratios within a multi-dimensional environment. Anyone familiar with the ratios that form musical intervals understands the degree of finesse and precision the ear has for ascertaining these ratios, even when the mind itself is ignorant of them. What art is there to cooking except the precise proportioning of all the ingredients in their exact order and quality of combination? Any time you weigh and evaluate something, you are using your sense of proportion. This sense exists because the principle of proportion governs almost everything in the universe.

Our left-brain sense of quantitative proportion provides us with a way to realistically deal with the concept of amounts in relation to each other. Children initially develop their sense of proportion by deciding what kinds of food and how much of each kind they would like to eat. Through food, our sense of proportion can be easily cultivated, if only because everyone has to eat.

Interestingly, it is easier to recognize when something is out of proportion than when a proportion is right. When something is out of proportion, it appears to stick out or feel wrong. When everything is in correct proportion, nothing calls attention to itself, and everything supports a lively, interesting, colorful balance. Not surprisingly, the sense of proportion is highly refined in the best artists.

It is a fundamental truth that all things interrelate. To know the sense of proportion is to understand the nature of how things relate to each other. When we use our intelligence to understand the relationships around us and the intellect to unravel hidden relationships, we are using our minds rightly.

There are two types of proportion that govern nature: spiritual proportion and musical proportion. Spiritual proportions govern relationships that can be expressed using "irrational" numbers. Musical proportions govern relationships expressed by "rational" numbers. One, two, three, and so on, are rational numbers, while *Phi* (1.61803398...), *Pi* (3.14159265359...), $\sqrt{2}$, and $\sqrt[12]{2}$ are irrational numbers. All living things manifest both types of proportion in near perfect balance. Trees express the musical ratio 3:4 and the spiritual ratio 1:1.618 (the golden ratio) in their patterns of growth. If you tap on the trunk of a tree and then on the first branch growing off that trunk, the musical interval is a perfect fourth (3:4). Tap on the first branch off that branch, and again the interval is a perfect fourth. By tapping on every subsequent branch, and you will find that the intervals that sound are all perfect fourths. If the interval is anything other than a pure fourth, that indicates a weakness in the tree. Grasses grow according to $\sqrt[12]{2}$ (the irrational number that defines the equal-tempered musical scale), and you can hear this phenomenon on reeds, rushes, bamboos, and segmented grasses.

Human beings and all living things with skeletons grow according to the musical ratios of the overtone series in the pitches of their bones, and according to the golden ratio (1:1.618) in the relative sizes of their bones. To discover the fundamental pitch of the bones in anyone's body, tap on the base of their sternum (breastbone). The collarbone usually sounds a perfect fifth higher than the sternum (the fifth being the second overtone in the overtone series). Add to this the fact that the fundamental pitch of any individual within any vertebrate species will be equal-tempered to an A–440 standard, and you have an explanation of how nature produces trillions of individual timbres within any community of organisms, such as a human population or a rookery of penguins. Only one bone needs to have a different ratio for the voice's timbre to be distinctly different.

Nature also uses musical proportions to govern the selection of mates. Pairing in the best relationships is invariably a perfect fourth because the perfect fourth (not being in the overtone series) makes both individuals equal in dominance. It is also how nature guarantees that the sounds an organism makes will carry, even in a jungle. In this way, music is the sole human activity wherein both musical and spiritual proportions can achieve perfect balance. When a piece of music demonstrates balance in both its construction and performance, the effect of hearing the music excites listeners.

Every decision involves evaluating one thing against another to arrive at an acceptable choice. People who are good at making decisions go through this process of evaluation quite deliberately. Usually, they are fully prepared to accept the consequences of their decisions, whether positive or negative. People who have difficulty making decisions often have a "seat of the pants" attitude about this process. They dislike reasoning out the options available to them or living with their mistakes when decisions turn out badly. Too often, people who behave this way also hate having their decisions criticized because any criticism of the decision is a major assault on their person, and they feel foolish. Their failure to use their sense of proportion generates the fear of looking like a fool that, in turn, results in mental blockage, intuitive paralysis, or creative sterility.

There are other types of proportion, like proportion based on the human value of desirable outcome. Capitalism is a system of economics founded on the desirable outcome of economic return for a specified investment. Religion is a system of beliefs founded on the desirable outcome of attaining heaven, Nirvana, or whatever. Educational systems are founded on the notion of the desirable outcome of possessing a given body of information. Politics is based on the desirable outcome of obtaining, using, and keeping power. In these and many other forms of human behavior, the driving force behind them is a balanced proportion between the feeling of need that excites desire and the means of achieving the desire. The sensation of proportion is employed to evaluate the relative amounts of the feeling of need and of the best method for relieving or fulfilling that feeling.

Whatever we decide for ourselves, we sense these feelings and urges, feel desires, and experience compulsions in a vague but precise way. It is the nature of all the inner senses that they are both vague and precise. They are vague because they are not easily put into words, and they are precise because they are apparent to us. If it were possible to easily discuss them, they wouldn't be vague. If they were not apparent to us, they wouldn't be precise. They await scrutiny to remove the vague and to give form or system to the knowledge they present.

THE SENSE OF HARMONY

The harmonic sense helps you find the balance point between states of tension. This experience is most readily observed in expressive speaking. Grammar, which governs the location of words, their declension, their tense, etc., leads the mind forward in thought and then refers the mind's attention back to the subject of the sentence. When a speaker fails to apply the principle of harmony, the listeners are required to supply it themselves. The harmonic sense, however, is designed to sense the stimulus, not supply it, so if a listener is asked to sustain this for too long, they begin to feel abused. When this happens, the mind assumes an "I don't care" attitude.

When we sense that a thing or act is harmonious, we experience an intense feeling of well-being. The Psalms, as found in the King James Version of the Bible, and the Sonnets of Shakespeare are breathtaking in the way they stimulate this sense. Bach's, Mozart's, and Beethoven's music is no less riveting.

Literature, art, music, cuisine, gardening, interior design, architecture, and psychology all involve the sense of harmony. Even the study of law is an investigation of how the harmonic sense was used by others in the past. In other words, anything that expresses tension is sensible to the harmonic sense.

The figure of Lady Justice holds the scales of justice that represent social harmony and the sword of truth that cuts both ways, and she is blindfolded to show her impartiality. But the most salient feature of this figure is that it is of a woman, probably because women are often known to be better listeners and less aggressive than men. When the scales are out of balance, the result is social unrest due to the perception of injustice by the populace.

It is interesting that people can astutely sense harmony in one thing but fail to use it in another area. You may be habitually sensitive to harmony in art, but that doesn't mean you are accustomed to using this sense to resolve arguments. When you focus on enlarging your capacity to sense harmony in everything you do, you can develop the habit of using this sense to the point that it is common for you to do so. The trick is to focus on the moment of resolution. Whatever is incapable of resolution or seems perpetually unresolved is also devoid of harmony, for it is that point of balance or resolution between tensions that defines harmony. The interim expressions of tension or force do not in themselves constitute anything but discord and strife. Usually, the forces involved are structures versus behaviors. When behavior is negated, harmony is absent; when structure is absent, harmony is negated. Thus, any work that expresses non-resolution stimulates the sense of harmony in the same way that starvation stimulates the sense of hunger.

Part of the reason why our sense of harmony is so profound is that each of us is born equipped to sense it in our bodies. One of the first and most important discoveries in my quest to learn what the best musical instrument builders of antiquity knew was the source of our sense of harmony. I was standing in the shower paying attention to the sound of the high-pressure water hitting my head when I noticed that if I moved so that the water hit a different part of my head, the pitch of the water stream changed. I wondered if there were any relationships in the pitches I was hearing or if they were merely random. What I noticed was that all the pitches were harmonics of a single pitch. I further noticed that when I tapped on all the bones in my arms and chest, I could hear that they were tuned to harmonics of a basic pitch in my body. I had discovered a phenomenon that no one before me had discovered, or if they had, they never wrote about it.

You are born hearing the sound of your voice, your mother's voice, and the voices of other people in your mother's environment. Through those sounds, your bones resonate with the harmonics of the basic pitch in your body. This attunes your sense of harmony because all the bones are harmonically related to your body's pitch. Your genetic material determines your body's pitch and the harmonics to which all the bones in your body are tuned. I further conjecture that personality is related to this phenomenon and this is the reason why babies are born with full-blown personalities.

The word *personality* comes from the Latin root *persona,* meaning *mask,* but it is also derived from the two roots *per,* meaning *through,* and *sona,* meaning *sound. Persona* means *to sound through.* It is the tuning of your body and your bones that sounds through to create your personality. Incredible as this may seem, it is possible to accurately predict the personality of an unknown person if their fundamental pitch and basic tuning of their bones are known. Similarly, once someone's personality traits are known, it is possible to predict what their body-pitch is.

We always have this sense of harmony, yet there are times in our lives when we lose track of it. That happens during adolescence when our bones are growing so fast that our sense of harmony is confused by the dissonances and cacophony caused by the rapid growth of our bones. During this time, our ability to know ourselves from month to month is challenged, and we experience what psychologists call an identity crisis. During this time, our sense of harmony is stimulated by the presence of others who are experiencing the same degree of disorientation as we are. Even our parents have trouble recognizing who we are because our behavior becomes so different as we learn to adjust to every change in the pitches of our bones.

This is also a stage when our bones break easily, the cause for which I discovered as a result of my violin making. This is caused by an acoustical phenomenon I call the *distortion resistance effect*. I discovered that the great violins of the eighteenth-century Italian masters are tuned so that the vibrating areas of a violin's plates are tuned to musical ratios. When a violin has been so tuned, the result is that the strings of the violin become difficult to make vibrate using the bow. With violins that are not tuned using this principle, it is much easier to get the strings to vibrate because they don't resist the distorting action of the bow. This is the distortion resistance effect, which is now being called the "Hill Effect" by other violinmakers because I happened to be the first to identify the phenomenon as a cause and effect. As the harmonically tuned plates of violins cause a strengthening resistance against distortion, so does the harmonic tuning of bones in the body cause them to be more resistant to distortion.

It's not until adolescent growth finally stops that we are able to sense again the same harmonic relationships of our bones, one to another, as we experienced before our bodies began to grow rapidly. Our sense of harmony is now stimulated by the absence of dissonance and disorientation that was caused by the cacophony of rapid bone growth, and we are again able to recognize who we are by the harmony expressed in our bones. From this point on, our sense of harmony is stimulated by the harmonic relationship between ourselves and others around us. If ignorant of the effect our sense of harmony has as it relates to our bodies, we might form relationships with others on a myriad of ego-related criteria, which brings about what is known in music as a false relationship.

If you are attentive to your sense of harmony, you are well advised to establish relationships based on this sense as animals in nature do. By understanding the profound effect the sense of harmony has on your life, you can learn to respect this sense and use it to guide you in a way that brings you the greatest happiness.

THE SENSE OF BALANCE

The mind senses balance in much the same way as the mechanism inside the inner ear senses physical balance. Though analogous, they are not the same. You can be thrown off balance by a thought. For example, questions designed to induce a state of doubt often have this effect, as do new ideas and statements that challenge our expectations. The mechanism that allows you to sense balance is the subtle equilibrium that exists between belief and knowledge, or between fear of uncertainty and expectation. When you believe something, it is because you do not know it, cannot know it, or do not want not to know it. When you know something, you feel sure enough to have certain expectations about what you know. Few of us have real knowledge such that we are not thrown off balance by something unexpected.

The purpose of the sense of balance is to help you correlate the outer world, which you cannot know, with your knowable inner world. You will feel the unease of imbalance when you have difficulty making this correlation. Unfortunately, the standard assumption about what humans can know is the opposite. That is, the outer world is assumed to be the only thing worth knowing because the inner world is subjective in nature. I call it unfortunate because this assumption arises from a mind that is afraid of the certainty of the inner world because that world is subject to interpretation—as though the outer world were not!

Balance is a state wherein the messages from the outer world coincide with those of the inner world. As long as there is a fundamental agreement between these two realms, whether right or wrong, balance is sensed. Should any conflict arise between them, imbalance predominates. For instance, so long as your attitudes agree with your experiences, you cannot be confused, and so you experience balance. You can have a totally wrong-headed attitude and inaccurate information and be happily sure of yourself. Again, balance is sensed. Couple wrong information with the right attitude or right information with the wrong attitude, and imbalance and confusion will ensue. Balance is not a smart sense, it only tells you when something is out of whack.

The danger of not paying attention to this sense is the ease with which it is possible to slip into self-satisfaction or derangement. The fact that most people do not succumb to either condition is a testament to the positive effect that our sense of balance has on our mental lives.

THE SENSE OF ORDER

The sensation of order involves apprehending sequences, placements, series, or any consecutive structures. Nature, where nothing happens out of its right or appropriate sequence, is constructed according to the principle of order. Babies are never born before they are conceived, and rain never falls where evaporation and condensation did not first take place. It is the rigor with which nature adheres to this principle that gives us the notion that we live in an ordered universe. Every day, in every way, our sense of order is confirmed by nature.

When we sense a breakdown in order, we feel violated. Our sense of order is violated when we hear an improperly constructed sentence because the correct word order for our language has been drilled into us. Whenever we learn something that is sequenced, our sense of order is being trained to recognize a correct set of steps or relationships. If we have been taught a skill or concept that involves a sequence, we tend to react strongly to any violation or alteration of whatever sequence we have learned, even if what we learned is wrong. The sense of order helps us schedule our days, create agendas, or plan and order lists of things to do.

The sense of order is complicated because it usually works in conjunction with other senses. For most of us, it is subordinate to the senses of logic and hierarchy. When involved in developing a new process, an inventor senses the order of events or items used in the process by creating a logical, hierarchical framework from which to function. Since much of human activity has to do with process and processes, most of us are well in touch with the sense of order.

If we lose touch with this sense, we lose track of what we are doing. For example, you have probably experienced thinking about needing to buy something from a store, yet when you arrive at the store, you cannot remember what you needed. In trying to remember, you construct a picture in your mind of what you were doing in the exact order you were doing it, and you are then reminded of the forgotten object, hopefully.

Successful people usually develop habits and strategies that use their sense of order to make themselves more efficient. This is especially the case when they jot down the things they need to remember in lists, appointment books, calendars, notebooks, etc. as a supplement to the sense. When we characterize someone as being organized, we are actually saying that the person has a strong sense of order.

My mother used to regularly switch the furniture around in her house in a never-ending search for the best arrangement of her furniture. Only now do I understand this behavior as her unfulfilled sense of order needing to be resolved. In size, kind, or style, the individual pieces of furniture she owned had little relationship to each other, so finding the ideal placement that best suited the way she lived was difficult. Her sense of order kept her experimenting with different possibilities during the entire time I lived with my parents.

Much of how we remember things has to do with the order in which they are committed to memory. Developing a good memory entails making up a system that ensures accurate recall. Most memory systems stress the importance of sequencing and relating information to most easily memorize it. Relying on the sense of order to give information context helps to fix it in the memory. Usually, the more complicated a memory task is, the more we rely on the intellectual senses to plant information in our minds.

Sensing order is first developed when learning language. As is now generally understood, once the word order for a language is determined, it becomes fixed in the brain. When that fixed order is scrambled—as in the phrase, "fell stumbling he"—the confusion created by the disturbed sense of order causes the words in the sentence to assume enlarged significance. Any sentence can be scrambled to highlight shades of importance of different words. In this way, authors can direct a reader's attention or propagandists can manipulate their audience's feelings. Writing that communicates efficiently deviates as little as possible from word order norms and avoids disguising word order with a mess of unnecessary words and phrases.

There is a link between intelligence and the sense of order. An intelligent mind understands the problem of resistance to new ideas, and it accepts the difficulties involved in expressing them. While an intelligent person tends to be less tolerant of expression that does not rigorously present information in an orderly fashion, the more intelligent that person is, the more interested they are in the ideas presented and the less interested they are in how the ideas are expressed. The sense of hierarchy suggests that content is more important than form, but only slightly. In an intelligent person, the sense of order is cultivated enough to help ideas along the path of understanding, but only as long as the ideas are stimulating or compelling. What this means is that intelligence, as far as it concerns order, can be increased by paying close and careful attention to this sense. This may best be done by reading the works of interesting thinkers who were not great writers. Like training for a marathon in weighted running shoes, reading about important ideas that are poorly presented (almost any philosophical work will do) challenges the mind and makes dealing with well-crafted presentations easy.

Methodology is another word to describe ordered process. A method is the sequence of events in a process or technique. Anything that involves manufacture is subject to a method. This is as true for building a house as it is for building a competent mind. To violate sound methodology for the sake of expedience or pleasure usually spells disaster. The same can be said of a spiritual path. What the best method may be for reaching the goals you set yourself is not always obvious. You must rely on your sense of order to guide in charting a course through the unknown.

THE SENSE OF FORM

The sense of form exists to perceive the general principle of form. The principle of form governs the shapes of things, concepts, ideas, and expressions. Without this sense, you would be incapable of recognizing a sphere, a cycle, a sonata, or a gothic cathedral. This sense apprehends the outer limits of a thing and appreciates the filling. Like biting into a piece of pie, the apprehension of the wedge shape remains abstract until the contents are absorbed. For shape to have meaning, it must be "handled" both from the outside and the inside. To see a great organ in a church without also hearing it is like trying to read a language that we can't understand. We see the evidence of the expression, but it says nothing to us. If the organ case is beautiful, it is as though the calligraphy of the foreign script is attractive, yet the words still fail to mean anything. Unless form is penetrated both inside and out, the sense of form remains un-stimulated. An inspired performance of a piece of music simultaneously reveals the outer and inner form of the music. When this occurs, the mind is "blown away" by the sheer beauty of the experience.

In art, the same experience happens when observing a painting that reveals both its outer and the inner form at the same time. When this occurs, the painting appears to leap from the wall. If you gaze upon such a picture, the corners of the frame will appear to be pointing outwards with great intensity. Interestingly, when only the outer form is revealed, the frame appears static, and when only the inner form is revealed, the corners point inwards. When I have pointed these effects out to others, they have no trouble seeing them. If you are not looking for it, you are not likely to notice it. It is also interesting to notice which painting masters were able to make this effect happen consistently (Monet, Renoir, and Van Gogh), occasionally (Degas, Cassatt, and Manet), or rarely (Pissarro, Gauguin, and Seurat).

A building that has been designed from the standpoint of its outer form somehow appears dated, even if it is brand new. A supreme example of this is the Pompidou Center in Paris. Like a disemboweled monster, its trendy corpse awaits burial—an act to which, until now, only the pigeons oblige by depositing their droppings. This building has to be seen in person to appreciate the full irony of the colossal joke. It is perhaps a divine comment on the building.

The cathedral of Notre Dame has more pigeon droppings on it than the Pompidou Center, but we don't notice them. I suspect that when the outer form and the inner form are expressed as an integrated whole, the result is an effect of such naturalness that the presence of bird droppings become as obvious as they would be on a tree. When a building fails to excite the sense of form, we only notice the things that are wrong with it. The Disney concert hall in Los Angeles is also such a building, which has the form of an exploded blunderbuss with shards going in every direction.

In the Olympic sports of figure skating, diving, or gymnastics, the judges appear to be forming their opinions based on the degree to which the sense of form is touched as the contestants deliver their routines. When the sense of inner and outer form is missing, the routine is judged on what went wrong, not on what went right.

The question of what constitutes inner form and what constitutes outer form would need a doctoral thesis to answer. But I can say in brief that inner form is that which makes outer form appear as it does. The ingredients that make up the inner form are principles, inner functioning parts, inner functioning spaces, inner requirements, inner materials, etc. The outer form is the most efficient shape required to adequately present or protect the inner form. In the case of gymnasts and dancers, the inner form is the imaginative conception of the performer, while the outer form is the performance itself. With a musical instrument, such as a violin, the inner form is the sound-quality that the maker is aiming for, and the outer form is the box that makes the sound.

The actual appearance of outer forms that reveal and conserve inner forms is almost unlimited. Consequently, the experience of seeing an object is new, even if we've seen it a hundred times before. When outer forms fail to reveal inner forms, the individual objects tend to look uninteresting. In fact, the appearance of such paintings, instruments, or buildings may be different, but the effect of beholding them is the same—it is dead boring.

The sense of form endows us with the ability to understand wholes when only some parts are revealed. In this regard, the sense is holographic. It allows us to form a picture, whether true or not, from scant information; like a blind man who touches an elephant's leg concluding that he is touching the form of a tree. It also helps us make sense of new ideas via metaphors. (A metaphor presents a formal comparison between dissimilar subjects.) We use other expressive devices, like analogy and simile, to aid in conveying new ideas to people who are unfamiliar with them. The success of these devices is dependent on whether the formal comparison they make reveals the inner nature of an idea.

Unfortunately, we are not taught in school to appreciate form or cultivate the sense of it to the extent required for a honed and conscious use. A message might eventually penetrate into the awareness of educators that the purpose of geometry is to build an appreciation of and make real the forms, both mathematical and rhetorical, it seeks to describe. To the ancient Greeks, it was geometry that made possible the construction of their buildings, ideas, and philosophies.

If you take the trouble to train your sense of form, you will be able to learn much faster, enjoy your culture to a greater degree, and become successful at anything involving this sense.

THE SENSE OF DEGREE

As there are degrees in the measurement of a circle, there are degrees by which we can measure the effect of anything. It doesn't matter what scale is used. It could be a graduated scale, a placement scale, a musical scale, or something like a circle. By consciously comparing every experience to similar experiences on scales of degree, you can develop a high degree of sensitivity to sensed differences. The alternative is to function at the level of pure preference and say, "I like this," or "I don't like that." If you determine to what degree you were moved by something or to what degree you experienced an effect, you create a handle on the experience that allows you to recall it with greater accuracy. Imagine seeing a falling star, having never seen one before. Let's say that this star was the most brilliant ever recorded. How would you fully appreciate the experience if you had not spent time looking into the heavens and noticing that all falling stars are not of the same size or brightness? By sheer quantity of experience, you develop an awareness of your sense of degree.

One event in life that makes us aware of our sense of degree is the onset of puberty. At that time, we change more quickly than ever before, and we are able to notice the appearance of each new hair in all the familiar places. We see our peers undergoing changes too, but at different rates than ourselves, and we have a hard time avoiding comparisons. It is about this time that the sense of degree starts to flower, and we become increasingly aware of differences between others and ourselves. The process of noticing differences begins slowly, accelerates, and then gradually tapers off as we become more interested in other things.

Many of the degree-sensing skills we could master during this period are neglected through ignorance and lack of interest, yet whoever goes on to develop a high level of consciousness regarding degrees of sensibility can master the subtleties in almost any field of endeavor. When mastery proves elusive, it is usually due to poor acuity in this sense.

The best way to cultivate the sense of degree is to rate every experience on a scale that is invented for the type of experience you wish to understand and manage. Part of the craft or science of anything is in creating scales as a means of measurement. In science, the scales are usually actual tools of measurement, while for the sense of degree, you are the tool, experimenter, recorder, observer, sensor, processor, and assessor all wrapped up in the same package. The more dimensions of experience you are able to determine and the more differences you are able to apprehend, the more refined your sense of degree will become. This is what makes a connoisseur.

Of all the senses, the sense of degree facilitates conscious self-improvement. However, when you learn that "judging is wrong," a lesson that is often taught in religious institutions, the development of your sense of degree is stunted. By stunting it, you are cut off from further self-improvement. The solution to this dilemma is to distinguish between judging and condemning. When Jesus said that we shouldn't judge because we too will be judged if we do, I think he meant the word *condemn*. It is an all too human tendency to condemn what we don't like. When we rate something as inferior, we also tend not to like it. In doing this, we condemn what we rate inferior as well as the inferior thing's maker. Therefore, to properly cultivate the sense of degree, it is imperative not to fall into the trap of also condemning what you may rate as inferior or those who are responsible for it. At the same time, you are justified in rejecting that which is sensed by degrees to be inferior. Failure to rightly follow this fundamental principle to the right degree results in professional or personal mediocrity.

THE SENSE OF CLARITY

Clarity is sensed as the sharpness and precision of a given perception. An idea may be sensed as clear when it has the quality of being seemingly irrefutably sensible. In the same way, an expression is sensed as clear when it is communicated undeniably. It is possible to sense clarity about oneself when both body and mind work together in unison. Clarity may also be sensed when intentions accord with actions.

It is not unusual to sense the deprivation of clarity more than clarity itself. Often, we perceive more from the standpoint of a negative, absent, or deprived sensation than from a positive, present one. For instance, it is easier to sense that things are muddled and obtuse than it is to sense that they are clear. Sensation of clarity, in such cases, is of the characterization of the input rather than of the input itself. That is, the sensation of obtuseness of an input is clearer than the input itself.

Clarity is charged with qualities of crisp, articulated forthrightness. There is nothing soggy about clarity. We are able to perceive the qualities of directness and precision in things that are sensed as clear. There is no beating around the bush. It is almost the experience of something being "in-tune" that the mind tastes when it savors the sense of clarity. These qualities of clarity are extremely desirable, especially when they are found in musical instruments. The multi-million-dollar price tags for which Stradivari and Guarneri's violins sell are indicative of the value our culture places on clarity, for the violins made by these two makers stimulate the sense of clarity in listeners as each note played is impressed on the eardrum as though it were finely and delicately placed there. The cost of diamonds is further evidence that our culture places a high premium on clarity.

People who can express their thoughts clearly are admired. Written material that doesn't require rereading to make sense of it is normally taken for granted because of the clarity of writing. It is the downside of clarity that when it is palpable, it tends to be taken for granted. Realizing clarity in work is extremely difficult to achieve; therefore, it should be recognized and acknowledged when it happens. This is a problem in anything that is made. When work is made to enhance the stimulation of many of the mental senses, the mind notices nothing special about the work and takes it for granted. Only when the opposite effect negatively excites the senses are we quick to acknowledge the void or the violation experienced. This behavior occurs because whatever is made to enhance the perception of something being right in the minds of the perceivers is treated in the way we tend to treat nature—as though there is nothing special about it. The higher the quality a thing is made to be, the more it creates the sensation of being right and fitting, and the more the mind assumes it to be part of the intellectual landscape and not worth mentioning.

It is important to acknowledge high-quality work when you experience it because, by doing that, you are acknowledging the Soul of the one who did the work. When you do that, you also encourage your own Soul. Your Soul witnesses the acknowledgment you are expressing, and it will discover a means to do likewise for you in your work, and so it is with every quality and sensation that you recognize and actively acknowledge.

THE SENSE OF CONTRAST

The specific function of contrast in nature is to guide the observer to knowledge of differences. Many survival strategies in nature avoid contrasts in order to hide in plain view. You can see this in insects, spiders, skates, octopi, etc. as they adopt the coloration and behavior of the landscape around them to avoid being eaten. Predators have to notice subtle differences (contrasts) not to be fooled by this ruse.

The sense of contrast helps you develop judgment and avoid being deceived by phenomena in the world around you. But to use the sense of contrast at all, you must notice enough to have a concept of what is normal. Without knowing what is normal, it is hard to detect subtleties, and you are limited to gross contrasts, such as bright light and dark shadow.

The problem lies with *normal*. What is normal? I once asked my physician that question when I wasn't feeling well. He had my blood tested, and the results came back as "normal," but I still did not feel well. "What is normal?" I asked. He responded that the tests are designed to chart the average spread of what a state of health looks like. When the tests show raised or lowered levels of some substance in a person's blood, it indicates that something is wrong with that person. My blood told him I was healthy, and I told him that I wasn't. Who or what was he going to believe? Piqued, I suggested that it was probably normal for physicians to ignore what their patients were telling them and to dismiss complaints as "all in the head" because the well-being of the tests were more important than the well-being of patients. Only then did he reframe his attitude about what was normal.

Again, we are back to noticing details. The reasons why things work or don't work are often noticed in the subtlest shades of gray. Mark Twain observed that "the difference between the almost right word and the right word is really a large matter—it's the difference between the lightning bug and the lightning."[20] If I were a great writer, I would have taken the trouble to cultivate this sense to detect the right word in every case, but nature endowed me otherwise.

Where musical instruments are concerned, I have cultivated a specific knowledge of the distinctions to be made between the right frequency and the almost right frequency. In my business, it is called tuning. In painting, it is about the right color or shade versus the almost right color or shade. In comedy, it is about the right moment versus the almost right moment for saying a punch line.

The sense of contrast needs a wealth of information about the normal state before it can notice increasing degrees of subtlety between the normal and the slightly different. Great artists will often express a more complete range of feelings for their perceivers by using a range of behaviors to play with the perceiver's powers of observation. For instance, keyboard players are generally accustomed to developing contrasting behaviors, like loud and soft (*Forte* and *Piano* in Italian, respectively indicated in music by *f* and *p*). In musical scores, a composer might want the players to play extremely softly, which the composer will show by writing *ppp*, meaning *pianississimo* or extremely soft. So, there is a range of contrast from loud to soft that looks like this: *ffff* – *fff* – *ff* – *f* – *mf* – *mp* – *p* – *pp* – *ppp* – *pppp* (the *mf* and the *mp* indicate *mezzoforte* or *mezzopiano,* meaning middling loud or middling soft).

Other types of contrast can be used in music, like *staccato* (which means to leave a sound abruptly, quickly, or shortly) or *legato* (which means to connect one sound with the next so we can barely tell when the last note ended and the new note began). Taken altogether, the number of distinctions made in touch by the above is approximately twelve. A good professional pianist should have about seventeen different levels of touch.

Perhaps the greatest pianist of the twentieth century was Vladimir Horowitz, and he is said to have had twenty-nine different levels of touch in playing the piano. He clearly saw it as his duty to create a range of behaviors with which he could

---

[20] Alex Ayers, ed., The Wit and Wisdom of Mark Twain (New York: Harper, 2005), 252.

play with his audiences' sense of contrast. Every concert was an opportunity to offer a feast of subtle contrasts to the Souls of his listeners. The effect on me of hearing Horowitz in concert was noticing how my energy level increased throughout the entire concert so that I had more than five times the amount of energy at the end than at the beginning. That was a pivotal aesthetic experience because it taught me that the function of art is to feed the Soul, which energizes the perceivers. It gave me a sensory model by which to realize if musicians are doing their jobs or not, and to what degree they are successful.

THE SENSE OF LIMIT

How do you know when you have reached the limit? How do you know when you have come to the end of something? It is a profound paradox that in the infinity of the universe, everything has definite limits. The question, then, is if there is a limit to the infinity of the universe.

Astronomers peg the age of the universe at about fifteen billion years because that is about how many light-years away current telescopes can detect distant galaxies. Before telescopes became good enough to see other galaxies in space, astronomers were saying that the universe was the Milky Way galaxy and that the age of the universe was probably about 4.5–5 billion years old because that is how old the oldest rocks on Earth appear to be.

As soon as the Hubble telescope took the astounding deep field photograph[21] that showed thousands of galaxies in a specific "empty" area of space, the number of galaxies astronomers were projecting that existed in our universe was in the trillions. From this and other photos, they were placing the age of the universe at fifteen billion years, give or take a few. With each advance in technology, the estimated size and age of the universe increases. What would the age of the universe look like if we were to instantly occupy a planet at the other end of the universe and make another photograph with the Hubble telescope pointing in the same direction as before (i.e., away from Earth)? I suspect we would instantly discover that the universe had to be thirty billion years old, and the number of galaxies would be trillions of trillions. Were we to do the same thing over and

[21] R. Williams, The Hubble Deep Field Team, and NASA/ESA, "Hubble Deep Field," *Hubble Space Telescope*, http://spacetelescope.org/images/opo9601c/ (accessed Mar. 15, 2018).

over again, we would keep changing the figure by adding yet another fifteen billion years to the age of the universe. The age of the universe is merely an arbitrary limit based on our present capabilities of technically aided perception. Naturally, all this presupposes that the universe had a beginning. Until the idea of the big bang was invented, astronomers thought the universe was a constant.

What we are repeatedly discussing here is the concept of limits. Human beings are exceedingly limited in their ability to acknowledge their own limits. The only way we can sense limits is to pay attention to the ends of things. That is, you know when you get to the limit of this piece of paper because the paper ends. You know what the limit of this sentence is because you get to the end of it. You won't know the limit of this book until you read to the end.

From a perceptual point of view, we need limits to make sense of things, and we invent limits to give order and definition to things. But reality doesn't need a limit on time or space, only *specific* times and spaces. We need limits to think clearly about things; otherwise, sentences could run on, and we would be forever focused on discovering the meaning of those sentences, like when reading Richard Wagner's philosophical writings. We need to know how things end so that we can understand processes. We need to know why things end so we can understand causes and effects. We need to know limits because that knowledge gives us the illusion of having more control than we do. Let's face it, we don't like the absence of limits because it makes us feel at a loss. This is why everything human beings do has a beginning, middle, and end. Form is the shape of limit.

Wherever there is a beginning, middle, and an end there is a story. But what if our sense of limit was designed not to restrict our sense of reality but to extend it? In *Morphic Resonance*, Rupert Sheldrake in which he discusses how changes in problem-solving behavior among animals of a given type in one locality appear to change the problem-solving ability of all animals of that type throughout the entire world.[22] In other words, if a sparrow in Central Park in New York City learns to solve a problem, like how to open spent popcorn containers left as trash in the park, all sparrows throughout the entire world will thereafter learn to open

[22] Rupert Sheldrake, *Morphic Resonance: The Nature of Formative Causation*, (Rochester, Vermont: Park Street Press, 2009).

spent popcorn containers and eat leftover popcorn. This example of morphic resonance or quantum behavior suggests that the limits of learning can be extended almost indefinitely.

Taking this idea of morphic resonance further, if the Egyptians solved the problem of how to make stable pyramids, every culture in the world would then be able to solve the same problem with fewer mistakes. Since there are so many examples of this kind of behavior in human history, they form a body of evidence for the existence of a force in the universe that doesn't need proximity for morphic resonance to happen. This means that we could project that all human-like beings (who occupy worlds that orbit stars of similar size to our sun and that are on evolutionary time-tables like our own) will have made pyramids, just as we see in the multiple pyramid-building cultures of human history. Granted, all those pyramids look slightly different, but a pyramid is a pyramid.

What is amusing to me is how our culture is so proud of all its technical advances over the last one hundred years, but in all that time, no one has been able to equal the violins of Stradivari or Guarneri. This inability of modern minds to figure out what the ancients figured out is *epochal arrogance*—the notion or feeling of the superiority of everything done in the present time. Epochal arrogance has existed during every period in history and is one of the cardinal causes of people's tendency to repeat the mistakes of past generations. We are living during a time when the entire body of knowledge about how to make antibiotics is disappearing because large pharmaceutical companies don't consider them profitable enough to continue making, i.e., the limit of profitability has been reached. It is like what happened with the violin making business around 1780, in Italy, when all the ideas, techniques, processes, and traditional methods for making violins were abandoned. The same thing happened in ancient Egypt with the pyramid builders. Within a short period of time, the art of pyramid building had reached its limit.

The sense of limit clarifies life. It exists to allow us to understand reality. It allows us to extend our abilities to apprehend more of reality than we normally limit ourselves to. Without this sense, little would make sense, be comprehensible, or pleasurable.

The purpose of my projection of a limitless universe was to show how the human mind seems to need limits. But there are parts of the mind wherein limits can be broken, as in the limitlessness of learning. Our imaginations are capable of expanding the limits of awareness, and the extent to which we can invent alternate realities is proof of this. Every invention that humans create expands the collective consciousness of a broken limit. Every improvement does the same. This book exists because of the invention of the computer. If I had had to write in long hand or use a typewriter, this book would never have come into being. Because of my literary impairments, I needed the aid of something with the capabilities of a computer to codify my thoughts. A limit was broken! And, if Mr. Sheldrake is correct, what I have written should make it possible for every person to become aware of their aesthetic self.

THE SENSE OF EQUIVALENCE

Our sense of equivalence accounts for our ability to create political systems in which all individuals are theoretically equal under the law. At the beginning of the twentieth century, there was a great experiment in equivalence established in Russia—Communism. Communism attempted to create an economic system based on equivalence. This idea attempted to put into place the notion that all work is equally valuable. In the throes of the experiment, people discovered that it wasn't working, so the Communist leaders forced everyone to accept the experiment as a fact of life at the risk of being punished if they resisted. The result was seventy years of disastrous dictatorship in both Russia and China.

The experiment in Communism proved that where wages for work is concerned, equality does not exist. The free market determines what work is worth, and our sense of equivalence determines how much we are willing to pay for that work. Using our sense of equivalence, we may decide that one hour of work by an experienced lawyer is worth the equivalent of fifty hours of work by someone cleaning floors in a fast food restaurants.

When we use instinct to divide substances in half, it is our sense of equivalence that is at work. A child is often taught to use their sense of equivalence when cutting a cookie in half, but they are then forced to accept that another child will get the first choice over which half of the cookie to eat. Knowing this increases the child's awareness of equivalence because it stimulates them in trying to cut exactly down the center so that no child gets a smaller or bigger "half." It is amazing how children respond to this particular sense. They feel deprived if their sense of equivalence has been violated.

Much of how we assess value is connected to this sense. We rate how one type of work has a certain monetary value and is worth more or less than other types of work. Similarly, we project the worth of a person based on what kind of work they do. This is the mechanism by which people make choices about the type of work they wish to do. This can become a problem when parents project onto their children a false sense of the value of work and laud certain types of work over other types. The result of this poor parenting is that children spend their lives doing work that someone else wanted them to do because of their prejudices. Life is too short to be living the lives that others want us to live. Every child deserves the possibility to choose the work they most enjoy doing, as long as they have the power to succeed in doing that work at the level of quality required.

It is a realization for each individual to experience that they do not have the drive, ambition, or skills necessary to do the kind of work they would love to do and that they need to choose work that better suits their personal inclinations. In such a situation, the sense of equivalence can drive a person to despair when they discover that they don't have talent equal to what others have, especially when the result is that they must give up a dream to do their desired work. That person may even use the sense of equivalence to measure their worth because they become so possessed of the notion that they must do or be something to consider themself worthy. These errors in thinking have to do with the mind and how it interprets value and worth based on the sensation of equivalence.

When we seek to do what is in our Souls to do and are content and happy to be doing that, then is this sense truly satisfied. It is a tragedy when a person's Soul seeks fulfillment in one kind of work, but social, parental, and cultural forces work against what that Soul would choose to do. Human institutions and parents need to discover what a child's Soul is meant to do and figure out a way to let that happen and encourage it. In this regard, I had especially wonderful parents.

THE SENSE OF NUMBER

The brain is constantly sensing number. My wife, Marianne Ploger, observed that the brain is a counting device because it is constantly counting the vibratory patterns streaming in from outside. Light, sound, taste, smell, regeneration, pressure, logic, harmony, integrity, honor, probability, and principle are all forms of vibration that are registered as senses and are perceived because they are all forms of vibration. Light and pressure are easily explained as vibration, while logic, honor, and principle are harder to explain.

Logic is like a static form of vibratory relationships. If I say, "A equals B, and B equals C, therefore A equals C," I am expressing a concept of equal relationships. Since everything in the universe exists as an expression of atoms and molecules in motion (vibration), and A refers to something, even a thought, then A represents a form of vibration that can be counted by the brain as it senses the concept. Similarly, *honor* and *principle* have an even higher rate of vibration because they refer to states of mind that need energy to illuminate the Soul. When we act honorably or perceive an honorable act, our Souls are thereby illuminated.

We use our sense of number to determine something like whether or not there is enough food in the refrigerator to last the next few days. Despite this being tricky to determine, the Soul does it by using the brain's sense of number to calculate at least six things:

(1) the number of individuals that need to eat
(2) the amount they are likely to eat if unrestrained
(3) the amount of food-stuffs available
(4) the kinds of foods that will appeal to some people more than others
(5) the types of dishes that can be made with the available food-stuffs
(6) whether any one food-stuff is closer to rotting than another

All these factors need to be carefully calculated so that none of the food is wasted and everyone is satisfied eating what is made. The mind is not normally able to deal with the complexity of such a disparate set of conditions, yet mothers do this all the time when deciding what to feed their families.

Another way the sense of number works is in the usual arithmetic manner, like when adding two numbers and identifying the correct sum. This is a crude form of sensing number that is simple enough for the mind to handle with significant ease.[23]

The ability to reach into a container and pull out the exact number of pins needed to pin an article of clothing that you are sewing is another way the sense of number is manifested. Similarly, reaching into a container of nails and extracting the exact number you need to build the substructure of a wall requires the sense of number.

THE SENSE OF ENCASEMENT

Encasement is a universal principle that manifests as something soft on the inside surrounded and protected by something considerably harder and tougher on the outside. The sense of encasement allows you to sense this condition in diverse forms. The amoeba is a single-celled organism that challenges the sense of encasement because the casing on an amoeba is a super thin membrane that moves and adapts itself to the environment. The earth is also an encased form, but of a far cruder variety than an amoeba. Likewise, all crustaceans are paragons of encasement because their shells act to enclose the softer muscles and organs of their bodies. Your brain is located in the skull that encases it; yet interestingly, the rest of your body is the opposite because your hard structure-forming skeleton is surrounded by softer tissues.

We use our sense of encasement to determine if and how things and ideas are constructed. The ultimate purpose of this is to decide how to act in relationship with things that may be encased or not. For instance, you appreciate how delicate an egg is because its encasement suggests that there is something soft and valuable inside. Were you to ignore the signs coming from handling the egg, you would likely break it and lose its food value.

---

[23] One way our sense of number is being seriously crippled is that learning to calculate in the head is now no longer being required of school children because we have computers to sense number for us. For centuries, the Chinese have had hand-held calculators (abacuses), but they still require every child to learn to add, subtract, multiply, and divide in their imaginations using an imaginary abacus with their fingers. Maybe we can learn a thing or two from the Chinese.

This particular sense makes you aware of structure in a manner that is easily perceived. Without it, your ability to appreciate non-formal structures would be seriously limited, and your appreciation of structures would be confined to things like those found in geometry.

Encasement is not just for solid objects. When words are put to thoughts, the sounds of the words encase the more fragile aspects of meaning. Ideas can also be encased in images. Feelings are encased in the affects used to project them. Intentions are encased in actions. Attitudes are encased in behaviors.

A lawyer would use this sense to discover if a prospective client has grounds to bring charges against another party. The client would need to have justification, or the case wouldn't hold up in court. Here, the law encases the offense. An actor would use this sense to decide if a particular role would suit him, relative to his career. A teacher might use this sense when searching for the best way to get her students to understand a specific concept. The students' learning behaviors encase the all the possible problems and workable strategies. A doctor would use this sense to determine the prognosis for the disease from which his or her patient is suffering.

Encasement lends structure to an array of different conditions and behaviors. An inability to sense encasement might lead a person to make decisions that are counterproductive because they are unable to formulate a means of thinking about problems as a whole. Often, discussing a problem with friends can lead a person to view that problem as if observing the situation from the sidelines. That, in itself, encases the elements so that they are contained enough to achieve a certain perspective on the problem.

Though it is not one of the more glamorous senses, the sense of encasement helps all of us organize our lives, thoughts, and actions. It does so because it is closely linked to structures and behaviors, as well as the sense of limit.

THE SENSE OF DIRECTION

You use your sense of direction to evaluate where you are going and how to get there. The sense of direction works in a geographical situation in much the same manner as it does in life. Without a clear sense of direction, you will have no idea where you are going or how to get there. If you live life without a clear sense of direction, your life becomes aimless and useless, even to yourself. Your sense of direction tells if you have taken a wrong turn or bucks you up when you feel as though you've lost your way.

For those of us who are blind in the sense of direction, as can happen with any sense, life is made all the more difficult because it has no direction or purpose. This is not to say that life has to have purpose, but whatever purpose we set for ourselves, the sense of direction will work when we become momentarily distracted. It will bring us back to the course or reset the course to make a necessary detour.

Since any of us could be blind in any one of the senses, it is important not to condemn others for a blindness from which we do not suffer. By understanding that each sense can be either missing, dormant, or active, you can have more compassion for others who are daily challenged by their blindness, be it in their sense of direction, their sense of degree, or their sense of sight. When you are able to distinguish between these three specific conditions that every sense may be subject to, you can illuminate the lives of others by rousing in them an awareness of each sense until full awareness is achieved. Until now, the only recourse was gratuitous criticism when there was a blindness or perceptual hole. In these cases, criticism is tantamount to bullying.

We each occupy a highly complex organism called the human body. That complexity challenges some, overwhelms others, and leaves many in a state of confusion. Those of us who step up to that challenge and work hard to pay attention are often inclined to ridicule others who fail to behave as we think they should. If you notice blindness in another, first make sure that you have none of your own. Remember, we are all pedaling as fast as we can in this bicycle race against time, even if that doesn't appear to be the case.

THE SENSE OF FOCUS

Focus is to the mind what glasses are to those whose eyes see imperfectly. The sense of focus brings thought, attention, awareness, and feeling into view more perfectly, but not flawlessly. Flawlessness is a condition rarely to be found anywhere in nature. *Perfect* merely means complete. The sense of focus allows you to perceive more completely than you would otherwise.

Those who wrongly use their sense of focus to notice the flaws in everything and everyone are like the movie critics who, incompetent to make a movie themselves, self-righteously harp at the flaws in the labors of others. Someone far greater than most of us once said, "the tree is known by its fruit." The function of criticism is to lead to improvement, not to diminishment. If you fail to grasp this, your misapplied sense of focus is rendered dull and useless for more important uses, like when a chisel's edge becomes dulled after being used in place of a screwdriver.

The function of your sense of focus is to make sure that you leave nothing out. It is with all your other senses that you can learn to know when that happens. Even so, the sense of focus can keep you rigorous and honest with yourself. It serves you well when you use it to decide on the most important events in your life because it makes sure you leave no consideration uncontemplated.

Reality, like life, is not fair. We are not all endowed with equal faculties or opportunities. When we focus on our senses or on helping others to focus on their senses, we are at least helping to level the racecourse so that everyone has the possibility of crossing the finish line.

It is important not to confuse the sense of focus or being focused with single-mindedness. An animal is single-minded when it becomes a predator. Single-mindedness could also be the cause of an animal's downfall should it fail to notice a predator that has its sights on it as a meal.

When we use our sense of focus, we are able to take in the whole picture as well as the details. We are not satisfied with the appearance of completeness—we insist on total completeness. Focus brings clarity to completeness because what is incomplete appears fuzzy to the sense of focus. We don't need extensive knowledge of a thing to sense fuzziness of incompleteness about it.

I have learned about this sense through the acoustical property of focus over a long period during my experiments in violin acoustics. The best violinists are able to detect the slightest lack of focus in the sound of a violin. Because I don't play the violin myself, I made it my job to figure out what was missing in the sound that caused it to be unfocused. Not surprisingly, the source of focus in a violin's sound turned out to be the degree to which every acoustical feature of a violin has been managed so that it emanates from the place where the sound was made.

The sense of focus can be trained in a variety of ways. Listening to the conversations of others and noticing the degrees of focus in the various points of view is one way to develop that sense. Comparing sounds from different sources, studying painting, and observing nature to notice how natural systems are designed to survive are all ways one can cultivate an awareness of this sense.

MINDING YOUR OWN BUSINESS

We cultivate a condition of "un-focus" when we insist on minding everyone else's business but our own. When we mind our own business, we make it a point to be clear in our minds about whose problems are whose. Busybodies make other people's business their own business. They are blind in their sense of focus because they can't notice the difference between what they are doing and what others are doing. So interested are they in what others are doing that they get nothing done except meddling in other people's affairs. Cultivating the sense of focus means attending to your own affairs and avoiding meddling in the affairs of others. Focusing on solving one's own problems is enough to keep any intelligent person busy for a lifetime.

Someone once said that the difference between a normal person and a genius is how long they can stay focused on solving the same problem. This is an interesting thought to contemplate because being focused is not necessarily the same as using the sense of focus. Being focused can represent a kind of mental myopia, but using the sense of focus never deteriorates to that level. On the contrary, using the sense of focus and being able to entertain a constant, consistent train of thought about a problem until it is solved requires *eagle vision.* This is a phrase coined by my wife, Marianne Ploger, to help her musicianship students increase their performance accuracy.[24] To describe mental myopia and how it relates to making errors in musical performance she also coined the phrase *chicken vision.* No better metaphor can be found that describes the two opposing states of focus and

---

[24] Marianne Ploger, "The Three Causes of Error," *The Ploger Method,* http://plogermethod.com/the-three-causes-of-error (accessed Mar. 15, 2018).

un-focus, or of a mind-set of paying attention as opposed to that of one made rigid by fear. People who exhibit the mental myopia of chicken vision make poor musicians. Eagle vision is required where breadth of attention is essential, especially when a problem may take years of experimentation to come to a good result, as it often does in the sciences.

THE SENSE OF GRAVITY

We have a sense of gravity to guide us towards what is real, meaningful, and true and away from what is fake, meaningless, and false. Here, the word *gravity* does not apply as it would in physics—it is more akin to the word *gravitas.* Thoughts and ideas have gravity, or gravitas. What imparts gravity are the universal principles. What steals gravity from thoughts and ideas are emotions and all the energies stemming from the primitive brain.

It is essential to distinguish between gravity and loudness. Loudness comes from the emotions and the ego. Unless these forces are held in check, they can deceive you into thinking that what is louder and more insistent in your mind has greater gravity. That is a description of something being more intrusive, rather than having greater gravity. A comparison that works is how the sound of a great clavichord, which is roughly the same volume as the sound of typing on a computer keyboard, has more gravity of sound than the loudest amplified sound of any electric guitar. Take away the amplifier, and the sound of an electric guitar simpers and whimpers with all the strength of a stretched rubber band. A great clavichord, as soft as it ever is, sounds majestic like a cathedral, yet charming like the thought of a kitchen filled with the odor of freshly baked chocolate chip cookies.

In nature, you can most acutely notice your sense of gravity at work. Experiencing the power of a great waterfall through its spectacular sight, its thunderous roar, the fresh smell of its mist, and the sensation of inevitability it stimulates sparks inspiration in the Soul as a sense of gravity. I have observed no scene of greater gravity than standing at the edge of the Grand Canyon to marvel at the majesty and depth of it all. Yet that pales in comparison to the sensation of gravity when observing the intricacy and completeness of an insect or spider that is no larger than the head of a pin. It's mind-boggling that nature can construct tiny living creatures of such complexity and completeness in every detail.

There is a tendency to substitute the word *deep* for gravity when hearing important, personally meaningful thoughts. Though the substitution is not altogether off base, the sentiment expressed only results from the sense of gravity when the sentiment is real and not used as flattery.

Because gravity is deeply connected to memory, it is easy to mistake memory instilled by fear as having gravity. Unless the experience was harrowing, like falling off a cliff or being severely abused by a guardian, painful or fearful memories have little gravity by themselves. It is how the Soul is affected for which the sense of gravity is best attended. Whatever enhances the Soul or its condition possesses gravity in its essence.

Chapter Ten

The Mental Senses of the Behavior-Sensing Right-Brain

Just as nature has equipped us all with at least seventeen left-brain senses that sense the structural aspects of reality, nature has also equipped us with at least fifteen right-brain senses that sense the behavioral aspects of reality. Remember that everything in the universe can be understood as being a form of structure (stars being spheres), a form of behavior (nuclear fusion), or a combination of the two that results in perfect balance. The ancient Chinese symbol for this dual nature behind reality is the Yin Yang symbol.

Figure 11. The Yin Yang symbol.

When the balance in nature is disturbed, the disturbance itself is always a form of behavior. The senses of the right-brain are needed to behold and appreciate these behaviors.

THE SENSE OF FLOW

The sense of flow relates to the nature of the connectedness of things. Those things can be ideas, rivers, traffic, time, planets in orbit, etc. We have a sense of flow to sense the universal principle of flow. This principle governs the manner in which everything in the universe connects to everything else. Our sun connects to our galaxy as well as to all the individual stars in it, and our galaxy connects to all other galaxies, including those that are thirty billion light years away and beyond. The universe is in a state of continual flux, flowing in every direction at once and at different speeds.

With the sense of flow, we perceive everything around us and inside us as being part of that continuum flowing at innumerable different rates. By sensing the things around us, we can notice patterns of organization in how things are different based on a given scale of time. We can notice that it is morning because the sun appears to be rising above the horizon. If cloud cover interrupts our ability to notice changes, we can project where the sun probably is because of our memories of its flowing movement across the sky.

Time is artificially divided flow. Without flow, time would not exist. Without flow, movement would not exist. When we sense time passing, it is because we are parsing out flow based on the manner in which everything has previously appeared to flow. So the sense of time is actually based on the carefully divided memory of flow that happened before. This is why being completely present feels timeless. By focusing on the present moment of how things are flowing, we lose the sense that anything ever happened before. This is how supper gets burned when you take a minute to focus on something more interesting. Before you know it, an hour has passed, and the food was long ago burnt to a crisp, yet you are always surprised because "it couldn't have been more than a minute or two."

The sense of flow informs us if others are well or ill because illness produces an interruption in a healthy flow of energy. This sense also informs us if others are mentally competent or incompetent, able or unable to focus, and think clearly or not. In traffic, when other drivers disregard the way traffic flows, we tend to assume that those drivers have no business being on the road because they violate our sense of flow with their erratic behavior that forces us to cease flowing or move out of the way.

The sense of flow also allows us to notice if and how thoughts connect because we are able to "touch" with our minds the logical flow of those thoughts and how they connect with all other thoughts we have had.

There exists in flow the absoluteness of truth. The philosophy of relativism suggests that truth is relative and is dependent on each person. Absolutism suggests that the truth is absolute and unchanging. Because of flow, we know that all things are changing, and since this is one truth that never changes, we know that truth is absolute. As for relativism, it is people who are relative because people change all the time; thus, their view of the truth, which is based on where they stand relative to the flow of reality at any given moment, is reliable to the degree they are free of vested self-interest.

Sensing flow of thought is how we normally "read" the thinking of others, respond to speeches, tell if music works for us, or listen to what others are saying. If there is any moment of cessation in the flow of thought, we will become disturbed by the feeling of blocked or stopped flow. Most of us are very sensitive to flow of these sorts.

When there exists a continuity of action without flow, like when actors are saying their lines without attempting to communicate with their audience, we feel left out because of the absence of flow of communication. Sensing flow creates the feeling of being a part of something. Observing action when no flow is intended or expressed makes us feel isolated. When flow is present, we feel somehow connected to what is happening. This is probably why so many people prefer to be spectators at a sports event rather than at a classical music concert. The players at the sports event understand where the game is going and intentionally play at their uttermost to move the game along, which keeps spectators riveted to their seats. In most classical music concerts, the music moves along only because the players maintain the music's beat. The problem is that maintaining a beat can be done by a machine (musicians are not required), and we rarely view the rhythm of a machine as flowing. When a machine becomes defective, we notice stoppage, but stoppage of action is not cessation of flow. Stoppage is a disruption of continuity, not of flow.

It is possible in music and in conversation to have a disruption of continuity of sound without a cessation of flow. For example, when a speaker pauses mid-sentence to think about what to say during a conversation, the continuity of speech is disrupted but the flow of thought is maintained. In this way, cessation of utterance becomes how thought flows.

For music to have flow, musicians must intend to deliver up musical thoughts for the consideration of listeners. Strict flow of musical thought, not beat, must be maintained or the music will be halting, even if the beat and notes continue to be performed. When players, sermonizers, teachers, musicians, and athletes intend their actions, that is when they connect with their observers through flow.

THE SENSE OF RELATION

The sense of relation enables you to notice that things connect, and it enables you to notice how those things connect. It is an absolute truth that everything interrelates, and it is the job of your mind to notice how this can be. Indeed, it is the most important job for which the mind was designed. The interrelatedness of everything is a major source of confusion in the mind, but for the sense of relation. By constantly seeking to understand how everything in the universe relates to everything else, you can become more intelligent and less confused.

It is a dull mind that is used for purposes other than noticing the intricate interrelatedness of everything. Sometimes success, or the lack of it, in noticing how everything interrelates accounts for why we might give up on life. Faced with so much for which to be responsible, we want a way out, or if we are unable to see the interrelatedness that others notice, we give up on the quest because it seems hopeless. It is precisely this that our minds evolved to resolve. Without the existential pressure to figure out why calamities appear from nowhere, we have a tendency to believe that such things are the wrath of God in punishment for our sins or sins of others. It is our ability to question reality that brought about our fundamental level of intelligence. This, and perhaps only this, is what sets humans apart from other life-forms on Earth. All other creatures go with the flow and accept where it takes them without forming assumptions about the nature of God.

The way things relate is governed by the universal principles. This is why using universal principles as our basis of inquiry will invariably lead to an increase in intelligence. How rocks and dogs are related is not just in the physical makeup of the molecules comprising them but also in the fact that they are expressions of complex processes brought about by universal principles. That we may view rocks and dogs as being so completely different that they share almost nothing to relate them is due to our entrenched laziness. What is obvious is that dogs and rocks are different, but what is not so obvious is that they both exist in harmony with the flow of reality, which is something that challenges our apparently superior intellects.

The point here is not to explain how dogs and rocks interrelate but to issue that challenge, the quest for which requires your sense of relation to be honed razor-sharp. Reality doesn't test you to declare you a winner or loser but to light in you the fire of spiritual inquiry. Not everyone is meant to keep that spiritual flame at a white-hot setting; though everyone, no matter their status, gifts, or condition, can work the bellows to generate that white-hot flame. As in most human endeavors, it is just a choice.

Relating to the spiritual realm is probably the most efficient means by which you are able to cultivate this sense of relation. Without this sense, you wouldn't be able to perceive "The Force," to use George Lucas' term from *Star Wars*. You can't feel The Force if you can't relate to it as a sensible phenomenon. By actively questioning how everything interrelates, from the grandest to the most minuscule, you can gain a palpable sense of everything's interconnectedness. You can sense how effects relate to causes, how qualities relate to universal principles, and you can learn to perceive these with clarity and certainty.

In many ways, works of art function like movies. But it is far easier to achieve a lively effect with movies than with paintings because of the nature of moving pictures. Since it is liveliness of effect that stimulates the viewer to relate to a work of art, making art that relates to the observer is far more difficult than making a pretty picture. As many aesthetic principles as possible must be present for a work to have an effect of liveliness. This is as true for a painting as it is for a building, a dance, an interior decoration, a sculpture, a book, a poem, or a piece of music. When universal principles are present and rightly applied in a work, the sense of relation is palpably stimulated in the observer because the observer has multiple possibilities of reference with which to relate to the experience. When few principles are present, the artist must appeal to non-aesthetic references to create in the observer a sensation of relation. This is the ploy used in collage, which functions on the hope that some of its images or texts will hit home with the viewer.

Great music speaks to the feelings of the listener. When the affects expressed in music are recognized at some sublime level, the effect is to draw tears from the listeners. The sense of relation connects the sounds heard to feelings felt or recalled.

THE SENSE OF RHYTHM

The sense of rhythm has two correlating aspects: measurement and the pattern of impression. Without measurement or a pattern to impress on an observer, there cannot be rhythm. If either the measurement or the pattern of impression is too complex or too subtle, the mind fails to recognize a rhythm. The seasons of the year are both measured and patterned—they are measured by the progression of the earth in its orbit around the sun and patterned by the earth's axial tilt. This produces a pattern of shortening days and gathering cold until the pattern reverses at the winter solstice for the days to lengthen until the time of the summer solstice.

Music trains one's awareness of the senses of rhythm, melody, and harmony. Where rhythm is concerned, the important consideration is the feeling that the measured pattern gives. For instance, a composer can write a waltz, call it a waltz, and still have the music played in a perfectly measured manner, which is boring. The result is not rhythmic until a pattern is perceived, and neither the metered notation nor the time signature guarantees the presence of a perceivable pattern. To be a waltz, the music must be played with the characteristic waltz pattern of stresses, punctuations, and elongations of the beat. In essence, it must feel like a waltz to be one.

It is the perception of a pattern that creates the feeling of rhythm. Until a pattern becomes palpable, the brain registers the effect as similar to being told what the pattern is but without experiencing the feeling of it. Unless the effect registered in the brain is the feeling of rhythm, rhythm doesn't exist (except as a concept). This is especially true where rhythms of a large scale are concerned. The rhythmic cycle of the solar system as the sun tears around the center of our galaxy is supposedly about two hundred million years. That amount of time is too long for a human being ever to feel its rhythm. The time it takes the earth to orbit the sun is 365 days, which is about as much as a human can handle from a feeling point of view. Were it not for the yearly pattern of changing seasons, that property of measured time would not likely be felt.

At its heart, nature is constructed of rhythm within rhythm within rhythm within rhythm, and so on, until the scale is reduced to such a degree that most people can't fathom the rhythm at all. This is the case with molecules, atoms, and subatomic particles. So, it should not surprise us when man-made institutions and behaviors are also cyclical or tend to appear rhythmical.

The spiritual dimensions of rhythm are as subtle as breath. If you focus on the rhythm of your breathing, you can notice that the natural rhythm is slower than the rhythm of your heartbeat. An adult heartbeat averages around eighty beats per minute, while breathing at rest occurs about thirty times per minute. When you focus on the physiological process of breathing, it is possible to notice that time spent inhaling to the time spent exhaling is a ratio of about 1:1.6 (the golden ratio). When you take the trouble to notice natural rhythms, you can see that they are everywhere. The subtler your observations are, the more that attention feeds your Soul.

The saying, "God is in the details," is not altogether wrong. One could also say that "in the details is where we find the spirit at work." The first saying tells us something, and the second is an instruction for what we find when we study details. The technique I use to study the details relating to my work is to imagine myself as being the size of a germ and riding on or watching a piano or harpsichord action in operation. By imagining myself becoming the size of a germ, I see details in such close proximity that I can notice rhythmic problems in the way all the parts move together or sense inertia problems that foul up the smooth rhythmic flow of the action. Because I can notice about ten times more with each observation from this vantage point, I know that applying this kind of attention will result in an enhancement of my ability to produce an action that players will describe as "playing itself."

Ideas also flow and develop in a specific rhythm. Pay attention to the nature and behavior of how ideas work, and thinking will happen by itself without you having to work at it. In this way, problems solve themselves. When this happens, it is a sign that your Soul is at work doing its job and you have successfully gotten out of the way.

THE SENSE OF TIME

When is the right time to ask for a raise? When is the right time to admit we have made a mistake? When is the right time to launch a new enterprise? When is the best time to make or effect a change? All these questions call upon the sense of time, and we could go on asking such questions to infinity. For the most part, there appear to be no fixed guidelines to how such questions might be answered. In the old days, people would consult an astrologer or a wise person. The astrologer would consult their charts and divine an interpretation of the right time to do this or that. The wise person was usually old enough to have spent a long time observing people's behavior so that they could predict the best time to take a specific action. Sometimes they were right and sometimes they were wrong. Today, psychologists, who have been trained in the business of understanding how people behave, have assumed the role of advisor. Like an astrologer or wise person, sometimes they are right and sometimes they are wrong.

The sense of time or timing is not an absolute sensation. The younger a person is, the slower time seems to pass. The older one is, the faster time flies. The more interested in something we are, the faster time goes by. The more bored we are, the more interminable events feel. This relativity of time is what makes determining the right moment so difficult, as well as the difficulty added by our feelings of anticipation or hesitation. The more we anticipate something, the longer it seems to take to happen. Any hesitation at all causes time to slip away until it is completely spent.

The sense of time informs us of the dearness of moments and the wastefulness of poorly spent time. We hate to have our time wasted, yet we think nothing of blowing off a whole month to do nothing productive. Clearly, how we perceive our relationship to time depends on how we choose to think about it or the attitude we hold about its importance.

That we interest ourselves in questions involving time is a result of the repetitive regularity of the movement of heavenly bodies like the moon and the sun. This has caused us to think about dividing the moments between recurrent events into roughly equal quantities. By extrapolation, we continue the business of dividing into smaller and smaller units until we arrive at a point where the units of time are so infinitesimally small that we can no longer imagine them.

Yet, without flow, time would not exist. Flow is what time is meant to express. To develop a sense of time without also developing a sense of flow makes no sense because it is flow which gives time meaning. Those astronomers among us are accustomed to separating time from flow by speaking about time in terms of light-years, which is a term that is as effortless to rattle off as it is impossible to imagine.

This unimaginable aspect of time at its largest and smallest expressions makes paying attention to the sense of time all the more valuable. Without the need to concern ourselves over the infinitesimal or gargantuan measures of time, we can focus on what time means for us personally. Since time appears to pass faster as we age, each fraction of time becomes more important to us. The younger we are, the less likely we are to value our time. That attitude appears to change the moment a major event occurs in our lives which instantly informs us of how short a lifetime is. So it seems that the more we value what little time we have, the faster time appears to pass; and the less we concern ourselves about exactly how long a life is, the slower time appears to pass.

How much we enjoy or dislike an experience alters our perception of time. Time passes rapidly when we enjoy ourselves because we experience the timelessness of the Soul. It becomes tedious and exhausting the more we experience feelings of distaste and boredom. Indeed, the word *interest* describes the experience of joy when attention is fixed on whatever has captured it. Interest comes from the

Latin prefix *inter*, meaning *between*, and the verb *esse*, meaning *to be*. To be between our attention and that which captured it is the experience of interest. It is during those moments that perception of time is suspended, which is why it appears to pass so quickly. Suddenly we become aware of time that felt like a few minutes when, in reality, an hour and a half had passed.

THE SENSE OF QUALITATIVE PROPORTION

This is the flipside of our structural, left-brained, quantitative sense of proportion. Qualitative proportion has to do with how things relate to each other.

Too often, when we talk about proportion, we don't actually mean proportion. Proportion is simply how one thing relates to another. If we say, "he blew that all out of proportion," we don't usually mean that he blew that all out of how one thing relates to another, we usually mean that he over-inflated his argument. When we say that a person has no sense of proportion, we actually mean that a person has no ability to grasp how one thing relates to another. When we use the word *proportion* considerately, we always mean how one thing relates to another.

Curiously, we mostly share a sense of what "feels" right (in terms of how one thing relates to another) because we also mostly share the criteria used for evaluating proportion. For example, commercials on television were first inserted at the beginning of a program, and then they were inserted a quarter of the way, halfway, three-quarters of the way, and at the end of the program. The norm at that time was of having single one-minute commercials. Later, to make more money, networks and stations began to put in two one-minute commercials during the break. After a while, they added another. Then they began dividing up programs into smaller segments with more commercials stuck in between until, like today, there were almost as many minutes of commercials as there were of programs. With the plethora of channels now available, there is hardly anything worth watching because the amount of program has been gradually reduced by time spent recapping what came before the commercial breaks. As the amount of program has reduced, so has the attention of viewers, who "channel surf" to find something interesting while the program they were watching is on a commercial break.

This behavior has caused programs to become structured more like commercials. They are created with the idea of selling the commercial rather than the subject of the program, so the program's language is overtly designed to make us continue watching the program after the commercials have ended, rather than to interest us in the program's subject. This is being managed to manipulate viewers into a state of unsettled repose, which makes them more receptive to the linear messages of the commercials. All of this naturally leads to the condition of having hundreds of channels with nothing worthwhile to watch. Somewhere along the way, viewers abrogated their sense of proportion so that they didn't have to pay to watch TV. Ironically, now almost everyone is required to pay to watch TV of which little is worth watching.

In every form of art, the sense of proportion is necessary. Yet, in the art of commercial programming, all the decisions are focused on getting viewers to abandon their sense of proportion because it is far easier to sell something unnecessary to someone who has suspended their sense of proportion. This is the driving force behind modern art. The proportionally blind are easy prey because they don't, won't, or can't account for the true qualitative value of things, ideas, attitudes, relationships, or activities.

To have a great sense of proportion is to be able to quickly assess the manner in which value relates to cost, worth relates to time spent, etc. A person with a great sense of proportion understands how the universal principles create value and worth, and how they manifest themselves both in nature and in the works of men and women. They are harder to fool when it comes to spending their money and are less inclined to value money more than time, things more than people, or arguments more than ideas.

The universal principle of proportion governs the manner in which nature grows. Aesthetic concepts, like the golden ratio (1:1.618), are not mere arbitrary ideas—they are scientific explanations for understanding how nature consistently knows what the exact balance point is between structure and behavior based on an object's function. Our sense of proportion is designed to inform us of these normally hidden realities.

|1.618|1.0 | 1.0 | 1.618 | 1.618 |
| 1.0 | 1.618 | 1.0 |
Sweet love, renew thy force; be it not said

| 1.0 | 1.618 | 1.0 |
| 1.618 |
Thy edge should blunter be than appetite,

| 1.0 | 1.618 | 1.618 | 1.0 |
| 1.0 | 1.618 |
Which but to-day by feeding is allayed,

| 1.0 | 1.618 | 1.0 | 1.618 |
| 1.0 | 1.618 |
To-morrow sharpened in his former might:

So, love, be thou, although to-day thou fill

Thy hungry eyes, even till they wink with fulness,

To-morrow see again, and do not kill

The spirit of love, with a perpetual dulness.

Let this sad interim like the ocean be

Which parts the shore, where two contracted new

Come daily to the banks, that when they see

Return of love, more blest may be the view;

As call it winter, which being full of care,

Makes summer's welcome, thrice more wished, more rare.

On the previous page, I have supplied *Sonnet 56*, by William Shakespeare, with a proportional analysis using the golden ratio applied to durations of gestures and phrases in the first four lines of the poem. I have preserved the line spacing throughout the sonnet for you to finish the analysis yourself, should you wish to.

Theoretically, it should be possible to write a credible sonnet using the structures from this analysis, assuming the affects and metaphors are apt and persuasive. The analysis is an intellectual framework or structure to facilitate behavior, and I wouldn't be surprised if this approach was used in Shakespeare's time to write sonnets until the practice was so ingrained that one could effortlessly write convincing verse. It is possible to make this kind of analysis of paintings, music, choreography, architecture, and so on, with the aim of sensitizing yourself to the inner workings of the great artists from the past.

By focusing on how things in nature are proportioned, and by applying that same technique of analysis, you can learn to create things that appear as though nature created them. By focusing on the principle of proportion and understanding how it works, you can build concepts, ideas, things, and conditions that mirror how nature might build those same concepts, ideas, things, and conditions. By carefully constructing your inventions to accord with the principles found in nature, your inventions will have the stamp of natural inevitability about them and should last throughout the ages. This is how great artists and musicians created masterpieces that continue to engage and appeal to our senses centuries later.

What is most revealing is how the French academic painters of the nineteenth century applied the golden ratio to their paintings with such a corrupt understanding that it resulted in stiff, dead compositions. Clearly, these painters knew they should be applying this important principle, but they chose to apply it without first understanding how nature applies the principle. Their repeated failure to effectively apply this principle indicates how mental conviction can easily override paying attention to the higher senses. In almost every case in which artists have allowed their mental convictions to take precedence over their senses, the results are as straightforward as they are boring. This is the preeminent error behind minimalism. In trying to be simple, minimalists succeed in making things that are minimally interesting, and no amount of conviction can change that.

Simplicity is an attitude, not a fact. In the arts, when simplicity becomes a fact, the effect is unidimensional. Only those artists who hold to an *attitude* of simplicity are able to create work that appears highly dimensional.

The attitude of simplicity places you in a position of unimportance and recognizes that there is nothing inherently interesting about yourself that would call for expression. This reduction of the self to the status of no importance, proportionally speaking, is a trigger that invites the Soul to take part in the work at hand. On the contrary, struggling to create simplicity as a fact keeps the intellect constantly engaged and busy, which eliminates the possibility of the Soul becoming involved in work.

Likewise, self-consciously constructed notions of beauty or ugliness make a highly uninviting environment for the Soul. The Soul is the true arbiter of what is beautiful, interesting, ugly, or boring. The mind and intellect are so easily deceived that they are wholly untrustworthy in matters of taste. Curiously, trusting the intellect or mind is the most common mistake made by artists, musicians, architects, designers, and performers of all kinds, and attempting to escape the stultifying effects of the intellect on one's work by "not thinking at all" is the second most common mistake. The Soul engages in work when we don't know what we are doing, but it expects us to learn from the serendipitous events during the work. Failure to learn sends the message that we don't take seriously what the Soul gives. The result? We become old and ignorant.

The sense of proportion informs our minds of how things relate to each other. The mind is expected to deliver cogent, well-conceived explanations for why an experience is perceived as it is. At that point, the self will seek to turn the mind's explanations into behaviors that can be repeated endlessly and mindlessly. Here, the sense of proportion needs to be engaged to notice the disproportionate participation of the self in work. By cultivating an attitude of simplicity, it is possible to set both the mind and self aside to invite the Soul to take charge.

The attitude of simplicity views the experience of work as a new, never before attempted act. This creates the mental environment of newness of experience, even if it is a strict repetition of what came before. It is this environment of undiscovered possibilities that tantalizes the Soul and lures it into action. For this attitude to work, it is imperative to adopt the principle of individuation. This means treating every repetition as a new and different expression of the same affect, effect, idea, or suggestion. Doing this means purposely making the same thing different in as many ways as possible. The craft aspect of one's work involves such practice. It is all in the details of what is expressed and observed. By practicing creating differences, the Soul is invited to create another more interesting, exciting, moving, and meaningfully different repetition that the self would never think of. That is the point of practice, as it is the point of holding an attitude of simplicity, requiring the mind to do the job for which it was designed, cultivating the discipline of setting aside the self, and paying attention to the sense of proportion.

THE SENSE OF EFFICIENCY

The sense of efficiency has little to do with accounting for amounts spent and results received. This is not to say that the sense of efficiency can't be used that way. Rather, there are so many other ways to cultivate this sense that are far more meaningful. By paying attention to how you proportion your time spent thinking, acting, and reflecting, you can then sense the value of thought, the importance of action, and the need for reflection.

This sense, perhaps more than any other of the mental senses, can make you miserable when it is violated by what you perceive. The example I like to use is as follows:

Imagine that you are an employer who hires someone to sweep your floors, and you are accustomed to paying your employees well for work well done. So you tell this new hire that if they sweep the floors, you will pay them x number of dollars to do the job, but you never explicitly say how you want the floors to be swept. The newly hired person picks up the broom and brushes it across the floor for two strokes here, two strokes there, and another two strokes six feet away, while pushing the broom in completely different directions for each stroke. It doesn't take long for you to get annoyed at the sweeper for not cleaning the floor. You, the employer, were unclear in your communication about what sweeping the floor meant, but equally clear in your imagination about what the sweeper was supposed to be doing.

This scenario is designed to illustrate exactly how frustrated and angry one can feel when the sense of efficiency is violated. Indeed, one can feel a great deal of anger at the violation of any universal principle, which is the truth of the matter for me. For years I puzzled over why I was so angry all the time. It was not until I connected my anger to the violation of my senses of universal principles that I found any relief. From that point on, a great deal of my anger abated, and the energy from the possibility of being angry became focused on understanding the connection between spiritual violation generated by neglect or ignorance of universal principles and the feelings of being raped or violated by that neglect or ignorance. This is also how I managed to work through a comprehensive list of all the senses. I thought about all the times when I could connect feeling angry from being violated to a specific moment in my life. As I detailed the myriad of moments, I also noticed that a specific feeling or sense was at the root of it all. This experience of being violated and the resulting feeling of anger is one I turned into a working principle. That is, if I am feeling angry, it is a signal to look for the source of violation. From this attitude comes almost everything good or of high quality in my work.

In the end, it is not how much you love a great result that counts, it is how much you hate mediocre or incompetent results that produces great work. This is why true artists of every kind have been considered by their culture as the "canaries in the mine shaft," and this is also why artists tend to be angry individuals. The more sensitive you are, the more likely it will be that you experience gross violations of your senses. The more awake you are, the more of your senses you are tuned into, and the more likely it will be that you experience violations of those senses.

Knowing that you have 133 senses that can be violated doesn't make living with them any easier, but by understanding how violation triggers these senses, you can make sure that you don't violate the senses of others in your work. As so many of the world's great spiritual teachers and religions have affirmed, do to others as you would have others do to you.

In the physical world, the principle of efficiency is expressed in the law of conservation of energy. In nature, efficiency governs growth in living things. When human beings disrupt the growth cycle of living things, they often unleash the negative consequences of such disruptions. The main negative consequence of human-caused pollution is cancer. Cancer is a manifestation of what happens when the principle of efficiency is violated so that cells multiply outside the bounds of their natural limit, which the principle of efficiency sets by containing or conserving the energy required to make those cells

In human cultures, the principle of efficiency works to limit the growth of human systems and organizations by causing them to break down once they have reached their capacity to serve the needs of the individuals within those systems. The moment individuals are required to serve a particular system rather than the purpose for which it was established, that system begins its decline. Economic cycles of boom and bust, of expansion and depression, and of glut and gloom are examples of efficiency at work. That is, when individuals begin to behave in a manner designed to buttress the boom, increase the expansion, or service the surfeit, the downward plunge is sure to follow as night follows day.

An example of how this works in practical terms would be the behavior of people in the fundamentalist evangelical movement who believe in the rapture. The rapture is a cancerous fantasy concocted in the 1830's and forwarded by people like Margaret MacDonald, J.N. Darby, and C.I. Scofield. The doctrine of the rapture suggests that Christian believers will one day be instantly assumed into heaven. As long as people who held this view applied it only to themselves, the fantasy was harmless. As soon as believers politicized the fantasy and used it as an excuse to vote proponents into positions of political power, it became dangerous because the part of the fantasy that describes the world of unbelievers going to hell became official policy. The political party in the USA that has become the right arm of this cancerous movement rapes and pillages as much as possible because, according to their fantasy, after they have been magically raptured into heaven, they aren't going to be around to pick up the pieces or be held responsible for their behavior. Their evil is in their willful blindness to the truth.

According to the conservation of energy, the actions of this movement could end in a global meltdown in which the earth's temperature rises, sea levels rise, and arable land becomes so parched that famine ravages the world. Those who set all this in motion will be the first to blame everyone but themselves for the disaster. Eventually, the truth will out, and the perpetrators of that fantasy will be held accountable, while the earth will likely recover by initiating some natural catastrophe that will bring everything back into balance. In the process, it will eliminate those who espoused that rapturous nonsense by every means possible. That will be the principle of efficiency coming to the rescue.

The sense of efficiency should be used to help us regulate how we spend our time, how we spend our energy, and on what we spend our time and energy. Life is short. Unless we make intelligent decisions about how we will manage these two single most important aspects of life, the chances are we will waste both of them. It's not that it takes a huge amount of intelligence to avoid certain behaviors that jeopardize our time and energy, but when we are young, we feel that time and energy are unlimited and boundless. That feeling is a fantasy fostered by a delusion of indestructibility. Unless time and energy are treated as premium, it is easy to fritter both away until one day we wake up and suddenly realize that we no longer have the time or the energy to do the things we dreamed of doing.

THE SENSE OF INTEGRITY

The sense of integrity is easily violated by whatever does not interrelate. Whatever interrelates positively stimulates the sense of integrity. What it means to have all parts interrelate is that it is possible to observe the same pattern of structures or behaviors in both the macro and the micro level. On observing a leaf, for instance, you can see how the whole tree mirrors the pattern of veining in how the branches relate to the main trunk of the tree. Snail shells grow from the tiniest, fully developed design by regularly adding sections, each of which looks like a slightly larger version of the one before it. The moons of Jupiter relate to the planet Jupiter as the planets of our solar system relate to the sun—that is, the planets are like moons to the sun. The structure of matter is constructed using that same solar system pattern. Indeed, scientific beauty comes from noticing these repeated patterns, and it is why some people believe in Intelligent Design.

The universal principle of integrity controls the manner in which everything in the universe interrelates, from the largest structures down to the subatomic level. Scientists are aesthetically drawn to these interrelated systems, behaviors, structures, and forms in nature, and they search for ways to describe them mathematically. Fractal mathematics is the mathematical expression of the principle of integrity.

Since it takes intelligence on the part of humans to develop these mathematical expressions, some scientists, whose agenda is to buttress the belief in God, point to evidence of the principle of integrity and conclude that there is a specific intelligence at work behind the way nature appears. The mere fact that something so simple yet profound as the principle of integrity is controlling how nature works may be mysterious on the surface, but as soon as we begin to use that same principle in our work, our thinking, our art, our behavior, and our lives, we realize how down-to-earth and un-mysterious the principle is. The principle only needs to be sensed and applied. Once it is sensed, it is known, and all the mystery disappears. This is the beauty of universal principles that control everything in the universe, and we have the joy of being able to harness the power of every one of them to create in our work the effect of it being a work of nature. If people choose to call the universal principles "God," they are using a name of endearment. Universal principles don't care what they are called.

In past centuries, people applied the universal principles more or less intuitively and did so with the attitude that the best a human being could do was to imitate God. It was the way people could honor their idea of God. Since the beginning of the twentieth century, this particular attitude has almost disappeared because the idea of God became literalized into a specific being that has human feelings and needs, which is an idea that is repugnant to many people. The behavior of literalizing things is an adolescent behavior that arises from the need to nail things down in a world perceived as being uncertain. The overwhelming need for certainty creates people whose thinking is opaque. Unable to live with uncertainty, they force everything to fit into a certain mold irrespective of the wisdom of doing that.

The fact that the universe is an uncertain place is a fact that we are obliged by reality to accept. To become a mature person means learning to live with and eventually to love the uncertainty that is essential to the nature of reality. To become a wise person means discovering the attitudes you need to live harmoniously with the uncertain nature of reality. It is a smart person who adopts those attitudes quickly, easily, and joyfully. The alternative is to live in a state of constant fear.

By knowing the universal principles through all our senses, we are empowered to make the best of every situation in a way that is both loving and accepting of reality. Deciding to live in love rather than fear is a choice we each must make. To activate the Soul in the most efficient integrated manner necessitates choosing to live in love.

THE SENSE OF INTENSITY

Have you ever noticed how almost everything in nature exhibits intensity? Stars exhibit intensity of heat and nuclear activity. Trees exhibit intensity of growth. In animals, intensity is expressed by "meaning business" in whatever they do. Intensity is striving to the uttermost. The major exception to this observation about nature is humankind. People have the choice not to behave intensely, and when they do behave intensely, they are often aggressive or destructive. We seem to reserve our intensity for endeavors that need it. This seems to be the major attraction we feel for making war and venting anger. Yet, when a person decides to behave in an intensely positive way, like when doing good, we treat that person as so special that they are raised to saintly or divine status. We do this, I suspect, to absolve ourselves of doing likewise.

Lack of intensity is a mark of mediocrity. Should each good act be done without intensity, the outcome is what we call normal. Likewise, when each bad act is done without intensity, we criticize the person for being stupid because they aren't even competent in their wrongdoing. Intensity informs our senses of what is perceived as competent or incompetent, healthy or unhealthy, or meaningful or meaningless. Intensity manifests itself physically in the form of muscle tension. Some people are so physically wound up that they become completely incapacitated. When this happens, it's called catatonia, and at the opposite end of the intensity scale is lassitude.

Ultimately, the purpose of art is to feed the Souls of the ones receiving that art by expressing universal principles. Since one of those principles is the principle of intensity, art must be intense for it to fulfill its purpose. For intensity in art to be recognized, it must appear to be struggling to the uttermost.

Intensity can also be manifested with subtlety. A fragrance that is constructed for human use can be made alluring by adding the smallest amounts of certain substances. The effect of this is what we would term *intensity of perception*; it is not the intensity of the fragrance itself. This is the basis of my definition of quality. Quality is the intensity of perception of a thing, work, or idea, etc. In other words, the higher the quality of an effect, the more intense the perception of that effect is. The poorer the quality of a thing, idea, or effect, the less intense the perception of it is.

Taking this idea of intensity of perception further, we can say that in any work, it is the presence of a universal principle or principles that causes the effect of perception. It is important to understand that liking or reacting to something are not the same as experiencing a perception of that thing. The greater the number of principles in a work and the more expressive of them that work is, the more intense the effect of perception is and the higher the quality it exhibits. Throughout history, the greatest artists, poets, and thinkers have been those men and women whose work has exhibited the greatest number of universal principles. Only since the early twentieth century have the standards of quality been dumbed down so that work expressing few, if any, universal principles is considered as being great. Though the intellect is easily fooled, the Soul is not.

THE SENSE OF DYNAMIC

The sense of dynamic is linked to our perception of change. Dynamic merely means *change* or *changing*. Our sense of dynamic is designed to detect the changes in our perceptions of reality, our environment, our thinking, our actions, and our attitudes. Noticing these changes is what makes us conscious beings, so you could say that consciousness is a product of our sense of dynamic.

It is an absolute truth that *everything is changing*. Indeed, the essential nature of spirit is change. The less a thing appears to change, the less spiritual it is. Hence, rocks are less spiritual than trees, trees less than insects, insects less than animals, and animals (as is so far known) less than human beings because human beings are the most changing of all. The aspect of change is related to the intensity of dynamic. Thus, the universal principle of dynamic acts on everything in nature and is the cause of the effect we sense and observe as change. This having been said, there are those among us who hate change. What does that say about them, in spiritual terms?

If change is the essential nature of all things spiritual, and our sense of dynamic is meant to keep us connected to the essential nature of the spirit, then it seems we are obliged by nature and the spirit to accept change as a clear sign of our spiritual manifestation. Although it may be argued that since not all change is good, the spirit must not be good because it is the author of change, we are forced by love of truth to accept that all change is good, even when our experience of it is marred by what we think is evil. Indeed, we owe our nature to spirit because we are finite beings endowed with Souls that are "quotes" from the spirit. To have a relationship with our Souls, to exercise our creativity, to grow in understanding, and to develop towards unity with our Souls is why we do art, music, dance, science, and so on. It is why we bother to think about why we do what we do. All this is made possible because of our senses, not because of our beliefs or how much we think we know. The sense of dynamic is pivotal to living at peace with change, even though we may not be happy with it.

Our relationship to spirit is governed by our attitudes towards change. We are not compelled to like change, but to accept it as a natural phenomenon that is often challenging. If we hold this attitude, it indicates how serious we are about having positive relationships with our Souls. To be truly creative means being serious about the relationships with our Souls. The message that we send our Souls is what we take seriously. Since the Soul is a microcosm of all that is spiritual in the universe, we must all take care to see that we reflect as much as possible how the spirit works to create the natural world. This is effected by love, not fear.

Our sense of dynamic is essential to our creative lives because it allows us to move from thought to action, attitude to action, feeling to action, and from action to improving results. We tend to think of dynamic as being something exciting, charged up, electrical, or riveting. For instance, we might speak of some person as having a dynamic personality. In these situations, the person in mind might have an irresistible attraction for us—for example, an enchanting smile or a loving countenance—but it is we who are changed, yet we attribute the dynamic to the other person instead of ourselves. If our sense of dynamic is awakened, we are able to sense the changes in ourselves and appropriately attribute each change to the parts of us wherein the change was sensed. Keeping these things clear informs the Soul that we are in touch with reality and not deluding ourselves. The Soul requires us to be aware of and engaged with what is real for it to give us the best possible insights, ideas, concepts, and understandings. Still, many people insist that behaving in opposition to the Soul is the right thing to do. This can only happen because of beliefs, which block the ability of the Soul to work in our lives.

It needs to be said that the power of religion to prevent people from experiencing a relationship with their Souls should never be underestimated. By religion, I mean everything based on beliefs, such as political beliefs, social convictions, philosophical propositions, and the entire gamut of intellectual theories. Belief, as a whole, needs to be replaced with inquiry; otherwise, it usually tends to be used as a justification for every behavior that inhibits the Soul. Inquiry liberates the mind and the Soul to discover truth, not proof to support preconceived notions.

The sense of dynamic can't compete with a detestation of the theory of evolution. The fear that empowers the feelings of hatred that many religious people have for the idea of evolution will, in the end, make it unlikely for them to experience partnership with their Souls. Evolution is merely an expression of how change happens, that's all. As dynamic provides the fuel for change, evolution governs how it unfolds. Without a refined sense of dynamic, understanding how changes happen is impossible.

THE SENSE OF PROPRIETY

Propriety is what is appropriate or fitting. Our sense of what is appropriate is largely determined by what our specific culture accepts as fitting. When we see conjoined twins, we are witness to an example of a violation by nature of the universal principle of individuation, but only in a physical sense. We know that two human beings should be distinct and individual. The universal principles inform our instinctive knowledge of this. Thus, when we see such a thing, we recognize it as being inappropriate because it doesn't fit from a perceptual point of view.

The sense of propriety is one that needs a great deal of training to avoid the fault of prejudice or irrational and faulty discrimination. This sense is so prone to producing bigotry and fear in us. It accounts for why, deep down, we all tend to be racists and fearful of change, difference, strangeness, and everything that is out of the ordinary. Properly trained, this sense would make us fearless of change, and we would rejoice in our differences and accept what is strange and out of the ordinary. Unfortunately, most people can only cope with tolerating what is out of the ordinary because they don't like what doesn't fit their preconceived notions of what is appropriate.

However, if we study the reality of it all, most of what we don't like or approve of reflects how fear controls our actions and thoughts. Thus, it is important that we consider how our sense of propriety is guided by our fears and not allow those fears to control our thinking or behavior. Truly appropriate thinking and behavior are based on love, which is accepting and caring in its nature. It is these loving attitudes that need to be the guide for what is right. We need to be ever on guard against fear tainting this sense.

THE SENSE OF CONTINUITY

Continuity is the quality of something that does not seem to stop or change as time passes. Continuity differs from flow in that what is referred to is usually events or things that are normally discontinuous. Your sense of continuity is challenged when you interrupt what you are doing, thinking about, or focusing on with any and every distraction.

One of the problems of our modern age is the easy availability of devices and possibilities for distraction. This leads to the inability to focus attention, and our inner life suffers from a vacuum of depth. Ultimately, this means that the world belongs to those who can direct and focus their attention, while those who can't do this are prey to have their attentions misdirected. For this reason, perhaps, it is important to make a habit of turning off all distractions. Distractions alone are enough to alienate you from your Soul. Practicing being undistractible enables you to sense interruptions in the continuity of observations, thoughts, reasoning, and development of your ideas. The importance of following through on what you get from your Soul requires you to be sensitive to the nature of continuity in all that relates to your life. Lack of following through translates into disruption of continuity in whatever you are doing. Similarly, lack of flow translates into being distractible.

We often hear the command, "Concentrate!" when children are spoken to by overseeing adults. It is wise to remember that children can intensely focus on things that interest them, so when we notice that children are distracted, it probably means they are bored by what is happening. If you have chosen to become a teacher of children, it is imperative to use inventive and cunning means of maintaining their attention. This is most easily done by remembering what it was like for you at that same age, how bored you were by what was happening, and what activated your interest and attention. Expecting the young to behave themselves by intimidation is both cruel and Soul-killing.

The mere presence of children is a stimulation of the sense of continuity because they represent the continuity of survival of our species. That is why their education is so important. A good education and a principled upbringing lead to happy, competent adults. Upbringing and education need continuity of intent to realize that aim.

In matters relating to art, music, and so on, the sense of continuity needs training to grasp the idea that it is not so much the objects of art and music that must exhibit continuity but the attention of the observers and listeners. Just as great teachers understand that it is their responsibility to effect continuity of attention in their students, so do great artists and musicians do all in their power to create that effect in the minds of their observers and listeners.

Experiencing an intense sense of continuity of attention is a marvelous experience to undergo. It feels like time has ceased, all worries are resolved, difficulties are eased, and all problems are solved, despite reality to the contrary. Lost in the experience of total attention, you are transported to a realm of timelessness until suddenly you are back to the awareness that continuity has been broken and timelessness was a fleeting moment. You remember those moments of total attention for a lifetime because of how intensely real they felt. Without the sense of continuity, you couldn't have such experiences.

THE SENSE OF DISTORTION

The sense of distortion is what guides your decisions when breaking rules. Distortion is a twisting, turning, bending, crushing, or smashing of the norm for the effect of engendering continuity of interest in something. Weather is a distortion when it is different from the normal conditions. If you expect that winter should be snowy, cold, and dry, then a sunny, warm, humid winter day is a distortion in the weather.

Doing something quickly that usually takes a long time to do is a distortion in the expectation of the length of time required to do that thing. Similarly, turning an idea upside down to inspect it from another point of view distorts the original point of view for the purpose of having a clearer idea of what is being observed. All these examples stimulate the sense of distortion. Without this sense, you would notice nothing except continuous differences, and you would never take note of what differences are more important to notice.

When we create distortion, we are disturbing the normal order of things. At its heart, nature is a balanced state between order and chaos. When we distort what we are doing, we purposely create chaos. If distortion does not serve to balance overbearing structure, then the distortion is gratuitous—it is done for its own sake and not for the sake of feeding the Soul. For this reason, the principle of distortion must be carefully applied. Aristotle used the term *poetic license* when referring to the act of distorting or creating on-purpose mistakes in a work. He considered such license to be inexcusable if the end result was not an enhancement of clarity.[25]

There is an important difference between physical distortion and perceptual distortion. Distorting something physically, like tying a knot in a length of rope, does not always constitute a perceptual distortion. If the rope was otherwise completely free of knots, it should be called a perceptual distortion because our perception has been guided to the presence of the knot itself. However, if there were ten other knots in the same length of rope, then the distortion is no longer perceptual because the presence of many knots means that knots in the rope are normal. Too many distortions create the effect of no distortion at all because the distortions become normal and thus boring. Conversely, the complete absence of distortions in all sensible matters guarantees boredom. This problem plagues modern architecture.

---

[25] Aristotle, *Poetics*

In music, singing pure tones creates the feeling of need to bend or distort them with vibrato, but singers too often use a continuous vibrato so that every tone is distorted. This engenders the feeling of need for distorting vibrato with pure tones. The problem with any aesthetic effect being applied uniformly is that every difference, every possibility, and every outcome becomes predictable and boring, like adding lots of salt to food so it all tastes of salt. By applying every technique possible to create and enhance differences, such that each becomes clear to the observer, we can use the effect of distortion to enhance whatever we are attempting to communicate. Should we fail to do this, we alienate the people on the receiving end of our efforts.

The same holds true in every field. Doctors who dose their patients without concern for how effective a medicine might be slather all ills with medication, rather than listening to what ails each patient. Teachers who slather every lesson with the same monotone delivery need to distort it with enthusiasm. Farmers who plant the same crop on the same ground every year slather the ground with chemicals, thereby forcing the dirt to act like fertile soil until it refuses to grow anything at all.

The sense of distortion is stimulated not by fulfilled expectations but by disrupted or denied expectations. It is not so much a question of the interjection of ugliness or turmoil in an otherwise placid environment than it is one of introducing an element of the unexpected that creates perceptual distortion. A physical distortion bends, twists, pulls, snaps, warps, and disfigures to attract attention. A natural distortion is one in which the forces of nature converge to push the physical limits of something to the breaking point. An intellectual distortion occurs when the element of illogic has been introduced into an otherwise logical discourse. Only when you have cultivated a high degree of sensitivity to distortions of the subtlest varieties is your sense of distortion refined.

Too often, those who mistake their interpretation of reality to be a clear reflection of actual reality use the word *distortion* pejoratively and tend to accuse anyone who contradicts that interpretation as having distorted the truth. Any interpretation of reality that does not accord perfectly with actual reality is an intellectual distortion. By understanding how we use and abuse the word, we can better develop our sense of it. By making mistakes, we learn the limits of distortion. By correcting our mistakes, we learn what Aristotle understood and meant by the proper use of error—that it should enhance clarity but be avoided otherwise.

THE SENSE OF CONNECTION

To be connected to something means to apprehend it intimately. We are connected to our family members by DNA and by intimate awareness of them over a long period of time. To sense a connection requires the element of time or a principled linkage. It is possible to share DNA with others in our families yet experience a remote sensation of connection because we spend no time getting to know them. A principled linkage involves the sensation of other mitigating, governing forces. Perceiving connections occurs through shared attitudes, idiosyncrasies, habits, and experiences.

Knowledge foreshortens the sense of connection, while fear or ignorance creates disassociation from the sensation of connection in proportion to the feeling of fear or condition of ignorance. The more we fear a thing, the greater our tendency to disassociate from it, but the more we feel bound to it. For example, being afraid of spiders would cause you to recoil from having anything to do with them, yet your fear enslaves you in how you react to their presence in your environment.

When people refer to a sense of community, they are usually referring to the sensation of connection perceived between themselves and others around them. The connection may be intellectual, emotional, physical, spiritual, or a combination of those four domains. There is no such thing as a sense of community; it is a misplaced reference.

The intensity of shared experiences, especially if they are negative, stimulates the sense of connection. Misery loves company! This is the basis on which group therapy is supposed to work. When experiences are positive, the senses of being are usually involved, which results in a powerful, intensifying effect on the sensation of connection because the most intimate means of connection are spiritual.

There is also an intellectual component to the sense of connection. Logic, for instance, depends in large measure on the sense of connection between elements that are said to belong to each other. Were it not so, if I said, "A = B and A = C, therefore B = C," you wouldn't be able to sense the relationship between B and C. Yet you conclude that B = C because of shared equality to A. I can remember, when learning algebra in high school, thinking that it was a leap to conclude that B and C were equal because the manner of what made B and C equal to A was never specified. It wasn't until my teacher said to me that the function of the letters and the signs in algebraic equations were to be taken at face value that I began to do well in algebra. Until then, I could think of a multitude of reasons why B and C could both be equal to A yet not be equal to each other. About fifteen years after I left high school, I realized that my learning style was the result of dyslexia. Until then, I thought I was just stupid when it came to academic subjects.

Regardless of my dyslexia, I never had a problem making things. Sensing connections was so effortless for me that I could look at a collection of parts, take one good look at a picture of what the final product was supposed to be and construct the apparatus without having to follow directions. I could sense how all the parts fitted together (i.e., how they were connected), and I assumed that everyone did things that way. Only after I began my career as a musical instrument maker did I realize how different my approach was compared to my colleagues'.

There is an abundance of connections to be sensed in the realm of art and music, and these are perhaps the most efficient ways to train the sense of connection. When drawing the human figure in every position, you rarely see the figure in its entirety. This means that you have to sense the connections of parts to parts, even when they are not visible. Both Leonardo da Vinci and Michelangelo Buonarroti understood the importance of training this sense so well that they took to dissecting human corpses to understand how the various parts of the human body are connected.

In music, the notes of the tonal scale have the property of hidden connection because all the notes in the scale relate to the tonic. The hidden connection is that the various tones relate to the tonic according to one of the basic musical ratios. Furthermore, another hidden connection for all the notes in the tonal scale is that they relate to each other and the tonal center in much the same manner that all the parts of a sentence grammatically relate to each other and the subject of a sentence. Atonal music, which has no tonal center, is devoid of such connections, and one is left wondering what connects to what so much so that a feeling of arbitrariness is the result.

When the sense of connection is denied, the feeling of arbitrariness is what we are left with. The feeling is so powerful and repulsive that most people work to avoid it. We don't like it when we are passengers in a car being driven by a driver who behaves arbitrarily. We don't like it when rules are applied arbitrarily. Connections are experienced as references to make sense of them. Remove the quality of reference, and experiences feel arbitrary. Where connections and references are concerned, we need to apply the Golden Rule: Do unto others as you would have others do unto you.

THE SENSE OF RADIANCE

Radiance is the outward manifestation of a principle, condition, or effect. It comes in many forms. The opposite of radiance is encasement. Usually, we find radiance where structure is on the inside and behavior is on the outside. Human beings are radiant creatures because their structure is internal, and everything behavioral occurs outside of the skeleton. Conversely, crabs and lobsters are encased creatures because their structure or skeleton is on the outside of their bodies. The sun is radiant, but the earth is encased. For a more detailed exploration of the universal principle of radiance, refer to page 121.

The sense of radiance is necessary to process thought that is designed to seduce. In general, language intended to manipulate people appears radiant. The structure of the message is hidden because it requires obscurity to succeed. The intention to manipulate is the structure behind manipulative words. By appearing radiant, words are attractive.

Too often, ideas that feel radiant are the result of delusion; hence, the sense of radiance is needed to distinguish between what appears radiant and what actually is radiant. The sense of radiance is a perception, not a feeling. When we experience true radiance, it becomes much less easy to be deluded by the appearance of it because the real experience is so intense. When the Soul imparts an idea, the experience is radiant. This is described in the story of Moses when he experienced the burning bush and a voice coming from the apparition. As with so many stories that presume to describe the radiant experience, it is ultimately the follow-through which tells the real truth. The more an experience reveals about the true nature of reality, the more likely that experience is radiant.

The enlightenment experience, as described by the Buddhists, is a moment of clarity and understanding of spiritual reality. The eureka moment, as described by scientists and inventors, is a moment of clarity and understanding of physical reality. The "Aha!" experience, as described by artists, composers, thinkers, and writers, is a moment of clarity and understanding of mental or intellectual reality. These people are all describing the moment when the Soul imparts an idea that brings into focus all that has happened to them and creates transformative clarity and understanding. Should such an idea occur to one who is not ready for it or who misinterprets the experience, the result is delusion.

Without a well-developed awareness of the sense of radiance, it is easy to "go off the deep end." As with so many of the senses, there are accompanying emotional components that often cause misinterpretation leading to delusion.

THE SENSE OF INFINITY

The behavioral sense of infinity detects the endlessness of possibilities in the face of terminate circumstances. Pessimists are probably blind in their sense of infinity because they typically gravitate to the most limited and therefore the worst possible outcome. Optimists have a heightened sense of infinity because they customarily resort to the view that every difficulty is merely a closed door to endless possibilities, so they work to open doors by overcoming the difficulties. Not everyone can be an optimist, and not everyone needs to be a pessimist. By applying the sense of infinity to difficulties in life, you may find a means to advantage yourself by the optimist's life strategy, even if you are not an optimist by temperament.

CONCLUSION

The senses of the behavior-sensing right side of the brain derive their clarity and force when the structure-sensing left side of the brain is involved in total perception. This occurs because of the corpus callosum, which is the structure that physically connects the two sides of the brain together. When you involve the senses of one side in making sense of the perceptions of the opposite side, you require that your brain grows connections between its two hemispheres. Sometimes the business of relating everything perceived with the senses of one side to the senses of the other side causes the brain to grow connections so fast it can make the head hurt. Even this is sensible in the front, central region of the brain. I call this *corpus callosating.* It is a sensation I try to create as often as possible. Like every process in the body which feels at first resistant, the more you do it, the easier it gets, and it eventually it becomes second nature. Involving sensations of both sides of the brain in every activity, thought, process, or method makes it easier for the Soul to draw upon the whole brain to create solutions or generate ideas that are sensible.

CHAPTER ELEVEN
The Imaginative Senses

The imagination is the Soul's playroom. It is my view that the imagination, when founded on reality, is linked to the corpus callosum, if not actually located in that structure. To develop your imagination, you should aim to grow as large a corpus callosum as possible and continue stimulating its growth to the day of your death. The only sure way to guarantee an unlimited source of ideas is to actively cultivate the imagination through growth of the corpus callosum by relating the mental senses of the left-brain hemisphere to those of the right hemisphere, and vice versa.

Even if I am wrong about the physical location of the imagination, I know that bringing together both sides of the brain in everything you do activates your Soul because your Soul loves to play in the one part of yourself reserved just for it. This means doing everything in your power to avoid cluttering it up with notions and delusions, of which a few can take up so much space in the imagination that little room is left for the Soul to play in.

When psychologists speak of the unconscious mind, they are actually referring to the host of motivations that load down our imaginations—the clutter of the unreal, the fake, the notional, the fanciful, and the hoped for. It is the job of consciousness to filter through everything and trash what is not real to get at the source of our nonsense. Once free of nonsense, there is little left in the imagination for the unconscious parts of our minds to grab hold of. Since the unconscious is connected to the ego and fear, once it is forced out of the imagination, the Soul will soon make itself at home.

THE SENSE OF MELODY

Our sense of melody is one of the first of the higher senses that we develop. We actually begin to develop it in the womb. It is crucial for feeling loved because with it we can sense the verbal and auditory signals of love. When mothers and fathers speak motherese with newborn infants, the infants are processing linguistic expressions from the standpoint of musical behavior. Since these infants cannot understand the words they are hearing, their brains respond to the musical tones and inflections in a manner that indicates they love hearing motherese. When infants respond to speech that does not have the expressive qualities of motherese, their response is flat, concerned, or anxious.

Motherese may be called the language of the brain, and since it is the same from culture to culture, we might well suppose that it is part of our genetic disposition. At birth, we recognize this language as being a source of safety and security, and we recognize non-motherese language as being threatening.

Since motherese depends on a highly variegated, melodious manner of expression, it is clear that the sense of melody is one of the first senses to be attended to by normal infants, which shows the importance of music and musical speech in our lives. Indeed, when parents do not or choose not to use motherese when speaking to their infants, they are unwittingly creating a feeling in their children of not being loved. Since we learn how to love and how to express love from motherese communications, our sense of melody is essential to living happy lives. Without the sense of melody or the loving expressions it reads from everything ever uttered to us as infants, we feel a deficit of love that is otherwise impossible to fill, and this can lead to a Pandora's box of mental problems in later life.

Like all the senses, the sense of melody can be ignored, but not without negative consequences. By cultivating a high degree of sophistication in music, we can make up for some of the deficits created when we were infants. It is interesting that in the USA, education devoid of music, music training, or cultivating listening to music is normal. When school budgets get trimmed, music, if it was being taught in the first place, is the first course in the curriculum to get cut, while the place of competitive sport is preserved. This indicates that American school boards consider happiness in life to be rather unimportant and aggressive Darwinian competition to be extremely important.

As adults, we suffer if our sense of melody has been allowed to degenerate due to lack of use. To understand why, we need to look at music and how it relates to language. The three cornerstones of music are melody, harmony, and rhythm. If any one of these three cornerstones are missing, is it still music? Musicians will point to music that is made of a single melody line and affirm that it is music. They would be right because a melody, no matter how simple, has an implied harmony and rhythm. Likewise, harmony also contains both melody and rhythm; and rhythm, at its best, contains suggestions of melody and harmony, depending on how pitched sounding the rhythm instrument is.

As there are three cornerstones of music, there are three cornerstones of language: meaning, expression, and syntax. If one of these three cornerstones of language is missing, can we still have language? Were we to remove meaning from language, all we would have is blather and nonsense. Remove expression from language and we have nothing, because expression is the vehicle for meaning. This leaves syntax, which is the means whereby expressions acquire references. Without references of one expression to another, it becomes impossible to make sense of anything expressed. For example, if we remove the effect of syntax from the sentence, "the cat walked across the room," we get, "room the walked the across cat." Without the references created by syntax, the sentence is a nonsense, despite us knowing what the individual words in the sentence mean. The effect of deconstructing language or music by eliminating one of the cornerstones is for everything to appear arbitrary and chaotic, which is appalling for the Soul to perceive because it is devoid of principles.

Music without melody is like language devoid of meaning—it is blather and nonsense. We have a sense of melody because we need to be aware of the presence of blather and nonsense. Why? Because that which blathers nonsense is insane, unpredictable, and possibly dangerous. The more arbitrary a person's actions are, the more dangerous that person might be to others. The more chaotic the conditions are within a group of people, the greater the likelihood of erratic, dangerous behavior gaining a foothold in the group. This is why mobs are so dangerous.

When we hear music that is arbitrary and chaotic, we respond as if the music signals danger. The effect on us is to excite the fear centers in our brains and create physical stress and tension as our bodies respond to the perceived threat. Conversely, when we hear music that is melodious, the parts of the brain which process structure and meaning are stimulated into activity, thereby producing feelings in us which language is incapable of producing. What is most interesting about the sense of melody is that it is the most palpable means of sensing how the brain processes sound. This depends, of course, on the ability of the performer to reveal the meaning behind the notes, harmonies, and rhythms that make up the melody. A metrically strict performance of a melody appears to be processed exclusively in the left hemisphere of the brain. When the performance of the melody is highly expressive of its meaning, it is possible to sense the attention-energy flowing from one side of the brain to the other and back again. The greatest performances of music cause this effect in the brain to be so obvious that it is like having music painted or brushed onto the mind's imagination.

The sensation of attention-energy repeatedly moving from one side of the brain to the other and back again is like swooning. Persons who are dominantly right-brained love this effect, while those who are left-brain dominant usually hate the sensation because it makes them feel seasick. Over the last eighty years, musicians who advocate a stiff and wooden way of playing music that purposely avoids producing the swooning effect have dominated the field of classical music. Because they have been "deaf" to the consequences of their unnatural style of playing, support for classical music in Western culture has dwindled to the point where now even the "deaf" struggle to understand what has happened. Little did musicians eighty years ago realize that when they changed how music was performed, most people in the audiences were dominantly right-brained when it came to listening to music and were quickly bored of music that left-brain dominant people happen to like. An audience once lost is almost impossible to regain. Musicians who earn their living by playing music composed before the mid-twentieth century must become reacquainted with their sense of melody and respect it. This is the only way to rekindle interest in the music they present for consumption.

The sense of melody is valuable to anyone studying languages of any kind, including computer-generated speech. Failure to recognize cultural modes of inflection, which are melody based, can lead to embarrassing gaffs or misunderstandings

What happens if a person has no sense of melody? It is unthinkable that this condition should ever occur in the brain. Were it to happen, that person would likely be unable to read shifts in inflection, which would render them socially incompetent because people unreasonably expect others to "get the message" from their inflections alone. It is a bad habit that is often practiced by people who prefer to communicate by indirection, and it leaves those who fail to "read between the lines" at a social disadvantage.

Sometimes we speak of people who can't carry a tune, sing in tune, or match pitch as being tone-deaf. My wife, Marianne Ploger, who has spent her career training musicians to know and understand what they are hearing in music, has found that these people are the opposite of tone-deaf. Her experience is that those who can't carry a tune are usually hypersensitive to sound, and they hear all manner of overtones as strongly as we less sensitive people hear a basic pitch. The result for them is confusion about exactly what the pitch is, so they vocally leap around trying to match some aspect of the tone or its overtones that they hear. Those who have trouble singing in tune are usually inexperienced at using their voice to match pitch. When this malady is found in a musician, the outcome is usually no career in music. Since everyone who can hear and who has normal vocal chords can learn to sing in tune, out of tune playing or singing is a defect that can be traced back to lack of experience or music teachers who can't be bothered to insist that their students play or sing perfectly in tune. In my opinion, nothing is more odious than hearing music played out of tune; it is like being served a meal in which all the ingredients were specifically selected to be rotten.

To a refined sense of melody, being in tune or hearing something in tune has the effect of stimulating the bones of the face, thus causing them to resonate. In many spiritual disciplines, chanting is thought to help focus one's thoughts. It does so by activating the bones in the face, which creates a feeling of being well-focused. This, in turn, creates a feeling of peace and well-being.

THE SENSE OF PROBABILITY

The sense of probability is perhaps one of the most important senses for thinking. With this sense, you can test ideas that are in your imagination. By testing the probability of ideas in your imagination, you are able to prevent waste of time, resources, or energy, etc. By letting your imagination run free with ideas, you can learn about consequences and effects and how they link to causes. As linkages are formed in the imagination, they are "scanned" by your sense of probability to notice their degrees of likelihood of being real. In general, if you sense that the likelihood is high that an idea will come to a dead end, you lose all interest in that idea. On the other hand, if you sense that an idea will probably turn out as being extremely useful, your interest in that idea will perk up and grow, and it encourages you to run more probability experiments to watch how the idea fares under various conditions. You do this entirely in your imagination. When an idea has gripped your attention with the probability of success, then you test it in reality to see if it actually works.

Without being able to do probability scans in our imaginations, creative thought would likely fizzle out in the minds of most people, just as discouraging and criticizing ideas in the imaginations of children causes them to doubt the usefulness of their imaginations. Parenting that encourages children to cultivate their imaginations produces creative adults that are competent to solve problems effectively. Parenting that discourages children's imaginations results in unhappy adults who are fearful of change and unable to effectively solve real-life problems.

Human vision and far sightedness spring from a cultivated imagination and a well-honed sense of probability. It is these traits that are becoming more and more necessary in our world today. Without a keen sense of probability, mistakes in judgment will occur with greater frequency, and decisions based on poor guesswork will have far-reaching consequences because so much of our world is becoming automated. Once a machine assumes responsibility for a task, it does its work independently of outside controls. The results of this happening become more probable as humans defer judgment to those running machines, and the probability of mistakes being multiplied exponentially skyrockets.

THE SENSE OF POSSIBILITY

Like the sense of probability, we have a sense of possibility. Should an idea appear to work, in all probability, we can scan the idea for its possibility of success and its possible undesirable side effects. Scanning or tasting an idea for possibilities differs from scanning or tasting an idea for probabilities. What is possible will probably happen, but what is probable isn't necessarily possible. For instance, it is possible that a trip to Mars by human beings will happen in the future. Since such trips are governed by things like the return on investment of time and money, the probability that such trips will occur becomes increasingly less likely. If robotics continues to advance to the point where sending robots to do the work of a human becomes possible, the probability of sending humans to Mars becomes so unlikely as to become impossible.

One way we use our sense of possibility is for detecting when to quit a project or when to start one. The limits of what is possible are based on intrinsic properties, such as time, resources, and human interest. In this regard, the senses of probability and possibility are different. Probability is a likelihood that we might conjecture, guess, or speculate about, whereas possibility has natural limits that influence the outcome and are based on knowledge.

The sense of possibility feeds the imagination with every conceivable option, especially when we refer to these as endless possibilities. It is a true irony that what appears to work for the imagination, in terms of endless possibilities, actually squelches the ability of the mind to make a decision regarding something specific. The mind, when faced with unlimited possibilities, has the greatest trouble making a decision. Freeing the mind requires that its choices are curtailed.

Applying our sense of possibility is how we manage to think outside the box, while we use the sense of probability to manage the size of that box. A person of good common sense knows the limits of both. Because the Soul cannot be limited, it is prudent to understand how to pose our questions about what is possible in a manner that includes all possibilities and entertains every probability. J.S. Bach was quoted as saying, *"Alles muß möglich sein."* That is, "Everything must be possible." Sir Arthur C. Doyle has Sherlock Holms saying, "How often have I said to you that when you have eliminated the impossible, whatever remains, however improbable, must be the truth?"

THE SENSE OF MECHANICS

The ability to visualize in three dimensions is linked to the sense of mechanics. The better trained a person's skill in visualization is, the more we characterize that person as having a good mechanical sense. They are often able to deconstruct and construct things entirely in their head. Indeed, the more finely honed someone's mechanical sense is, the more intelligent they are thought to be. This is the reason why academics revere those who have this ability. By using a keen sense of mechanics, one can take a few lines drawn casually on a piece of paper and make huge intuitive leaps to seeing the whole object working entirely in the imagination. Bach, Mozart, and Beethoven had that ability where music was concerned. Da Vinci, Edison, and Tesla had that ability in the realm of machines.

When I speak of the imagination as being the playroom of the Soul, I mean the specific ability to construct things entirely in the imagination. For your Soul to be able to play with ideas, concepts, and constructions, you must first have paid full attention to all the details. If one detail is missing, the ability of your Soul to play will be materially compromised. When complete attention to detail has been forthcoming, and you are still unable to construct a proper object or objective, it is then up to your Soul to provide the missing feature. Here is where allowing the Soul to do its work by assuming the role of active observer is extremely important. Once you have done all you can on your own initiative, the Soul takes over and finishes the work. Your best effort from that moment on is to stand by and watch as the Soul begins the process of rearranging all the factors into a completely new order that makes total sense, but that you would never have thought of on your own.

Watching the Soul in this process leaves one in awe. It is this process that sits at the center of every religion. It is this process that people have sought to capture in religious doctrines and creeds, hoping to get control of God. Every true spiritual leader has understood the ephemerality of this experience and understood that the only way to approach it is by maintaining an attitude of love and care. Each, in their own way, understood that it was through *knowing* that this experience could be managed, but never controlled. In reality, this process is possible for everyone to experience because it is subject to a set of rules.

The sense of mechanics is one of the pivotal senses needed to provide the impetus for the Soul to explore its playroom. Whether the vehicle is visual, auditory, kinesthetic, intellectual, or attitudinal is not particularly important because they all derive origin in the playroom of the Soul. By understanding the term *mechanics* as a structure and its workings, we can accept that the sense of mechanics includes everything understood or understandable, no matter its form.

THE SENSE OF SIMILARITY

Similar means "akin to" or "alike." The sense of similarity helps us notice similarities in things that appear totally dissimilar. We often confuse the sense of similarity with the sense of logic. Where the two senses converge is in discerning the logically dissimilar as similar by noticing how the surface dissimilarities obscure underlying similarities. For instance, what is similar between a pyramid and soda straw? Two unrelated similarities come to mind. The pyramid is a four-sided triangular form and the straw is a cylindrical form, yet both are similar in that they both are forms. Further, just as the pyramid could have been understood by its makers as a conduit for the Soul to pass from the earthly plane to the spiritual plane, the soda straw is a conduit for liquids to pass from one container to another. So, the sense of similarity can help you "think outside the box."

From a cognitive point of view, the brain makes sense of things not by how they are the similar, but by how they are different. Light and shadow highlight this point. In a landscape filled with light, those elements that are in the shadow will be the first thing we notice because they are most dissimilar. Our sense of contrast is the sense that brings this to our attention. Those things that are contrasted are easy to perceive, so we need the sense of similarity to bring to our attention those things that appear dissimilar but may be viewed as similar. This is one major way in which the mind notices subtle interrelationships of things. Our sense of similarity helps us keep the mind trained on noticing and processing things for which it was intended to notice and process.

We do ourselves an injustice when we allow the sense of similarity to govern our prejudices. When we limit our preferences to matters, things, or people that are familiar to us, we are limited indeed. The Soul rejects the prejudiced and bigoted mind (in that way, the Soul is prejudiced). A right use of the sense of similarity is to find the common elements that make all that seems unusual, foreign, or dissimilar to be viewed as somehow similar. By practicing sensing similarities as well as differences, it is possible to develop an open mind. Cultivating an open mind is the technical practice of being in Love Mode, which is required to activate the Soul.

THE SENSE OF DIFFERENTIATION

The sense of differentiation is not the same as noticing how things are different. Noticing how things are different is what the brain does because the body needs to unambiguously know those things that are familiar from those things that are unfamiliar. In an environment full of unfamiliar and possibly dangerous things, survival hinges on eliminating the unfamiliar from our diet to avoid eating something poisonous. Taken further, survival depends on our ability to differentiate between what is familiar and what is similar. Those who can't distinguish the subtle differences between certain kinds of red berries by sight or by taste might make the fatal mistake of eating yew berries instead of cranberries.

Distinguishing slight differences is what our sense of differentiation is designed for. Carl Linnaeus, the eighteenth-century Swedish botanist, revolutionized the science of botany by declaring that all plants could be accurately classified by something as simple as counting the sexual organs found in the flowers of plants. Before that, most botanists were amateurs whose real profession was as clergymen in the church. These amateurs sought to classify plants according to how similar they appeared to other plants in growth pattern and leaf or flower structure. When Linnaeus proposed his system of classification based on the sexual organs of plants, the idea of it scandalized the amateur botanists because it was based on sex organs. Linnaeus' system eventually became recognized as the one sure method for classifying plants. Just recently has his method been supplanted by DNA testing. As more botanists are trained to collect plants' DNA and process it to classify as of yet unclassified plants, finer and finer differences will emerge to reveal new species and families of plants. Science would be in a sorry state without our sense of differentiation.

THE SENSE OF ANALOGY

We make analogies to clarify points we wish to emphasize. For example, I have used the analogy that the Soul system is like the digestive system to explain the process whereby our attention-energy feeds the Soul, just as the digestive system feeds and processes food for the body. However, it must be remembered that it is extremely easy to make up false analogies. Although they sound good on the surface, a false analogy is fraught with underlying problems. Our sense of analogy is there to help us detect analogical fraud.

Logical fallacies, of which false analogies are one of many, abound in our market-driven environment. These fallacies are used as an easy way to convince unthinking people of almost any idea or policy that salespeople and politicians want.

Without a finely-honed sense of analogy, false analogies are difficult to detect because they have been constructed to appeal to people's basest instincts and biases. The impulse to believe is a base instinct because the act of believing is far easier than the act of knowing, which is not an instinctive act.

The Soul and the truth go together. If an analogy is true, it might indeed emanate from the Soul. False analogies are barriers to the Soul in thinking.

THE SENSE OF METAPHOR

Metaphors are to poetry as analogies are to prose. Where analogies appeal to thought, metaphors appeal to our sense of metaphor and the feelings generated by poetic expression. Metaphors are the language of the spirit because everything in the spiritual realm is ineffable, i.e., beyond the ability of language to accurately describe or express. For this reason, we use metaphors to discuss sensations, feelings, spiritual reality, and emotions.

Music, in a sense, is continuous metaphor in sound. Metaphors in music are called *affects*, which act like emotions but are only suggestions of them. This chord or that melody sounds like flowing water, the effect of which makes the listener feel calm and refreshed at the same moment. Every subtle change in chords or their progression in time creates a different effect of which affects are the metaphor. Ditto for each subtle change in melody.

By learning to think metaphorically, you can train your sense of metaphor and simultaneously create a clear pathway into the imagination for your Soul to follow. Speaking or thinking in the language of the spirit and the Soul is giving a direct invitation for your Soul to speak or think for you. This is when the opportunity to learn from the Soul is apparent. Learn what it thinks, then think on all you can learn from it.

THE SENSE OF SUFFICIENCY

The sense of sufficiency amends the sense of limit (p. 221), and vice versa. Sufficiency is less than limit, but more than enough. To know when something is sufficient, it must first be sensed in the imagination. It is not as simple as knowing that a glass is full.

How do you know when you have had sufficient experience at doing something? In ancient times, the best advice given to students was to find a skilled master of a specific craft or trade and stay with that master as long as possible (even twenty years was considered an insufficient time to learn all that a master could teach). Today, young people think that taking a six-hour course or training for a year is sufficient for learning all they need to be competent. Anxious to improve their earning potential, they join the ranks of the dangerously ignorant when they try to make a living using the little they know, while they are convinced that their education was sufficient.

It is in the nature of mastery that what is masterfully done appears to be easily done. Little do aspiring masters realize how much knowledge is required to do something (apparently easily) that is extremely difficult. As Michelangelo once wrote, "We cannot surpass what we do not at first equal."

In another vein, you use your imagination to sense the completeness of a specific task. You sense if the work was sufficient. If you are insensitive to this sense, you will fail to appreciate every aspect involved with a task and wonder why the work at hand doesn't pan out. Over the last thirty-five years, I have repeatedly noticed in myself that I think I've arrived at the final solution only to discover that there are more aspects to ponder. If it takes thirty years to uncover all there is to know about a subject, the first fifteen years of that is required to learn 95% of what is important, the next five years is spent learning the next 3% of what is important, and the remaining 2%, which is the most important knowledge of all, requires another ten years. The subtler the knowledge, the longer it takes to uncover it. When you teach all that you know to someone, who might learn it in six months or a few years, their lack of appreciation for the knowledge causes them to dismiss much of it as unimportant.

Imaginatively underrating what is sufficient is perhaps the best way to fully comprehend how much is yet to be learned in some skill. This is a means to combat the condition of not knowing how much there is to know.

This sense is also applied to the areas of judicial discretion, legislation, economic decision-making, and behavior modification, for a start.

THE SENSE OF WORTH

The worth of something is a justification of its importance or quality. Worth is sensed as extrinsic, whereas value is sensed as intrinsic. When we are in a position requiring us to determine the worth of something, we invariably consider the question on the basis of what we are willing to pay for it in currency, time, energy, substance, or knowledge. Value, on the other hand, is usually considered to be intrinsic to an object itself and is beyond price. For example, the value of a trinket or object owned by a loved one may be far greater than it's worth on the open market. The act of weighing the factors involved in worth is something we do in our imaginations. In general, reciprocity is involved, so it seems that the senses of worth and reciprocity are linked.

Because worth is connected to specific amounts, determining worth also requires using the senses of probability and possibility. People who are particularly good at pricing objects have a well-honed sense of worth as concerns the probable or possible price that an object might fetch.

Rarity can be a worth-determining extrinsic property. The harder a thing is to find or possess, the more worth is attributed to it. This is one of the reasons why the paintings of a great artist fetch high prices, while photographic reproductions of those paintings are relatively worthless.

Another extrinsic property used to determine worth is an understanding of the skill required to make an object. That which requires virtually no skill to create is usually considered to be worth less than an object that requires great skill in its creation. Hence, a hastily decorated Easter egg is considered to have less worth than one made by Fabergé, but if a person was starving, the Easter egg might have significantly greater value than that made by Fabergé.

Worth is also figured according to amount or size. A small meteorite is worth less than a large meteorite. Although this might be because large meteorites are rarer than small ones. The extrinsic worth relating to size has more to do with the mind's perception of anything larger as also being worth more. When the perception of worth related to size is trumped by the perception of preciousness, the issue of size relative to worth inverted. Compare the worth, for instance, of a Stradivari violin with a Stradivari cello. The Stradivari cello is much rarer than one of his violins, yet it is his violins that are perceived as being more precious (though perhaps not to a cellist).

Worth is also calculated based on desirability. The more desirable an object is, the greater its worth is perceived to be. Hence, a sculpture of mediocre quality, made by a famous movie star who has a fan base in the millions, might be considered worth more than a high-quality sculpture made by an excellent but relatively unknown artist. Great collectors of art often have a sophisticated appreciation for works of superior intrinsic value. Collectors take advantage of unknown artists and buy their work while it remains affordable. By the time the artists have become famous, the collectors have amassed enough work to be worth millions.

Finally, both worth and value come together according to the expression of universal principles intrinsic in an object. The greater the number of principles expressed, the higher the quality that is perceived. The higher the perceived quality, irrespective of size, rarity, skill, or preciousness, the more a thing is worth. As time goes on, those things which are perceived to be of higher quality gradually acquire greater worth, though their intrinsic value has not changed at all. This is because the number of people able to appreciate objects for the principles they express has radically increased through time.

What of the worth of an idea? What is the worth of a true thought? Our sense of worth functions as a guide to appropriate action when applied to ideas and thoughts, as well as to things.

THE SENSE OF SIMPLICITY

One of the rarer senses is the sense of simplicity. The stronger the intellect, the less likely it is to have a developed sense of simplicity. To cultivate the sense of simplicity, you are required to habitually curb any tendency towards the grand and complicated. It means to cultivate a focus on essence and what is direct. While the grand and complicated are more impressive to many, simplicity is the realm of the real connoisseur. Lincoln's *Gettysburg Address* is an exercise in simplicity. The single true statement, clearly and simply expressed, trumps the finest fantasy clothed in the richest highfalutin language. Eloquence is greatly overrated when it is found in those who are in love with the sound of their own voice.

In simplicity, you hear the sound of the Soul speaking. The Soul generally expresses itself in the simplest terms possible, while the intellect adores its own erudition, and the ego can't get enough of talking about itself. By listening carefully, you can train your sense of simplicity as you learn to delineate these three aspects of yourself.

Simplicity is largely unadorned, essential, clear, direct, and comprehensive. By filtering your experiences with this understanding, you can learn to put away needless complications and restrict your dependence on them.

The best training you can undertake to cultivate the sense of simplicity is in the art of mindfulness. Next to meditation, mindfulness hones the everyday awareness of excess.

THE SENSE OF PROFUNDITY

Getting to the core of any matter or delving below the shallow surface of any subject is what *profundity* means. When we hear a profound thought, we tend to classify that thought as deep. The more a thought expresses the truth behind the universal principles, the greater the depth we perceive in it. The sense of profundity leads us to either seek more of the same or avoid it altogether. This effect is relative to the degree to which we apply ourselves when pursuing a line of profound thinking. Some people are instantly overwhelmed by the profound because they are unfamiliar with it. Most are able to handle being in that realm for a short while. Very few seek to be in that realm most of the time.

Contrary to popular opinion the realm of the profound is neither complicated, complex, nor hyperbolic. The more a thought or an idea is based on universal principles, the more profound it is. This in no way means that thought will be easy to understand. We can sense the profundity of a thought long before we are able to understand it. Thoughts which emanate from the Soul are often the most difficult to understand.

The ease of understanding a thought is inversely proportional to its profundity. This often leads to a convoluted expression of certain thoughts in hope of appearing profound. Works on music theory or educational theory are particularly prone to obtuse language for the sake of appearing thoughtful, while the reality is that it is usually a cover-up for the loss of having anything useful to say. All one needs is to hear the compositions composed by music theorists in comparison to those composed by great composers. As ever, I use Bach as the supreme example of clarity, simplicity, profundity, and directness. In his text, *Precepts and Principles for Playing the Thorough-bass Or Accompanying in Four Parts,* he spells out on a few sheets of paper the entirety of his music theory.[26] That work

---

[26] J.S. Bach, *J.S.Bach's Precepts and Principles for Playing the Thorough Bass or Accompanying in Four Parts*, translated by Pamela L. Poulin (Oxford: Clarendon Press; New York: Oxford University Press, 1995).

is complete in every way, except that he doesn't include anything about his personal process of composing music using those principles.

THE SENSE OF SIGNIFICANCE

Significance is outstanding, pertinent, and specific. Without these three traits, significance cannot exist. Our sense of significance is brought to bear on matters that immediately concern us. When we speak of something as being significant, we are usually referring to these three traits. If nothing stands out to our perception (i.e., it is not outstanding), we consider what we are taking in to be irrelevant. If it is not pertinent to our immediate situation, we may consider it to be relevant, but not at that particular moment. And, if something that appears to be outstanding and pertinent fails to ring true to us, we can't say that it is significant. When all three traits are present—outstandingness, pertinence, and specificity—we experience a strong stimulation of this sense and can say that what we sense is significant.

This sense is special to the imagination because signs and symbols are the stuff of this realm. I refer you to the sense of metaphor. Signs and symbols are metaphors connecting the mind, through the imagination, to what is real in the world of objects, ideas, and feelings.

Much meaning is contained in the quality of significance because meaning conveys that the attention paid to something only scratches the surface, and it will become deeper and more profound on closer inspection.

THE SENSE OF ELASTICITY

That which is elastic has the property of springing back to a previous shape or condition after being distorted. A rubber band is elastic because no matter how stretched or twisted it may be, it will always resume its former shape unless it breaks. When we take a new idea, add to it, and twist it out of shape, we do so to gauge the elasticity of the idea. The more elastic a thing or idea is, the stronger it is to our sense of elasticity. Many ideas and thoughts can't stand up to being twisted out of shape in the imagination. Those that can stand up to deformation are the ones we tend to respect.

We use our sense of elasticity to detect the health of objects, ideas, and concepts. Without this sense, we would spend much of our time guessing about things, and thinking would become onerous and clumsy. Just as little children will take a new toy and do everything in their power to pull it apart, we play with ideas and things in our imaginations to notice what abuse they will bear. Parents view this behavior in children to be negative because they see the behavior as destructive, not to speak of costly. Yet those "destructive" children are probably doing to their toys what they will eventually do with ideas and thoughts handed to them by adults. If this is true, then parents need to watch this behavior and teach their children to do it to ideas as soon as possible.

From the famous Ten Commandments, the two commandments that exhort us not to have gods before God and warn us against creating graven images are both referring directly to our sense of elasticity. By avoiding creating gods of ideas, things, and beliefs, we also avoid creating things that will break under the distortion of thoughts to which we are exposed. Similarly, when we avoid making graven images of those ideas, things, and beliefs, we are able to think more flexibly, and our thoughts are more able to tolerate being distorted while still remaining inviolate.

The problem many people have when it comes to being creative is that they craft their ideas into gods and graven images, both of which easily get broken when exposed to the rigors of mortis in the imaginations of others. When they watch their ideas being shot down, they become extremely upset because what got destroyed was their god and graven image. By avoiding worshipping or idolizing ideas, thoughts, and inventions, they can become living, working, useful things as they go through the refiner's fire of criticism and reworking. People who take little offense when their ideas are subjected to criticism use their sense of elasticity to bounce off the criticism and learn to create work of greater quality.

The universal principles of distortion and elasticity work together as polar opposites. The greater the distortion applied to something, the closer to breaking point it is brought. If a distorted idea, thing, or hope manages to snap back unbroken, it is likely that it will be stronger than before. Similarly, people who are able to snap back from being taken close to breaking point usually become stronger from the experience. When life casts difficulties in your path, it is prudent to remember this.

THE SENSE OF GESTURE

The mathematics of gesture is expressed in logarithms to describe the amount of increase or decrease of something, but that doesn't explain the vast array of what human beings experience as gesture. Gesture is the language of attitude and meaning. Every attitude manifests itself in a gesture. Our sense of gesture is designed to help us read a gesture and comprehend the attitude that produced it or the meaning behind it. The Nazi salute is converted from the heinous mentality of racism into the command to "Stop!" by changing the position of the hand from 45° to 90°, relative to the ground. Maintaining that hand position while moving the arm to a position of 90° to the body changes the meaning from "Stop!" to "stay" or "stay away." Moving the arm in an arc across the chest, with the hand still at 90°, means "you're dismissed," or "get out, you're bothering me."

In art, the sense of gesture is essential to creating work that has meaning because much of what we communicate in the gestures we present are the attitudes which others read from our work. Angular gestures communicate anger and distemper. Rounded gestures communicate loving attitudes. Heavy gestures communicate oppressive attitudes. Long gestures communicate attitudes of patience and endurance.

During the Baroque period, from 1600 to 1750, artists, musicians, architects, and so on were all expected to know, understand, and use the language of gesture to communicate attitudes. Those who were not competent to do this were understood as being mere technicians. Since that time, this objectively understood language of gesture has been gradually abandoned in favor of self-expression. The inevitable result is that art has become less and less meaningful or relevant. When it has been meaningful, that meaning has been either unintended or accidental. Since everything done expresses the attitude of its maker, the unintended attitudes tend to be solipsistic, narcissistic, and egocentric, which is not very interesting or pleasant for the observer.

When an artist's work shows no gestures at all, the attitude expressed is one of indifference to the receiver. This attitude communicates that the receiver is so irrelevant as to be dead. The attitude expressed by sharp points and geometric angles is like the attitude of a vandal attacking the viewer with knives, ready to inflict imprisonment on the observer. There is no art when the observer is treated in an unloving manner by the artist. The function of art is to create love where love did not first exist. It is through the sense of gesture that we become aware of this.

THE SENSE OF IMPRESSION

When you are impressed by something, you respond automatically to it. With this particular sense, you discover the necessary forces in your life that lead to creativity. Being jaded means having lost the ability to receive an impression. It is an unfortunate reality that those who are inured to impression, either positive or negative, also experience little creativity, much less a relationship with the Soul.

Since a relationship with your Soul involves receiving impressions from it, it is imperative to cultivate a high degree of sensitivity to your Soul's impressions. This has the effect of sensitizing you to other impressions from the external world, which can be devastating if the events and actions that make the impression are negative, but as long as you are aware of the dangers, it is possible to take them in your stride. The alternative might render you impotent.

Sensing impressions from the Soul and responding automatically to them is what this sense is intended for. I've used the analogy before of the Soul's impressions being a thousand times fainter than the taste of a few grains of salt. Indeed they are. Cultivating this sense means purposely magnifying the subtle and sublime until they become commonplace.

Chapter Twelve

The Moral or Ethical Senses

You might be confused about what I mean by *moral* or *ethical*, so I will discuss briefly what I mean by these words. Traditionally, morals have been the territory of religion, as ethics have been the territory of philosophy. The aim of morals and ethics is the same—providing a foundation for living a good life. So, for the sake of simplicity, I will refer to these senses as *the ethical senses*, but you can understand that the term *moral senses* could equally be applied.

For each culture, what is deemed ethical and moral has been largely a matter of what happens to work within that culture's religious and philosophical framework. For instance, in a culture of headhunters, killing is deemed a good thing. In our culture, killing is considered bad unless the government says it is a good thing to do, like in war or capital punishment. Among the Jains of India, killing of any kind and for any reason is bad, period.

What this means is that morals or ethics are relative to time and place. In the early part of the Judeo-Christian tradition, the killing of disobedient children, adulterous wives, homosexuals, and pork eaters was considered good behavior because it got rid of people who disagreed with the rules of behavior set down by the lawmakers and the priests who followed them. We no longer kill people for those behaviors, maybe to the regret of the puritans among us. Yet those same puritans are as shocked as anyone when they hear about honor killings in other countries. So it seems that morals and ethics are right and proper for those who believe their morals and ethics to be the best available. Since that includes just about everyone in the world, it would also seem that the greatest good is tolerance of differences, stupidity, nonsense, beliefs, lifestyles, etc., as long as they don't cause anyone harm. Intolerance is the greatest evil, except for when it is intolerance of intolerance. Otherwise, practicing tolerance with patience and good humor is the highest ethical standard.

Only when the culture of tolerance breaks down because too many people fail to accept that standard of behavior do morals and ethics become a topic of discussion. The trend over the last five hundred years is for people to become increasingly tolerant until they are too tolerant from a puritan's point of view, whose desire in life is to sterilize the world of disapproved behaviors and people. It is not enough that humanity has learned over centuries of cruelty and evil what the costs of intolerance are. It seems that the human family must repeatedly learn this lesson because of our tolerance of the intolerant ones among us. For this reason, I hold that our tolerance for what others do or think should extend only to those who practice tolerance. We need to be totally intolerant of those among us who insist on being intolerant and teach intolerance to others. Intolerance festers like a cancer in the minds of the discontented until it metastasizes into a political party of leaders who spread their venom of intolerance into the law. This is exactly what occurred in Germany in the 1920's and 30's with the Nazis, who were arch-puritans. If it requires yet another world war to eradicate the attitude of intolerance completely, that is what will happen. In the end, intolerance is the greatest of all evils because it justifies the cruelty and venom that are its spawn. That is why intolerance must be treated with intolerance.

What does this mean for the ethical senses? What it means is that great care must be exercised in the training and conditioning of our awareness of those senses. We need to understand that the impulse to sterilize the world of those who disagree with us lurks in each of us, most especially during adolescence. During adolescence, the ethical senses become part of the development of every human being, and the impulses stemming from those senses need to be carefully guided lest the influence of intolerant power mongers and puritans gain a foothold in adolescent minds. We are all responsible for taking care of the minds of the young, or they will become the pawns of those who occupy the "dark side of the Force," to quote George Lucas. This means that everyone is responsible for warning the rest of when and where intolerance is metastasizing.

The ethical senses are the backbone for how we relate to others with whom we must share the planet. When these senses are violated, it can be the cause of altercations and war. The problem with these senses is that they are highly susceptible to corruption from beliefs of all kinds. If we are to live together at peace on Earth, we are obligated to question our beliefs so that we maintain the ability to clearly read the truth from what our senses are informing us. Here lies the problem. Beliefs that feel right and secure are often those that spring from intolerance. So it is of utmost importance to inculcate the habit of questioning everything in the light of what will make the future more harmonious for everyone. Despite the fantasy of leaving Earth to populate distant worlds—supposedly after suitably despoiling our own planet—we are stuck here, so we had better get used to the idea and learn to live with each other in ways that are increasingly harmonious.

Entertaining nonsense notions like that escape fantasy seem all too pervasive, and it has the effect of letting people think that they are going to escape the spoilage of the earth that has been accelerating since the beginning of the industrial revolution. Human beings are designed to live on Earth and nowhere else. We aren't going to magically redesign ourselves using genetic engineering because we aren't smart enough to do a decent job of it. If we can't do a decent job of living responsibly with each other in the world we were designed for, a job that we can actually accomplish, there is no way we will be able to solve the problems of adaptation to a completely different environment. First, we must be able to prove that we can live in harmony on an Earth that hasn't become a sewer because of our predatory ignorance and stupidity. Then, just maybe we can let fly the notion of visiting other planets many light years away from Earth.

To make sure we put first things first, we need to learn to be aware of our ethical senses; otherwise, there is no hope for humanity, and another more appropriately fitted species will replace us. From the point of view of the aesthetic self, the evolution of any new species hinges on the specific senses or equipment needed to successfully adapt to new conditions in the environment. Having the equipment for adaptation without the senses needed to effectively use it is an evolutionary dead end. On the other hand, having the senses to effectively be aware of the need to adapt guarantees the development of adaptive behavior. This view of the mechanism behind evolution is based on my observation that change stimulates an organism to respond, and the only successful response is an adaptive response. Where human beings are concerned, the adaptive response occurs in the brain and, as such, requires little new structure. The brain rebuilds itself to adapt to most situations, as long as it has the time to do so. In human beings, all that is required for the brain to begin rebuilding itself are the attitudes of foresight and the projected need for adaptation. While those two requirements are rare to be found in any human population, it is true that every human being is supplied with the equipment for fulfilling those two requirements. That equipment is the aesthetic self. The process used by the brain to rebuild itself for adaptation is jumpstarted by the ethical senses.

THE SENSE OF RESPONSIBILITY

The sense of responsibility makes you aware of how your behavior affects the rest of society and the world. When you have your sense of responsibility violated, it usually occurs because someone has behaved irresponsibly towards you. When your sense of responsibility has been touched, it often happens because you witnessed responsible behavior in another person towards you or others. Touched or violated, the sense of responsibility calls to attention your relationships with others in this world.

The question of human adaptability depends on how tuned humans are to this particular sense. As the population of the world increases, greater demands are made on available resources, and how we each respond to the new conditions determines our ability to adapt. We are responsible for what happens to all of us, and the sense of responsibility calls that to our attention.

Of course, you can ignore this sense and prey on others as you please. This course of action is commonly used by those who put getting ahead in this "dog eat dog" world above their responsibilities as citizens. The consequence of this course of action is alienation from the Soul for those involved, which is a consequence that can go unnoticed for a lifetime. Like the frog that sits contentedly in a pan of cold water while the fire below heats up the pan until the frog is finally cooked to death, behaving in violation of the sense of responsibility feels normal to many people, and they will continue to escalate their irresponsible behavior until it gets the better of them. Eventually, when they need the power of the Soul, the Soul can't recognize who they have become, and so will be of no use to them.

The other side of the sense of responsibility is the person who is so acutely aware of this sense that all other senses are ignored. Such a person is so worried about not being responsible that they might try to become a saint and do everything in their power to redress the fear of violating this sense. In so doing, they forget to live life to the fullest because doing so might be construed as selfish behavior. Spending a life trying to avoid violation of any of the senses is clearly not a user-friendly way to live, and it can be as alienating for the Soul as being a predator. A predatory person feels no guilt for squashing others in their attempt to get ahead, while the saintly wannabe feels guilty for breathing because they might steal air needed by someone else.

My wife, Marianne Ploger, one of the wisest people I have ever met, noticed in her music teaching that there are two distinct groups of students. The irresponsible group she calls *shysters* and the overly responsible group she calls *vigilants*. Shysters try to get away with doing as little work as possible and are full of excuses for why they can't do the work. The vigilant students work extra hard but still can't perform because they are so tied up in knots. For both groups to flourish in what they are doing, the shysters need to learn to be vigilant, and the vigilants needs to learn how to be shysters.

Here are four tricks to living happily with a healthy sense of responsibility:

(1) Be clear about what problems belong to you and what problems belong to others. Pay attention to solving your problems first and wait to be asked for help when others need help solving their problems.

(2) Cultivate an evenly spread attention of all the ethical senses, not just the ones which are being violated or which are ignored because you are preoccupied trying to solve other people's problems.

(3) Pay attention to all that is happening around, and decide what you need to keep yourself upright. It is not good if you neglect an important matter only to find that having done so causes you to be overturned by a perfect storm.

(4) When you have done what is needed to keep yourself intact, then respond to what others need. If you see a person drowning, be sure to put on your life vest before you jump into the water to save them lest they drag you to the bottom of the lake.

Among believers in reincarnation and karma, it is often assumed that if you see a person drowning, you may be interfering with their bad karma by attempting to save them because drowning might be what that person needs to balance their karma. I would say that maybe it is your karma that needs to be balanced by you helping to save a drowning person. These beliefs are often made into convenient excuses for not dealing responsibly with others. The key to understanding how to act always boils down to the question of how it will affect the relationship with your Soul.

Not everyone who asks for help needs it. Someone might be asking for help because they are lazy. The sense of responsibility helps answer such questions. If you turn down a request for help, you are not irresponsible if you have considered the matter and decided not to be forthcoming. In most cases, it is important for people to suffer the consequences of their decisions and actions. What spoils a person most is to never experience the consequences of their decisions and actions. Parents who protect their children from these necessary experiences violate their children's Souls because each time their children fail to experience the consequences of their actions or decisions, it sends a message to their Souls that reality is not important, which makes their Souls unnecessary. The result of this is that the ego is empowered, and the Soul is disempowered.

The most extreme outcome of an empowered ego is to become a predator. Predatory behavior is not limited to criminals. This behavior can be found in religious people who self-righteously determine that they are the best judges of morality. Politicians become predators when they carelessly enact policies that cause the deaths of innocent people or that unleash the predatory tendencies of people who run businesses that pollute the physical and spiritual environments. Those who cause loss of life or loss of relationship with the Soul do irreparable damage to the populace. It is this behavior that causes any civilization to decay. So long as governments are established to preserve the integrity of each citizen's Soul, that nation will remain intact. Sometimes this means attending to the senses of balance, reciprocity, justice, and integrity in the Souls of the majority by removing the person whose aim it is to violate and damage the Souls of others, even if that person happens to be king, president, or prime minister.

Responding sensibly might also mean sacrificing your life to preserve the integrity and good of the whole. The problem with this scenario is in determining who is the best judge to make such a decision. Ultimately, being responsible means being considerate by asking questions and answering them from the Soul's point of view. Depending on the occasion, sacrificing your life could be real or metaphorical. Devoting your life to creating works of art is not the supreme sacrifice one can make, but it is a sacrifice nevertheless because to create art is to devote your life to the works of the Soul. Having no guarantee that your work will ever be appreciated during your lifetime is a sacrifice of security, respect, and esteem. Vincent van Gogh lived and worked his whole life without these values. But for the intervention of his brother, he would have been without the means to buy paints, brushes, and canvases. Now his work stands as a testament to the triumph of his Soul and his responsibility to it.

THE SENSE OF HONOR

The sense of honor does not involve loss of face or suffering damage to the ego. Honor requires steadfastness in the face of insult, slowness to rash action, and a clear and determined integrity. It is characterized by an abiding esteem and long-lasting consideration.

You honor your Soul when you abide by your promises and vows. For this reason, it is important not to make promises or vows lightly. You honor the Souls of others when you are steadfast with them, especially when doing so is not easy. By honoring the Souls of others, you guarantee that your Soul will honor you. Failing to honor the Souls of others brings dishonor to your Soul.

In the area of sports, honor is called sportsmanship. In the area of business, honor means upholding agreements. In the area of academics, honor means never stealing or taking credit for the other people's ideas. In the area of work, honor means fulfilling the job's requirements to the best of your abilities. In the area of human relations, honor means keeping your word. In the area of politics, it means living up to the highest standard of conduct. However, all these different meanings have one result, which is to honor the Soul in yourself and in others.

Exactly what does it mean to honor? First, to honor is to consider and respect; second, to behave loyally and faithfully in word and deed; and third, to place the needs of the Soul before the needs of the self. If you have made agreements with others, honoring those agreements means holding yourself to those agreements, even if doing so costs you in time, energy, and resources. Failing to act honorably communicates to the Soul that you don't consider honorable behavior to be important enough to uphold. The Soul, in turn, will see no reason to uphold and honor its responsibilities to you, and it will withdraw from you. This is the reason why making vows is a serious matter, for a vow dishonored irretrievably damages your relationship with your Soul.

For most cultures, honor and saving face or avoiding disgrace and embarrassment are the same thing. This way of thinking is as petty and groveling as it is weak and cowardly. The ego is the only aspect of the self that can be embarrassed or disgraced, and it is the only part of the self that needs to save face. For the ego, loss of face is tantamount to death, and since the entire aim of the ego is survival, to lose face, be disgraced, or be embarrassed is the same as a lethal threat. This is the motivating force behind the aggression that often accompanies slights and insults, even ones that are wholly unintended. The person who learns self-management so they can weather a hailstorm of insults understands the importance of honoring the Soul within.

To behave honorably, when it comes from the Soul, moves the Soul to action. Behaving dishonorably alienates our Souls from us; it leaves us barren and spent like misers in a pigsty. Having purloined the treasures of other people's Souls, the spent Soul hides in horror of the unclean act. Throughout history, many of these dishonorable acts have led to sumptuous rewards for the thief and poverty and ruin for the creator, but it is indeed fortunate that the spirit puts all to right in the end. So, take care of your Soul by honoring the Souls of others.

THE SENSE OF RESPECT

Respect literally means to look again, look back, or review. Your sense of respect is stimulated positively when you have the sense that another person has considered you, and it is violated when another person treats you dismissively.

There are many reasons why others may treat us dismissively, but they all boil down to the reality that they don't respect us. In general, people tend to respect those who respect themselves. Without self-respect, we can't expect others to respect us, and we also tend not to be bothered much when we are treated with disrespect or dismissiveness. We may certainly register the disrespect of others, but we tend to view their behavior as one of their problems, not ours.

Your sense of respect is essential for having a healthy relationship with others and, more importantly, with your Soul. Indeed, it is more important to respect others than it is to like them. It is often the case that when others oppose us, we tend to lose respect for them. This is the ego acting like a sulking child. It is foolish to assume that others are obliged to respect you because you respect them or because you think you deserve their respect. Likewise, it is foolish to assume that someone's Soul doesn't deserve your respect because you don't like them. Nature is no respecter of persons. Just as we don't usually feel that we deserve to be respected by nature, we also ought not to feel that we deserve the respect of others, if only because it is unreasonable.

How you respect the relationship with your Soul is ultimately how others will respect you. When you hold your relationship with your Soul in the highest esteem, that fact shines through every facet of your being so that even those who don't know you can perceive this aspect in you.

The specific quality that appears to mark a person for respect is the degree to which that person means business in all they say and do. This quality extends to animals. We tend to respect a dog, cat, or bird that appears to mean business. We know we don't want to mess with that animal in a manner that violates it. I have seen how cats and dogs show great respect for hens that have chicks. A mother hen that means business is not a creature you would cross; if you do, you will live to regret it.

The issue of respect reflects the quality, or lack of it, of the relationship you have with your Soul. Today, it is not a foregone conclusion that people consider their Soul. When little is known or understood about anything, the usual regard is no regard at all. Though people may talk casually about the Soul, they don't normally harbor any lingering ideas about its purpose in life. The field of psychology has more or less reduced the matter of the Soul to a mere philosophical concept. If others could be reduced to a mere philosophical concept, the chances are that we would all have a lot less respect for each other. Fortunately, we are more than that and are worthy of respect more than niceties. Dispensing with the niceties of interaction and expressing worth and respect is a way to save valuable time that should not be viewed as dismissiveness.

THE SENSE OF DUTY

Duty, for some people, is a powerful sensation. They feel compelled by their sense of duty to fulfill obligations that others in the same position might not feel obligated to fulfill. We all have a sense of duty. It is that feeling of obligation that makes us take the trouble to vote in elections even if we don't want to. Our sense of duty is the driving force behind the manner in which we honor our commitments, fulfill our obligations, and abide by our agreements.

Duty carries moral imperatives based not on explicit directives, but on intuitively sensed responsibility to others. Being a parent means fulfilling your duty to care for and support your children. Being a child means fulfilling your duty to care for and support your parents in their declining years.

Your duty to yourself is to explore, uphold, investigate, and increase your knowledge of the relationship with your Soul. When you do this by investing yourself in a religion, you satisfy your perceived obligation. Some people fulfill this obligation by reading about spiritual matters. Others fulfill it by assuming full responsibility and doing this duty directly themselves, rather than learning how others have done it or choosing to adopt a set of religious doctrines and practices. It is of no concern to the Soul which way this duty is fulfilled as long as the end result enhances your relationship with it. In the end, the Soul is not fooled.

THE SENSE OF LOYALTY

Loyalty is based on faith. There are two kinds of faith. There is faith that is based on belief, and there is faith based on knowledge. Faith that is based on belief has its foundation in the hope that what is believed is true, whereas faith that is based on knowledge is founded on the intuitive understanding that faith itself is irrelevant, which is to say that what is known may also be intangible or unprovable. Thus, loyalty based on faith founded on belief is steadfast only to the point when what is believed is no longer held to be true. Loyalty based on knowledge is always steadfast, and it is this kind of loyalty that rises from our sense of loyalty. What we sense to be true, though we can't ever prove it so, remains incontrovertible, and thus we remain steadfast in our loyalty to it. We sense loyalty as a connection requiring obligation, and we act on that sensation based on the nature of our faith. In the case of loyalty based on belief, should either the belief or the sensed connection be broken, the loyalty will also be broken.

The sense of loyalty also applies to receiving the loyalty of others. Being sensible to the loyalty others have in us means considering and respecting that sense in others and abiding by the bonds which connect us.

The problem with loyalty exists when it is demanded or required. Once we are required to be loyal, we cannot be loyal in any real sense. Conjured, obligatory loyalty is fealty. Hence, an oath of loyalty to one's country is a bond of fealty, not loyalty, because it makes vassals of those who take the oath. An oath of loyalty to an idea, such as the United States Constitution and the Bill of Rights, is about pure loyalty because the Constitution does not demand an oath. The sense of loyalty serves to distinguish and discern between the right and wrong of such questions.

THE SENSE OF DISCRETION

To have discretion is to have the ability to discern what is responsible or socially appropriate. The sense of discretion must be actively cultivated to have any sophisticated sense of it at all. The complement to the sense of discretion is the sense of propriety because situations requiring discretion have many levels of urgency, from negligible to absolute, based on what is most appropriate to the situation. Since trust is based mainly on the attribute of discretion, to ignore the sense of discretion will result in never being trusted. People who have cultivated a fine sense of discretion tend to be well trusted by those with whom they work and live.

The Soul knows your level of discretion and governs its interactions with you based on its ability to trust you. If others can't trust you to be discreet, what reason should your Soul have to trust you? It is not merely a question of being confident in your ability to withhold, it also includes being confident in your ability to act as you say. When the Soul gives an idea, and you fail to use that idea to the fullest, you are being indiscreet unless you made it clear that you would not oblige your Soul regarding that idea. What your Soul needs is the confidence that you will respond by applying yourself to what it gives you. It is your sense of discretion that informs your Soul with what, when, and how much it can be forthcoming.

The sense of discretion is used to precisely measure all the senses of the ethical self. If you don't cultivate this sense, you will tend to rely on approximations of these senses, instead of precise measurements. As long as you never encounter difficulties arising from errors in these approximations, you might never know the difference. Interrelationship mishaps occur because of such errors.

Where the term *discreet* is used to replace the intention of hiding the truth, for good or ill, the sense of discretion is violated. Too often, good and useful words are perverted to take on base and unethical meanings to such a degree that they can no longer to be trusted to mean what good they can mean. Using the sense of discretion as a filter to ferret out those perversions is the best possible use for that sensibility. Being unwilling to use your sense of discretion in that way makes the sense useless to you.

THE SENSE OF HUMOR

Without a sense of humor, life can be pretty bleak. Overly cultivated ethical senses have the defective tendency of turning us into prigs or stuffed shirts. There is nothing more odious than a prig or stuffed shirt, except someone who claims to be a paragon of virtue but who is bigoted, self-righteous, and judgmental (the three cardinal signs of a person who has no relationship with their Soul). Evidently, these holier-than-thou types forgot to cultivate their sense of humor when they were cultivating the other ethical senses. If you want to find a person who is spiritually ill, look for one who is humorless. Humorlessness is a serious spiritual defect because it makes you a burden to other people, who are then forced to edit everything they say and do for the sole purpose of not offending you because you might treat everything as a possible slight.

You don't need to be good at telling jokes to have a good sense of humor. Rather, it means you can enjoy them. Having a good sense of humor means that you are hard to offend, while those who do not have a refined sense of humor are usually easy to offend. The reason for this is that a person who has a refined sense of humor and is in relationship with their Soul realizes that everyone is pedaling as hard as they can to do the right thing, and when that pedaling fails, it is best to help them laugh at themselves.

Interestingly, when jokes are well constructed, humor is replete with universal principles. It is this confluence of qualities that makes laughing at jokes and other forms of humor so healthy and loving. When we make light of dangerous or serious situations, it doesn't reduce the danger or seriousness, but it does help our minds avoid being stiff and over-reactive.

Laughter can also be viewed as an important medicine because it gets our diaphragms moving vigorously. It is fear that causes us to clinch our diaphragms, and a diaphragm that is forced to exist in a constant state of tension creates illnesses of all sorts as it binds up both the mind and the body. By getting our diaphragms in action, our minds become unbound, our thinking becomes clearer, our actions become more graceful and integrated, and we feel happier.

Still, the sense of humor is about more than laughter or keeping balanced in a world of tension and strife. Humor was once a word that referred to four distinct emotional (not necessarily psychological) conditions of the Soul that were sometimes referred to as the four temperaments. These four states are melancholic, choleric, phlegmatic, and sanguine. Psychologists of today might wrongly be tempted to restate these temperaments as depressive, irritable, indifferent, and cheerful. Melancholic temperaments tend to introspection and contemplation. Cholerics are passionate and energetic. Phlegmatic people are characterized by their calm, unruffled natures. Sanguine folks tend to be gregarious and sensuous.

Having a sense of humor involves your ability to sense and autocorrect any imbalances experienced in yourself. When you sense a surfeit of passion, you might view that state as being inappropriate for an occasion that requires a more contemplative approach. When you detect too much inner calm at a time when you need to be more gregarious, you can take steps to lift your internal energy level to respond to the situation.

Taken from an intellectual point of view, this might look irrational, but viewing everything from an intellectual point of view is also irrational and unbalanced. The sense of humor is designed to balance all the inner forces and to inform your awareness of imbalance. Though all this might appear to be plain old common sense, in a world that has been increasingly drifting into blind intellectualism, it is common sense that is needed to pull us back to reality. Remember, the mind and intellect are a dangerous pair because they are fully competent to create any rational-sounding argument for committing or believing error.

So you don't get the idea that I reject the intellect, let me say that the job of the intellect is to notice the interrelationships of everything. For the intellect to do its job, it must ask lots of questions and process every possible answer to grasp the rational foundations of truth or error, but when the questions become speculation for the pleasure of speculation, then the intellect becomes a plaything that has no more use than a rubber duck in a bathtub. Aware that thousands of people in the world love to use their minds as playthings, I would emphasize that speculation is belief and, as such, is a Fear Mode mental state.

Does this mean that all speculation is worthless? No. Because we are limited in our awareness of reality, we are obliged to speculate about aspects of reality of which we are unaware. The difference here is between the attitude of inquiry about the interrelationships of real things and the attitude of pointless speculation about fantasies. Our sense of humor is there to grasp the distinctions between different kinds of speculation and to help us avoid being sucked into the vortex of pointless meditations, all while still maintaining a certain lightness of being.

THE SENSE OF COMMITMENT

The sense of commitment enables you to think more freely and with greater agility. This behavior stems from the fact that a brain forced to work in an environment that is uncommitted is a brain that is divided. Commitment focuses the energy of the brain to make thinking faster, easier, clearer, and more often right. By using your sense of commitment, you can sharpen your wits faster and better than by doing anything else. The more absolutely you are committed to whatever you are doing, the faster and sharper your mind will become. Breaking commitments you have freely made causes your mental energy to be dissipated because the brain needs to be constantly reminded of what it is supposed to be thinking about.

When you use your sense of commitment to determine the strength of that sensation as it relates to your path or goals, you can autocorrect any deviation in your commitments. This is what the sense was designed for. One of the greatest errors a person can make is to wander through life avoiding commitments—it is as though that person is spending a life rather than living it. Fear of commitment is a paralyzing fear that strangles the inspiration of many would-be creators.

Being creatively blocked is usually traceable to a lack of commitment. Finding no focused commitment to guide how the brain works, the brain freezes into a stall. The reasons for lack of commitment may be many, but they are all excuses. As the saying goes, "there is no such thing as a good excuse." Without commitment, we are forced to function on the "hope that springs eternal in the stupid head."[27]

---

[27] I noticed early in my career how often those around me made their decisions on the basis of hope. I also noticed how often those decisions brought them nothing but more reliance on hope. Thus, I took the well-known saying and adapted it to accord with reality. I could see clearly how

The true nature of commitment is found in the attitude of burning the bridges behind you so that turning back is not an option. I call this attitude *zero options thinking*. If you give yourself even one alternative to a course of commitment, the chances are that you will use that alternative rather than focus on your commitment. It is a good idea to determine all the options and alternative courses of action before making a commitment, but once the commitment is made, all other options are then closed. A feeling of total efficiency is then created in the mind because the Soul can quickly sort out all the available possibilities and produce the best one for the purpose.

One of the cardinal curiosities about zero options thinking is the degree of intensity it endows the thinker. When all other options are closed, the road ahead is the only one you can take. This means you can embrace the difficulties and upcoming decisions without questioning whether the basic direction was right in the first place. Those who dally with every option and possibility dither away a lifetime unsuccessfully trying to get something accomplished. Once the course is charted, holding to that course will reveal the wisdom of taking it. This suggests that asking the greatest number of questions at the outset is the best policy before committing to a decision.

What about holding a commitment to a course that is clearly wrong? This is a double-edged sword. To whom is it clearly wrong? The intellect often fosters doubt by trying to second-guess the commitments of the Soul. This is usually a tactic applied by the ego to divert attention back to it. The other edge of the sword is that the course might indeed be wrong. Fearful of loss of face, you might stupidly continue on that course just to prove that it was the right decision. If you are smart, you admit it was the wrong decision, reassess your options, and then commit 100% to the new course.

In science and art, there is nothing wrong with being wrong. You don't want to prematurely abandon a course of action because you don't understand why it is

---

their proclaimed interest in acoustics was just a tissue of hope, not commitment. I wasn't any smarter than those around me, but I was definitely more committed, and I understood how their desire to understand something about acoustics was not based on well-founded experiments. They were choosing to function on delusion, not on evidence.

right or because you are working intuitively. If the course was intuitively clear to begin with, then holding to that course would eventually reveal the truth and abandoning it prematurely would be wrong. This also reveals another of the purposes behind the sense of commitment, which is sensing differences relative to commitments.

THE SENSE OF DISCRIMINATION

The word *discrimination* has been so twisted out of shape that it no longer means what it should mean, which is the ability to distinguish, discern, or perceive. Since the 1960's and the civil rights movement in the United States, the word *discriminate* has come to mean to behave in a bigoted manner. The result is that people since that time have lost the power to distinguish, discern, or clearly perceive reality around them, so focused were they to haul into court anyone behaving in a prejudiced manner. The interesting thing about this is that losing the ability to distinguish or discern reality leads to narcissism. When deprived of a word that means to distinguish, discern, or perceive, it reduces the ability of the mind to use that word as a tool for doing those things. When the mind is thus rendered impotent without the powers of discrimination, it is allowed to focus on the self. That sounds like narcissism to me. Indeed, people became more narcissistic since the 1970's as they have developed a kind of self-infantilization resulting in a rise in egoistic, predatory behavior that pollutes the political, social, and economic environment.

When you are able to discriminate the thoughts of others, you are able to winnow the wheat from the chaff and sort out your own thoughts more rigorously. This ability means that it is harder for others to snooker you, and you are less prone to indulging nonsense. Your Soul needs you to filter and eliminate what is bad and useless so that only the good and useful remains. The more junk that gets through to the Soul, the more thinking becomes polluted and the more useless the mind is to the Soul. The Soul needs the mind to be as free as possible from junk thought, false ideas, false concepts, notions, sentimental fantasies, and wrong information. The Soul only uses thought that is true, language that is connected to reality, and attitudes that are as free of nonsense as possible. So it is incumbent on you to filter out nonsense as much as possible. This cannot be done without the sense of discrimination.

THE SENSE OF VIRTUE

Everything known or believed vibrates at frequencies that may be read as true or false. Likewise, everything can be calibrated on a scale of zero to one hundred for how true it is, and from zero to negative one hundred for how false it is. Zero indicates something that is neither true nor false. Reality reads zero all the time because reality is neither true nor false—reality is what is, and knowledge or belief has nothing to do with it. What we make or interpret from reality is true to the degree that everything we interpret from reality is known. When Columbus set out with the belief that one could sail west to arrive in India because he believed that the earth was a sphere, he merely showed that it wasn't flat when he discovered the New World. It was the voyage of Magellan that finally proved that the earth was a sphere because the men on that voyage sailed around the globe. The people who insisted at the time that the world was flat were interpreting the fact that the horizon appears straight from ground level. They were functioning in the negative one hundred range. Columbus brought that number up to zero, and Magellan's men brought it up to positive one hundred.

The sense of virtue works much the same way. *Virtue* means truth or righteousness. Interestingly, the word *virile* shares the same root word as virtue. Since virile refers to manliness, this means that one must be righteous and in touch with the truth to be manly. The alternative is to be a male, which only indicates a biological functionality.

We use the sense of virtue to discriminate between the true, the not true, the not false, the false, and every shade in between. Without a sense of virtue, reality is a matter of opinion and truth is relative. When someone holds reality to be a matter of personal opinion, that person has completely shut down their sense of virtue. For them, their sense of virtue doesn't exist.

The Soul knows the truth, so to hold the view that the truth is all a matter of personal opinion means that the Soul is irrelevant. If the Soul is irrelevant, it is like having no Soul at all, and that is to have the ego as the only means of expression.

The sense of virtue needs always to be at the forefront of our processing and making sense of the world. What we take into ourselves needs to be finely filtered to remove every trace of idiocy we are exposed to. By this means are we able to give the Soul the intellectual tools and the knowledge it needs to serve up what we need from it. Those people who live by their sense of virtue never seem to run out of inspiration.

THE SENSE OF CONTINENCE

The word *continence*, in this sense, does not mean being able to avoid urinating or defecating uncontrollably. Here, continence means to contain or command yourself. It means being able to sense when your ego is getting out of control and then rein it back into its hole. We use the sense of continence to herd and hold back the various aspects of ourselves until we release them as is needed.

The intellect can easily get you into as much trouble as can your emotions or your instinctive impulses. Saying or asking something at the wrong time, even though it may be worthwhile uttering, is one example of how the sense of continence is applied in daily interactions. Likewise, expressing an appropriate emotion at an inappropriate time, or vice versa, is another example.

Some people have a highly refined sense of continence and harbor their impulses and actions until they sense that the time is right. (This is the moral behind the story of Ulysses, who found his home overrun with moochers and conspirators upon return to his kingdom. He wisely waited for the right moment to reveal who he was and then cleared his home of the moochers and conspirators.) Others let everything hang out and always seem to be saying or doing something that indicates they can't be trusted. When we speak of self-restraint, we are actually talking about using the sense of continence. Both reticence and impulsiveness are signs that the sense of continence is not being attended to. Reticence bespeaks a fear of action or participation, while impulsivity is often read as the sign of a fool.

People who have a highly refined sense of continence always seem to be able to say the right thing, at the right moment, to the right person, and for the right reason. They know the motives and patterns of other people's behavior, and they observe by what means each is convinced or persuaded and what predilections and preferences need addressing to answer any possible objections. They listen carefully to what people say and intuit their real meanings by studying their body language and habits. They carefully plan their strategies to avoid the traps caused by unforeseen problems. They also pick the location and environment to create a relaxed surrounding to broach whatever it is they wish to persuade others of.

When we witness this behavior in a person, we often attribute that behavior to political talent, but nothing could be further from the truth. We all have the sense of continence; it is just that most of us don't bother to pay close attention to it. In this regard, those who we call talented have spent hours paying attention to this particular sense, and they have observed how not paying attention to it sabotages their goals and desires.

Perhaps the best example of one who always seemed to be in touch with his sense of continence was George Washington. It is interesting that at the age of sixteen, he guided himself and his behavior according to a set of rules of conduct taken from *The Rules of Civility and Decent Behavior,* which is a set of 110 maxims to teach proper behavior in young men that he copied out in his own hand. George Washington was keenly aware of the importance of exercising control over himself, even when he was a teenager.

THE SENSE OF DECENCY

When we think about or discuss decency, we often refer to sexual behavior and attitudes. We say that a person who makes sexual jokes in mixed company has no sense of decency. This is true, perhaps, but decency extends far beyond the scope of inappropriate remarks. Our ethical senses are what we need and use to get along in a civilized society. Tracts that sought to teach young men about what was considered decent and indecent have been written and rewritten over the last five hundred years to curb offensive behavior. The one which George Washington used, *The Rules of Civility and Decent Behavior,* was one of many.

Curiously, behaviors which parents teach their children to avoid are often habits and behaviors that occur naturally. By removing natural habits found in young children, the risk is to create in them a fear of social appearance. It would be better to teach children to study the behavior of others and themselves to notice what behaviors demand their attention, what the effects of those behaviors are, and how those behaviors steal attention from more important matters. This course of action would make a scientist of every child.

The sense of decency extends to the area of politics. Some politicians consider war to be a decent way of managing dominance and power in the world but consider intimate same-sex relationships to be indecent, or some believe capital punishment to be decent and abortion to be indecent, and vice versa. Any waiver of our sense of decency from what is true weakens our ability to sense what is truly indecent.

THE SENSE OF VALUE

Where the sense of worth is an imaginative sensation, the sense of value is an ethical sensation. Here, the idea of *value* refers specifically to intrinsic qualities. What has intrinsic value is whatever exhibits the greatest number of universal principles or positively stimulates the greatest number of specific senses in us. On the other hand, extrinsic value is what appeals to our preferences and fulfills our notions of what is ideal.

When we make value judgments about things, people, behaviors, and ideas, we too often resort to extrinsic values as the basis for such judgments. This closes down the possibility of learning how to judge these matters by intrinsic values. So many of the true or intrinsic values have been lost in the political quagmire brought about by religion.

THE SENSE OF RIGHT

Of all the senses, the sense of right is probably the most dangerous of all. It is dangerous because it may be easily confused with the feeling of self-righteousness, which stems from the ego. Self-righteousness arises from the ego's attempts to survive. Like the raving self-righteous, we tussle with our image in the mirror. We observe behavior that felt right to do at the time but that we also know is wrong. Our survival instinct corrects this conflict by causing us to blindly focus on that behavior and seek to stamp it out in others more than in ourselves while hoping and believing that we won't have to suffer the consequences of our behavior.

To avoid falling into the trap of self-righteousness, you first need to recognize how the ego converts your sense of right into a range of emotions and attitudes that can become your undoing. Specifically, those emotions and attitudes are crowned by intolerance for all disagreement. By intolerance, the mind is shut against truth and reason. When disagreement can't be resolved by rash judgments, intolerance becomes subversive. When subversion doesn't work to eliminate "the unrighteous," outright belligerence and aggression come into the act. Each time a self-righteous person's convictions fail to persuade others who disagree with them, the person's self-righteous bullying escalates. This is the underlying process that results in terrorism.

The problem is that to those who are self-righteous, the feelings they experience are firm convictions that their way is the one right way to be. They give little or no thought to the matter of their bullying. In their opinion, they are clearly right and perfectly persuaded of it.

It is by this predictable cycle of escalating intolerant behavior that most of the misery humans have inflicted on each other has occurred. The anger, aggression, and venom that go with the feeling of self-righteousness grow from what begins as mere irritation or offense. In every case, it is the ego that interprets offense as a direct assault on survival. It is the utter stupidity and incompetence of the ego (which can't differentiate the feeling of being offended from a lethal assault) that makes it so dangerous. Historical highlights of when the venom of self-righteousness poisoned humanity may be found in the bigoted purges of Jews, witches, heretics, etc. Without exception, the actors in these pogroms are religious zealots, whether or not their religiosity is political, economic, academic, or theological.

The spiritual condition from which the followers of these diverse religions suffer may be called *self-righteousitis*, which is a word I coined to indicate an inflammation of the feeling of being right. There is one cure for those who are afflicted by this malady, and it is called tolerance. Unfortunately, it is the nature of tolerance to tolerate intolerance that becomes the undoing of any society based on tolerance. When the number of intolerant people increases enough to threaten the tolerant attitudes of a society, then that society is doomed to tyranny by the intolerants. For this reason, every society that advocates tolerance must enforce radical measures to eliminate intolerance.

In contrast to this negative side, the sense of right is important for assessing ideas, thoughts, intentions, actions, attitudes, methods, systems, solutions, questions, and all other forms of conscious mental processes to "taste" the quality of right from those various sources of thought. The sense of right is extremely useful for determining the validity of any of the many senses by which you experience reality.

In many situations in life, the number of variables leads to a multiplicity of possible outcomes. When choosing how to arrange the furniture in your home, for instance, each piece of furniture adds to the number of possible arrangements. Your sense of right is there to help you filter through the plethora of possibilities and come up with the best solution for that particular set of variables. This is a mundane example, but it clearly describes the manner in which we most often apply our sense of right to situations occurring in day-to-day existence.

The better a person becomes at making decisions, the more likely that person is aware of and is actively using their sense of right. There is a right time, a right place, a right order, a right moment, a right size, a right amount, a right action, a right idea, a right way, a right aim, a right connection, a right purpose, etc. for which the sense of right is best applied. Learning to sense what is right about any situation is how experience becomes the best teacher. Anyone who has been mentored well will understand that the focus of mentoring was about instilling in the recipient how to make the right decision in a given situation.

It is the sense of right that ultimately resides behind the phrase, "Let your conscience be your guide." When you understand this, you are able to hone the sensibility of your conscience so that the manner in which it guides your decision-making is quickened and made more accurate and precise. Remember, decision-making is your Soul's job.

Chapter Thirteen

The Intuitive Senses

The intuition is the mouthpiece of the Soul, just as the imagination is its playroom. The Soul is the part of you that makes decisions, and to make the best possible decisions, it requires you to filter your experiences through all seventeen intuitive senses. Like filtering water to purify it for drinking, you need to filter all you experience using the intuitive senses to be able to make the best decisions possible.

THE SENSE OF JUSTICE

The intuition's experience of balance comes in the form of our sense of justice. Some people prefer to refer to this as the sense of fairness or fair play. Sorry to say, we have no sense of fairness; we have feelings of fairness that arise from a complex of senses that feel similar to a sensation of justice (probably because the sense of justice is a part of that complex, which also includes the senses of proportion, number, balance, worth, value, consequence, and gesture). On the other hand, our sense of justice is stimulated specifically by the sensation of balance in the realm of human relations. As often happens, when a woman in the workplace excels in every area of her work and shows great skill in making decisions yet is passed over for promotion in favor of a less competent man, merely because she is a woman, her sense of justice has been violated.

Justitia, the symbol of justice, holds a balancing scale (the Scales of Justice) and a double-edged sword (the Sword of Reciprocity) that cuts both ways, for or against, to create the necessary internal sensation that justice has been served. Human societies need to know that justice is blind to the status of individuals and that when a wrong has been done, the sword will cut down the wrongdoer according to the nature of the wrong. When this sense is left unsatisfied within a society, that society is in deep trouble because people will no longer abide by the law, and they may take out their vengeance on whoever is believed to be the wrongdoer. So it is that our sense of justice is perhaps the most important sense to pay attention to for maintaining societal peace and stability.

When voters witness politicians getting huge payoffs in the form of corporate campaign donations, each voter has two choices—to vote or not to vote. The feeling of pointlessness results when they know that their vote won't count for much because the politician who has the most money to spend on campaigning can repeat their lies more often and more convincingly to get elected. The decision not to vote involves a capitulation of the voter's right to choose the person they feel is most qualified to be in office. A democracy in which voters sense the injustice of their election system will not long be a democracy because it is ripe for perversion. The sense of justice of the body politic needs to be constantly monitored by those in power, lest they end up on the chopping block.

On the other side of the coin, it is important that each individual pays attention to the sense of justice to make sure that it is not merely the ego that feels wronged. Since the ego will stupidly feel as if it is under lethal attack when someone looks the wrong way or says something offensive, we all must be on our guard against the rantings of scorned egos.

THE SENSE OF TRUTH

Truth stimulates our sense of it, so when someone says, "to tell the truth," "the truth be told," "truthfully speaking," or "to be perfectly honest," it usually means that they are not being truthful or honest. That person obviously feels the need to convince you that they are telling the truth. If they were telling the truth, that alone would stimulate your sense of truth.

Saying "the truth hurts" is too true. This points us to one way of telling if we are being lied to—it feels good. Because most people normally function through their egos, they will invariably feel under lethal assault when hearing the truth about themselves. Usually, the truth is that which the ego desires least.

For this reason, telling the truth all the time will get you into a heap of trouble. The trick to staying in the realm of the truth is not to judge other people. Let other people figure the truth out for themselves, and if that takes them a lifetime, that is their problem. Your problem is to know the truth about *Truth*.

There is a great difference between facts, the truth, and *Truth*. Facts appeal to the emotional and physical selves, the truth appeals to the intellect, and *Truth* is exclusively reserved for the spiritual aspect of one's being. Facts spell out what is real or not real. The truth expresses the mechanics behind facts, while *Truth* helps us understand the nature or meaning of facts.

Fact: The sun rises. The truth: The sun rises in the east in the morning and sets in the west at night. *Truth*: Both are false statements because the sun doesn't actually rise; it appears by day and transverses the sky from east to west due to the earth's rotation. It took the better part of the time that humanity has been on the earth for that *Truth* to be utterable. When the Catholic Church charged Galileo Galilei of heresy for advocating the Copernican view of the cosmos, which is the truth about the real relationship between the earth and the sun, that was the moment that many thinking people decided that the Church did not stand for *Truth*, and the Church's stock lost most of its value. By declaring itself as sole arbiter of the truth and then persecuting the world's most famous scientist for expressing *Truth*, the Church basically put itself out of the truth business, and it has never recovered from that one act of brutality. The same game is being played today in the evangelical "Bible churches" when they lobby hard to eradicate the teaching of the Theory of Evolution from school curricula.

The *Truth* is that evolution is a universal principle. The principle of evolution is the force in nature by which nothing happens magically. All things evolve, which means all things are changing and growing from one state to another by small increments. The more spiritual a thing is, the more or the faster it changes. The less spiritual a thing is, the more resistant it is to change. When a thing is unspiritual, be it an act, a thought, an organization, a group, an individual, an object, or anything whatsoever, it evolves negatively. A word we use for that is *devolution*. Dead bodies don't evolve, they devolve.

Pitting yourself against *Truth*, the truth, or even a simple fact is a battle you will lose. You would be choosing to deny and separate from your sense of truth. Separation from *Truth* means exactly what it says. It means fighting against the force in nature that governs the universe and everything in it, from the largest to the smallest, from the strongest to the weakest, and from the most complex to the most simple.

For example, in the former USSR, Communists pitted themselves against the universal principle of individuation by forcing everyone to be economically equal. They pitted themselves against the spiritual forces that make human beings unique creatures with individual strengths, weaknesses, and abilities. These differences make each person economically unique, and no amount of state policy can remove that condition. We now know that a system so perverse lasts until the originators die and they get replaced by people who are more pragmatic, who sense the truth, and who respond to reality. We can't fight nature and win.

THE SENSE OF PURPOSE

The sense of purpose corresponds to the sense of focus. It gives clarity to thoughts and actions. Purpose is the rationale or reason behind the act of doing something. We use the sense of purpose to understand the motives and reasons for why we do what we do. We also use it to detect motivations in others, and we scan thought to discover motives that are hidden from us. If you scrutinize your thinking about some course of action, your sense of purpose allows you to uncover ways of thinking that you are unaware of.

THE SENSE OF PERFECTION

Perfection is probably one of the most troubling ideas that humans ever conceived. It means to be *made through* or *complete*, but it has come to stand for something altogether different—it has come to mean flawlessness. When the idea of perfection has been perverted to mean flawlessness, it is because the ego is fed by that idea. Those who work to create flawless perfection are ego feeders. The Soul is spoiled by flawlessness. For the Soul, perfection is nothing more or less than being complete and natural. Those who make the mistake of viewing perfection as flawlessness set themselves as false judges of other people's actions and works.

By viewing perfection as complete and natural, your sense of perfection can scan all thoughts, actions, ideas, works, and behaviors to see how complete they are. When you sense a thought to be somehow incomplete, you can set it aside for consideration until your sense tells you that it is now complete. Without naturalness, perfection is merely mechanical completeness and is not persuasive.

Work of great perfection doesn't mean it is more complete; rather, it possesses an order of naturalness that takes completeness to a level not normally achieved. To many connoisseurs, the violins of Stradivari and Guarneri are examples of perfection, yet I have seen violins by both these makers that can hardly be called flawless, though Stradivari's violins come close to it.

Years ago, when I visited the home of the violinist, Georgio Ciompi, I was able to closely inspect his Guarneri violin. I noticed that the edges of his violin did not describe a smooth curved arc—they were undulating all along the perimeter of the violin. Work of this kind could only be termed crude and incompetent by the false standards of modern violin craftsmanship. Even the purfling, the strips of wood inlaid along the edge of every violin, followed every inconsistency expressed by that wandering edge. In fact, because Guarneri couldn't get the purfling to follow the curves of the purfling channel, he broke the purfling and crammed it in the channel anyway. Work of this purposeful crudity is a joy to see, especially because the violin sounded fabulous. It demonstrated that Guarneri was a maker of sound in the form of a violin, not a violinmaker. It was clear that the sound was perfect and that the violin assumed its appearance accordingly. This is also an example of paradox.

THE SENSE OF PARADOX

Paradox means to have opposites in one. Sometimes reality is easier or more interesting to view and understand when the opposite of reality is used to describe it. The Yin Yang symbol is an ancient representation of the concept of paradox.

Other examples of paradox are great violins sounding like human voices, black holes so dense in mass that even light can't escape, carnivorous plants, life that feeds on poison, a work of art that feels alive, a bright night, a dark day, a wonderful catastrophe, and so on.

The sense of paradox is designed to apprehend and perceive the paradoxical nature of reality. With the sense of paradox, you can sense the importance of dirt to the existence of purity, the weakness of strength, the emptiness of plenty, the greatness of simplicity, the obscurity of the obvious, and the wisdom of the fool. Two works by M.C. Escher, *Relativity* and *Waterfall*, are excellent visual representations of the principle of paradox. In *Relativity*, Escher has drawn a building with stairways that lead to the walls of other stairways that lead to yet other walls or floors that lead nowhere, or that loop back on themselves.

Stimulating the sense of paradox is of great importance where the creation of art is concerned. To be considered art, an observer must experience that an object appears or feels alive, which is a paradox. What creates the sensation or feeling of being alive in a work of art is the number of universal principles that are expressed in it. The greater the number of universal principles expressed in a work, the more alive it seems to be and the greater that work of art it is.

THE SENSE OF AWARENESS

Awareness is normally what we think of when we recognize a sensory experience, but to have a sense of awareness means that we can experience all the levels of knowing. The difference between knowing and being aware is subtle, but it is clear to those who have sensed awareness in themselves. For teachers, there is perhaps no experience in teaching that is more fulfilling than to witness the awakening of a student's sense of awareness. Until whatever is taught becomes palpable and dimensionally real to us, our learning is purely academic and has no bearing on real life. The moment we experience the value and importance of what we learn is the moment that we sense our awareness of what was learned. It is the

"Eureka!" moment when the lightbulb goes on in the head. It is a moment of enlightenment.

Is it possible to have an enlightenment experience and not realize that it happened? The answer is yes. Every time a great idea occurs to you and you pass it off as being nonsense, crazy, or unimportant, you missed a moment of enlightenment because your ability to pay attention to the sense of awareness was dulled by distraction or because you were too filled with vested interests. Awareness has to be cultivated for it to integrate with intelligence.

THE SENSE OF VITALITY

Vitality is used to mean *living essence.* The word *vital* has a pulsating or intensely gripping aspect to it. When you sense that kind of energy within yourself, even in a relaxed state, it is because of your sense of vitality. This sense is also used to detect that pulsating or intensely gripping aspect in other people and in things.

A musical performance without vitality is a flat experience. For a performance to stimulate our sense of vitality, the performer must exhibit that quality. Some performers are able to project vitality, while others try to fake the effect. Real vitality cannot be faked. When vitality is present, it is often called charisma. However, since a person can have charisma and be at death's door, it is erroneous to say that vitality is charisma.

Charisma is the result of universal principles having been applied. In the case of life, the application of universal principles manifests as charisma. Where truth is concerned, the application of universal principles manifests as the intrinsically real and palpable. Vitality in art reflects the spiritual nature of the artist, who probably is or was charismatic. This is true even if the charismatic person happens to be the embodiment of evil. People will often follow one who is evil if that person stimulates their sense of vitality. Stimulating the sense of vitality makes people feel powerful, and the feeling of being powerful is both an ego-feeding narcotic and a delusion. Politicians too frequently exploit people by this method.

THE SENSE OF KNOWING

There are seven distinct levels of knowing that we are able to sense. Each level processes our experiences at a specific degree of refinement, of which the seventh level is the most refined. For example, by using a filter with seven layers of increasing fineness, the process of purifying water might be as follows:

(1) Remove logs and branches from the water.
(2) Remove leaves and other debris.
(3) Remove the remnants of leaves and particles.
(4) Begin to remove clay, silt, and organic materials from the water.
(5) Remove every particle that might color the water.
(6) Filter out bacteria and other microscopic pollutants.
(7) Filter out viruses and dissolved molecules, like heavy metals and salts, that would otherwise pollute the water.

What would result from this filtration process is pure water. Likewise, what results from the seven levels of sensation of knowing is knowing in its purest state.

The first level of knowing that we can sense is connected to our five physical senses. When something stinks, you know it stinks. You don't believe that something stinks, you know it. Anyone who has had the misfortune of being close to a skunk when it has released its defenses knows what I mean.

If you are questioned about having experienced the stench of a skunk, you know that you know the smell of that odor. This is the second level of knowing—you know that you know. This knowledge is extremely difficult to prove to anyone who has not themselves known the smell of a skunk. Nevertheless, you know that you know, and you are disinclined to be dissuaded from that knowledge.

The third level of knowing might be what we call *legally provable knowledge*. This level is more or less verifiable, in that you know that you know what you know. You are sure, when asked about it, that the smell you encountered was definitely that of a skunk and not of chocolate chip cookies. The chances of having been fooled by a counterfeit odor mixed up in a laboratory are unlikely because that is not a smell that a person would wish to create to deceive people.

The fourth level of knowing involves your awareness of knowing that you know what you know. This awareness is like the effect of sitting in front of a mirror, with a mirror also behind, and seeing yourself seeing yourself seeing yourself in the mirror. We are aware of these levels of knowing in that manner. The value of this level of knowing is that the attention paid to it feeds the Soul with attention-energy. What makes this level of knowing to be food for the Soul is that it requires a certain perspective and disinterest to be in touch with it.

The moment you are able to notice that you're aware of knowing what you know and that you know it, you have refined your level of knowing to the fifth level. At this level, you have perspective, you have no vested interest in knowing, and you also appreciate that you are knowing. Appreciation implies that you savor the awareness of knowing as you might savor the smell of a rose.

At level six, you experience a simple awareness of that appreciation. You are able to register the knowing of all previous levels, but you are no longer interested in them because you focus on the raw experience of your awareness of appreciation. At this level, the food you are generating for your Soul is rich and full-bodied. The reason for the richness is the degree of purity obtained from interest in the less refined levels of knowing.

By the time you have filtered out even your awareness of appreciation for knowing what you know and knowing that you know it, you reach the seventh and final level of knowing—knowing as a state of being that is without the need to realize that you appreciate knowing at the more mundane levels. Language becomes incompetent to describe this experience. It is pure and simple knowing without the need to characterize, judge, or evaluate the experience. This level is the most nutritious as food for the Soul. The energy provided stimulates the Soul and invites it to enjoy the feast.

By learning to reach down to that purest level of knowing, you become accustomed to the rarity and subtlety of the experience and are sensitized to your Soul's communications. The more sensitized you are to your Soul, the louder its voice (your intuition) becomes and the easier it is to listen to and understand what it's expressing.

The more you make a habit of paying attention to this seventh level of knowing, the more assertive your Soul becomes. When the moment is right, if you invite it to play in your imagination, it will be ready to play, eat, and converse.

THE SENSE OF UNITY

Unity is a condition in which all things refer to a singularity. In music, unity is a result of all the notes in a diatonic scale referring to the tonic. In cosmology, unity is a result of all planets referring to the star or solar orb around which they revolve and all the stars in a galaxy referring to their galactic center. Unity in a class or group involves a common trait or behavior that holds that class or group together. For example, shared values hold a family together; shared interests hold a club together; shared aims hold a society together; and shared principles hold a nation together. We also sense unity in a shared purpose, philosophy, location, etc.

When a shared element is no longer able to hold a group or class together, the group disintegrates. We experience our sense of unity both in accepting the elements that bind a class or group together or in rejecting those same elements. Accepting those elements stimulates our sense of unity in the positive, while rejecting them stimulates our sense of unity in the negative.

When sensing thought, we experience how a thought is similar or dissimilar to other thoughts we have encountered. The sense of unity helps us filter through thoughts more quickly to decide if a certain thought is worth entertaining. Unity informs our perception of class or group. Disunity is sensed when a condition of "each to their own" is perceived.

THE SENSE OF TRANSPARENCY

The quality of transparency is present in thoughts and things by a scale of degrees. The more transparent, the higher on the scale a thing is. A true vacuum, without molecules of any kind, is likely to be the most transparent thing possible. Likewise, purity of intent renders thought transparent. The opposite of transparent is opaque. The more opaque, the lower on the scale of transparency. Theoretically, a black hole should be the most opaque thing in the universe.

When a thought is transparent, its meaning is exoteric and immediately comprehensible. When a thought is opaque, its meaning never becomes clear, and it exists in obscurity. A person may be characterized as being transparent when their motivations and intentions are immediately comprehensible and are made evident by their behavior or attitude. An opaque personality suffers from behaviors or attitudes that obfuscate and prevaricate so that nothing is made clear about that person except their opacity. We sense transparency as being clear and direct, and opacity as the opposite.

Transparent personalities often alienate those who are more opaque because their directness is interpreted as aggression and is felt as a violation of one's ego. Opaque personalities have trouble getting to the point, and they communicate by indirection and innuendo, which is usually indicative of one who doesn't know what is happening and won't admit it.

The sense of transparency informs us of where on the scale of transparent to opaque the object of our attention exists. We usually use this sense to filter out all that is opaque to get at a real description of what is happening.

THE SENSE OF DIMENSION

The degree to which our culture is influenced by the language of science, most especially of physics, is the degree to which we have been taught to think and perceive in a manner lacking in dimensionality. In physics, there are four dimensions: three dimensions of space (up-down, forward-back, and side-to-side) and one dimension of time. The problem here is that scientists are taught to keep things simple because matters get complicated when they do not. To abstract reality and reduce it to four dimensions is to ignore every other dimension of reality:

- Each of the specific wavelengths of light that produce color
- All forms that produce infinite timbres and tones of sound
- Every flavor combination that we are able to taste
- Every chemical that combines to create a different smell
- All the various grades and types of surfaces that result in unique sensations of touch

It turns out that we live in a universe of such dimensionality that we feel compelled to simplify everything to the point that what we perceive about reality is limited to the names we give it.

Our sense of dimension is there to help us appreciate every dimension perceivable. It picks up the slightest differences in vibration that present us with yet another dimension. With this awareness, we can create works that express as many dimensions as possible. Doing this makes for work that is infinitely interesting for others to behold, just as nature is infinitely interesting to behold.

There is a tendency among serious minded folks to dispute the value of an experience because it isn't profound enough—the "all that glitters is not gold" argument. Well, gold also glitters. In glitter is a multitude of dimensions of the same thing, which is why we are inexplicably attracted to it. True, it is simplified to one effect, but what an effect! The light being reflected and tossed about stimulates our sense of dimension to the point that we are distracted from the fact that it may be only one type of glitter. Simultaneously dazzling the sense of sight and the sense of dimension dazzles the mind and creates a condition in the Soul of being suspended in time. During these occasions, we are able to notice our sense of attraction.

THE SENSE OF ATTRACTION

That which attracts the attention stimulates the sense of attraction. There is a specific structure and order in the way the sense of attraction is stimulated. If you notice how and when your attention is attracted, you can construct this structure and order for yourself. Tests that have been conducted using infants of a certain age as subjects indicate that preverbal brains are first in the order of attraction. How long an infant focuses their attention on stimuli indicates the strength of the brain's level of attraction. The nature of an infant's emotional reaction indicates the primitive brain's interaction with that stimulus. Crying indicates that the stimulus is perceived as fearful and anxiety-inducing. Rapt attention and smiling indicates attraction, and so on. The manner of stimulation also influences the way the sense of attraction is captured, encouraged, or inhibited. Too rapid and sudden stimulation will cause fear and anxiety; too slow, and the brain becomes bored.

It is the nature of all art that artists must become scientists of this particular sense. The success of an artist depends on their ability to stimulate this sense in a way that motivates others to want the source of that stimulation. Advertising specialists have made the science of the sense of attraction their own private realm for study. Anyone who wishes to excel in that realm needs to learn how the sense of attraction responds to every type and manner of stimulation. They need to know how the sense of attraction of people in every age group is to be stimulated or repelled.

Our sensory nature is highly dimensional, and so too is the manner in which we respond to stimulation of every kind of sense. What attracts our sense of humor might repel our sense of right, and that same thing might also attract our sense of dimension and repel our sense of harmony. In this way, our attitudes act as a filtering agent governing by what and how intensely our senses are stimulated and attracted or repelled.

THE SENSE OF MEANING

By the sense of meaning, we read stimuli as making sense, and thus being comprehensible and understandable, or as not making sense, and thus being nonsense. Unlike the sense of attraction, the sense of meaning specifically stimulates the intellect and spirit. If the stimulus is experienced as being nonsensical to the mind, the stimulus is dismissed by the mind. If the stimulus is experienced as something sensible, then the sense of meaning helps us further focus on every aspect of that stimulus.

What the sense of meaning can't do for us is to put incoming stimuli into a sensible form—that is what the intellect is designed for. The intellect looks to the intuition for the potential of a stimulus to be meaningful, but that is all. When you intuitively feel that something you have encountered is of deep or important meaning for you, that is your sense of meaning communicating to your mind that it should pay attention to what is being taken in.

Nonsense is the result of no sense having been made of an input. It is like asking a question and receiving the answer in a foreign language. When we say, "it's all Greek to me," we are saying that what we have taken in is read by our sense of meaning as being nonsense.

This particular sense could be detrimental to your well-being if you think so highly of your ability to detect nonsense that you dismiss ideas, explanations, solutions, and possibilities that could prove useful to you. Those who practice this habitual dismissiveness suffer from a closed mind. Your sense of meaning is there to help you detect the subtlest hints that what you are exposed to could be valuable and useful, it is not to build barriers against a truth that might offend you or that you can't instantly understand.

THE SENSE OF CONDITION (OF MENTAL STATE)

How are you to know if the dog barking at you is ready to attack or is merely barking out of habit to anyone who happens to be in its vicinity? How do you know when a person asking a question is doing it to irritate you or to relieve the suffering produced by not knowing the answer? You know these states of mind because you have a sense of condition. By reading the signs from the nature of expressions, you then respond appropriately or inappropriately.

Your sense of condition reveals to you the true nature of whatever it is that you encounter. When you ignore this sense, your behavior and decision-making suffer. So, to respond appropriately to your sense of condition, you need to make a practice of questioning your preferences, desires, hopes, dreams, attachments, and infatuations to stay open to whatever you might glean from a given experience.

Often, when a person appears to be a good judge of character, we are acknowledging that person's ability to accurately detect someone's real quality or condition from what, when, and how they speak, their accompanying body language, their manner of delivery and the attitudes expressed by that manner, and any specific physical mannerisms that might indicate a person's condition. All of these things are being processed by the sense of condition.

THE SENSE OF VIBRATION

The sense of vibration does not refer to physical vibration. Every thought uttered bespeaks a certain vibration of intention. One could call this the qualitative registration of an attitude. Actors need to have a highly refined or trained sense of vibration with which to read the lines of a script in several dozens of ways on command. In like manner, we all have the possibility of accurately grasping the real substance of a person's thoughts because we do not have a preconceived notion of what we are paying attention to. When we have a preconceived notion about a person based on their manner of dress, we can be easily deceived. Likewise, if we hold a false notion of a person based on their speech habits, we will likely be fooled into thinking that they know more or less than they do.

Accurately gauging the attitudes of whoever happens to be engaged with us in work, conversation, or play helps us to respond in a manner congruent with the person's true intent.

THE SENSE OF PRINCIPLE

A principle is a force that governs. What that force governs could be anything. The sense of principle is there to help us register and comprehend governing forces. For instance, Newton's law of motion, which says that for every action there is an equal and opposite reaction, is the universal principle of reciprocity applied to physical objects in space. It is that same force of reciprocity that is behind the impulse to give a gift in return for having received a gift. Anytime we are able to produce yet another example of the reciprocating force at work, it is because we are applying our sense of principle to various situations to notice how that same principle is behind the behavior or structure. This applies to every one of the thirty-five universal principles.

When there exists a phenomenon for which we have no immediate explanation, our sense of principle assists us in uncovering another as of yet undiscovered universal principle. Should we think that we have discerned a new principle, those to whom we describe the nature of this principle will invariably use their sense of principle to ascertain if the force described is a true and distinct universal principle.

In general, people who have a refined sense of principle also happen to be the most likely to be called brilliant or talented. Those who have little sensibility for principles and how they function play an important role as technicians and number crunchers.

THE SENSE OF CONSEQUENCE (CAUSE AND EFFECT)

The sense of principle is easily confused with the sense of consequence. This is because universal principles are also ultimate causes for every real or natural effect. However, not every effect is real or natural. Many effects, like being sent to prison for committing a crime, are unnatural or man-made. The effect of egg white turning opaque in a hot frying pan is not a natural effect, though it is real. Naturally, egg white, with the yoke, turns into a bird after the egg is subjected to an appropriate time span of incubation.

The sense of consequence exists to inform the mind and conscience of the necessity of considering actions and behaviors. In the case of committing a crime, the consequence would probably be time spent in prison. In the case of incubating an egg, the consequence would be for a chick to hatch.

When people behave without scrutinizing their behavior to register what the possible consequences might be, the likelihood of unfortunate outcomes increases exponentially. It is in the nature of the ego to act without regard for consequences because thinking takes time, and the ego needs to act fast to keep us alive.

Playing chess is an excellent means of refining the sense of consequence. Each move has the potential for a multiplicity of outcomes, so the player who has the most sophisticated sense of consequence will likely win the game. Cooks need a refined sense of consequence to plan a complex meal and serve the food, all hot, at the same time. This is not an easy outcome to manage without a highly refined sense of consequence.

One might ascribe our sense of consequence to the imagination rather than the intuition. The reason I grouped this sense with the intuitive senses was that, time and again, my understanding was enlightened by the sense of consequence through my intuition. For example, if I was experimenting with acoustics, I was often struck by a solution to an acoustical problem not by the solution itself, but by the instant, intuitive recognition of what the consequence would be.

Chapter Fourteen

The Senses of Being

The senses of being are focused entirely on registering the state of being as manifested by thoughts, attitudes, physical condition, and motives. These senses are the least attended to because they are so ineffable. To speak about them is more difficult than speaking about any of the other senses. What does it mean to have a sense of energy, and how is that different from a feeling of energy? Although difficult, it is possible to discuss these senses, just as it's possible to sense thought as it occurs in the brain. The various subtle energies that flow within the body, brain, mind, and heart are nevertheless quite palpable when the mind is quieted and turned to focus on these specific sensations.

A good example of what I am talking about is found in the following experiment: Sit quietly and think the question, "What?" and notice where in your head this thought appears. Try to push or make that thought appear in a different location in your head. Then think the question, "Why?" and notice where in your head that thought appears. Again, try to push or force that thought to appear elsewhere inside your head. Do this before you read the next paragraph.

If you were able to quiet your mind and still the turmoil of thought normally happening in your brain, you might have noticed that the word *what* appears on the structure-sensing side of the brain (for most people, this will be the left side). The word *why* likely appeared somewhere on the behavior-sensing right side of the brain.

What requires facts and information, but not meaning, which is why it arises in the structure-sensing side of the brain. *Why* seeks answers that are about meaning and relation, which is why it arises in the behavior-sensing side of the brain. Now, if you ask "How?" you may notice that this question appears in the frontal area of the brain, midway between the two hemispheres. This is because that question seeks resolution by calling on both hemispheres to contribute to the answer.

Even if you found the above experiment difficult, it should show you that the ineffable senses of being can be sensed, especially if your mind quiets and focuses on these senses.

THE SENSE OF ENERGY

The energy to which this sense refers is the mental energy experienced when an idea of significance occurs or when an idea is recognized for the first time. The quality of this energy is the more palpable and easily recognized form of the same kind of energy that normally experienced in the head when thinking. Somehow, this energy has the property of being more distilled and therefore easier to perceive than the kind of energy sensed when thinking normally, yet both are sensed with that same sense. This is why we can recognize the sense of energy as distinct from sensations like having a headache.

I suspect that this sense of energy will be the means by which people will notice and distinguish other mental, imaginative, ethical, intuitive, and being types of senses. As I said earlier, I doubt that the number of senses I have detected is the sum total of all the senses with which human beings are endowed. Others who are more sensitive than I will likely discover senses that have not pertained to my specific experience. I do not consider myself to be the most sensitive of people, at least not compared to my wife, who is far more sensitive than I am.

As I have posited before, it is in these types of inner senses that human evolution continues to take place. When one of the human family detects another undiscovered sense and brings it to the attention of all, the brains of all living humans who are informed of that sense will soon evolve the necessary connections to reorganize their brains. It will be enough that everyone who pays attention to that newly discovered sense to detect it within themselves will eventually evolve the brain material and sensitivity needed to make it useful. Thus, over time, the human brain continues the evolution of our species. Aside from progressing human evolution, I see no reason for needing this particular sense of energy.

THE SENSE OF BEING

The term that we normally use to articulate this sensation is *self-respect*, so I gave considerable thought to whether this sense would more rightly belong to the ethical senses. I placed it with the other sensations relating to being because the quality of the experience is more ineffable than the experience of the ethical senses.

I have noticed that people who have a deficiency of self-respect tend to recede from being in their faces, which is especially noticeable in their eyes. Their eyes bear the signs of receding from the front of their face, probably as a result of shame. We almost never find this effect in babies' eyes. This particular effect appears to start in adolescence and is accompanied by defiance and disdain towards others. Photos of adolescents from the late nineteenth century rarely exhibit this phenomenon, but I have noticed this disturbing look in some young people since the late 1970's, which I attribute to the affects in the rock music that many of these kids listen to.

More interesting is how easy it is to notice this effect in the eyes of hardened criminals. It is as though their eyes have receded so far from the front of their faces that we see the eyes of their egos, like their eyes have migrated back and down towards the primitive brain. I once met a man who exhibited this effect. Since the man was a total stranger to me, I had no idea about his character, though he seemed to be a nice enough person when I met him. I later heard that he made a habit of being unfaithful to his wife and that he was manipulative of those with whom he worked.

I am reminded of the story called *The Picture of Dorian Gray*, by Oscar Wilde, in which the main character strikes a bargain with the devil to keep his good looks. That bargain allowed Dorian Gray to keep his comely appearance yet notice every alteration of his image as it appeared on his portrait. Every act of cruelty and brutality Dorian committed turned the portrait increasingly ugly and contorted until he couldn't stand seeing it. He eventually attacked the portrait with a knife to destroy it. At that moment, Dorian discovers that he has killed the portrait of his Soul. Dorian dies, and at the moment of death, he assumes the visage of his tortured Soul, while the painted portrait reverts back to a picture of Dorian when he was young and exceedingly handsome.

Your relationship to your sense of being is like the relationship that Dorian Gray had with his portrait. It is there to remind you of the nature of your true being because it stays the same while your body grows, changes, ages, and deteriorates. Should you do things for which you are ashamed and notice the growing disparity between your being and sense of being, you are then reminded by that sense of being to avoid damaging your Soul or the Souls of others.

THE SENSE OF ATTENTION

If you were not able to guide and direct your attention, you wouldn't have a sense of it. Like other animals, you would be your attention, and your attention would be directed by your instincts to food when you are hungry, to water when you are thirsty, to sex when your hormones require it, and to sleep when you need it.

Humans are able to direct attention. For example, you can focus your attention from one eye to the other. You can shift your attention at will to move your fingers and toes independently. You can do this because you sense what your attention is, but only if you use the experience of guiding, directing, focusing, or shifting attention to bring the sense of attention to your attention.

Since the Soul is the part of you that makes decisions, in the ultimate sense, unless you abrogate that duty and give it to your ego, your body, or your mind, deciding what to focus your attention on in the first stages of your life was an act of your Soul. The entire thrust of spiritual development may be understood as a process designed to get back to the state where the Soul makes your decisions. Without your sense of attention, this would be almost impossible.

The sense of attention is also responsible for being able to detect those energies and impulses that arise from the Soul when it needs to be attended to. These energies and impulses manifest themselves as non-physical urges or needs, like a form of aching. For some people, this may be experienced as the ache of deprivation, while in others, it is experienced as a drive or as being driven. For me, the experience manifests itself in an unstoppable surge.

By clearing the mind and emotions of vested interests, recognizing these diverse types of experiences that come from the Soul can be more readily accepted and acted upon. Unless you are clear about what does and does not come from the Soul, you risk acting on impulses that are entirely ego-driven. These same kinds of urges, needs, surges, achings, or drives are how the ego seeks to stay in charge of making decisions. The fundamental difference in these two sources is in the volume and intense nature of the impulses. That which emanates from the ego is powerful, loud, and demanding—in some cases, brutal or abusive. That which emanates from the Soul arises as a subtle suggestion, at one end of the scale, or as a constant, inevitable force at the other. What comes from the Soul never becomes brutal or abusive, nor does it ask that you behave that way to others.

When we read of the wrath of God in the various religious texts, those references are actually references to the reaction of the writers' egos to violations of their ethical senses. Ultimate reality is incapable of emotions because it doesn't have a primitive brain and it is too busy with the act of creation to bother with subjective feelings. It is the sense of attention that allows us to know what is true and what is not true because we are able to experience reality as if in the third person. This is what makes spiritual people seem so dimensional, wise, and loving.

THE SENSE OF PERCEPTION

Perception is a perplexing word. According to its roots, it simply means *to take through*. Perception, when translated into German, is *Wahrnehmung* (pronounced var-nay-mung), which means *truth taking*. What is more curious is that in English, the word *perception* has come to mean *interpretation*. This definition appears to have strayed far from its original meaning if the more ancient definitions are any indication. That is likely the result of the philosophy of relativism distorting what is real to make it more palatable to our egos.

I once heard someone respond to a critical comment of mine by saying, "Well, your reality isn't my reality!" This reaction was so apt in highlighting how far relativism has dumbed down people's ability to perceive. Millions of people today would see nothing problematical about that reaction. What the reaction is saying is that the truth is irrelevant—what feels good to you isn't what feels good to me, and the only relevant thing is how I feel. This is a classic example of the ego taking control of a situation in its outstandingly stupid manner.

The sense of perception informs you of when a perception has taken place. It is also your means of recognizing the truth when you encounter it. In general, the recognition of the truth precedes the perception of it. These experiences are usually so intertwined with other matters more demanding of attention that we are unable to focus on the fact that we have experienced a perception.

Still, it is with the sense of perception that you can register the volume or loudness of perceptions in the scheme of other mental activities. By placing all manner of mental activity on a scale of loudness, you can learn to register and more easily identify perceptions when they happen. The loudness of thoughts next to that of perceptions is as the sound of a roaring jet engine next to a whisper. From the loudest to the quietest, the different forms of mental activity are as follows: emotions, thoughts, ideas, attitudes, perceptions, and intuitions. This is one means by which you are able to distinguish between the wants of the emotional ego, the intellect, and the intuitions of the Soul.

The sense of perception also has the requisite sensitivity to notice degrees of truth. The more laden with truth a thought appears to be, the stronger the perception is sensed. Falseness appears as a void to the sense of perception. These are the parameters within which the sense of perception functions.

THE SENSE OF ATTITUDE

For every thought that exists, there exists an attitude behind it. The sense of attitude allows us to discover the hidden attitudes that are behind thoughts. We could say that the sense of attitude is used to "taste" attitudes. Without this sense, we wouldn't be able to grow spiritually because spiritual growth occurs when we have successfully adopted or acquired another right attitude. Whoever acquires the most right attitudes is the most successful human being. Throughout history, the people who are remembered longest are the ones who spent their lives seeking to understand and use the attitudes needed for their Souls to make their decisions.

The fact that men and women have chosen to record the deeds of people that demonstrate a lack of spiritual depth is an unfortunate quirk of aesthetics. People like to read about conflict because conflict is more aesthetically interesting than no conflict. The problem is that conflict usually entails egos more than Souls. In myth, however, the conflicts recorded are often those between egos and Souls. These mythical stories encourage you to answer the call of your Soul, and they teach the attitudes needed to let that happen. Anytime attitudes are being taught, the sense of attitude is being stimulated.

The process for exercising your sense of attitude is to take a statement made by a spiritual person, and ask the question, "If I were to make that same statement and know what I mean by it, what attitude would I need for exactly those words to pop out of my mouth?" Answering this question requires that you puzzle through a variety of different attitudes until the right one occurs to you. This involves using the sense of attitude to detect and project the thoughts that would arise from having a specific attitude.

THE SENSE OF EMOTION

You might think that we wouldn't need a dedicated sense of emotion because emotions often feel so intense; however, the sense of emotion exists so we can distinguish between subtly different emotions, like infatuation, affection, desire, love, and lust. We don't need this sense to identify and articulate obvious emotions. But what of the difference between not wanting to bother someone and the fear of being rejected by someone? What of the difference between feeling uncertain and feeling the conflict of vested interests? These questions refer to subtle differences.

If we were always able to be perfectly clear about what we feel, we would not need the sense of emotion, but few of us ever acquire that level of clarity. In general, women are more attuned to these subtleties than men (probably because women have evolved to be that way for survival). This doesn't mean that males can't also cultivate that same degree of sensitivity to emotion, though I suspect that testosterone makes it difficult. When men learn to become sensitive to emotions and their various shades, they become wiser because they are better able to understand the other half of humanity.

THE SENSE OF THOUGHT

Sensing thought is not the same as thinking or being aware of thinking. The sense of thought enables us to capture the faint suggestions that our Souls occasionally give to us when we are in need. During those times, we tend to be emoting or machinating so loudly that it is a wonder anything from the Soul can get through. This sense makes it possible for us to tell the difference between conscious thought and unconscious thought.

Being human is a complex business, and we need all the help we can get to pilot ourselves through the maze of thoughts and emotions that are normally undifferentiated. This sense is linked to the right-brain due to the importance of sensing meaning from thought, so I was first moved to include the sense of thought in the behavioral, right-brain senses. What pressed me to include it in the senses of being is Descartes' saying, "I think, therefore I am." Although that statement is crude, it is true, and it is our sense of thought that makes it so.

THE SENSE OF INEVITABILITY

This sense detects outcomes as being unavoidable, certain, or destined. Some of these outcomes are obvious, while others are obscure and mysterious to us—we sense them, although we are unable to say why. Mechanical or chemical outcomes are the easiest to grasp as inevitable. For instance, when you first witness the mixing of hydrochloric acid solution with sodium hydroxide solution, you would never guess that the inevitable outcome is harmless salt water had you first observed their corrosive effects when poured on a slab of meat. Before the invention of modern chemistry, these various reactions would have been treated as magic because the experiment does appear to be magical. Once you understand how chemistry works from a technical point of view, the magic seems to vanish as the outcomes of chemical reactions appear inevitable.

When we sense the inevitable in processes, it is because we are intuitively aware of that consequence. We may not be able to explain why we sense the inevitable, but the sensation is nevertheless strong enough to be called to our attention. For example, when under Republican administration, Congress has altered laws to remove restrictions on the activities of financial institutions, but they didn't also remove the insurance programs that existed to bail out those financial institutions should they fail. It was clearly inevitable that greedy speculators would enrich themselves by gambling with the money belonging to account holders, and it was clearly inevitable that those financial institutions would fail and have to be bailed out by the Federal Government. None of the people who voted for those stupid laws were held to account for that inevitable outcome. In this case, greed trumped the sense of inevitability. When greedy men and women use government to enrich themselves, the inevitable consequence is despotic corruption.

In spiritual terms, feeding the Soul by paying attention to all your senses has the inevitable consequence of enlivening the Soul and encouraging it to participate in all that you do. Similarly, paying close attention to all your senses has the inevitable consequence of banishing fear and anxiety. Even attention paid to fear itself will preserve your integrity if that fear is justified.

THE SENSE OF INFINITY

Infinity is a universal principle. The young man who brought this sense to my attention was James Raynor, then a student at the University of Wisconsin–Stevens Point. The moment he brought infinity to my attention, I knew he had said something important. I gave considerable thought to what he had said and concluded that he was right. Infinity is not just the state of having no end; infinity is possible within strict limits. Take, for instance, the mathematical symbol for infinity. This symbol (∞) is limited yet infinite—if we are to put any trust in the definitions of mathematics. This also makes infinity paradoxical.

The sense of infinity exists to sense the true nature of the Soul. The Soul is infinite yet bound in the body. The infinity of the Soul is what belief in an afterlife is all about. Should the question of the infinite existence of the Soul arise, it stands to reason that the essential nature of Nature is that all matter transforms—it is not destroyed. Just as the living body transforms to a corpse at the moment of death, the Soul must also transform unless it did not at first exist, or it was made not to exist.

The sense of infinity is the counterpart to the sense of limit. Where limit contains, infinity releases. Infinite limits or things that are limitedly infinite are paradoxes.

Hence, a circle is the perfect paradox. It is defined as a single line made up of an infinite number of points equidistant to a central point. In a real sense, the ancient Greeks were the first to develop a cogent description of the universe. They imagined reality as a series of spheres each containing another sphere, like a Russian doll. The earth was, to the ancient Greeks, a sphere, and the night sky was the inside of another sphere that contained the moon and the earth. Since a sphere is a set of infinite circles sharing a single point, it makes perfect sense to describe reality as a series of spheres sharing a single point because it provides a way of grasping and comprehending the infinitude found in the night sky.

Modern cosmologists are essentially saying the same thing, but they choose to move the shared point to someplace out in the universe that, until now, has no known specific location. That shared point was the moment of origin called the big bang. The concept of the big bang is how today's cosmologists express their limited understanding of a universe in which everything appears to be expanding.

THE SENSE OF UNIVERSALITY

We use this sense to extrapolate out from our experiences to a universal application. When we read about principles, the description of them is normally mundane. Laws are not principles; laws are abstracted from principles to facilitate their application. Thus, the laws of motion articulated by Isaac Newton were abstracted from the principle of reciprocity. The laws of gravity were abstracted from the principle of attraction. The laws of thermodynamics were abstracted from the principles of contrast and efficiency. These laws are universal because the principles from which they are derived are universal. As the field of cosmology develops due to our increasing understanding of the universe, we are becoming more accustomed to sensing the universal nature of forces, principles, ideas, behaviors, and structures.

THE SENSE OF ORIGIN

Ur is a word that means beginning or origin. The philosophical quip, "Which came first, the chicken or the egg?" is meant to stimulate a sense of origin in us. How do we think about our origins? We don't need to have an answer to this question, yet our sense of origin exists to deal with developmental processes. I am reminded of James Burke's book and video series titled *Connections*, which sought to show how everything comes from something that came before.[28] He was challenging people's sense of origin. That, more than the content of his work, was the true value of it.

Which came first, the universal principles, or the big bang and the universe that took its form from the universal principles?

THE SENSE OF ULTIMATE

How do we know that we have reached the limit of something? With material things, it is easy to say. We reach the limit of making cookies when we run out of cookie dough. How do we know when we have reached the limit of an idea and where it can take us? We cannot reach any specific point where all that can be understood about an idea is finally comprehended.

To train our sense of the ultimate, we have the great music of Bach, Beethoven, Handel, Mozart, etc. Every idea worked out by these great composers was taken to its ultimate conclusion. Just as we develop an idea in conversation or in writing, we also develop a sense of ultimate conclusion when nothing more can or need be said about an idea. Sensing that ultimate point is difficult, especially in the field of painting. It's all about knowing when to quit. Great artists begin their careers overworking their paintings, but they eventually learn to know exactly when they have reached the ultimate point of effect. If they go beyond that ultimate point, they will be subject to the effect of diminishing returns. Without the sense of ultimate, there would be no great artists of any kind.

THE SENSE OF SACRED

The sense of sacred is often misconstrued or mistaken for the mundane behavior of holding things or ideas as sacred. We tend to make whatever we happen to venerate into a sacred object of worship. This is called idolatry, and it is about as far from actual sacredness as one can get. Anything can be converted into an idol for worshipping—a person, an object, an idea, a feeling, a desire, etc. Just because people make idols, it doesn't mean that these forms of idolatry are sacred in themselves.

---

[28] James Burke, *Connections* (New York: Simon & Schuster, 2007).

Recognizing the quality of sacredness comes from a deep understanding of what is holy from the Soul's point of view. Too often, we attribute holiness to people, things, or experiences that are merely awe-inspiring, but acting like something is sacred doesn't make it so. When we mistake doctrines, teachings, and rituals relating to beliefs as sacred, we are setting up the ego as God because all doctrines, teachings, and rituals are man-made designs to provide comfort for our fears. To treat these things as sacred is like saying that our fearful emotions are sacred.

Our sense of sacred is exclusively for the relationship we have with our Souls. Everything else is theology, and like so many man-made mental constructs, theology is not very useful. The most sacred moment of all is the moment a person awakens to the relationship with their Soul. The teachings, speculations, practices, or rituals relating to that moment are not sacred. Only that specific moment is sacred because it is that moment when a person becomes aware of the Soul with a big S. Experiences that build on that moment are also sacred, but only to the individual. Trying to initiate that moment or build on it is not enough to call it sacred. Where sincerity is concerned, a miss is as good as a mile.

We live in a world where the sacred has been made pat and the Soul made irrelevant. This will not change until Soul-based values have been restored to first position in our scale of what is sacred. If religions continue serving up hope in place of sensing, rituals in place of attention, doctrines in place of understanding, beliefs in place of knowing, and theology in place of perceiving, it will be a long time before these things improve.

THE SENSE OF ENIGMA

Enigmas are puzzles and mysteries that endlessly intrigue but rarely enlighten. The purpose of having a sense of enigma is to eradicate enigmas. Every serious puzzle or mystery solved is one more source of belief converted into a source of knowledge. It is better not to create myths about what we can't answer or solve; rather, it is enough to say that we can never answer that question or solve that mystery. Creating false or incomplete answers and solutions is to fabricate doctrines that obstruct the truth. False or incomplete answers and solutions are the enemies of science because they possess every negative attribute of beliefs and believing.

The sense of enigma is designed to help us isolate false and incomplete answers so that we may better see the truth. It aids in determining what is knowable and unknowable so that we don't waste our time speculating about things we can never know, no matter how entertaining that pastime may be. Within our brains, there is enough that is both unknown and knowable to keep humanity occupied for the next one thousand years, so there is no need to bother with what can never be known.

THE SENSE OF TRANSCENDENTAL

Transcendental experiences are exceedingly rare for the average human being. To experience them, you must be competent to recognize them; otherwise, the experiences are wasted. One of the central reasons why transcendental experiences are rare is that they are sought for in the realm of belief and not in the realm of knowing.

It is important to remember that emotions and feelings most often occur when our senses have been stimulated in a particular way. Violations stimulate our senses in a way that causes pain, hurt, anger, guilt, and shame. Stimulations that cause pleasure, joy, elation, affirmation, and happiness arise from our perception of other people's respect, appreciation, and love for us. When that respect, appreciation, and love comes from the Soul, the experience is transcendental. This can only happen when we become one with our Souls.

It is fascinating to listen to the music of Antonio Vivaldi because his music, at its best, expresses the feelings of a transcendental experience. During the Baroque period, the transcendental affect was the most revered of all the affects that art or music could express. Examples of this affect can be found in Baroque paintings that depict apotheosis, transfiguration, or the assumption into heaven of some Biblical figure. Without the ability to sense the transcendental, those paintings and pieces of music could not have been created.

The specific affect of transcendence is one that combines rapture, silence, unmitigated joy, and reverence all at the same time. It totally consumes the attention and pricks the sense of responsibility to convey that experience in one's work, whenever possible.

THE SENSE OF RELEVANCE

We have a sense of relevance to maintain a quality of focus that keeps what we do to the point of our aim. Some people appear to be blind in this particular sense or are so insensitive to relevance that they have no idea what it means. This sense is designed to connect the past with the future, for what arises out of necessity from the past is the present which brings about the future. That which is arbitrarily interjected into the present is largely irrelevant, so it is with our sense of relevance that we detect arbitrariness—the product of whim.

This sense appears to work best in situations where outcomes of death might result if behavior and thought is not relevant to preserving life. In matters where death is not a factor, irrelevance flourishes because whim is viewed as a satisfactory guide. Specifically, the realm of the arts is one in which self-expression is more valued than relevance. In our present culture, artists are viewed as doing something irrelevant. Thus, for every artist, their central question needs to be how to stay relevant to society and culture at large.

For each person, the question is simple. To be or not to be relevant? The path that leads to relevance requires the traveler to ask and answer four simple questions:

(1) So what?
(2) Why bother?
(3) Who cares?
(4) What am I going to do about it?

It turns out that these simple questions are difficult to answer. If the answer goes something like, "that's what I feel like doing," then irrelevance is close by. The higher-minded the purpose to which these four questions are applied, the more likely it is that relevance will be the result. Benefiting humankind is perhaps the best way to guarantee being relevant.

This is not to say that everyone in the world is obliged to be relevant. People have the right to do with their lives as they please. We are not all made the same, and what works for one may not work for others. Just as beauty needs ugliness to be taken seriously, relevance needs the presence of the irrelevant to clarify the importance of relevance.

In a similar way that creating beauty is vastly more difficult than producing ugliness, being relevant is vastly more difficult than being irrelevant. Perhaps if our sense of relevance were more immediate and sensible to us, more of us would choose to be relevant. But our sense of relevance is neither immediate nor sensible, so we should not judge the choices others make for their lives—we don't live in their shoes. Nevertheless, we have a responsibility to question each other's behavior, lest we become like lemmings and follow the herd only to fall into the ocean of ignorance and drown.

THE SENSE OF VERITY

Sensing verity and telling the truth are closely linked. It is through lying that the sense of verity becomes calloused. The more you lie, the more difficult it becomes to know what the truth is. Your conscience, or sense of verity, is your ability to inwardly know what is true. The willingness to act on the sense of verity is identical to being guided by conscience.

Since most people already know about the conscience (though not many people follow the advice to be guided by it), why not call our sense of verity our conscience? Conscience is a much less specific term because our conscience calls on a dozen or so senses, including the sense of verity. Hence, verity is a specific sense that contributes to conscience. This sense is what we use to detect every property, aspect, or inkling of truth in every form it assumes. In this sense, truth is not restricted to the philosophical, it also includes the material, intellectual, emotional, and spiritual.

Because we live in an age in which truth is considered by most people to be relative, matters of conscience no longer assume the strength of conviction as they did in ages past. The ability to rationalize a lie into a "truth" that works for the individual has led to many abandoning the value of conscience. Plagiarism, even in academic situations, is rationalized as academic freedom. Ideas are no longer respected as property, and as the internet invades the realm of ideas, idea-stealers get credit merely by repeating ideas without giving due credit to the originators of those ideas. Ownership of inventions is falsely claimed by spiritual vampires who need the marketing hype to sell more product. All this goes on at the expense of these spiritual predators' Souls, as though it were nothing more than a simple case of "I forgot" or "I would have thought of it myself, it was so obvious."

The sense of verity is not fooled, and neither is the Soul of a predator. Turning lies into personal truth will inevitably rust one's spiritual gears until the machine comes to a dead halt. When that happens, there is no turning back. Abandoned by the Soul, predators always run afoul of their own machinations. All that we think and do against our aesthetic selves is eventually brought to the surface when we least expect or want it. This is not a prediction or a condemnation. It is merely an observation of human nature.

Chapter Fifteen

Sensory Clusters

Our experiences of the world are so rich and multidimensional that the simplest act, like drinking a glass of water, is almost overwhelming to put into words. The external factors involved with drinking a glass of water consist of the following:

- the source of the water
- the quality of the water
- the motives for drinking the water
- the properties of the glass used to hold the water
- the movements of fetching the glass
- the movements of filling the glass
- the movements of lifting the glass to our mouth
- the movements needed to swallow the water
- the movements of returning the glass to its prior place

The internal factors are as follows:

- the experience of the act of drinking the water
- the taste of the water
- hearing all the sounds of this experience
- the effect of the drinking
- the feelings experienced drinking the water
- the feelings experienced in the aftermath

All these factors, and the above lists are by no means exhaustive, contribute to the simple act of drinking a glass of water and could be easily communicated in a court of law if you were obliged to tell the truth, the whole truth, and nothing but the truth:

Q. Where did you get the water?
A. I got it from the faucet in the sink in the kitchen.
Q. What can you say about the water quality?
A. I found that the taste was spoiled by the presence of too much iron in the water.
Q. Then why did you drink the water?
A. Because I was thirsty.
Q. What can you tell us about the glass you used, if you did use one?
A. It was dirty, but my hands were dirtier, so I used the glass anyway.
Q. Did you try to clean the glass before you filled it with water?
A. No, because I was not sure that there would be enough water to clean the glass and drink my fill.
Q. Did you then fill the glass?
A. No.
And so on...

Do these questions and answers get to the whole truth of the matter? Some people will answer in the affirmative. Others might doubt that an affirmative answer would be telling the whole truth. No questions were asked about the source of the water, or why you drank the water from that particular faucet. If the water came from a mountain spring, an oasis waterhole, or from an outdoor pump at an old farm, a wholly different experience would entail; but in every instance, the experience would be a series of *sensory clusters.*

A sensory cluster is an effect that is formed when multiple sensations from multiple senses are beheld at the same time. For example, six musical instruments heard to notice the qualities of unity, harmony, clarity, focus, etc. would be a sensory cluster. A sensory cluster takes in all or many of the senses at the same time and is therefore difficult to describe in any terms except the most general, like, "I ate a piece of mincemeat pie." In the single act of tasting a mincemeat pie, a sensory cluster can occur if the person eating the pie pays attention to multiple senses that are simultaneously stimulated. For example, they could pay attention to:

- the proportions of salt, sweet, sour, savory, and bitter;
- the olfactory gesture that occurs when eating something that smells intense;
- the degree of chewiness;
- the rolling of the food around the mouth; and
- the qualities of transparency, intensity, temperature, clarity, radiance, relation, harmony, awareness, consequence, and focus.

How can these senses have anything to do with eating a piece of mincemeat pie, you might ask? When food tastes transparent, it is because the ingredients keep their integrity as they are blended together. In the case of a transparent pie, the flavor of the dough would not overwhelm the flavors of the mincemeat, as often happens with poorly made pies. If the dough is too strong, it is because the flavor of the flour is too intense. When all the ingredients are correctly proportioned, but the sizes of the pieces in the filling are either too large or too small, the quality of clarity of flavor of the individual ingredients is destroyed. If certain substances, like brandy, have not enhanced the flavors, those flavors will not radiate throughout the entire mouth and sinuses, and the pie will taste ordinary. If there is too much cinnamon, it will be out of proportion relative to the other flavors. If all the flavors are clear, and the ingredients are properly proportioned and balanced, the effect in the mouth is radiant and the awareness one has is of a harmony of flavors. Anyone who has experienced truly great cuisine or home cooking can never get that experience out of their head because the effect is heavenly. The effect may last only as long as it takes to consume a piece of pie, but those few minutes can create an impression of such intensity that it awakens the mind to the possibilities in every future sensory experience.

What I have described is a sensory cluster due to the depth of attention paid to as many senses as possible. It's not a sensory cluster if the perception has not been created, even if the same number of senses have been stimulated. It becomes a sensory cluster when the person sensing has participated in noticing the depth of the experience. A sensory cluster feeds the Soul because as much energy as possible has been issued in the form of attention.

Despite the focus of attention on sensory clusters, the truth is that not much of what we experience is particularly useful unless we take care to measure our sensations. A sensory cluster can be quickly reduced to a simple experience if the person experiencing it doesn't bother to grade the experience on a scale. Rating or grading experiences is the fastest way to make use of sensory input. We are asked to do this when we visit the doctor for problems with pain. For example, your doctor might ask, "What is your present pain level, on a scale from zero to ten?" During a recent visit to my doctor, I reported that the pain I was experiencing was 3.75 on a scale from zero (no pain) to ten (unbearable pain). That was when I discovered that I wasn't allowed to have a 3.75 pain level—it had to be either three or four. Obviously, my doctor had never encountered someone who was skilled at specific sensory grading.

To better manage sensory experiences for others, which is a requirement for anyone who cooks, it is essential to place every specific sensation on a graduated scale. People who really care about the quality of their work equate caring with the precise measurement of sensation.

Knowing, Believing, and Spirituality

Chapter Sixteen
The Spiritual Foundations of Knowing

OF LOVE MODE AND FEAR MODE

The basic foundations for knowing or believing resides in one of two modes in which humans are being or functioning. *Being* relates to the nervous system that each of us is born with and how incoming impulses from outside and inside are biologically processed. *Functioning* refers to how each of us chooses to behave in response to our states of being. We can't change what we are born with, but we have absolute control over how we choose to behave. This is where the two modes of being or functioning come in.

The first mode is what I call *Love Mode.* It is a mode characterized by a high degree of sensitivity and paying attention, and its purpose is to embrace reality. The central properties of this mode are positivity and openness of being. The second mode is what I call *Fear Mode.* Fear Mode is characterized by a hyper-degree of emotional reactivity and self-protection, and its purpose is to forbid reality from encroaching on one's insular shell. The central properties of Fear Mode are exclusion and retraction. The metaphor here is that of sea anemones, which have an impulse to withdraw into the safety of their shells the instant a sensation is detected.

At one extreme, in the direction of Fear Mode, there is a degree of hyper-reactivity such that every sensation causes a person to recoil from reality to avoid being overwhelmed. At the other extreme, there is the open and accepting nature of Love Mode, where every sensation is the cause of distraction to the point that learning is made virtually impossible. Most of us live somewhere between these two extremes.

What we are born with is something we are unable to change. So the question arises, how can we make a go of life given that we are stuck with whatever our biology deals us? Each of us answers this question in the way we behave. Our behavior is largely, but not entirely, governed by how we were treated after we were born as well as by our natural inclinations or talents (what I call *dominances*). Still, people who have been badly treated by others don't necessarily become brutes themselves, nor do people who have been treated well invariably treat others well.

Behavior displays function and function marks character. A choice to function in Fear Mode (and it is just a choice) marks character with the traits of negativity, closedness, anger, hatred, pessimism, sentimentality, egoism, judgmentalism, possessiveness, and addiction because we have chosen to be easily hurt or offended. Choosing to function in Love Mode (that, too, is just a choice), marks character with the traits of positivity, acceptance, optimism, openness, authenticity, nonjudgmentalism, generosity, and freedom from attachments.

In Fear Mode, the brain is restricted in what it can take in and make sense of. In Love Mode, the brain is unrestricted and can embrace reality and everything about it, both the good and the bad. In Love Mode, we are free to pay attention to whatever we choose. In Fear Mode, our attention is perverted by our traits of character. It is the choice to function in Love Mode that makes knowing possible because attention is ours to direct when we are in Love Mode. What we pay attention to is what we know, most especially where the senses are concerned, and it is the quality in every experience that materially determines how much we know of what we know.

OF QUALITY

Paying attention lives and breathes because of quality. Things of low quality destroy interest in paying attention. Things of high quality simulate interest in paying attention. The best and most useable definition of quality I have evolved is this: *Quality is the intensity of perception of an effect.*

When we speak of quality or qualities, our reference is usually to the effect itself, and here lies a source of massive confusion. Quality is the level of intensity of perception. The effect itself is something quite separate. The effect, which is the cause of perception, is what we usually and mistakenly focus on. We focus on the effect because it usually has more substance than our sensations have, but it is actually a distraction. It is easy to notice and talk about the effect, so that is what we normally do. However, if we choose to focus on the sensory experience, we can begin to understand what quality is and how it works, and we can invent ways of increasing it.

What our Souls contribute to our work normally results in work of better or higher quality. Too often, we look for our Souls to produce a miracle, like magic. By this way of thinking, we infantilize ourselves because it is both silly and reduces us to believing in magic, like when we believed in Santa Claus. Since all quality emanates from an intelligent application of the thirty-five universal principles, most people would give up on trying to intelligently apply that many principles simultaneously while they work. However, what may challenge the intellectual mind is child's play for the Soul. The Soul is made of those universal principles, so dealing with and applying them is no more work for the Soul than breathing is for the body or adding 2 + 2 is for the mind. The Soul knows best how to apply the universal principles, and it is for that purpose that we need to engage the Soul in whatever work we are doing. As long as we don't violate anyone in the process, the Soul will oblige us if we have followed the creative mechanisms that govern our relationship with it. Focusing on quality is one of the easiest ways to lure the Soul into working with us.

In music, an example of a quality, in the conventional meaning, is tone quality. If we apply our definition of quality to this term, we would have to say that tone quality is the intensity of perception of the effect called tone. More specifically, as we tend to use the term *tone* when referring to the sound of good musical instruments, tone quality is the intensity of perception of the fundamental pitch in the sound of an instrument. Another example of a quality in music is rhythm. Rhythm is the intensity of perception of the effect called swing. Poor rhythm means that the effect of swing is perceptually flat. This could be described as a physical motion that is uniform and undynamic, though cyclical or mechanically circular. Rhythm, like tone, is a specific effect. Communication is also an effect, but it is a general one. When specific effects are presented together, a general effect is the result. Weather is another example of a general effect. It is constructed of specific effects like evaporation, condensation, atmospheric pressures, clouds, winds, temperatures, and precipitation.

Similarly, Love Mode and Fear Mode are general effects that are produced by the combination of specific effects called attitudes. Our attitudes are our answers to questions we have about reality. The quality of our lives is dependent on our perception of reality as being either benign or malevolent, for us or against us, or something to love or fear.

Chapter Seventeen

The Foundations of Belief

A belief of any kind is a mental construct designed to give form or substance to whatever happens to be unknown. This, unfortunately, is not how most people use the word because they usually treat what they believe as being irrefutable or unquestionable. That is, believing, as it is practiced, is the mental act of forming, accepting, or acceding to a mental construct as being absolutely true.

Believing doesn't require any burden of proof, just as the truth of a belief is not required for that belief to be accepted. The mind is extraordinarily competent at inventing thousands of ways to rationalize beliefs of all kinds. A mind predisposed to believe doesn't need the truth to accept a belief as being true. For this reason alone, it is advisable to distrust the mind.

So we humans find ourselves choosing belief over knowing as a basis for forming our views of reality because belief usually happens to agree with what we want or wish reality to be. What this means is that the belief one holds is largely irrelevant because it is in the nature of beliefs that they are all equally right if consummately justified and equally wrong *because* they are consummately justified. In other words, it doesn't make much difference what a person believes because any belief can be justified for the sake of it being accepted. Truth or reality has nothing to do with believing.

THE STRUCTURAL FOUNDATION OF BELIEF

The structural foundation of belief is found in the brain. Located above the brain stem are structures including the thalamus and hypothalamus. These structures govern the autonomic systems of the body, such as the respiratory, excretory, and circulatory systems. The key word in the description of these structures is *autonomic*, which means to function involuntarily or without interference from the mind. Every system that is needed to maintain physical health is autonomically controlled by these and similar structures, which are collectively called the primitive brain. It is so-called because it is a part of the brain shared with all other brain-possessing creatures. Indeed, this part of the brain is so primitive that it is found in both fishes and reptiles. For this reason, it is sometimes called the reptilian brain.

The function of the primitive brain structures is to keep us alive and healthy so that we can survive and reproduce. They work by being extremely fast in responding in fear to situations that might get us killed. That is, if you are walking along and a wild animal leaps out of the bushes, your primitive brain will instantly come into action so that you can protect yourself by fighting or fleeing. The primitive brain doesn't need anything but the merest sudden motion for it to pump hormones into your body that support your need to stay alive.

Thus, it is my understanding that all belief has its beginning in these primitive brain structures because the only thing required of a belief is that it helps us deal with a situation as fast as possible and with as little effort as possible. The smallest motion of a blade of grass is enough for us to assume that an animal is about to attack us. Likewise, the slightest hint of criticism is enough for our egos to act as though we are in mortal danger.

By working on the assumption that a moving blade of grass or the slightest hint of criticism is a lethal threat, the primitive brain can respond with extreme speed to fight or flee. Without the trait of extreme speed, our primitive brain structures would be quite useless, especially if our lives were constantly in danger. The problem for most people in the world today is that their lives aren't constantly in danger. The more civilized society is, the less we have to fear from nature. Nonetheless, we are endowed with primitive brain structures that behave as though we still live in a dangerous environment, and these brain structures generate fight or flight responses to situations that aren't remotely dangerous, like when experiencing humiliation.

Most of us have felt the flush of anger or resentment when on the receiving end of criticism or belittling. It would be an odd person who did not experience these feelings under similar circumstances. Ironically, the primitive brain structures that are designed to protect us in threatening situations are the same structures that make fools of us. When under the influence of our primitive brains, we tend to behave no more intelligently than apes.

THE PSYCHOLOGICAL FOUNDATION OF BELIEF

The psychological equivalent of the reptilian brain structure is what we have come to know of as the ego. Fear is the emotional energy that feeds the ego and keeps it in working order. Your ego, if given a chance, will guide decision-making to make sure that everything you do feeds it so it can always be prepared to keep you alive. By cultivating a strong ego, you can be sure to dominate situations that might otherwise cause you to be killed.

The ego is completely stupid and incompetent at everything other than ensuring survival. It is so stupid that it can't tell the difference between real danger and fake danger. Real danger is a snake that could be poisonous and rearing to bite. Fake danger is hearing a critical comment from another person. To the ego, any action, behavior, or words that it finds offensive are the same as a lethal threat and it reacts to make sure you stay alive in an unoffended condition. When others criticize you or what you have done, and you feel offended or under attack, those feelings are the result of your ego making sure you fight or flee. When afraid to be in a dark room, that feeling is caused by your ego attempting to make sure that you won't come to an unpleasant end.

Politicians often play to our fears so that we vote for them. They are communicating with our egos in a manner designed to get us to act on our fears and vote for them. They understand that nothing they say needs to be true; it only needs to spark fear in us for us to go and do what they want. Politicians who do this are agents of the ego and are no different than a raging tiger or a poisonous snake, except that the tiger and the snake are more honest. Indeed, all evil springs from fear and an empowered ego.

Your ego can lead you to believe anything it needs you to so that you can have a feeling of certainty and security while your body is alive. This is how religion and politics are the fruit of the ego. Religions and political systems don't need to be true for the doctrines and policies they espouse to make humans feel more safe and secure. Religions generate doctrines that are extremely easy to believe in so that each religion survives and leads people into believing whatever they need to believe to feel safe and secure while living in fear.

Anything that dispels fear and requires us to work at dealing with our fears will disempower our egos. Beliefs that spread fear are malevolent, and those who spread such beliefs are evil, irrespective of who they are. Fear is no respecter of persons, and evil is no respecter of fear mongers.

THE STRUCTURAL FOUNDATION FOR SPIRITUAL DISEASE

Brain structures such as the thalamus and the hypothalamus are important to our physical survival but are also inextricably linked to spiritual ill health. How is this so? Spiritual health results from paying close attention to all the senses. Everything depends on what we pay close attention to and on how we respond to the objects of our attention. Paying attention and loving are one and the same thing. What we pay attention to is what we love, like it or not, and this is what determines the quality of our spiritual health.

If we choose to pay attention to things and matters that are easy to focus on, we risk spiritually poisoning ourselves if what we choose to pay attention to is the product of ego. Paying attention to the faults of others and constantly complaining about them means we love those faults because they give us something to complain about. The more we complain, the more we love and glorify faults and the people who have them. Similarly, if we choose to pay close attention to creativity, how to be creative, and those who are creative, we then love and glorify those aspects of creativity and we can learn to be more creative ourselves. The more we focus on those aspects that increase our creativity, the more we glorify being creative, and the more creative we will likely become.

Developing right judgment about what to pay attention to is crucial. It is best to focus on the senses because the senses do not lie. Senses sense—they do nothing else. The mind lies and deceives itself, but the senses cannot be deceived. Only the mind that interprets what is sensed can be deceived. Its interpretations are usually based on vested interests, and those are predicated on what we happen to believe. If we make a habit of allowing ourselves to be distracted from paying attention to our senses by paying attention to our beliefs, we become highly susceptible to self-deception.

Believing is the fastest way not to think. In cultures that reward believing as a way of life, the only form of freedom available is slavery to the ego. Odd as it may sound, it is an irony that in America, where the notion of freedom is a national anthem, the freedom to believe anything produces slaves of so many, who then cling to their beliefs more passionately than in just about any other democracy in the world.

Everyone knows how the mind has the wondrous power of reason. If that wondrous power is used to rationalize a belief, idea, concept, notion, feeling, interpretation, or desire about something that is not true, it can make a person delusional or dangerous. It can cause a person to become a spiritual bully, like the religious zealots who made a sport of burning as a heretic anyone who disagreed with their way of thinking. Still today, being a heretic in countries where religious leaders control the state can be a ticket to suicide.

BELIEVING IN SOMETHING THAT IS TRUE

Even belief in something that is true is problematic. True beliefs are not as toxic to the Soul as false beliefs, but it is the act of believing that is the problem. The mere act of believing creates a link to the primitive brain that imperils a person's spiritual integrity. Since the function of spirituality is to know reality in all its intricate detail, and not just physical reality but psychic, intellectual and spiritual reality too, any belief hinders knowing. Believing inhibits or blocks knowing. Without knowing, there is no such thing as understanding. The only recourse to not understanding is hope, and to rely on hope is to rely on beliefs that may or may not be true. Those who function on hope do so because they have abandoned all possibility of knowing and are condemned to believing.

THE COMMONEST TYPES OF BELIEF

The most common type of belief is God-based religious belief. Religions range from pantheistic to monotheistic and from pagan to what believers call "true religion." The problem endemic to every so-called true religion is that the believers are convinced that their form of true religion is the only true religion. In most religions, the aim is to inculcate in people the rules for correct behavior according to the religion in question. Correct behavior means correct sexual behavior, personal habits, moral behavior, thinking, and doctrines. Religions function on the assumption that certain behaviors are acceptable to the god or gods involved. The idea is that people are supposed to appease the god of their religion by behaving according to that god's dictates. Failure to do so is a sin; thus, the concept of sin applies to behaviors that are forbidden. The design behind these various rules and regulations is not to have a thriving relationship with the Soul, rather, it is to avoid a miserable afterlife or guarantee a wonderful one.

Furthermore, religions typically resort to using mystery as an explanation for what can't be known and manufacture doctrines to provide pat answers to questions believers might have. Mystery allures and seduces the mind, but it is a poor substitute for real understanding. The point of all these religious doctrines and mysteries is to make believers feel safe and secure while living in fear. Religions are predicated on the importance of being in and living in fear.

The exact opposite of religious belief in God is the religious belief in no God. Adherents to this odd religion profess a doctrine of the non-existence of God. They believe fervently in the rectitude of their doctrines, and many of them take the trouble to evangelize their beliefs to anyone who will listen. Like many theistic religious believers, atheistic believers are possessed of the conviction that they must spread their beliefs to others, and they take pride in demolishing what they see as errors in other people's beliefs.

Science, too, becomes a religion when it is reduced to theories that can't be proven or demonstrated with the weight of evidence (beliefs), or when scientific debate regarding theories, not facts, competes to be the dominant rationalization of a belief. What passes for science is too often fantasy and speculation. Fantasies and speculations are the scientific equivalents of religious doctrines. Science is perhaps more informed than religion, but its beliefs are still fantasy and speculation nonetheless.

Political beliefs become a religion when the facts and principles behind the social or economic reality don't support a particular political point of view. In this regard, both Capitalism and Communism are political religions, each of which has its peculiar doctrines for running a society. Capitalism has just recently become dominant as the worldwide economic and political religion only because Communism could not sustain itself in a free and open society. That is, Communism only worked when it was imposed on society by force and intimidation. Practically, Communism worked by turning many of its believers into bullies and predators, a fault that Capitalism also seems to endow in its most ardent believers.

It is almost axiomatic that when any religion becomes dominant in a culture, many of its believers become bullies and predators who care nothing for how the religion affects people individually, socially, or spiritually. Where the religion of Capitalism errs is that its doctrines are not founded on humanity's best attributes; rather, Capitalism is founded on humanity's worst attributes of greed and rapaciousness.

The political and economic system that properly accounts for the Souls and the egos of humankind and is based on the universal principles will be the most productive, creative, and easily understood by everyone. That system will also eventually dominate and strictly regulate the predatory and egocentric nature of humankind to make sure that the works of the Soul are not violated in any way.

It is not enough to say this once: Beliefs are not the problem, rather, it is the *act of believing* that is the problem. Beliefs are the symptom of believing. Believing keeps us stuck in our primitive brain structures because it requires no attention on our part. All that is required is to hear or see something that seems good to us and then believe it, whether or not it is true or actually good for us.

Those who study the brain and have mapped its processes can prove that we activate most of the brain on any given day. What they don't say is how much of the brain is consciously available for use. This is key. The brain is doing far more than its owner can ever be aware of. Anyone who has suffered a stroke and has had to relearn to consciously manage all the functions needed to move one leg can tell us how much work it is to do the simplest movements. The brain doing all that processing, which we take for granted, in no way translates into having all that processing power accessible and available for our conscious use. The brain that runs on automatic is no more useful to its owner than a computer that is without a keyboard or a computer frozen in a crash mode. Believing, at its best, is like using the original Apple *MacWrite* program, created back in the 1980's, on one of today's computers equipped with two superfast processors and several terabytes of solid state memory. Such a primitive program would run at lightning speed on today's computers, but we couldn't do much with it. The believing brain has all that processing power, but most of it can't be utilized. Just as it takes a huge amount of work and attention to produce programs that use such a computer to its full capacity, knowing requires a huge amount of attention and careful mental work to make the full capacity of the brain's resources accessible and useful.

Naturally, I expect most people who prefer to function in a belief mode to complain about these comparisons. It is in the nature of the primitive brain to treat what I have written as a lethal threat to the ego, but it won't change the truth. Being restricted from having useful access to 85% of your brain means that you are forced to live a 15% life, which is like being a slave. Living an 85% or even a 100% life is what you were designed by nature to live. For anyone choosing to live such a life, throwing off the constraints of the primitive brain begins by paying attention to all the senses. It is no more mysterious than that. When we do this, we activate within our brains a knowing mode or state of mind as opposed to a believing mode or state of mind.

Cultivating a knowing state of mind is within the ability of every person to undertake, but don't underestimate the amount of work it takes. It is hard work to keep our egos at bay and question everything, and it is challenging to live happily with the unknown before us. But each person who takes on that challenge can expect the rewards that come with paying attention and knowing. Since the rewards depend entirely on what one pays attention to and the quality of that attention, the rewards will be different for each person. To each, the rewards will be fitting and right.

WHAT ABOUT THE SENSE OF EMOTION?

It is my observation that we have no sense of emotion. I say this even though I have listed the sense of emotion as one of the being senses in Chapter Fourteen. That particular sense detects emotions being experienced from the strongest ranting down to the subtlest desire, but that is all it does. Mostly, our emotions are experienced as reactions to sensory clusters or are sensory clusters themselves. What this means is that we experience felt emotions as not one discreet sensory experience, but as a large number of simultaneous sensory experiences.

Anger, for instance, is generated in the brain and is initiated by an ego reaction to a physical assault, real or fake, or a violation of one or more senses. The sensational cluster involving anger might include the senses of pressure, temperature, intensity, focus, territory, gesture, and so on. The sense of pressure might be experienced in the mouth, the arms, the abdomen, the throat, the chest, and the fists. It might also be experienced as the increase in blood pressure that often accompanies adrenaline responses. As the body cranks up its mechanisms for initiating the fight or flight instinct, the senses of intensity and focus are stimulated, which causes a fighting gesture or, if those senses are overwhelmed and disoriented, a flight response.

This single example demonstrates how emotion stimulates a complex of sensations and how the sensations generate the appearance of emotion. Actors must learn to use those same sensations to instantly call up any emotion or complex of emotions in a way that makes the audience believe that the emotion they are acting is actually felt. For an actor to become so involved in the life of the character they are playing can be dangerous because those emotions might cause them to enact negative behaviors which their character would commit. This is why it is important for actors to distinguish between emotion and affect. Affect is the *suggestion* of an expression of an emotion. The emotion is the feeling itself.

In all matters involving art, it is affect rather than emotion which is the currency being spent. For the suggestion of the expression to be convincing, an actor needs to be an astute scientist of human emotions to transpose all the sensory experiences generated by emotions into the form of affect. Failure of an actor to be convincing, that is, received as real, is usually the result of poor observational skills. This usually causes the actor to overact, which may work for young children, but not for intelligent adults.

In all this discussion of emotion, the point is to understand our emotions and what triggers emotional reactions. It is important to note that our beliefs constitute the single most delicate trigger for our emotions. A person who chooses to believe nothing has no reason to react violently when insults are leveled against what their beliefs might be. They also have no reason to feel elated when accolades are offered for what they have done. When choosing to believe nothing, a person has no feelings that can be hurt, and it is possible for them to acknowledge emotions without taking them seriously.

Feelings that cannot be considered as emotions are what I have termed *ammotions*. Ammotions are conventionally called the positive emotions. Since the word *emotion* has its roots in the meaning *to move away from*, a new word needs to replace it when the meaning is *to move towards*, as in love and loving. With ammotions, such as love or enthusiasm, the sensory clusters might involve many of the same senses as with anger but with a totally positive mental state. In anger, muscle groups tend to pull downwards and become increasingly clinched, but in love or enthusiasm, those same muscle groups tend to rise upward. Likewise, we experience sensations of tension in anger, but release in love or enthusiasm.

Ammotions have a nonreactive quality to them—they are responsive but not reactive. Love initiates a response to stimuli, whereas fear initiates a reaction against stimuli. Ammotions in the negative range might be characterized as being understandingly yet firmly opposed while always maintaining self-control.

Knowing is an ammotional state brought about by disciplined attention-paying. Believing is an emotional state that arises from a conviction regarding the strength of that state. That is to say, tepidly held beliefs have a flaccid feeling of conviction about them. At the other end of the emotional scale is a raging and rapacious certainty about the truth of one's convictions. It is perhaps a truism to say that the more ranting one's certainty is about solidly held convictions, the less likely they are to be true. This is not to say that the truth doesn't need to be defended ardently and earnestly—it does.

Where knowing can easily tolerate doubt, believing abhors doubt just as nature abhors a vacuum. Knowing tolerates doubt because what is real and true will stay real and true. Doubt, from a knowing point of view, is a minor detour from arriving at the truth. Doubt puts beliefs and believers on trial, which ramps up the ego to protect beliefs from becoming extinct.

Once we make the choice to know instead of to believe, the shift away from rampant emotionalism sets in because knowing is extremely difficult to attend to and focus on when feelings are running high.

Chapter Eighteen

The Problem of Dominances

I must credit my wife, Marianne, for many scientific observations she has made and shared with me over the thirty-four years we have been together. It was she, from her experience as a teacher and as a perceptual and cognitive scientist, who got me interested in the idea of dominances.

Just as there is right-handedness and left-handedness, which indicate hand dominance, there also is right and left-footedness to indicate foot dominance. These attributes are genetically encoded and can't be altered. They can be denied, like when left-handed children are forced to write with their right hand, which is a medieval practice that was still enforced in schools as recently as sixty years ago.

Just as there are hand and foot dominances, there is brain dominance. Some people are born left-brain dominant, which means that the structure-sensing processes of the left-brain are what they excel at. Other people are born right-brain dominant, and those people have better perceptual acuity in sensing behaviors and qualities.

Every one of us has a dominant eye, a dominant ear, a dominant nostril, a dominant side of the tongue, and a dominant external physical sense. When it comes to the eyes, our brain-eye connections are designed to split up the business of seeing, such that one eye sees certain colors more easily than the other eye. Splitting up the business of seeing extends to one eye being dominant for certain levels of depth perception, while the other eye handles what the dominant eye fails to behold as easily. For instance, divide the view before you into three levels of perception (foreground, middle ground, and background). Then divide each of those levels into three more (forward-foreground, middle-foreground, and back-foreground; forward-middle, middle-middle, and rear-middle; and forward-background, middle-background, and rear-background to infinity). You will notice that one of your eyes will behold each of these levels more easily than the other eye. Similarly, your ears will split up the business of perceiving sounds of voices, music, timbres, noise, etc. One ear will hear vowels more easily, while the other will perceive consonants more easily.

Furthermore, we have dominances in the emotional, intellectual, spiritual, and physical aspects of being. All these types of genetic dominances exist to make certain that each person or creature born is unique. It is exceedingly rare to find two people in the same place who have exactly the same dominances.

In the same way that it is a real struggle for right-handed people to write with their left hand, it is a struggle for visually dominant people to relate to their physical senses. Aurally dominant people have trouble relating to their sense of sight, and emotionally dominant people have difficulty making sense of how spiritually dominant people process reality. In other words, dominances are both a blessing and a curse. To have easy dominance in one part of your being is to have a weakness with which you struggle in another part.

A compassionate person accounts for differences in ways of processing reality through understanding that not everyone shares dominances. A compassionate person seeks to help others in comprehending the fullness of reality by using the dominances of each individual to best effect. Those who use their particular set of dominances to bully and belittle others are an all too common bane of humanity.

To fully appreciate how these dominances function, it is important to realize that each dominance has subdominances within it. Your right eye may be more sensitive to the color yellow and less sensitive to the color red, for instance. In other words, your right eye may be yellow dominant and red recessive. I suspect this subdivision of dominances also transfers to the body's muscle and nerve groups. For instance, it may be easier for your right eye to move up and down than to move from side to side.

Much of what we call talent relates to natural dominances, and with every subset of dominance, there are inborn proclivities. When educational systems reward left-brain dominant students, they are saying, in effect, that being right-brain dominant is bad because right-brain dominant students don't tend to be talented at academic subjects (although they excel in the arts and graces—those human endeavors that make life more bearable). Educational authorities may not mean to send that message, but for those on the receiving end of lower grades, what is learned is that being right-brain dominant is not as desirable as being left-brain dominant. The result of this situation is that the right-brained are often stigmatized as second-class students for most of their school years, if not for their whole lives.

With every dominance and subdominance, there are drawbacks. A person who has no problem with learning from books may experience serious problems relating to people. The dominance that makes learning from books easy also makes it difficult to understand how that learning connects to real life because that dominance is localized in the brain, and without significant exposure to dealing with real-life situations, such a person can become what is known as a "bean counter" type individual. For this reason, it is important for dominantly left-brained individuals to experience an education that is rigorously right-brained and vice versa. Without an education that balances the brain's dominances, strengths, and weaknesses, students have a harder time developing into balanced and compassionate people.

EMOTIONAL DOMINANCE

People who process their world through their emotions also tend to focus their attention on the past because memories have a strong emotional component. The stronger the emotional tags are for a particular memory, the stronger that memory will be. For that reason, physical or emotional injury tends to produce the most intense memories. Those who are emotionally dominant have difficulty understanding others who do not share that dominance, and they tend to feel that those who can't or don't share their way of viewing the world lead impoverished lives. This is likely due to how recalling the memory of something that made them feel alive effectively replaces an uninteresting or unchallenging present, so memories become a replacement for real life.

Having a good memory has little to do with being emotionally dominant, but acquiring a better memory involves learning to tag memories with emotional cues because the speed of recall is related to the strength of emotional connection to memory. Since emotions are intimately connected to pleasure and pain, emotionally dominant people also exhibit a strong tendency to focus on their experiences of pleasure and pain. The practice of forming therapy groups is a response to those who have experienced trauma. This response allows them to connect to their emotions about the experience or learn to let go of the emotions that have held them captive.

A sign of a well-integrated and mature emotional being is acknowledging emotions without being held captive by them or letting them dictate behavior. Other signs would be working through emotional distress by seeking to understand its cause and accepting that feelings are transitory and fade in time. Being emotionally disintegrated and immature usually results in mental disorder or a descent into cruelty or narcissism as the affected person becomes a victim or a tyrant.

PHYSICAL DOMINANCE

Being physically dominant doesn't mean having a gorgeous body. It means relating to reality through the physical body, rather than through emotions or the mind. This dominance usually manifests itself in the need for physically moving. Physical activity is essential to one who is physically dominant. If you are athletically inclined, it is probably because you are physically dominant or because that component is a secondary dominance in your personality. It is extremely rare for a person to be exclusively dominant in any one of the various types of dominance.

The need to constantly move is a manifestation of physical dominance. Children who are constantly fidgeting in class or who are wrongly identified as suffering from ADD or ADHD are more likely than not to be physically dominant. Allowing these children to learn while on the move is better than medicating them into a stupor to please parents or teachers, but they need a teacher who is also physically dominant or one who is at least understanding of their needs. To intellectually dominant or left-brained individuals, these children are just being disruptive.

People who are physically recessive can be content to stay still and enjoy the sensation of not moving. They are not usually good at or interested in sports. The disadvantage of being physically recessive is that, during the aging process, physical motion becomes increasingly difficult, so taking regular exercise is doubly important to avoid the tendency of being a couch potato.

INTELLECTUAL DOMINANCE

Because the brain has two hemispheres conjoined by the corpus callosum, intellectual dominance comes in two forms: right-brained and left-brained. Though the right-brained form is often incorrectly considered the feeling side of the brain, it is more correctly considered the behavior-sensing side of the brain. Likewise, the left-brained form is usually considered the analytical side of the brain, but it is more correctly considered the structure-sensing side.

People who are right-brain dominant tend to focus their attention on how things change, what those changes mean, and how to relate to those changes. They are more interested in how things relate to each other than in the things themselves. For them, meaning is more important than facts. A process will hold their interest more than any one step in that process.

Those who are left-brain dominant seem to find specific facts or structures more interesting than what is going on with those facts. This type of brain dominance prefers keeping track of, controlling, and managing details more than understanding what the details signify. Structures fascinate those with this dominance, and sometimes the desire for order, regularity, control, and predictability overwhelms them. For these people, this proclivity is both natural and preferable because of how their brain works most efficiently.

Sometimes quirks occur in nature, and the structure-sensing side of the brain will be on the right and the behavior-sensing side will be on the left. This is not a mistake; it is a result of how nature is always aiming for maximum differences between individuals. The processes that bring this impetus for uniqueness are hardwired into the workings of nature through the principles of individuation and dimensionality.

Intellectually dominant people usually live in their heads, just as physically dominant people live in their bodies, and emotionally dominant people live in their hearts, metaphorically speaking. This behavior is connected to genetically determined dominance and is unlikely to change. When conflicts occur in personal relationships, those conflicts are usually a result of an unfortunate pairing of dominances that are in diametric opposition. If one person in a relationship is emotionally dominant and the other is intellectually dominant, the chances are that the intellectually dominant person will eventually become a bully to the emotionally dominant person or that the emotionally dominant person will use manipulation to control the one who is intellectually dominant. Most successful human relationships occur when dominances complement or mirror each other.

Over the last century, psychologists have developed various psychometric tests to help them understand how individuals work. Terms like *analytical*, *intuitive*, *feeling*, etc. suggest how people are the products of their dominances. It is true that these dominances can't be altered, but we can use our free will and choose to focus attention on our weaknesses rather than on our dominances. In this way, we can become more balanced human beings.

SPIRITUAL DOMINANCE

Spiritually dominant people view their relationships to others and the world through different colored glasses, i.e., attitudes, such that they can rapidly change attitude as the situation warrants it. While they relate to the world through their senses, it is attitudes that are the currency of those who are spiritually dominant. People with other dominances tend to view the spiritually dominant as inscrutable, unpredictable, or even untrustworthy. It is not for want of sound character, but rather that spiritually dominant people are unattached to their attitudes and tend to readily abandon attitudes that don't work when dealing with specific problems in the real world. Those whose dominances are other than spiritual have a more difficult time unloading themselves of useless attitudes; instead, they assume that their attitudes are an immutable part of their character. For those with emotional, physical, or intellectual dominance, criticism of a useless attitude tends to be viewed as a personal attack. Spiritually dominant people are always on the lookout to notice any new attitudes that will help them solve their problems faster and more efficiently. They are not at all sentimental about their attitudes (or anything else, for that matter).

In other views of human personality, spiritually dominant people might be called pragmatic or synesthetic in their approach to problem solving. They live in their senses and draw on them to gain feedback from their environment. They are generally not attached or attracted to beliefs of any kind and instead prefer to rely on their senses for knowing. Spiritually dominant people who do exhibit such attachment usually have a strong secondary dominance, like emotional or intellectual dominance.

It should never be assumed that spiritually dominant people are spiritual in the conventional sense. Many are agnostic or profess atheism yet are exemplary in their conduct and how they treat others, though their ability to read attitudes is a trait that can enable them to manipulate others with greater ease than those who are not spiritually dominant.

DOMINANCE COMBINATIONS

The words people use to discuss what interests them is a giveaway for their dominances. Emotionally dominant folks use the word *feel* a great deal. Intellectually dominant people talk a lot in terms of *thinking*. Physical dominance is usually described in *actions, motions,* or *motives.* Those who are spiritually dominant often talk in terms of *points of view.* Obviously, it is important to have as broad a balance as possible in all the dominances. A person who is lopsidedly dominant will not be well-balanced enough to thrive in the world.

So, whatever combination of primary and secondary dominances we have, we can achieve the greatest benefit from seeking to enhance our non-dominant sides. This way, we can become more fully integrated and balanced human beings.

Just as oil and water do not mix, certain combinations of dominance are not likely to fare well in long-term relationships. Perhaps the most difficult relationship combinations occur with people who are spiritually dominant. This has less to do with the dominance being spiritual than it does with their particular outlook on life. To the emotionally dominant, spiritually dominant people come across as being detached, indifferent to feelings, oddly rational but without professing interest in their intellect, and happy as clams to sit and think rather than taking in some fresh air and getting exercise.

Nature creates this multitude of dominances to ensure that no two individuals are exactly alike. It does this because the greatest strength is found in diversity. In nature, what can kill one of many similar individuals can easily destroy the entire population of those individuals. No species can survive if its genetic pool has dwindled to the point that individuals being born no longer have the intensity of diversity needed for the survival of that species. So, by creating hundreds of thousands of possible combinations of dominances, nature is making sure that each individual is made as capable of surviving as possible.

When people group themselves together to exclude others who happen to be different, they are unwittingly ensuring their collective extinction. Individuation in nature is governed by the universal principle of individuation, and when people violate any universal principle, they take upon themselves the consequence of that action—extinction. The Soul is rarely found to be active in groups where diversity of opinion is restricted because such restriction is based on Soul-quenching fear.

It is important to bear in mind that while we have these dominances, the Soul does not have dominances. The Soul is not left-brain dominant or right-brain dominant, and neither is it male or female, because the Soul transcends dominance and gender.

The purpose of thinking about and understanding dominances is that it helps us avoid judging others who don't behave the way we would. Too often, when children are raised in a judgmental environment, that environment poisons their relationship with their Souls. For children, their clear perception of the world must be affirmed rather than invalidated or dismissed. Children most need to be listened to with an awareness of how to help each child manage all aspects of mind and body so that they can access the Soul when the time comes. Remember, no greater evil can be inflicted on a human being than to have the relationship with their Soul be impaired or, worse, intentionally destroyed.

Understanding how our dominances affect our ability to learn and thrive in certain situations or inhibit us in other situations makes it more readily possible to access our Souls. Sometimes, all it takes is the suggestion to explore our dominances that will lead to a better our understanding of ourselves.

Chapter Nineteen

Faith, Belief and Knowing

Belief is about what is not known. Knowing is about what is known. Knowledge is mostly collected opinions about why things are the way they are. If opinions are not based on reality or truth, they cannot be considered knowledge—they are beliefs in disguise.

As for faith, there are four kinds. **(1) Faith, as it relates to belief,** is the hope that what is believed to be true actually is true and includes trust in the positive consequences of that belief. This is religious faith. For example, people who believe Jesus is their savior have faith in the words of Paul, the founder of the Christian religion. Their faith is placed in their belief that what Paul said is true.

People adhere to religious beliefs more tenaciously than to other kinds of belief, probably because there is no way to say definitively if they are true. It is also probably the hope of a heavenly afterlife that underlies that faith. In other words, if the idea of going to heaven were not dangled in front of them as a reward for believing a particular doctrine, religious believers would not hold so tenaciously to those beliefs.

Another example of this would be the faith a person might have who was adopted but was never told this by the adopting parents. One day, when the genetic father or mother shows up and announces that person's true parentage, the adopted person would likely have a crisis of faith regarding their adoptive and biological parents. That person assumed all along that the people who raised them were their birth parents. Their trust or faith that all the words and actions of the adoptive parents were true or real would be shaken.

(2) Faith, as it relates to knowing, is a trust in the positive consequences of paying attention. Every time you jump in the car to drive somewhere, you are exercising faith in your ability to arrive at your destination unhurt and alive, as long as you pay attention to your driving and to what is happening on the road. Should you have an accident on the road while paying attention to driving instead of sending text messages, you would probably assume that the other person was at fault. Even if the accident had been caused by you because you had a momentary lapse of attention, you wouldn't necessarily lose faith in your driving ability. As soon as the car was repaired, you would be out on the road again.

(3) Faith, as it relates to collective opinion about why things are the way they are, is based on the presumption that the information and calculations used to form those opinions will prove to be right. When people used to think that the earth was flat, it was the consensus of opinion that if you sailed too far from land, you would drop off the earth. As long as you avoided sailing so far that you could no longer see land, your faith in this collective opinion would remain intact.

(4) Faith, as related to the sense of principle, arises when anyone applies a universal principle in the hope that it will create the result one might expect from its application. This kind of faith acts like all the others, but it overarches them because it presupposes an acquaintance with and an awareness of a principle and its consequences, which suggests the possibility of a positive outcome but does not guarantee it. In simpler terms, faith in one's belief in a doctrine, such as belief in God, is like faith in one's knowledge of a principle. You cannot prove that God exists in the same way that you cannot prove the existence of a universal principle. Faith, in these two instances, is placed in something that can't be proven. Likewise, faith in knowing by paying attention is like faith in the act of applying a principle because both types of faith are placed in the benefits of mindfulness in a reality that also can't be proven. Faith in universal principles is like faith in a physical law of nature—that is scientific faith. Both of these faiths are based on the assurance that the principle, like the natural law, will only work as well as one's understanding of these realities.

When Christopher Columbus set out to find a better route to the riches of China, he was placing his faith in the idea that the earth was not flat but was round like a ball. He had no proof of this; he only had the words of several scientists or thinkers. His faith in the general principle of form was so intense that it allowed him to override what everyone else was saying, which was that the earth is flat. It's true, the earth is flat; all you have to do is look out over the ocean to see that the horizon is flat and straight, but Columbus' faith in the principle of form told him that if he sailed west, he would eventually arrive in the East, in China. The rest is history.

DOUBT

What is intriguing is the relationship between faith and doubt. Faith, as it relates to belief, is intolerant of doubt. Faith, as it relates to knowing, dispenses with doubt. Faith, as it relates to physical laws, like the laws of thermodynamics, makes doubt irrelevant. Faith in universal principles tolerates and invites doubt.

The reason that faith in universal principles invites doubt is that doubt creates the foil against which principles can be understood more clearly. This is to say, when a universal principle has been applied, the result appears so natural that attributing it to a universal principle might seem doubtful to a bystander. The presence of that doubt is an aid in confirming reality, especially if the same application is made in the same manner to the same kind of thing with an identical outcome. Doubt becomes a partner in understanding the importance of the principle. If the same exercise is undertaken but without applying the principle, and an inferior result is the consequence, then doubt is transformed into faith.

Doubt, as it relates to physical laws, is irrelevant because the connection between the calculation of what will happen and the actual outcome are easily accepted and understood.

There are three kinds of doubt. The first kind of doubt is designed to lead to knowing. This doubt involves questioning everything while remaining open to all possible answers to arrive at an understanding of what it is we need to know.

The second kind of doubt is a form of religion. Both believers and non-believers practice this doubt. Believers in a religion doubt the validity of the point of view of non-believers and vice versa. In other words, Jews, Christians, or Muslims doubt that atheists are right about the existence of God. In like manner, atheists doubt that Muslims, Christians, and Jews are right about the existence of God.

The third kind of doubt is a belief that only material things are knowable and therefore credible. Practitioners of this third kind of doubt use it because of the feeling of superiority it produces in them. They deceive themselves by choosing to accept nothing that can't be materially seen, measured, or touched.

Faith, as it relates to reality and the sense of principle, accepts and cultivates the first kind of doubt as a necessity to be able to know reality, thereby making faith unnecessary. The nature of that doubt is a serious yet lightly imposed doubt about everything, even about things that are already known. This kind of doubt helps us avoid arrogance about what we think we know, and it keeps our focus on reality and the truth, not on the explanations that may or may not be true.

This kind of doubt is systemic, without being dogmatic, and general, so as not to force everything to conform to its specific notion of what reality is. It is a healthy mind that questions the true and the untrue without preference or prejudice. This is the purpose of the blindfold on the statues of Justitia. It forces her from taking sides until the truth is told. This is also what the phrase, "the benefit of the doubt," is referring to. If it can't be demonstrated beyond a shadow of a doubt, the accused must be judged as not guilty. It's an irony that a system of justice based on doubt is what we all put our faith in.

Chapter Twenty

What Does It Mean to Be Spiritual?

Being spiritual means being aware of the reality of the Soul in all its dimensions. Merely believing in that reality is not being spiritual. To be spiritual, one must partake in a relationship with the Soul. This is most easily articulated by saying what is *not* being spiritual.

As I have already asserted, being religious is not being spiritual. Forcing a notion of spirituality into religion allows us to feel justified when behaving in ways that accord with religion but are unspiritual. Does this mean that people cannot find their version of spirituality in religion? No. It means that their version of spirituality may not be the real thing.

Being spiritual does not mean being nice, though being nice can't be ruled out as one of the behaviors of a spiritual person. It does not mean believing a set of doctrines about spirituality. It does not mean being kind or generous. It does not mean being perfect. It does not mean reading about spirituality or studying sacred texts, nor does it include talking, however eloquently, about being spiritual. It does not include setting oneself up as a moral authority or trying to lead others to become more moral. It doesn't even include being pious and thinking about spirit. Being spiritual is not about any of these behaviors.

Spiritual behavior has no doctrines, no vested interests, no rituals, no ulterior motives, and makes no demands on a person, other than to pay attention to reality using their senses. It doesn't require a person to accept what others say is true, so don't take my word for it.

Since we are inculcated into thinking about being spiritual as the practicing or exercising of conventional spiritual behaviors, imagining how to be spiritual without all these behaviors is difficult. These behaviors are designed to produce the *appearance* of spirituality, but they are not spiritual.

To be spiritual, at its essence, is to pay attention and listen to your senses. The senses are your connection to reality. When you pay attention to your senses for the purpose of beholding reality, you are behaving, as much as is possible, as a pre-verbal infant behaves. When babies are awake, they give 100% attention to their senses. They have no other choice. They are as naked spiritually as one can be. For them, everything is taken in without judgment or editing. This is why babies are as close to unity with their Souls as one normally finds in a given population. They are born in Love Mode, and only by experience do they learn about fear.

Being intimately acquainted with your Soul is the point of paying attention to your senses, and it is the point of being spiritual. A person who has achieved unity with their Soul so that they think the thoughts of their Soul may rightly be called spiritual. Such a person might not be likable. It is one of the unfortunate realities that many historical people who achieved unity with their Souls somehow managed to get themselves killed because they told the truth that others didn't want to hear.

Indeed, the desire to be loved is a trap frequently fallen into by those who fancy themselves as spiritual. The desire to be loved motivates people to abandon their focus on the truth because the truth often hurts or makes them feel offended, guilty, or ashamed. You cannot seriously intend to pay attention to reality and hope to be loved by anyone, perhaps other than someone else who is also seriously attending to reality. This means that to be spiritual, you have to abandon all expectation or desire to be loved by others. Human beings are designed to love, not to be loved. It is a spiritual person who conducts their life to fulfill this design.

To love means to pay attention. Loving and paying attention are one and the same thing. Loving attunes the brain of the lover to the meaning of the reality before them. Since it is impossible to truly pay attention and not be responsible towards the object of attention, loving and being responsible are two halves of a whole state of spiritual being. Don't take my word for it. Discover it for yourself.

Being responsible entails having the ego under careful management. Every slight, hurt, criticism, violation, or assault is an opportunity for a spiritual person to assert their management of their ego. Those who are quick to forgive others and themselves for not being spiritual enhance their management of the ego within.

Spiritual necessity demands that you live in the present, while nursing grudges shackles you to the past. As long as you are shackled to the past, you cannot be present, and you cannot maintain management of your ego or let go of past actions. Those who forgive themselves are more able to understand the benefits which forgiveness bestows on the one who forgives. This is what *love others as you love yourself* means. To adopt all these attitudes equips you to live in a world without the security blanket of belief. Don't take my word for it. Test it for yourself.

Being egoistic and being spiritual are opposites in the same way that believing and knowing are opposites. It is the ego that wants to be loved, that seeks attention, that eschews responsibility, that puffs itself up, that seeks to convince others of its spirituality by religious discipline and practice, and that needs to feel safe because it fears assault from every quarter. In spite of all this, the ego has a rightful place and a function at which it excels—to save the life of the body when it becomes necessary, nothing more.

Being spiritual in work means doing what is required to feed and nourish the Souls of others by the work we do. Specifically, this means seeking every way to apply universal principles and establishing the highest possible quality in the work we do. It also means never being satisfied with whatever level of quality we have achieved because it is always possible for quality to increase.

Being spiritual in our relationships means treating others in a way that honors their Souls by entrusting their Souls with the truth. Should others reject that approach because they prefer to keep their egos in charge, then that is their decision. Attempting to affect their decision is unspiritual because who is to say that decision is wrong for them?

Being spiritual requires one to resist correcting what is perceived to be wrong in others, but it does not mean that the truth need be silenced—it only may be necessary to leave it unarticulated. At the same time, it is necessary to discern and articulate the difference between being wrong and being harmful. As long as a person chooses to do what is counterproductive to knowing reality and harms no one else in the process, it is important to have an attitude of live and let live. Everyone has the right to be wrong, and it is wrong to force others into our preferred version of what is right.

Where another person's notions directly result in harm to others, that person's notions need to be opposed vigorously. This view of what it means to be spiritual is not as unusual as you might think, but it is unusual to find it realized in most human beings.

Those who are spiritual, in reality, are mostly focused on the uninterpreted, unvarnished truth, and they are almost impossible to offend. It is the ego that reacts strongly to offense, therefore they hold their egos well in check because they realize that knowing the truth requires it.

Being spiritual means resisting the urge to condemn others because it is only a spiritual person who knows how difficult it is to know the truth. It means accepting that what others can't understand may be beyond their capacity to accept, even if they did understand it. It means loving unconditionally without needing to affect others. It means tolerating the differences between ourselves and others, and not allowing the intolerance of others to spread. It means being responsible, but not ignorantly so. It means being sensitive to deception as the need arises. Above all, spiritual people are quick to forgive. Don't take my word for it. You must decide for yourself.

The overriding persuasion found in all spiritual people is an aim to be at one with their Souls. Spiritual people do not allow others to affect the relationship with their Souls. They prefer to think the thoughts that their Souls think, act as their

Souls would act, and be as their Souls would be. That is, they prefer to be as wholly in touch with the truth and reality as possible.

SO WHAT? WHO CARES? WHAT OF IT? WHY BOTHER?

It is now up to you to decide how you want to answer these four questions. I answered them, finally, by writing this book and addressing everything in it to the Souls of my readers. I have provided you with my answer to "So What?" by recording what I have learned about how the Soul works and how to optimize your relationship with it. You now have the information you need to feed and nourish your Soul so that when you are ready, willing, and able to do what it needs of you, you can save precious time and grow that relationship quickly and efficiently.

My answer to "Who Cares?" is this: If humankind is to evolve beyond this egoistic, adolescent stage, each one of us needs to realize a strong relationship with the Soul so it can guide us to deeper and more profound understandings of whatever we choose to do. Believing in magic, the recourse of an infantilized self, no longer cuts it.

To do this (my answer to "What of it?"), we need to recognize that the Soul is a manifestation of a spiritual system that functions using all 133 of our senses and, like any other of the many systems within us, it is one that we need to keep our Souls alive, fit, and thriving. Just as we don't need to believe anything to realize the importance of the digestive system, we also do not need to believe anything to realize the importance of this spiritual system, of which the Soul is the driving force and intuition its manifestation. If you take the trouble to give your Soul the nourishment it requires, it will come out and play!

As to the question of "Why Bother?" we need to understand that human evolution is a choice we, as members of the human race, must make. Each of us is either going to be a partner in that evolution, or not. Any person who decides to cultivate a close and intimate relationship with their Soul becomes a partner in the evolution of the human species. Those who prefer not to become a partner should not be penalized; they need to be allowed to have that experience and all that comes with it.

THE CONSEQUENCES OF PARTNERING WITH THE SOUL

The more aware you are of all your senses, the healthier your Soul will be and the more available it will be for you. Having a healthy Soul means that you will be harder to deceive, and being harder to deceive means that spiritual predators will find it increasingly difficult to thrive in this world—spiritual predators are empowered by self-infantilizers who insist on believing in magic. So as you sense and identify spiritual predators, you avoid becoming their victims, and you can help others avoid becoming their victims too. By knowing spiritual predators as they really are, you can learn how to love them. Yes, love, as in paying attention. Just as you can love and pay attention to those you have affection for, you can and also love and pay attention to those who intend to harm you. A predator might someday learn to understand and acquire compassion.

Most importantly, all of us need to learn how to love our real home, Earth, because we are stuck here along with everyone else, like it or not. Our evolution is not going to be of the physical kind for us to venture out into space and turn it into a dump, as we have so far done on Earth. We must choose to either make Earth a garbage heap or a garden wherein each one spiritually flowers and bears fruit of the highest quality.

As human populations continue to increase, we must use the earth's resources wisely, according to the universal principles that made them available to us in the first place. Failure to do this is no longer an acceptable result unless we all decide to go extinct together. That need not be a hatchet over our collective heads; merely, it is a possible outcome of not making this decision together and choosing not to use sound, mindful judgment.

Finally, the real measure of our intelligence has nothing to do with our ability to figure more stuff out, make more stuff, or discover more new stuff. The real measure of our intelligence is the speed at which we adopt better and more sensible attitudes with which to solve our problems. In other words, the most intelligent person is the one who can adopt a new and better attitude the fastest.

The best way I know of learning how to do this is in doing some kind of art because the arts are a testing venue for learning how to solve fake problems, quickly adopt more sensible attitudes, and develop judgment by competently using the 133 senses. Those who have mastered an art are rendered more capable of sensibly solving humanity's real problems, which require the application of sound judgment.

All of this can be done by any one of us, irrespective of our innate intellectual capabilities. We need only exercise the good judgment required to make the best possible decisions for the whole human family. That is what the *day of judgment* means. Those who exercise sound judgment will prevail, and those who don't will not. That day is now.

BIBLIOGRAPHY

Aristotle. "Poetics." *The Internet Classics Archive.* http://classics.mit.edu/Aristotle/poetics.3.3.html (accessed Mar. 15, 2018).

Ayers, Alex ed. *The Wit and Wisdom of Mark Twain.* New York: Harper, 2005.

Bach, C.P.E. *An Essay on the True Art of Playing Keyboard Instruments,* Translated by William J. Mitchell. New York: W. W. Norton, 1948.

Bach, J.S. *J.S. Bach's Precepts and Principles for Playing the Thorough Bass or Accompanying in Four Parts.* Translated by Pamela L. Poulin. Oxford: Clarendon Press; New York: Oxford University Press, 1995.

Burke, James. *Connections.* New York: Simon & Schuster, 2007.

David, Hans T., Arthur Mendel and Christoph Wolff, eds. *The New Bach Reader.* New York: Norton, 1998.

Doczi, Gyorgy. *The Power of Limits: Proportional Harmonies in Nature, Art, and Architecture.* Boston: Shambhala, 1981.

Edwards, Betty. *Drawing on the Right Side of the Brain.* London: Souvenir Press Ltd., 2013.

Holt, Lunstad J., W. A. Birmingham and K. C. Light, "Influence of a 'warm touch' support enhancement intervention among married couples on ambulatory blood pressure, oxytocin, alpha amylase, and cortisol." *Psychosomatic Medicine* 70 (2008): 976-85.

Ploger, Marianne. "The Three Causes of Error." *The Ploger Method.* http://plogermethod.com/the-three-causes-of-error (accessed Mar. 15, 2018).

Sheldrake, Rupert. *Morphic Resonance: The Nature of Formative Causation.* Rochester, Vermont: Park Street Press, 2009.

Trut, Lyudmilla and Lee Alan Dugatkin. *How to Tame a Fox (and Build a Dog): Visionary Scientists and a Siberian Tale of Jump-Started Evolution.* Chicago: University of Chicago Press, 2017

Williams, R., The Hubble Deep Field Team, and NASA/ESA. "Hubble Deep Field." *Hubble Space Telescope.* http://spacetelescope.org/images/opo9601c/ (accessed Mar. 15, 2018).

Made in United States
North Haven, CT
09 January 2022

14480561R00209